IS LAW
DEAD?

Edited by

EUGENE V. ROSTOW

Simon and Schuster : New York

Law, Order, and Enlightenment © 1971 by Peter Gay

The Rightful Limits of Freedom in a Liberal Democratic State: Of Civil Disobedience © 1970, 1971 by Eugene V. Rostow. First published in *Trial*

In Defense of Anarchism © 1971 by Robert Paul Wolff

Freedom, Consent, and the Costs of Interaction © 1971 by Charles Dyke

Taking Rights Seriously © 1970, 1971 by Ronald Dworkin. First published in *New York Review of Books*

Civil Disobedience © 1970, 1971 by Hannah Arendt. First published in *The New Yorker*

Changing Patterns of Social Cohesion and the Crisis of Law Under a System of Government by Consent © 1971 by David M. Potter

The Roots of Social Neglect in the United States © 1970, 1971 by Robert L. Heilbroner. First published in *TRANS-action*

The Historical Roots of American Social Change and Social Theory © 1971 by Harold Cruse

Revolution © 1971 by Michael Harrington

Public Safety as a Public Good © 1971 by William H. Riker

FIRST PRINTING

SBN 671–20866–7 Trade
SBN 671–20867–5 Clarion
Library of Congress Catalog Card Number: 78–139657
Designed by Irving Perkins
Manufactured in the United States of America

TABLE OF CONTENTS

PART II : The Capacity of the American Social Order to Meet the Changing Demands for Social Justice Through the Methods of Law

FOREWORD

by Whitney North Seymour

The Association of the Bar of the City of New York, founded in 1870 to cleanse the city of corruption, has been steadily engaged for a hundred years in trying to make law and legal institutions work and to see that they do so in the public interest. The handsome Assembly Room of the Association, where this symposium was held, has heard the voices of many of the leading judges and lawyers of America and elsewhere since the old headquarters building was constructed three quarters of a century ago. The Association's work, and the many memorable debates, lectures and other occasions there, underline the belief of lawyers in the vibrancy of law.

Challenges to that belief have lately erupted all over America, from many sources. Some embraced hatred and violence, oblivious to the lessons of history. It was thus in order that, in its centennial year, the Association should ask itself whether its premise, faith in law and in the value of trying to mold it and its institutions to fit the needs of a changing society, was still valid. It would have been easy to get leading lawyers who would massage its ego by praising its history and viewing the future only with blandness. On the other hand, it would also have been easy and, at the moment, almost fashionable, to arrange a symposium of merely angry people, some of whom would denounce the past as irrelevant and, using the graffiti of the day as their literary vehicles, brazenly order our institutions to stand against the wall, as their contribution to reform. But we are indebted to the Association's Centennial Committee, chaired by Merrell E. Clark, Jr., for the decision to grasp the nettle more firmly and imaginatively. Their concept was warmly supported by an Association Special Committee appointed to help with the

7

planning. They decided to draft former Dean Eugene V. Rostow, of the Yale Law School, a wise and widely experienced lawyer and former public official, who was an extremely knowledgeable member of the intellectual community, to bring together a broad spectrum of experts, legal and lay, to discuss the subject. One of the best contributions was the suggestion of Senior Federal Judge Edward J. Dimock, a well-loved member of the Centennial Committee, that Dean Rostow's symposium should be on the challenging subject: "Is law dead?"

The actual production confirmed the wisdom of this approach. Dean Rostow, using his diplomatic capacity for cajolery and persuasion, induced a notable company, representing all major schools of thought, to provide papers and to deliver them. Interstices of the production were filled by short turns from an outstanding group of discussants. I can testify to the quality of the performances, because as presiding officer (under the benevolent eye of then President Plimpton), time restrictions had to be applied rather firmly. No doubt encores by most of the speakers would have been sought by the audience, if it had been given any encouragement.

It is no part of an introduction to say in advance whether one agrees with the speaker or not. As I listened to some of the speakers, I found myself thinking occasionally, during the more abstruse passages, that, in some ways, Dean Rostow rather resembled Gilbert K. Chesterton who, in his fine introduction to his life of George Bernard Shaw, said: "Most people either say that they agree with Bernard Shaw or that they do not understand him. I am the only one who understands him, and I do not agree with him." When it was over, I asked myself, as the reader may after completing the book, how shall one answer the question, "Is law dead?" I concluded that my own answer was that it clearly was not, and that while in some areas it was, perhaps, breathing hard, it would continue to live to serve the public interest at least until another centennial, if we remained steadfast in shaping it to America's needs and did not let the divisions and aggravations of the moment divert us from the task.

July 28, 1970
New York, N.Y.

INTRODUCTION

The Association of the Bar of the City of New York is one of the finest professional bodies of our law—highbrow, research-minded, and action-oriented. As a rightful part of the *noblesse de robe,* it is serenely confident of its ability to take on dragons, and to slay them. It is characteristic of the Association that it chose to celebrate its centenary by asking the most topical and yet the most fundamental of all the questions that could be put about the condition of society today: "What is law?" "What is it for?" And "Can it meet the challenge of these turbulent times?" And it is also characteristic of an Association which has long honored Judge Benjamin Cardozo that these questions were posed in the perspective of a particular theory of law: "What is law, what is it for, and is it up to its tasks, as part of the American social process, and as the institution above all others through which we seek to fulfill our changing ideals of social justice?"

Against the background of our present discontents, there are no issues of greater urgency. In bringing together the men and women who undertook to answer these questions, in two lively days of discussion on April 30 and May 1, 1970, the Association sought a representative and strong-minded panel. The ideas they canvassed at the convocation, and have set out more fully in this book, have become the core of the vocabulary of social conflict. And I, for one, am convinced that the crystallization of a new state of public opinion on these issues, after the widest possible consideration and debate, is the key to the renewal of social peace.

Any day's newspaper provides the text. *The New York Times* of April 22, 1970, introduces our themes as well as any other. The story reported local reactions to events at Isla Vista, California, a college town beset by nights of rioting, culminating in the death of a student who had been helping other students put out "fires set by bands of marauding demonstrators." Some of the militants were said to advocate street fighting as a way of radicalizing the community. "Basically, the issue is how to build a mass movement," one said. "The mass of left liberals are not ready for street fighting." A freshman is quoted: "When I saw the kids trying to burn the bank, I thought they were insane. But then the cops came in and they were obviously looking for trouble. . . . Later they used tear gas on campus. I just can't support a government that sends in troops to do things like that." Another student commented, according to the reporter, "I don't go in for this window breaking and violence. But maybe there isn't any other way to get changes. Maybe the only way to end the war is to burn down all the Bank of America buildings."

At New Haven, as the convocation met, my own university faced the test which so many others have had to endure in recent years. The nominal occasion was a murder trial. Several members of the Black Panther party were charged with killing one of their number on the ground that he had informed the police about a series of bombings carried out by Black Panthers. A brilliant campaign had generated an epidemic of anxiety, fear, guilt, and concern within the University, and elsewhere. There were rumors that Yale and New Haven would be invaded by organized militant groups, and stormed. Some thuggery and several episodes of arson had already occurred. Once again, we saw that these contagious fevers do not respect the generation gap. Otherwise serious scholars wondered whether it is wise or moral to try men duly charged with murder, and whether possible error on the part of a judge warranted burning a few buildings, or jail delivery.

We know, of course, that moods and events of this kind are phenomena from the realm of mass hysteria, like the Tulip Mania, the Dance of Death and the South Sea Bubble. We know also that the driving force behind many of these episodes is not social protest but the attractions of violence, adventure and excitement as sport—the powerful and fundamental lure which has drawn men for centuries to hunts, wars, crusades, and expeditions of exploration or of conquest. Perhaps it is quixotic even to try, through disciplined intellectual effort, to examine what Mill called "the necessary limits of individual freedom arising out of the conditions of our social life," [1] that is, the idea of "civil liberty" within organized society, in Rousseau's phrase, as distinguished from "natural liberty" in a state of nature.

The City Bar Association consists of worldly lawyers, beyond surprise at man's capacity for folly, sin, and irrationality. It says much about the ultimate idealism of the legal mind that the leaders of the Association did not respond to the prevailing atmosphere with a shrug of sardonic resignation. On the contrary, they based their centennial program on a premise of unabashed faith in the potentialities of reason, and in the goodness of man. They assumed that most men desire to be upright citizens, but that they are confused and uncertain in the face of arguments like those reported in *The New York Times* story I have just quoted. It followed, in their minds, that a careful analysis of what lies behind these assertions is not only possible, and worthwhile, but indispensable; and that the most practical contribution the Association could make to the peaceful resolution of this time of troubles would be to seek coherence—and, conceivably, even a degree of consensus—at the level of first principles.

Those who planned the Centennial Convocation, and this book, soberly recognize that our credo and our institutions are being tested with a vehemence the nation has not known since the Civil War. They understand, and understand with sympathy, that in many sectors of our national life angry men say the pace of change is too slow. The peaceful methods of law and of democratic politics, these protesters assert, have failed as an instrument for the ordering of progress. Some deny the idea of law itself as the compass of our social system.

Five turbulent upheavals are occurring simultaneously. Each by itself could well require the best efforts of a generation; their confluence strains the sinews of society.

The first and most fundamental is our vast national effort—more than a century after Appomattox—to make good, at long last, our promise of equality for the Negro. This process has been gaining momentum for a generation. It has been given a powerful new

[1] J. S. Mill, "On Social Freedom," ed. by Dorothy Fosdick (1941), p. 31. See also pp. 35–36, 37–40, 61–66.

impetus by the judicial decisions, the legislation, and the social experience of recent years. It touches every aspect of our law, our politics and our settled patterns of habit. And it provokes dangerous conflict, especially in our cities where so many black citizens now live.

The second is the accelerated pace of urbanization—the immense movement of people to cities, and to urban areas. Many are the rural poor, and especially the black poor, ill-equipped for the requirements of urban life. Their presence has led to counter-shifts of population, tending further to divide communities on racial lines. The pressures arising from these processes have precipitated a mounting urban crisis, which seems beyond the reach of our traditional methods of local government in many large cities.

The third is the renewal of doubt about the foreign policy the nation has followed since 1945. That policy has imposed burdens unfamiliar to our history—thirty years of conscription, a succession of costly military campaigns, the prospect of apparently endless crisis ahead. We are living through another intense round of the debate we have pursued at intervals since President Wilson urged his countrymen to ratify the Covenant of the League of Nations, fifty years ago. This round of the debate, like its predecessors, has sharply divided the country. It is given a special quality of urgency by the anguish of Vietnam, the condition of international politics, and the shadow of the nuclear weapon.

Fourth, the demand for higher education, and for better education of all kinds, has outstripped the capacity of our educational system. Since our people know that education is the key to their advancement, and to the advancement of their children, the many shortcomings of the educational system produce widespread bitterness.

And finally, a fraction of our youth, like their counterparts in other countries, feels frustrated or alienated by their experience. They are the first generation of a world society in which the authority of the family, the church and the nation-state has been radically diminished; the fear of unemployment has been weakened or destroyed as a sanction for work; and the consciousness of good and evil has faded. The idealism of many young people is aroused by injustice, by the malfunctioning of institutions seeking to meet the challenge of change, and by the specter of war. All too often, their education has not prepared them for the world as it is. Many are shocked and bewildered to discover that their society is not Utopia, and that, in the nature of societies, it cannot be made over into Utopia quickly. Few are trained to understand why war and near-war have come to be the dominant feature of the human condition in our time. And a considerable number tend to dismiss the experience of history as the misguided chronicle of people less moral, less idealistic, less humane, and less civilized than the youth of today.

The stress of these linked processes of change has produced waves of riots and of disobedience to law which have become the most critical social problems of our time. Their character has been highlighted by a series of assassinations which shocked the nation. Furthermore, many believe there may be significant connections between such social and political phenomena and the increase in ordinary crime, and especially in crimes of violence.

These social storms, and the violence they have generated, have created a climate of doubt about the most basic issue a free society ever confronts: the citizen's moral relation to a valid law.

The nation has had a long and bitter experience with civil disobedience, in the open resistance of the South for more than a century to the commands of the Fourteenth and Fifteenth Amendments.

The resistance of the South was justified by moral claims, asserted with passionate conviction: The Amendments had been ratified by coerced legislatures—that is, by legislatures voting under the pressure of military occupation; they were contrary to the word of God, which declared blacks to be "hewers of wood and drawers of water"; and it was against conscience in any event for the majority of the nation to impose its will on a considerable dissenting minority, and to disregard the strongly held mores and beliefs of a region.

The civil disobedience of the South to the Fourteenth and Fifteenth Amendments was carried out by political means, reinforced by mobs, arson, murder, lynching, and intimidation. These tactics "succeeded" in a pragmatic sense—that is, they produced a state of policy which could not have been achieved by political means alone. But Jim Crow and the Ku Klux Klan have left behind a poisonous legacy, which will require the best efforts of a generation to clear away.

Now, as the South has begun to accept the law of the nation, the practice of civil disobedience, and the jurisprudence invoked in its behalf, have suddenly spread. Earnest men claim that the citizen has a right—even a duty—to refuse military service for a war he disapproves and, more generally, that his own feelings of injustice and unfairness, if strongly enough held, justify illegal action on his part. The precedent of Nuremberg, and Gandhi's example, are invoked in support of draft resistance and cognate acts of disobedience to valid law. Some defend arson, trespass, and other forms of violence as protest, and on the ground that they might hasten the reform of institutions and policies, such methods are justified as means, in their view, by the fact that they might produce desirable ends. A few embark on campaigns of subversion or "confrontation" designed, they say, to weaken or destroy important institutions of society, and society itself, on the ground that they, or others, are aggrieved, excluded, or unfairly treated, and that society itself must be deemed hopelessly and inherently unjust.

Taken together, this is a formidable array.

This volume is addressed to two issues: first, the citizen's moral relation to the law in a society of consent; and, second, the capacity of the American legal and political order to meet the felt needs of our people for social justice.

The two problems are reciprocal. We believe they must not be studied in isolation from each other: The idea of order without justice is odious.

The first of these issues is the subject of Part I of this book. It is one of the oldest and at the same time most novel dilemmas in legal and political philosophy. The American constitutional order rests on an explicit answer to the question—the theory of the social contract, dear to the men of the Enlightenment who made the nation. In their view, the Constitution was made by the people, not by the states, through a unique constituent act. "We the people of the United States," in their memorable phrase, meeting in special assemblies, entered directly into the covenant of the Constitution, committed to the proposition that the just powers of government derive from the consent of the governed. It follows that in the kind of society they wanted to achieve, the citizen was bound—morally bound—to obey the law he helped to make.

Where does their theory stand today, in a vast pluralistic society, far less homogeneous than the thirteen British colonies of the Atlantic seaboard in the late eighteenth century? What are its alternatives? Can it, should it, be used to explain the citizen's moral relation to the law in the last third of the twentieth century?

But even if a study of the problems considered in Part I of this book resulted in universal agreement on the proposition that the citizen of a free society owes his fellows a moral obligation to obey the law—a most unlikely outcome—the problem of disobedience and violence would remain. Moral rules and principles, however universally accepted, are never universally obeyed. Life and literature would be more tranquil, but less interesting, were this not the case. Whatever one's school of philosophy may be, we know that when our society, by a considerable margin, fails to satisfy the mores of our people, violent and illegal protest has occurred in the past, and will continue to occur in the future. We have had a long history of protest going beyond the limits of law—rebellions by debtors and taxpayers, the Ku Klux Klan, labor conflicts, farmers' protests and draft riots, to say nothing of the Civil War itself—as antecedents for the diverse phenomena of protest we have endured during the last few years.

Part II of the book is therefore devoted to another theme: Can our political and legal system satisfy the legitimate demands of modern society for social justice in peace, and without regression or collapse?

Thus the concern of the Association has been not merely to justify the ways of law to the community, but to vindicate the law as a means of achieving justice—not merely to defend the law, but to help make it worthy of defense, as the supreme and all-embracing instrument of social progress, and of social peace.

It is an old and harsh social truth that unless the leaders of a society lead, there is little hope either for the institutions placed in their trust, or for the society itself.

In organizing this convocation, the Bar Association met its responsibilities under that rule.

I should like to thank many who have helped make my task easier. First, I should name the Honorable Francis T. P. Plimpton, president of the Association, and Merrell E. Clark, Jr., chairman of its Centennial Committee, and the members of that committee: Arthur A. Charpentier, the Honorable Edward J. Dimock, Henry N. Ess III, the Honorable Samuel I. Rosenman, Oscar M. Ruebhausen, the late Harrison Tweed, and Bethuel M. Webster. Together we worked out the first plan for the convocation and for this book, in a spirit of adventure which was a joy. Then, as is the custom of the Association, a special advisory committee on the program itself was established, under that wise and cheerful warrior, Whitney North Seymour, whose company, and that of Mrs. Seymour, I have enjoyed on many occasions in the past. He assembled an outstanding group: G. Wallace Bates, Aaron Benenson, the Honorable Herbert Brownell, Judge Edward J. Dimock, John Doar, Edward J. Ennis, Jack Greenberg, the Honorable Nicholas deB. Katzenbach, Professor Louis Lusky, Barbara Scott Preiskel, Judge Scovel Richardson, Judge Francis E. Rivers, Alan U. Schwartz, and Asa D. Sokolow. We met several times, and conferred more often on the phone, to put the enterprise into its final form.

Financial support for the convocation was generously provided by the Ford Foundation, the Beinecke Foundation and the Vincent Astor Foundation. Without their contributions the convocation could not have been held. We are grateful to those charged with responsibility for these institutions for their help, their encouragement, and their confidence.

The convocation attracted a most gratifying audience, and (a signal which always delights the managers of such enterprises) an audience notably larger on the second day than on the first. All the participants, I know, found the *assistance,* to use the apt French word, of our interlocutors an exhilarating feature of the experience.

Paul De Witt, the executive secretary of the Association,

smoothed our path in a hundred ways, both in his advice about the program and in his hospitable direction of the convocation itself.

Finally, I should like to give special thanks to Neal Steinman, a student at the Yale Law School, who advised and helped me in all phases of the project with the zest, concern, and scholarly scruple which have always been—and I hope will always be—the hallmark of that great breed.

EUGENE V. ROSTOW

August 15, 1970
New Haven, Connecticut
Peru, Vermont

PART I

The Citizen's Moral Relation
to the Law in
a Society of Consent

CHAPTER I

LAW, ORDER, AND ENLIGHTENMENT

by Peter Gay

In celebrating its centennial at a critical juncture of American history, this Association may look upon its past with great pleasure. But it cannot rest with self-congratulation alone, no matter how well deserved. For there are powerful reasons why it must look upon the present with some dismay. An Association like this one, dedicated as it is to the care and feeding of the law, cannot remain indifferent to the reputation that the law enjoys in our time—if "enjoys" is the word I am groping for. That fine old phrase "law and order" has fallen into widespread, almost cynical contempt. Whatever may divide Americans today, southern sheriffs or northern liberals, members of the Young Republicans or of the SDS, all define "law and order" as a code phrase concealing, or rather all too plainly revealing, its opposite: illegality and chaos. This is a deeply troubling state of affairs. The loss in respect that law and order have suffered among wide circles in our country make both into victims and, worse, threaten to make us all into victims sooner or later.

It cannot be my purpose to spell out in detail what you all know. Nor could it be to offer a program of social, economic, legal betterment; we have perhaps far too many of those already. As an eighteenth-century historian principally interested in the Enlightenment, I want simply to remind you of a few principles that we may be in danger of forgetting. Indeed even lawyers and philosophers of law, who should know better, are in danger of forgetting them. The relevance of the Enlightenment to our time is of course that the legal philosophy which dominated it underlies the Constitution of the

United States. Nor is such recall mere antiquarianism: The principles that mattered then matter now.

For the men of the Enlightenment law and order was of critical importance. This importance emerges in the writings of the philosophes of all countries—lawyer and non-lawyer alike—in the writings of Montesquieu, of Voltaire, of Beccaria, of Bentham. While their legal thought differed, sometimes in striking ways, they all agreed that while not all societies under law are good societies, no society *not* under law can be a good society. There is a famous passage in Jean Jacques Rousseau's *Social Contract* which demonstrates with peculiar clarity just how serious the law was to the social philosophy of the Enlightenment: "Man is born free, yet everywhere he is in chains," Rousseau writes in the opening of his first chapter. "One thinks himself the master of others, which still leaves him more of a slave than they. How did this change come about? I do not know. What can make it legitimate? I think I can resolve that question." Like many other pronouncements of Rousseau's this one, too, is not wholly free from rhetorical extravagance, and thus ambiguity. But it forcibly suggests, and the rest of the *Social Contract* amply confirms, that Rousseau was groping for the solution to an ancient problem in political and legal philosophy: how to establish a sound theory of obligation. A sociologist and a political scientist may explain why people, in fact, obey the state. It might be the thirst for community, habit, or fear. But the theory of obligation raises a far more difficult question: Why *should* men obey? Obedience and its counterpart, domination, must be made legitimate. Power must be replaced by authority.

Rousseau's solution to this old problem was bold and highly original. It consisted of making the lawgiver identical with the law obeyer; in his system ruler and ruled are the same person. No other philosophe followed Rousseau in adopting this particular solution; while he was a democrat though not a liberal, most of them were liberals though not democrats. But all philosophes shared Rousseau's passionate concern with the question. And so should we. We hear many voices—voices indeed of normally responsible persons—urging us to disobey the law or forgive those who disobey it. The question "Why should we—or under what conditions can we conscientiously—respect law and order today?" receives peculiar poignancy when the chief spokesman for law and order appears to be the Vice-President of the United States. It is because the Enlightenment attempted to answer this delicate question in ways that remain significant to us now that I have made their answer my central concern this morning.

Let me begin by drawing a distinction central to the Enlightenment's philosophy of law: that philosophy was both formal and substantive. In its formal side, the law concerns itself with its very existence and its shape. In its substantive side, the law concerns itself with its content, its sociological presuppositions, and its social consequences. The formal philosophy of law, the philosophes held, begins with the proposition that life under law is the essential and irreplaceable precondition for the life of reason. A law is a publicly stated rule known to all and understood by all; it sets down what conduct is permitted and what conduct prohibited. In addition, it sets down, normally in great detail, penalties for prohibited conduct—for housebreaking, for perjury, for treason. Finally, the law provides for its own amendment; it specifies the rules under which it can be changed. The significance of these formal properties should be evident. The rule of law permits individuals living under it to predict the consequences of their behavior. The first implication of such a rule is the total unacceptability of ex post facto legislation. To make illegal retroactively conduct that was legal at the time it was performed is to make rational prediction a sheer impossibility. Society is a game with rules laid down in advance. Such rules make for clarity. They dispel confusion. What is more, this kind of formal rule alone may guarantee orderly social change. It informs both those content and those discontented with things as they are how they may go about keeping, or changing, things.

It is obviously essential to the rule of law that the mode in which the law is written and promulgated is practically as important as the law itself. In his great, short treatise, *On Crimes and Punishments,* which summarizes the Enlightenment's philosophy of law, Beccaria insists that the laws of a country must be written neither in the jargon that is the property of the specialist, nor in Latin which is the monopoly of the learned, but in ordinary language.

The laws must be clear, perspicuous, translucent; they must be what Beccaria calls "a solemn and public book." This is why Beccaria, in company with the other philosophes, rejoiced in the advent of printing; to him printing meant above all an unprecedented possibility of diffusing the public law among the widest possible public. "The larger the number of those who understand, and hold in their hands, the sacred code of the laws," Beccaria wrote, "the rarer crimes will become, for there can be no doubt that ignorance about, and uncertainty of, punishments enhance the eloquence of the passions." Hand in hand with the publicity of its details went the certainty of its application. Like some Supreme Court Justices of recent decades, and like Professor Alexander Bickel, the philosophes wanted the justices to obey the law they were supposed to administer. This meant that for the philosophers of the Enlightenment judicial interpretation of law, or leeway in assessing the nature of crime or dealing out penalties, must be restricted as closely as possible.

The essential virtues of this kind of formal thinking about the law should be evident enough although they do appear in danger of being neglected these days. But it would be a mistake to suppose that the philosophes confined themselves to formalism. Indeed if formalism were all that the Enlightenment had as its philosophy of law, we should instantly observe two grave defects in its thinking. Formalism, standing by itself, appears to assume that all men are educated enough to understand, and rational enough to obey, the laws as they are laid down. Implicitly or explicitly, such an assumption discriminates against the poor who have, through the centuries, had infinitely smaller opportunity to acquire control over the passions than their richer fellow citizens, and infinitely less opportunity to learn the intricacies of the laws they are supposed to obey. The poor, the uneducated, the unstable, and, as we are daily being reminded in our country today, the blacks and the Puerto Ricans, have two strikes against them before they swing at the first pitch. Nor is this all. In its silence about the *content* of the laws, the formal theory of law opens wide the possibility of injustice masquerading as justice—which is to say, class justice. By definition, despotism—rule without law—is impossible under this formal legal philosophy. So, too, is favoritism, which is the breach of law in behalf of one or another chosen subject. But the ideological use of law in behalf of one group against another, one class against another, one race against another, is not merely a distinct possibility but, in most societies, an extreme probability. One need not be a cynic to observe that in most societies at most times the laws tend to be made by the few for the few. As Adam Smith candidly put it in *The Wealth of Nations,* "Civil government, so far as it is instituted for the security of property, is in reality instituted for the defence of the rich against the poor, or of those who have some property against those who have none at all."

The philosophes were aware of these risks, and therefore paid close attention to the other, the substantive, side of the law. They did so in three ways. They argued, first of all, that law must not merely be an aid to rationality, but must itself be rational. Now a "rational" law is one that is designed to fulfill its own proper purposes—to act only in those areas in which it makes a real difference and to act in behalf of the subject for whom it has ostensibly been promulgated. Let us remember the starting point of the Enlightenment's inquiries: By refusing to take for granted the need for obedience, the Enlightenment insisted that any call for obedience must rationally justify itself. Beccaria, for one, argued that philosophy must begin by establishing the right to control and to punish. "Every act of authority of man over man which does not derive from absolute necessity is tyrannical." Montesquieu, who was Beccaria's master in so many things, had said the same thing in slightly different words. The philosophes liked to equate reason and nature. One striking and amusing instance of this is Diderot's *Supplement to Bougainville's Voyage.* This unique production, part book review, part imaginary dialogue, prompted by Diderot's reading of Bougainville's report on his voyage around the world, depicts an idealized Tahitian society which knows no such foolish European institutions as monogamy, or dread of incest. Father and daughter, brother and sister, copulate freely. But not completely freely. Theirs is a libertarian society; it is bathed in the beneficent sun of the South Pacific and blessed with the absence of confusing and hypocritical Christian superstition. Yet there are limitations placed on the sexual conduct of the Tahitian. The rules they obey are rules they derive from nature. Their society is not a paradise, or a primitivist Utopia—if Utopia and Paradise are places where one does anything one likes. As Diderot fancies his Tahitians, they impose strict taboos on intercourse before maturity has been reached, since such intercourse violates the unmistakable precepts of nature. But the introduction of Christian teachings, with their irrational insistence on such unnatural behavior as celibacy and with their equally irrational confusion of the realms of guilt and innocence, only multiplies crime and miseries, depraves the conscience, corrupts the mind—and all because the rule of reason has now disappeared: "People will no longer know what they must do or not do; guilty in the state of innocence, tranquil in the midst of crime, they will have lost the North Star that should guide their course." Perhaps the simplest and briefest way of expressing the rational quality that, the philosophes thought, must underlie and justify the law is the principle formulated by Beccaria. The aim of the law, he said, is to provide "the greatest happiness divided among the greatest number." This means that law should not be regarded as a form of vengeance by which an injured society avenges a God who has been insulted, or a rich man who has been robbed. In our own time, I suspect, the philosophes would go partway with Professor Dworkin in arguing that civil disobedience that hurts no one else and interferes with no one else's rights should be regarded as generously as possible. One consequence of this attitude toward the law was, in the Enlightenment, the insistence that there should be a close relation between crime and punishment; in contrast with traditional and then prevailing codes of law, the philosophes argued that the smaller the crime the smaller the punishment should be. The reason for this proportionality was aesthetic and moral, but beyond this it was quite simply utilitarian: A crime is, by definition, an act that harms society, and society does have a stake in preventing harm to itself. But this prevention must be as economical as possible. Hence, crime of whatever kind must be repressed by as lenient a punishment as is practical and useful. The free employment of the death penalty, which abounded in the eighteenth century and was in fact extended, particularly in England, in crimes involving property, must be used sparingly if ever. It is unnecessary, irrational, and besides it has pernicious consequences: It sanctions violence officially and thus makes violence respectable. All of this means that we must carefully examine our catalogue of crimes to see that conduct called "criminal" really *is* criminal. The philosophes had no doubt that blasphemy was not a crime. Blasphemy is the insult that a mere human being offers to God. Now, as Montesquieu persuasively argued, it is to have a low conception of God to think of him as being easily hurt, and of being incapable of taking care of himself. In the same way, the philosophes made light of such "crimes" as homosexuality between consenting adults, loose speech, and related forms of behavior which could be shown to harm no one but, perhaps, those who engaged in them.

For the philosophes, the rational work of the law was supported by the efficient action of law enforcement agencies. It is here that the role of the police, which, I need not remind you, has become one of the most controversial of all questions in our time, becomes absolutely decisive. The philosophes thought that the most effective deterrent to crime, and with it the most significant aid to rationality, was the certainty with which crime was detected. It was obvious to the philosophes that a harsh penalty for crimes that are rarely solved was ineffective, while in contrast a mild penalty for crimes solved rapidly was effective indeed. It should hardly be necessary to add that the police could protect the laws all the more efficiently for being freed from wasting its time with nonsense. In some of the noblest pages written in the eighteenth century, Montesquieu condemns the facile and irresponsible use of the word "treason"—that is, of speeches or even thoughts with no discernible social or political consequences. In state after state, he noted, the government employed such repellent instruments as *agents provocateurs* whose job it was to stir up talk against the government in order to sniff out opposition. For Montesquieu the crime of treason was a possibility. But it had to be defined and circumscribed with the greatest care and prosecuted only when it had been firmly established. And, just as the philosophes insisted that the law be rational in what it prohibited and how it was enforced, so they insisted that crime itself be established by rational needs. This made them avid reformers of court procedure, and eloquent opponents of the use of torture either as a means of gaining information or as a method of punishment.

The purpose of this substantive aspect of the law was, of course, to secure to it the kind of voluntary respect that reasonable men will give to rules that seem to them both sensible and fairly administered. Its second aspect, to which the Enlightenment paid unremitting attention, was the question of education. The uneducated preoccupied, almost haunted, the philosophes. Most of the poor in their day, especially on the Continent, were of course illiterate, and could hardly benefit from the most clearly written of legal codes. The class distance between rich and poor, between peasant and lawyer, was so wide that one might almost speak of two conflicting or competing species in one political arena. While the philosophes did not have Utopian expectations of what education might accomplish, they did expect that education could narrow these gaps. And one major purpose of education was precisely to permit the subject to enjoy the protection of the laws rather than simply to feel their sting. Many of the philosophes, like Bentham, thought that the law itself could act as an educator. They did not have perhaps much faith in lawyers, and therefore they would, I think, have been delighted to see law students intent upon devoting a substantial share of their working time to social service. To take the case of the defenseless, to speak for the inarticulate, to help those who have seen the law only as the enemy, is to use the law as an educator in society.

There was still a third way in which the philosophes tried to infuse substance into legal forms. Anticipating and, as it were, refuting in advance the German legal idealists of the nineteenth century, the philosophes argued that a state could run like a perfect legal machine with no favoritism, no corruption, no delay, and yet be eminently unjust, even if the suffrage was wide. If society is both socially and economically a steep hierarchy—and surely all societies before and most societies after the Enlightenment were just that —then the large mass of those who only toil will neither have the knowledge to understand, nor the time to make, the laws. Nor will they have the funds to protect themselves against its clutches.

Rousseau's political writings are a treasure-house for this argument; there are certain kinds of inequality that make nonsense of the best intentions and most far-reaching legal reforms, and will distort the rule of law into the rule of privilege. Rousseau was careful to distinguish between inequality imposed by nature and therefore acceptable, and inequalities smuggled in by society and therefore illegitimate. He insisted that if society contained people rich enough to buy others, and people poor enough to be compelled to sell themselves to others, it could never be effectively just. Thus it was necessary to have a relative measure of social and economic equality not merely for the sake of abstract right, but for the sake of concrete power before the law. Rousseau also insisted, more persistently than the other philosophes, that such concrete power would best be achieved by universal participation in law-making. "To be general," Rousseau wrote, "it is not always necessary for the will to be unanimous, but it is necessary that all votes be counted; any formal exclusion breaches generality." This kind of analysis would be pushed further in the nineteenth century, especially by Marx. It has become extremely fashionable in our time. But the roots of this substantive philosophy of law, which is designed to make the formal philosophy of law work, must be sought in the Enlightenment.

I need not waste time praising the substantive philosophy of law. Its capacity as the critic of ideology and the unmasker of privilege is well known and thoroughly appreciated. The point that matters is that for the Enlightenment the formal and the substantive sides of law were indispensable to one another. Form without substance, the philosophes reasoned, is empty. It has no way of criticizing, let alone rectifying, those evils that have insinuated themselves into the law through regular procedures. But they also reasoned that substance without form is capricious. It has no way of producing, let alone guaranteeing, improvements that will bear the stamp of legitimacy. Granted, it is tempting to see form as the enemy of substance. If the regular channels of procedure—speechmaking, editorial-writing, peace-marching, voter-canvassing—seem to be clogged; if the formal, legal means of persuasion, no matter how patiently employed, fail to persuade; if the free press voices only one opinion and the political party system offers no alternatives—then, the argument runs, we must discard forms for the sake of substance. Sit-ins at lunch counters in the South were illegal, but they produced the kind of change that no amount of lobbying and letter-writing ever produced. Sit-ins at college buildings are illegal, but they are producing the kind of university reforms that no amount of peaceful student protest ever produced. In a word, where forms are ossified, they must be broken.

This argument is perfectly understandable, familiar, plausible, and specious. The question of just when a citizen legitimately disobeys authority troubled the Greek political theorists, found room in the political writings of Thomas Aquinas, and dominated the agonized dilemmas that a religiously divided Europe imposed on religious men in the late sixteenth century. The answers differed: There were many who held with St. Paul that "the powers that be are ordained of God"—that rebellion is never permissible, since the worst of tyrants is still somehow God's instrument on earth. And even those who licensed rebellion, like John Knox in Scotland or the Huguenot theorists in France, surrounded their justifications with high fences of caution and reserve. In the very act of giving reasons for disobedience, they were gravely conscious of the enormousness of their daring.

The doctrine of civil disobedience from Thoreau to Martin Luther King essentially translates this religious question for use in a secular world. Like the attack on form, this doctrine, too, is understandable, familiar, and plausible. But it is not specious. Its advocates respect form while challenging it, and thus they participate in the life of reason: They act, vigorously but sadly, and accept the consequences of their actions. Thus they preserve an order they feel compelled to improve, and keep open the way to further orderly improvement. We all know the colloquy between Thoreau and Emerson, when Emerson went to visit his friend in prison. "Why are you in jail?" Emerson asked. Thoreau asked in reply, "Why are you out of jail?" In this famous moment, form and substance met and merged.

It would be an error to associate the advocates of civil disobedience with those who champion the sovereign disregard of legal form. A Gandhi, who accepts jail, is on a different level from those who take part in a sit-in, who first obstruct others from doing their work and then demand amnesty. We may understand the latters' impatience—the newspapers, every day, bring news that make many of us very impatient indeed. We may even share many of their aspirations. But their arguments stand on a lower level of logic and ethics than those of the civil disobedience movement. It is not simply that their contemptuous view of the law deprives the lawbreaker of his dignity, and his act of lawbreaking of its meaning. Worse than that, their reasoning is an invitation to the reign of political irresponsibility and moral arrogance. It is one thing to be tired of a persistent policy, to be furious at the foot-dragging pace of social change; it is quite another to jump from such feelings to anarchism. For the justification for anarchism is the anarchist's confidence that his own judgment is superior to the constituted process within which change legitimately occurs. This is to put violence in the place of persuasion, elitism in the place of debate, the cynical exploitation of legal technicalities in the place of authentic respect for a system of order—in a word, it is to put will in the place of reason. Those who despise form *know* that they are right; like Robespierre, they are pure, and, being pure, they are dangerous. We must learn to beware of men who do not see that legitimate rights may be in conflict and who, in the name of extending freedom to all, abridge the freedom of others, forgetting that the only remedy for flawed laws is better laws—legally arrived at.

This is how I read the Enlightenment's view of the law, and this is why I think its view of importance to us. I feel apologetic about coming before you with such commonplaces. But, as I said at the beginning, we must look at the present with some dismay. And one reason for this dismay is that I should find it necessary to remind you of such commonplaces.

COMMENT

by Harris Wofford, Jr.

Let me be loyal to our profession and try to apply the Enlightenment principles given by Peter Gay to an actual case and controversy: the murder trial of Black Panthers in New Haven, and the response by Yale and by the Vice-President of the United States.

The news accounts suggested that it was possible—on May Day 1970, which we like to call Law Day—on the New Haven green to see the fall of the American Winter Palace, with a majority of Yale students swept along by their own aroused sympathies and by the revolutionary rhetoric of a wave of visitors, with the faculty falling apart and unwilling to defend the rule of law, and with the chaplain contending that though there was a murder, our society's pervasive discrimination makes a trial of those indicted legally right but morally wrong.

Before Bill Buckley writes another book against Yale, let me add a few notes from *The Harvard Crimson*, commenting on a riot in Cambridge. This is what the editorial chairman of the *Crimson* wrote:

> The wholesale window-breaking and looting . . . made the night successful. Such activity *does* raise the price of imperialism and racism. . . . Where have the years of marching gotten us? Who has a plan up his sleeve that he can guarantee will work better to keep Bobby Seale from being executed? The smashing and looting . . . are desperate measures, but what is left but desperation after every other kind of protest has failed to stop the killing in Asia and at home? (Frank Rich, April 20, 1970)

And the *Crimson* concluded that "On May 1, in New Haven, the widening of support for violence; the new excitement of looting (which, like it or not, proved in the long run to be a successful tactic of the 1965 ghetto riots)" and other factors "can lead to no other outcome than wholesale violence."

Closer to home, for several hours at Hunter College recently I saw the ugly face of anarchy as a moderate students' rally was disrupted and taken over by a militant minority who drowned out any dissenting voice or attempt at discussion by chanting "Same Old Shit." Law is not dead on these campuses but it seems to be in very bad shape.

What has given birth to this strange madness of revolutionary zealotry, and what can we do about it?

Peter Gay has given one clue, in suggesting that anarchy has two faces and that the other face of anarchy is not a bearded student making nonnegotiable demands, but the clean-shaven bureaucrat who makes a mockery of authority, the official who emphasizes order over justice, who espouses neglect as a strategy, and who has no better case for law than the refrain "The law is the law is the law."

"Law and order," Professor Gay says, has become a code phrase that "really stands in all eyes for policemen clubbing students, government officials . . . employing electronic snooping, governors seeking to stifle dissent . . ."—and he should add Vice-Presidents, or at least the only one the United States has got, a man who is deliberately using the power of the Vice-Presidency to purge university presidents and destroy the autonomy not just of news commentators but now of the Academy itself.

It is this kind of contempt for law, abuse of office, and arrogance of power that is turning off and deeply alienating so many of the best minds of the younger generation. To paraphrase Ramsey Clark, the worst kind of contempt for law is the contempt by those sworn officially to uphold it.

Let me be fair to Mr. Agnew. We *are* caught in a vicious circle. The Vice-President is right that "civil disobedience has degenerated into criminal violence." He is right that "anarchic dreamers" in some cities and on many campuses are a threat to the rule of law which Peter Gay calls "the essential precondition for the life of reason." And I think he is right that the laws should be enforced, whether those brought to trial are white or black, young or old. For those who turn to bombs and guns and arson belong in jail or a hospital—at least I don't know any other places for them—and police and judicial process are the only recourse in such cases.

But the Vice-President is wrong and compounds our predicament, I believe, in lumping together *civil* and *uncivil* disobedience, in not dis-

tinguishing between violence and nonviolence, in treating peaceful protesters as beyond the pale of reasonable dialogue. When he castigates
"the whole damn zoo" of "deserters, malcontents, radicals, incendi-
aries, the civil and uncivil disobedients," he is dangerously polarizing
our politics and competing from the Right with the unreasonable
rhetoric of the Left.

What is the appropriate response? I sometimes wish a sense of
humor and British calm would suffice, and that we could just copy the
bobby who stands at Hyde Park Corner saying to protesters who come
down the street, "All those who favor beheading the king, move into
the park and let the traffic pass." But letting the traffic pass—business
as usual—will not work when we are already caught in a massive
traffic jam—when our society's capacity to deal effectively with the
pending life-and-death issues of war, race, pollution, population, and
education is on trial, when the very air we breathe, water we drink, and
land to live on now depend on the revival and vast extension of the
rule of law.

Here, it seems to me, Kingman Brewster was pointing in the right
direction, as he has done so often in recent years, when he joined the
dialogue at Yale, agreed that the issues raised by the students deserved
the full attention of the community and gave as his personal response
a pledge. "I personally want to become more effective," he said, in improving the condition of the blacks in America. Write that large and
it is the kind of response required. We of the legal profession, and we
educators, must do more—much more—to make American law and
education more effective—much more effective—in meeting all the
public problems mounting around us. Only reason applied on an unprecedented scale through the art of politics can solve these problems,
and law, as the men of the Enlightenment used to say, is that Reason
Writ Large, Man's Second Reason, our form of public reasoning.

It is Peter Gay's emphasis on this relationship between law and
learning that seems to me most helpful in his paper. His reminder that
some of the best minds of the Enlightenment "thought that the law
itself might act as an educator" is most timely. Certainly the Supreme
Court has been a powerful educator throughout our history, and especially in the last decades, and persuasion seems to be the central
principle of the whole federal and republican system, with separation

and division of powers, checks and balances, and freedoms that all promote, even require, reasoning through law. This states an affirmative and creative case for law, an enlightened if not the Enlightenment view of law which—applied in effective action now, as Ralph Nader is doing, and Martin Luther King did—should appeal to many being repelled by the negative and narrow view of law propounded by the Vice-President.

In summary, the argument goes like this: Law, the great teacher, in its very commands is asking questions, the most serious questions our society can ask, the ones to which we attach public sanctions. As Peter Gay put it, "In refusing to take for granted the need for obedience, the Enlightenment insisted that any call for obedience must rationally justify itself." In thus asking us to judge and choose, the law enables us to be free—to be rulers who rule ourselves. Each law in this view asks every citizen: Is this a good, a just law? The citizen is required to respond, one way or another. If he concludes the law is just, his response should be obedience. If he concludes it is unjust, he has a responsibility to try to change it, and, along with a whole series of other political efforts to change the law, the possible ultimate alternative of disobedience must be entertained.

From St. Thomas up to Gene Rostow today, most men of law have reserved disobedience for extreme cases where a person's religion or conscience or other claims of a higher law were so violated that the high price of anarchy, including possible violence, was worth paying. But Socrates and Gandhi, and in our time Martin Luther King, saw a way of sailing between this Scylla and Charybdis. In the *Apology*, facing curtailment of his freedom of speech by actions of the majority in Athens, Socrates said, "Men of Athens, I honour and love you; but I shall obey God rather than you . . . and if this is the doctrine which corrupts the youth, I am a mischievous person." Then in the *Crito*, dealing with the issue of whether he should seek to escape the penalty, Socrates decided to drink the hemlock, so as not to break his social contract with Athens and thus subvert the very process of law which he respected as a mother from whom he got all his freedom.

This is the civil disobedience which Gandhi and King offered as a new political alternative. It affirms a moral relationship to law based on a serious and continuing dialogue in the form of a very direct registering of consent and dissent. By specifying and emphasizing the *civility*, that is, nonviolence and respectful—Gandhi insisted cheerful—acceptance of the law's sanction, this course seeks not to abolish the law but to fulfill it. The voluntary suffering of such jail-going is undertaken as a hopefully potent form of persuasion within the pale of our legal system.

But let us be clear. This is not a soft doctrine. It presumes that the laws will be enforced. It claims no right to amnesty. It deeply respects the Law, even while disobeying a particular law. As Gandhi told the judge before whom he was first being tried in India, "If you agree with me, resign your office; if not, do your duty and please impose the maximum penalty."

Civil disobedience is indeed full of paradox, for one man's natural law is another man's poison, and it is particularly difficult in America, where the appeal to higher law is almost written into the Constitution by the very ambiguity of such promises as due process, equal protection, and freedom of speech. Martin Luther King usually discovered that what he started as civil disobedience turned out, in the courts' ultimate decisions, to have been quite legal constitutional testing of invalid statutes or state actions.

Nevertheless, King represented a valid and, I think, still very promising approach in the politics of protest. In the effect on law there is a world of difference between the nonviolent direct actions of Dr. King and the actions of the Black Panthers, between Dr. Spock and Abbie Hoffman. Wouldn't Martin Luther King, alive and leading nonviolent action, even back in the Birmingham jail, do more to restore faith in law than any amount of "law and order" imposed by police or National Guard gas, clubs, or guns? King said he never felt more a partner in the making of American law than when he was in jail protesting one.

A wider and better understanding of the difference between civil and uncivil disobedience, a special respect for those who practice true *civil* disobedience, and an imaginative application of law as dialogue could help provide a partial antidote to the present spirit of anarchy. Kingman Brewster, in refusing to disown our sons and daughters, in respecting the students' avowed commitment to nonviolence, and in

seeking to turn the confrontation into an occasion for serious consideration of the substantive issues presented, has been taking this course.

If anyone does turn to violence, Mr. Brewster will, I feel sure, invoke
appropriate sanctions of the law, as President Wexler at Hunter College has done so courageously, when and as necessary. For law does
not lose its teaching power merely because on occasion its full sanctions must be applied; on the contrary, as the strongest form of education we have, part of its teaching comes from its very enforcement.
Perhaps one reason civil disobedience on campuses has tended to de-
generate into criminal violence is that those in authority have themselves lost faith in law, or at least lost their nerve.

Instead, we need the kind of persistence in dialogue that Mr. Brewster under great pressure has demonstrated. For, as he said last week,
our chance of solving the problems before us "will depend greatly on
two things: first, whether or not the younger generation feels that the
critic, the skeptic and the heretic are still welcome, even honored and
respected, in the United States; and second, whether or not they feel
that the channels of communication, persuasion and change are truly
open, as the Bill of Rights intended they should be."

In passing I should note a personal dissent. I disagree with Mr.
Brewster's expression of skepticism about a fair trial for black revolutionaries at a time, it seemed to me, when a defense of our courts was
called for. But the attacks on the Panthers and the Panthers' own violent
language have certainly aroused widespread passions and prejudices,
among both whites and blacks who might sit on juries if not on the
bench. So Mr. Brewster has raised an important point, or rather the
Panthers and other would-be revolutionaries by their actions are
raising an important point, and we cannot simply rest content with
pride in the creative role that courts have played in this whole area in
the past twenty years. How *do* we deal fairly with this unusual challenge by disrupters who range from serious revolutionaries to very sick
adolescents?

I do not know, but to keep our law alive I think we must give new
vitality to political dialogue, and new demonstrations of the affirmative,
enabling role of law. If we believe in a civilization of dialogue, we
must accept a law that teaches by posing questions and being ques-

tioned. Therefore, we should listen attentively to our republics of
learning called colleges and universities, especially when we disagree—
which I expect now to do as Gene Rostow, my teacher, disagrees with
me.

CHAPTER 2

THE RIGHTFUL LIMITS OF FREEDOM IN A LIBERAL DEMOCRATIC STATE: OF CIVIL DISOBEDIENCE[1]

by Eugene V. Rostow

I. INTRODUCTION

As Geoffrey Woodhead points out, any book is "the child of its time." Even classical scholarship invariably reflects not only the pre-occupations of the scholar's world, but also his own reactions to that world.[2] If, as Woodhead shows, this is the case for the study of Thucydides, it is hardly remarkable that the focus of concern has recently shifted in the literature of liberty. The contributors to that literature are usually men and women devoted to the expansion and protection of personal freedom. For many centuries, they have written almost exclusively about the obligation of the liberal state to respect the moral autonomy of the individual. They have preached toleration, and attacked beliefs which they thought had become superstitions, restraints which no longer deserved the support of opinion. Today, for the first time in modern history, there is widespread interest in the reciprocal issue—the rightful obligation

[1] This paper draws on "The Consent of the Governed," a Fourth of July oration delivered at Monticello under the auspices of the Thomas Jefferson Memorial Foundation in 1968, and reprinted in the Autumn 1968 *Virginia Quarterly Review;* on "Chief Justice Warren and the Gift for Action," a speech given in 1968 and printed in the Spring 1969 issue of the *Yale Law Report;* and on a memorandum prepared for the National Commission on the Causes and Prevention of Violence in 1969.

[2] Geoffrey A. Woodhead, *Thucydides on the Nature of Power* (1969), pp. ix–xii.

of the individual to the liberal society in which he chooses to live.[3]
The reasons for the change are self-evident. All over the world—
at least in societies which have or wish to achieve liberal governments—difficult problems have arisen in defining the boundary between individual freedom and public order.

In drawing that boundary, cultures like ours tend to resolve most
doubts in favor of individual liberty. We are still dominated by the
optimism of the Enlightenment, and its faith in the perfectability of
man. And we believe that the continuity of American society, and
of our constitutional system, is the order of nature. We never really
doubt their toughness and tenacity, and their capacity to brush off
any threat. Still, though our law goes to great lengths to protect the
individual against the state, it has hardly abandoned its inherent
right to protect the state against the individual, or the hostile group,
and to insist on some deference to the prevailing code of social
morality.

[3] Among recent articles and books, these exemplify the resurgence of interest in the problem of obligation: M. Walzer, *Obligations: Essays on Disobedience, War, and Citizenship* (1970); H. W. Jones, *The Efficacy of
Law* (1969); A. Fortas, *Concerning Dissent and Civil Disobedience* (1968);
J. P. Plamenatz, *Consent, Freedom and Political Obligation* (2nd ed. 1968);
G. Woodcock, *Civil Disobedience* (1963); H. A. Bedau, ed., *Civil Disobedience: Theory and Practice* (1960); W. O. Douglas, *Points of Rebellion*
(1970); H. L. Nieburg, *Political Violence* (1966); C. Cohen, H. A. Free-
man, and E. Van Den Haag, "Civil Disobedience and the Law," 21 Rutgers
L. Rev. 1, 17, and 27 (1966); C. L. Black, "The Problem of the Compata-
bility of Civil Disobedience with American Institutions of Government," 43
Texas L.R. 492 (1965); M. Keeton, "The Morality of Civil Disobedience,"
43 Texas L.R. 507 (1965); P. Freund, "Civil Rights and the Limits of Law,"
14 Buffalo L.R. 199 (1964); J. Goldstein, "Psychoanalysis and Jurisprudence," 77 Yale L.J. 1053 (1968), esp. pp 1064–1071; H. Pitkin, "Obligation and Consent," 59 Amer. Pol. Sci. Rev. 990 (1965) and 60 Amer.
Pol. Sci. Rev. 39 (1966); F. A. Allen, "Civil Disobedience," 36
Cincinnati L.R. (1965), H. Prosch, "Towards an Ethics of Civil Disobedience," 77 Ethics 171 (1968); Kent Greenawalt, "A Contextual Approach to
Disobedience," 70 Col. L. Rev. 48 (1970); C. Blackstone, "Civil Disobedience: Is It Justified?" 3 Georgia L. Rev. 679 (1969). The three collections
of value-oriented papers on *Philosophy, Politics and Society,* ed. by Peter
Laslett, and then by Laslett and W. G. Runciman (1956, 1962, and 1969),
represent the movement, and have given it momentum. *Essays in Legal
Philosophy,* edited by R. S. Summers (1970), should also be noted, as should
James Finn, ed., *A Conflict of Loyalties, the Case for Selective Conscientious
Objection* (1968).

Cultures of pessimism, on the other hand, tend to give greater weight to the claims of order. They start from a Hobbesian view of human nature. They never confuse men with angels, and they live with nightmare memories of civil war, revolution, and tyranny. Their instinct is to keep the dark side of mankind in tighter rein, and, if choice be necessary, to sacrifice some individual freedom to the hope of social peace.

If men live together in society, the fact and the mode of their cooperation necessarily limit their individual freedom. How a society fixes these inevitable outer limits of individual freedom is one of the few issues of public policy on which it is legitimate to distinguish a "liberal" from a "conservative" position. The terms are so fashionable, and are invoked so often, that they have lost nearly all their meaning. But in this area—that of marking the zone of toleration, and of freedom protected from the state—these cherished words do apply. I should make it clear that I approach the subject as a liberal who believes in the widest feasible zone of personal freedom for the individual as a good in itself—indeed as one of the highest goals of law in human society. I approach it also as a student of the social process who is convinced that the law of a society must reconcile the claims of liberty and of order in accordance not with my personal norms of social justice, and my vision of the future, but with its own—the spirit of its law, in Montesquieu's phrase, its superego, in effect, and the compass of its quest for the grail.[4] If the law deviates from that course, society is subjected to severe and potentially dangerous tension.

American constitutional law has witnessed a remarkable enlargement of the realm of personal freedom during the last forty years. Viewed in perspective, the growth of our law of civil liberty and of civil right, starting about 1915, and gaining momentum steadily after 1930, is an achievement of merit, however much remains to be done. Now, like other open societies, we are being forced to re-examine the rightful limits of personal freedom—right-

---

[4] The phrase is Lord Radcliffe's, from *The Law and Its Compass* (1960). I have commented on the problem in "The Enforcement of Morals," Cambridge Law Journal 174 (1960), reprinted in *The Sovereign Prerogative* (1962), p. 45.

ful, that is, for our society, living in harmony with the code of its particular, and particularly libertarian, constitution.

The degree of stress in this process of re-examination is notably acute for the United States, as compared with other democratic societies. Our society is being subjected to the pressure of deep and disturbing psychosocial transformations. Several are unique to the American scene.

And in the United States, as in other countries, social protest is being expressed and dramatized in new and sometimes disturbing styles.[5]

Wherever men look, they witness happenings which affront their sense of the right order of things—bombings, strange increases in the common crimes, turbulence at the universities, draft resistance, the rhetoric and sometimes the pantomime of revolution. In turn, these storms have stirred an intense preoccupation with the ancient philosophical problem of man's moral relation to the law.

I should make it clear at the start that the subject of this paper is the model for right behavior which should prevail in a liberal civilization, and particularly in the United States. A generally accepted model for exemplary behavior has a profound influence on the pattern of actual behavior, although even the most upright and responsible citizen doesn't always succeed in living up to it. The influence of legal and moral norms on society does not depend on whether laws are fully enforced or fully respected at any given moment. The critical issue, as Weber pointed out, is "the 'orientation' of an action toward a norm, rather than the 'success' of that norm." [6]

In this perspective, and for this purpose, how should we evaluate the claims being put forward in the name of civil disobedience?

---

[5] The creation and development of the twentieth-century style in social disruption is brilliantly reviewed by Norman F. Cantor in *The Age of Protest* (1969), and by George Dangerfield in *The Strange Death of Liberal England* (1936). These themes are traced more deeply in Norman Cohn, *The Pursuit of the Millennium* (1957) and John Passmore, *The Perfectibility of Man* (1971).

[6] Max Weber, *On Law in Economy and Society,* ed. by Max Rheinstein (1954), p. 13.

II. The Case for Civil Disobedience

Is the highest form of moral liberty, as Rousseau contended, "obedience to self-imposed law," which alone makes man truly his own master? [7]

Or is there an inalienable right of civil disobedience which citizens of conscience possess because they are moral beings—a right to disobey valid laws they do not approve, and to engage in organized programs of unlawful conduct (including some recourse to violence) by way of protest against such laws?

There are, of course, now as always, cynics, immoralists, and criminals among us, and genuine revolutionaries as well—romantics with a burning desire to destroy society in the name of anarchy, communism, nihilism, or even vaguer doctrines of purification and rebirth through the purge of fire. But their efforts rally significant support only because many people are in doubt about the extent of their duty to obey valid laws they oppose. The pervasiveness of such doubts has been a factor leading to violence, or weakening the restraints against it, particularly in the cycle of troubles which have beset our universities, and spread from the universities to other areas of society.

An extensive literature asserts that there is a right of civil disobedience, and that the more disturbing features of the movements of protest to which society has been subjected—the turbulence, the violence, the shouting down of speakers, the campaigns to discredit authority and even due process of law—are all moral, legitimate, and indeed legal exercises of a kind of personal freedom which the law should now recognize as subsumed within the idea of liberty protected by the Constitution. Some proponents of civil disobedience contend that even if some of the occasions on which this "right" has been exercised have involved acts which in their view should be recognized as "excessive," and therefore "technically" illegal, society should be wise enough not to prosecute the men, women, and children of superior virtue who are responsible for them. They do no more, it is urged, than apply the tactics of the

[7] *The Social Contract* (1762), Bk. I, Ch. 8.

civil rights movement, and the philosophy of Martin Luther King, Jr., in other settings. If it was right, and legal, for black students to sit at the counter of a lunchroom in North Carolina twenty years ago, and ask for food despite a state law forbidding its sale to them, it is argued, then it must be also right, and legal, for Harvard students to sit in the dean's office and demand an end of R.O.T.C., the abolition of grades, or the employment of more blacks on Harvard construction projects.

Besides, it is said, even if some of the manifestations of civil disobedience go "too" far, one should put the blame not on those who have committed the "excessive" acts, but on the society whose callousness to injustice has driven morally superior persons to such extreme behavior. In any event, they contend, the "excessive" protests are redeemed by their beneficent effects. They dramatize the views of the protesters for the media, and they jar our stolid and harassed institutions into reform.

Other arguments and analogies are advanced to justify the recognition of at least a limited legal and moral right of civil disobedience. The Nuremberg Trials are often invoked to support the contention that in the United States men are bound to disobey laws they believe to be unjust, and to organize illegal protests against them. Similarly, one finds many references to Gandhi, Thoreau, and George Washington as proponents and exemplars of civil disobedience.

Finally, some of the more analytical supporters of the idea contend that society should recognize a limited and entirely nonviolent right of civil disobedience for men who disobey the law to advance not their own moral principles but those of society itself, when in fact, or at least in the firm and sincere judgment of the demonstrators, the laws have deviated from the community's sense of justice.

In a few cases, philosophers advance norms of their own, rather than those they conceive to be implicit in the moral code of American society itself, as the proper test for the citizen's obligation to the law in a society of consent. A few would make obedience to law a prudential matter for the individual, an issue of convenience, of balancing the advantages and risks for him, rather than an ethical question. Others argue that the individual does face an ethical prob-

lem in determining his relation to the law, but that the ethical problem must be resolved—by the individual, or perhaps in the end by
the law-making agencies of society—on utilitarian grounds ("the
greatest good for the greatest number"). Another group would
claim a right of disobedience for the individual because in practice
the law does not reach a standard of tolerance and perfection which
is advanced as the only true test and bench mark of justice.

Others argue that while the social-contract theory is morally persuasive as to laws the free citizen has helped to make himself, it
cannot bind the citizen to laws made by his elected representatives.

Finally, a few would contend that while the social-contract argument is unassailable in its own terms, the United States is not a
society of consent—that power is so concentrated, politics so corrupt, opportunity so limited, and freedom so illusory, that America
must be regarded as the equivalent of Hitler's Germany, or the
Soviet Union.

These are the main themes of the case for civil disobedience
which have impressed and shaken public opinion without quite persuading it. Many of the writers, clergymen, professors, judges, and
philosophers who support these views command wide respect. For
our culture, there is deep resonance, calling up the memory of
heroes and martyrs, in the comment of one of the leaders of draft
resistance that what he did "may be a crime, but it is not a sin."

III. The Obligation to Obey Valid Law in a Society of Consent: The Major Premise

It is the thesis of this paper that our society—as a society of consent—should not and indeed cannot acknowledge a right of civil
disobedience; that the moral and philosophical arguments advanced in support of such a right are in error; and that the analogies invoked in its behalf are inapplicable.

The major premise of my argument is the corollary of Jefferson's
magisterial sentence, which echoes Locke, Rousseau, and a long
line of philosophers stretching back to Plato at least: The "just
powers" of government derive from "the consent of the governed."

It follows, I should contend, that in a society of consent the powers of government are just in Jefferson's sense: that is, they are legitimate, because authorized and renewed by procedures of voting all must respect. As a consequence, a citizen of such a society owes his fellow citizens, and the state they have established together, a moral duty to obey *valid* laws until they are repealed or fall into desuetude. I stress the word "valid" in the preceding sentence, to distinguish situations—of the utmost importance for our legal system—where the citizen is testing the constitutionality of a statute, an ordinance, or an official act. I cannot regard such tests as acts of disobedience to law.

For me, this proposition is the beginning, not the end, of the problem. It does not of itself permit us to resolve all the questions which are necessarily involved in defining the citizen's obligation to the law in a society of consent. But, I should contend, it is the right place to start such an analysis.

The individual owes other moral duties in his life—to his God, his family, his work, his conscience. Sometimes—often—there is conflict among the moral claims upon a man. But if man lives in a society of consent, and above all in a society of equality and of liberty, his relation to the valid laws of that society should be regarded as moral in character, and entitled to great weight in the hierarchy of moral claims he must face in the course of his life. If a man decides to commit an act of civil disobedience—for example, because he feels that what the law requires would breach his obligation to God—our culture would acknowledge at most his power, but not his right or privilege to do so. In such cases, the citizen faces a moral dilemma—he may resolve it in one way or another. But I can find no basis for saying that society has acknowledged, or must acknowledge, or should acknowledge his "right" to decide to violate the law. If the citizen should violate the law, then he should in turn acknowledge that he thereby breaches a covenant with moral dimensions, and is not committing a purely technical offense. To be sure, he would contend that he is breaking the law in order to avoid what he would regard as a greater sin. But the law too has a moral content; it represents the moral judgment of the majority, and its sense of justice. Under such circumstances, the individual should at least respect his duty to the law he has helped to make by accepting its penalties.

Most philosophers have concluded that the citizen's relation to the law in a society of consent is a moral obligation, and not simply a matter of convenience, of habit, or of fear. Different theories have been put forward to account for the moral element in the citizen's obligation to the law in such societies. On analysis they turn out to be contractual in character, if not always in language. The moral obligation to obey the law, they say, is in the end an instance of the moral obligation to keep one's promises, particularly one's important promises, on which others have relied. Some writers stress the importance of an explicit promise, like a formal oath. Others infer a promissory obligation either from the citizen's voluntary participation in a society he is free to leave, or from the reliance of other citizens, who have obeyed the law, on the expectation of his obedience in turn. The citizen, these men say, has accepted the benefit of the laws, and of the obedience of others to them. Therefore he owes his fellow citizens, and the law, a reciprocal obligation.

The benefit theory of the social contract, while perfectly familiar as contract doctrine, proves too much. It does not permit a discrimination between the citizen's obligation to the law in a tyranny and in a democracy. But that distinction is surely the heart of the matter. The citizen accepts some benefits—i.e., fire protection or education—from the most despotic regimes, and may be deemed to have consented, or at least submitted, even to slavery.

But the essence of Jefferson's thesis is that unless the citizen can participate responsibly in the making of the laws, he is not morally bound to obey them.

It may be more direct, and more realistic, to draw the moral element in the citizen's obligation to the law from the necessary conditions of social cooperation within different kinds of societies. The obligation to the law of a citizen in a liberal, democratic society is necessarily greater than that of a citizen under conditions of tyranny. The spacious tolerance of a free society is possible only if the laws are generally accepted and respected voluntarily, so that the role of force and coercion in the society can be kept to a minimum. The idea of a free society posits a much higher degree of civic responsibility on the part of each citizen than the concept of a tyranny or a system of paternalism. When a man elects to be a citizen of a society of consent, he necessarily undertakes a personal and far-reaching obligation to the laws, and his fellows do likewise. No such society could fulfil its aspirations, nor indeed remain free very long, unless this obligation were respected.

Thus the substantive content of the social contract is not the same in all societies, although in all—even in prisons—there are some links, some rules which define the relations of members to each other, and to the whole. For a society of consent—and particularly for the liberal and egalitarian democracy of the United States—Jefferson's axiom demands that the citizen take a high degree of responsibility for the law. In the words of the famous first sentence of Montesquieu's *Spirit of the Laws,* this approach defines the citizen's duty to the law of a free society as "a necessary relation derived from the nature of things," that is, in its broadest sense, a law.

The modern, secular world has long since rejected the divine right of kings. The proudest claim of the legal tradition we inherited is that the king is under the law. Locke's theory of the social compact has become the prevailing political theory of modern times and the only modern rival for the doctrine that power proceeds from the barrel of a gun. I agree with Professor Rawls that it is the appropriate basis, both in ethics and in political theory, for the concept of political obligation in a democracy.[8] As Professor d'Entrèves has said, "The principle of equality, together with the related notion of consent as the foundation of power, is the essential component of the idea of legitimacy in the modern world." [9]

The notion of the social compact is of course a metaphor. The social contract is hardly a formal document to be interpreted like a

[8] John Rawls, "The Justification of Civil Disobedience," in Bedau, *op. cit.* (note 3), p. 241.

[9] A. P. d'Entrèves, *The Notion of the State* (1967), p. 199. He warns, and warns wisely, that "equality has its perils, and . . . consent is no sufficient guarantee of the preservation of the basic values of democracy, since it is possible to consent to anything, even to being no longer equal or free."

deed. But the phrase embodies the idea of an understanding none-theless, a core of quintessential ideas, values and customs, defining the ultimate norms of the society, and binding all who share its culture. That body of shared values—what Cicero called the con-cordia of society—is the foundation on which any community is built. It involves a commitment on the part of each citizen to play the game according to the moral code of the community as a whole, and to respect the equal rights of all his fellow citizens.

The social contract binds the state as well as the citizen. The two sets of obligations are reciprocal. Neither can exist without the other. But the citizen's obligation continues as long as the state re-mains faithful to the fundamental rules.

The social contract is the organizing principle of society. It does not vanish when either party—the state or the citizen—breaches one or another of its covenants, so long as the basic pattern remains vital. Even the most perfect of democratic societies is capable of error, and indeed capable of error which violates its own code of social morality, or higher ideals urged by individuals in the name of moral advance. But unless such errors breach the essential terms of the social contract itself, and destroy the capacity of de-mocracy to correct its errors, they do not weaken the citizen's moral obligation to obey valid law, nor do they dissolve the social con-tract.

The question is always one of degree. If, for example, a Presi-dent should dismiss the Supreme Court and the Congress, and at-tempt to rule by decree, all would concur, I should suppose, that the United States had become a different country, and that the so-cial compact itself was in gage. But an individual is not justified in concluding that the state has abrogated the social contract because he feels, and feels passionately, that injustices are unremedied, or not remedied fast enough. Human society has never achieved Uto-pia, and it is not likely to do so soon. The test proposed by Jeffer-son is still persuasive. Governments are instituted among men, he argued, to secure the unalienable rights of man. It follows, he said, that men are justified in altering the form of their government when it becomes destructive of these ends, and in revolution itself when "a long train of abuses and usurpations, pursuing invariably the same Object, evinces a design to reduce them under absolute Despotism." [10]

As Professor Rawls has written, "Even under a just Constitution, unjust laws may be passed and unjust policies enforced. Some form of majority principle is necessary but the majority may be mistaken, more or less willfully, in what it legislates. . . . Assuming that the Constitution is just and that we have accepted and plan to continue to accept its benefits, we then have both an obligation and a natural duty (and in any case the duty) to comply with what the majority enacts even though it may be unjust. In this way we become bound to follow unjust laws, not always, of course, but provided the injustice does not exceed certain limits." [11]

The moral duty to obey valid laws is expressed and explained in somewhat different ways.

The purely legal tradition is that each person is bound by ties of allegiance to the sovereignty of a nation, to its laws and to its social code, by the fact of residence or citizenship. Allegiance, the lawbooks have said for centuries, is the reciprocal of the protection each person receives through living in an organized community.

The nature of a citizen's adherence to the social compact of a free society is expounded as a matter of consent by Plato in the *Crito*.

The most famous and most influential denial of Socrates' argument is that of Thoreau. His essay "Civil Disobedience" and his "Speech in Defense of John Brown" assert the theory that a citizen of superior virtue—the rare man of conscience, a member of the "wise minority," in his phrase—has the right and indeed is under a duty to disobey valid laws—like tax laws—when his conscience, and his conscience alone, tells him that important policies of the society are wrong.

The *Crito* presents Socrates on his last day. Crito had come at dawn, to offer Socrates a chance to escape so that he could live safely in exile. In answering his friend's urging that he should leave prison, despite the decision against him under the laws of Athens—

[10] The Declaration of Independence.
[11] Rawls, *op. cit.* (note 8), p. 245.

a decision he regarded as erroneous and unjust—Socrates speaks for the laws, in declaring man's ultimate duty to obey the decisions of a reasonable legal system he has voluntarily accepted, when he has failed to convince the authorities of law that they are wrong.

Since the literature of the subject contains little beyond a few grace notes that are not dealt with in these essays, I can summarize the debate by presenting an imaginary dialogue between Socrates and Thoreau.

SOCRATES: In leaving the prison against the will of the Athenians, do I not wrong those whom I ought least to wrong? Do I not desert the principle that we are never intentionally to do wrong, and that injustice is always an evil and dishonor to him who acts unjustly?

THOREAU: But the mass of men serve the state not as men mainly, but as machines, with their bodies. In most cases there is no free exercise whatever of the judgment or of the moral sense; but they put themselves on a level with wood and earth and stones. Such command no more respect than men of straw or a lump of dirt. They have the same sort of worth only as horses or dogs. When power is in the hands of the people, a majority continues to rule not because they are most likely to be in the right, nor because this seems fairest to the minority, but because they are physically the strongest. Can there not be a government in which majorities do not virtually decide right and wrong, but conscience?

SOCRATES: Suppose I do play truant, and the laws and government come to interrogate me. "Tell us, Socrates," they say, "what are you about? Are you not going by an act of yours to overturn us—the laws, and the whole state so far as in you lies? Do you imagine that a state can subsist and not be overthrown, in which the decisions of law have no power, but are set aside and trampled upon by individuals?"

THOREAU: In fact, I quietly declare war with the state, after my fashion, though I will still make what use and get what advantage of her I can. The authority of government, even such as I am willing to submit to, is still an impure one: To be strictly just, it must have the sanction and consent of the governed. It can have no pure right over my person and property but what I concede it. I please myself with imagining a state at last which would not think it inconsistent with its own repose if a few were to live aloof from it, not meddling with it nor embraced by it.

SOCRATES: "And was that our agreement with you?" the laws would answer, "or were you to abide by the sentence of the state? For, having brought you into the world and nurtured and educated you, and given you and every other citizen a share in every good which we have to give, we further proclaim to any Athenian, by the liberty which we allow him, that if he does not like us when he has become of age and has seen the ways of the city, and made our acquaintance, he may go where he pleases and take his goods with him. But he who has experience of the manner in which we order justice and administer the state, and still remains, has entered into an implied contract that he will do as we command him. And he who disobeys us is, as we maintain, wrong, because he has made an agreement with us that he will duly obey our commands; and he neither obeys them nor convinces us that our commands are unjust; and we do not rudely impose them, but give him the alternative of obeying or convincing us; that is what we offer, and he does neither."

THOREAU: But there are nine hundred and ninety-nine patrons of virtue to one virtuous man. All voting is a sort of gaming, like checkers or backgammon, with a slight moral tinge to it, a playing with right and wrong. A wise man will not leave the right to the mercy of chance nor wish it to prevail through the power of the majority. There is little virtue in the action of masses of men. Any man more right than his neighbors constitutes a majority of one already. Why is the government not more apt to anticipate and provide for reform? Why does it not cherish its wise minority? It is not a man's duty as a matter of course to devote himself to the eradication of even the most enormous wrong; but it is his duty at least to wash his hands of it.

SOCRATES: But I of all men have acknowledged the agreement, made at leisure, not in haste or under any compulsion or deception. If I flee, the laws will say, "Consider, Socrates, that if you do escape you will be doing us an injury. You would be breaking the covenants and agreements which you have made with us, and wronging those whom you ought least of all to wrong, that is to say, yourself, your friends, your country, and us, the laws, whom you would be doing your best to destroy."

THOREAU: Any man knows when he is justified, and all the wits in the world cannot enlighten him on that point. The murderer always knows he is justly punished; but when a government takes the life of a man without the consent of his conscience, it is an audacious government, and is taking a step toward its own dissolution.

SOCRATES: Who would care about a state which has no laws?

Professor Rawls, who approaches this subject very much as I do, would, however, justify narrowly limited forms of civil disobedience "in a reasonably just (though of course not perfectly just) democratic regime" [12] when they are entirely peaceful; when the actors fully accept the rightness of their punishment; when acts of disobedience are limited to dissent on fundamental questions of internal policy, and especially to "the liberties of equal citizenship"; and when they consist of political action which addresses "the sense of justice of the majority in order to urge reconsideration of the measures protested and to warn that, in the sincere opinion of the dissenters, the conditions of social cooperation are not being honored." [13]

In Professor Rawls's sense of the term, civil disobedience is "disobedience to law within the limits of fidelity to law"—that is, disobedience as a means of appealing to the majority, or to the courts, in the name of the sense of justice of the community as a whole.

I have one fundamental difficulty with Professor Rawls's definition. How are we to determine whether the "firm" and "sincere" minority is right in its view that the measures adopted by the majority violate the sense of justice of the community as a whole? Presumably, the majority has already decided the contrary. It has not as yet been persuaded by the arguments of the minority. Professor Rawls seeks to distinguish the grounds for civil disobedience he

[12] *Ibid.,* p. 240.
[13] *Ibid.,* pp. 246–247.

would have society respect from purely individual views of social justice, or views based on considerations of interest. But I, for one, can find no substance in his distinction.

I can understand the difference between the opinions of an individual about the morality and justice of a given measure, and the view of it that would be taken under the code of morality of society as a whole, as applied and interpreted by mass public opinion, by elections, by the President, by governors, by legislatures, by customary procedures of bargaining and informal adjustment, by courts, and ultimately by twelve men in a jury box. I can also understand that the dissenting individual would claim—with complete sincerity—that he was interpreting the community's sense of justice more correctly than the majority. Indeed, I often reach such conclusions myself about particular laws, policies, and judicial decisions. But if the majority does not come to agree, how can Professor Rawls's distinction justify civil disobedience in the one case, where the minority appeals to the community's sense of justice, but not in the other, where dissent rests on explicitly individual ethical views? Aren't the minority views quite as "individual" in the one case as in the other? I can find no halfway house, or Third Thing, between the two concepts. I conclude that while Professor Rawls would not allow civil disobedience to go as far as Thoreau, he would, like Thoreau, condone civil disobedience when the individual, and the individual alone, firmly, earnestly, and sincerely decides that he is right, and the majority wrong, in interpreting the community's sense of justice. Such arguments confuse "is" and "ought"—that is, they confuse the law (and morality)-that-is at any time with the law (and morality) an individual thinks preferable.

Professor Wolff's admirably clear paper in this book accepts the social-contract theory of obligation, but only for a limited case of no practical significance. His argument merits careful examination, for it is scrupulously put, and helps to define the philosophical difference between anarchism and all other theories of social life. And Professor Wolff's confession of doubt, at the end of his essay, highlights its moral and intellectual significance.

Wolff starts from a most particular premise. Using Rousseau's language, but not his analysis, Wolff says that when men submit to laws they have made themselves, they are "as free as before." Thus he would acknowledge a *moral* obligation to obey the law only for small communities where every citizen votes on all the laws, and a single negative defeats any measure. Even if the principle of majority rule is built into the social contract—as is surely the case for the United States—he argues that a free man who promises to obey the decisions of the majority forfeits his freedom, and his moral autonomy, exactly as if he had promised to obey "a king, or a priest, or a slave-master." He concludes therefore that in a representative democracy the citizen has no moral obligation to obey the law, although he may generally do so on grounds of convenience, prudence, and deference to the correlative interests and rights of his fellow citizens. For Wolff, the citizen is morally bound by a promise to obey a law only if he has himself formally voted for it, and, presumably, for each application of it as well. Then, but only then, does a moral obligation to obey the law flow from the promise of a morally autonomous man—a promise freely and directly given.

But should we—must we—accept Wolff's formula as the only valid test for determining when the citizen has a moral duty to obey the law?

Wolff starts with Kant's idea that the moral autonomy of the individual is both the end and the means of a just society. He agrees with Kant and Rousseau that a morally autonomous and responsible man ought to keep the promises he has made to those with whom he shares the benefits and burdens of social life. But tentatively, at least, he rejects Kant's view, and Rousseau's, that the idea of moral autonomy within a just society is compatible with the practice of representative government, based on the majority principle. Instead, he insists that the citizen who lives in an organized society retains his moral autonomy only if he is "as free as before": that is, as free as Robinson Crusoe.

I agree with Wolff that the citizen "loses" some freedom—as compared with Crusoe—by promising to obey majority decisions on matters which the society has committed by agreement to its government. I should go further. He would "lose" quite as much freedom, in Wolff's sense, in a society where every citizen had a veto over policies desired by his fellows. I should suppose that the individual can never be as free as Crusoe in an organized society, however libertarian.

What follows?

Rousseau's metaphor is hardly a usable standard for so fundamental a discrimination. It is a romantic fancy dear to the vocabulary of the Enlightenment, and integral to the task of turning men's hearts from God to Nature's God. The notion of man living in a state of nature was a step toward liberation from theology, Reason's substitute for the Garden of Eden.

But for all its charm, this whimsy cannot provide a convincing ethical criterion by which to measure man's obligation to the laws he has helped to make.

In the first place, as Hobbes showed with devastating force, the state of nature is hardly an idyll, once there are two Robinson Crusoes trying to adjust to each other's freedom, but a brutish condition of war and chaos in which the individual can never live tranquilly, confident that his rights will be respected. Methods for adjusting competing claims of freedom and autonomy would be needed even in Wolff's ideal state of natural anarchy, in order to avoid dominance by one citizen over another. If the citizens of the anarchy agree upon an acceptable method for reconciling conflicting claims, and establish limits for conflict, so that one will not be able to indulge his autonomy at the expense of the autonomy of another, won't they be smuggling the social contract in at the back door, in the sequence of constitution-making which all the classic political philosophers described as the process of transition from the state of nature to commonwealth? And if they agree on a majority principle, or on judicial protection of individual rights, in order to assure each citizen an equal or an optimal degree of freedom, won't they necessarily cross the line Wolff has drawn so clearly? [14]

[14] These problems are examined in the papers of Profs. Dyke and Riker, in this book, and in K. J. Arrow, *Social Choice and Individual Values* (1951), esp. pp. 30 ff.; J. Rothenberg, *The Measurement of Social Welfare* (1961), Ch. 13, and "Conditions for a Social Welfare Function," 61 J. Polit. Econ. 389 (1953); and R. Wollheim, "A Paradox in the Theory of Democracy" in P. Laslett and W. G. Runciman, eds., *Philosophy, Politics, and Society,* Second Series (1962), p. 71.

But these refinements of the concept of Robinson Crusoe's autonomy are the least important aspect of the problem.

By living in society, man is necessarily less free than if he were living in a state of nature. This is what Rousseau meant by his distinction between "natural" and "civil" liberty. One should qualify this comment by recalling that there are many freedoms, and other amenities, which can be enjoyed only in organized society, so that it is by no means obvious that the sum total of freedom and of moral autonomy is necessarily less in society than in the woods; in large societies than in small; in cities rather than in the provincial villages of the countryside. It is hard, after all, to exercise one's moral autonomy save in facing the dilemmas, and making the choices, which arise from the presence of others, each also seeking to use his freedom.

Living in society, men enact laws in order to make freedom and serenity possible, and to secure other ends as well: decency, amenity, and social justice, for example. Each society will differ, as I remarked earlier, in its aspirations with respect to the degree of freedom and serenity to be sought for the citizen, and in its conceptions of decency, amenity, and social justice as well. Assuring the individual the moral autonomy of Robinson Crusoe is not the only concern, among the activities of society and of its government, which should be considered to have moral validity.

In this connection, the phrases of the American social contract are striking. The Declaration of Independence states the theme, with great but not exclusive stress on the protection of individual rights:

> We hold these Truths to be self-evident, that all Men are created equal, that they are endowed by their Creator with certain unalienable Rights, that among these are Life, Liberty, and the Pursuit of Happiness—That to secure these Rights, Governments are instituted among Men . . .

The Constitution enlarges and qualifies the thesis:

> We the People of the United States, in Order to form a more perfect Union, establish Justice, insure domestic tranquility, provide for the common defence, promote the general Welfare, and

secure the Blessings of Liberty to ourselves and our Posterity, do ordain and establish this Constitution . . .

The real problem in judging the ethical quality of social arrangements is not whether they achieve for the citizen the degree of moral autonomy which Robinson Crusoe possessed. Such a test would be chimerical, to say the least. Society must fulfill many functions and accommodate many jarring claims. In human societies, individual freedom and moral autonomy should not be viewed as absolutes, but as matters of more or less. Valid provisions made by the majority to provide for the common defense, for example, may well qualify individual freedom. It is not reasonable to judge the moral rightness of such accommodations by an absolute or Utopian standard.

Jefferson's standard—the standard of the American code of social justice—is drawn from two aspects of the idea of "consent." First, the individual has consented to the social compact: he has given his Platonic promise to obey the laws of the state where, as an adult, he has freely decided to stay. And, second, the society to whose code he has adhered is itself a society of consent.

The first meaning of the word "consent" in the previous paragraph would apply to the individual in any kind of society—tyrannical, oligarchic, or dictatorial—if he had freely accepted its rules. But "consent" in that sense is not enough to explain Jefferson's doctrine that the consent of the governed confers "just" powers on the government. He was talking about a particular kind of government, and a particular ideal for government—a vision of the enlightened republic as it emerged from the pages of Locke and Montesquieu, and the American experience. That ideal contemplated special arrangements to secure liberty—a wide dispersal of authority, and an independent judiciary to protect "the unalienable rights" of man, and to enforce other agreed limits on power against abuse by a transient majority. The citizen was free to come and go, with all his property. He could participate actively in public life, through rules and systems which minimized the risk of tyranny. Both aspects of the idea of "consent" are fundamental.

In the theory of American democracy, then, "consent" is more than a ritual acceptance of the social compact, done once in a life-time. It is not, in Wolff's phrase, equivalent to accepting the rule of "a king, or a priest, or a slave-master." On the contrary, it is con-sent to the initiation of a process of continuous citizen involvement in government, through which the mandate of government is regu-larly renewed from the only rightful source of its authority—the consent of the governed.

That theory, then, answers both the questions Professor Berlin regards as fundamental to the definition of liberty: "By whom am I to be governed?" and "How much am I to be governed?" [15] Other modern democracies differ from the United States somewhat in the way these two questions are answered. But all such differences among the societies of consent are within a narrow range on the spectrum. All provide for procedures of law-making by elected rep-resentatives of the people, and all assure the individual an exten-sive zone of privacy, and a degree of protection against coercion by the state or by private groups.

For Jefferson, for the ethical code of American society, for most philosophers of law and politics in the liberal tradition, and indeed for most philosophers in all but the anarchist tradition, the case for accepting the idea of majority rule as morally valid in this context —that is, as an appropriate foundation for the citizen's moral obli-gation to obey the law—has seemed persuasive. Must we reject it, as Professor Wolff contends, because it does not leave the citizen "as free as before"? I cannot. The moral autonomy of Robinson Crusoe does not strike me as an operational idea—a concept with sufficient content to be used as a norm. And, even in less poetic form, the moral autonomy of the individual is not a sufficient test for the purpose, standing alone.

Men seek many goals by working and living together in society. As Berlin says, "The extent of a man's, or a people's, liberty to choose to live as they desire must be weighed against the claims of many other values, of which equality, or justice, or happiness, or security, or public order are perhaps the most obvious examples. For this reason, it cannot be unlimited." [16] The theory of liberty on

[15] I. Berlin, *Four Essays on Liberty* (1969), p. xlvii.
[16] *Ibid.*, p. 170.

which the argument here is based accepts "the fact that human goals are many, not all of them commensurable, and in perpetual rivalry with one another." [17]

For me the key question in judging the moral quality of a society —that is, in deciding whether its laws merit obedience—is how it reconciles these conflicts, whether under stress it genuinely remains a society of consent, with a powerful internal gyroscope capable of restoring its equilibrium and holding it to its course. To say that such questions are questions of degree, not matters of Yea or Nay, is not to deny the possibility of distinguishing between freedom in Denmark or Britain, for example, and freedom in the Soviet Union. Drawing the line is sometimes difficult, although it is easy in the case I mention. But making important judgments is generally difficult. I cannot believe it is wise to approach the task by trying to apply a single rule, even the magnificent standard of moral autonomy, at least as Professor Wolff has defined it.

Professor Dworkin also asserts that in a society of consent the citizen has the right to disobey valid law, or at least certain classes of valid law, but on different grounds.

Professor Dworkin prefers to analyze these problems of right and obligation without reference to the idea of a social compact. I do not believe, however, that he has altogether succeeded in this effort.

Professor Dworkin takes the institution of individual rights—the focus of his essay, as given—as a "practice," he says, not "a gift of God, or an ancient ritual, or a national sport." Without referring either to custom or to covenant, he then accepts, equally as given, the professions, put forward by those who would describe American society as generally but not perfectly moral, that our legal system recognizes certain basic human rights, and enforces them in behalf of the individual against the government. The existence of these rights, he says, is "in part" the basis of the claim of such men that the law deserves respect (and perhaps obedience as well), although Dworkin dissociates himself from their views.

Rights of this kind—rights like freedom of speech, equality, and due process—Dworkin says, can be considered "strong" when one

[17] *Ibid.*, p. 171.

has a right to do something—for example, to gamble—and it would be wrong for anyone to interfere without special grounds, even though he (and the community) thought the actor was morally wrong to gamble.

Both the legal system and the prevailing moral code of the United States claim to regard basic civil rights as "strong" in Dworkin's sense. Legally, we say that the government bears the burden of proof in justifying the constitutionality of legislation or executive action that affects civil liberties protected by the Bill of Rights, and that such legislation or executive action does not come before the courts with the advantage of a presumption of constitutionality. On the contrary, modern cases treat such laws as almost presumptively invalid. And morally, the pattern of our silences reveals the depth of ingrained habits of tolerance, and the vast patience of society with words and acts which arouse, offend, and disturb.

But Professor Dworkin says something more. I am not sure, however, after analyzing his writings on the subject, and discussing them with him at length, exactly what his next step means.

His argument follows this course: A citizen has a moral (and I believe he also means a legal) "right" to do an act even though the act is against the law, when he would have had the right to do the act, in Dworkin's "strong" sense, if it were not unlawful.

His text suggests two possible sources for such a right—Natural Law or the Social Compact. He speaks often of an individual "having" rights of this order, or of his "having" them except for, or despite, the contrary claim of a valid statute. This language must reflect an inarticulate Natural Law premise—that man is endowed with certain "unalienable rights" by his Creator, or by a code of pure reason, and not by the constitutional customs of his society, embodied in its social compact. On the other hand, Dworkin also calls the protection of individual rights against the state a "practice," not a gift from God—language indicating that he regards man's rights against the state, and the extent of their protection, as a particular attribute of a particular society: that is, as derived from the customs, and embraced within the mores, or the social compact, of that particular society. This, I take it, is the import of what he means when he says that the source of the individual's right is the fact that the society professes to take rights seriously, and should be urged by concerned citizens to live up to that profession.

I should put the latter point in this way: the source of a citizen's civil rights can only be the social compact of his society, which assures the citizen that this or that class of rights, and his personal freedom generally, will be respected by society and the state, and protected by the courts even against legislation. Indeed, I should go further and class the putative abolition of the Bill of Rights as so basic a change in the social contract as to alter the foundation of society.

"If a man believes he has a right to demonstrate," Dworkin writes, "then he must believe that it would be wrong for the government to stop him, with or without benefit of a law. If he is entitled to believe that, then it is silly to speak of a duty to obey the law as such, or of a duty to accept the punishment that the state has no right to give."

I made the same point, in the vocabulary of my own analysis, in urging that in American society constitutional test cases, and the conduct necessary to initiate them, should not be regarded as acts of civil disobedience, or breaches of the social contract.

But when, in Dworkin's analysis, is a man "entitled" to believe he has a right, for example, to demonstrate, despite a law or an interpretation of law that says his demonstration is a riot? Dworkin says the right survives "contrary legislation or adjudication." So the issue that emerges—and the issue on which Dworkin's case turns—is to define the circumstances which "entitle" a man to believe that the government is wrong in trying to prevent him from demonstrating, even though the Supreme Court has said it is right to do so. Dworkin's answer is that the individual is sometimes "right" to reach this conclusion, sometimes "wrong," but that usually the government should not prosecute in such cases, even when the actor is "wrong," provided he does not use or incite violence. Dworkin does not take the view that even basic civil liberties are absolutes and can never be validly qualified by the assertion of other morally valid social interests. For example, Dworkin says that censorship may be morally and legally justified in wartime, and that the law of defamation is morally right, according to his own moral standards.

In terms of what standards, and what processes of reasoning, does Dworkin reach this conclusion?

Taking rights seriously, he says, is important to any society which wishes to respect the dignity of the individual, and his moral autonomy, in Kant's sense. Dworkin does not comment on Kant's argument that in a society which does respect the moral autonomy of the citizen, the citizen has a moral duty to uphold the promises he has freely made, and to obey valid laws enacted by representatives he has chosen, under a procedure he has accepted. In the passage I have just quoted, however, to the effect that the right survives "contrary adjudication," Dworkin inferentially rejects Kant's reasoning, although he nowhere explains why.

The ultimate paradox of Professor Dworkin's paper is that he nowhere identifies the source of the rights whose protection he is discussing, unless his reference to the enforcement of personal rights against the government as a "practice" is a clue. He offers a theory of rights (and, presumably, of obligations as well) which he says is an alternative to the social contract theories he regards as inadequate. But he never tells us directly what his alternative is, nor does he set out the propositions with which it is built.

Dworkin says we should take rights seriously, in his "strong" sense, for two reasons: (1) because we claim that taking rights seriously is a desirable feature of American mores, and one which some philosophers (but not Dworkin) believe to justify a general rule of obedience to law; and (2) because taking rights seriously respects the moral autonomy of man, a goal for government to which Dworkin himself attaches great importance, although he carefully points out that in his view it is not the sole legitimate goal for social action.

As I pointed out earlier, I can identify only two sources for moral principle—the code of morality of a given society at a given time; and the opinions of individuals who are more or less effectively detached from the attitudes of the society in which they live. Individual views may be put forward in the name of revelation;

reason; instinct; prejudice; the good-faith opinion of reasonable men, or men of superior virtue; a vision of natural law and natural rights, existing above and apart from the code of social morality, but somehow manifest, at least to an elect; or one or another of the great philosophical traditions—idealism, utilitarianism, positivism, and so on.

Dworkin concludes that a citizen has a "right" to disobey a law, or at least a law which he thinks interferes with one of his "strong" rights against the government, even though he may be "wrong" in thinking that the law does in fact interfere with his "strong" right. For example, the citizen may regard the state as wrong in prosecuting him for rioting, because in his view he was doing no more than exercising his right of freedom of speech with a vigor that suited his own personality and life style, and the passion of his convictions. Although the citizen may be "wrong" in concluding that the state is "wrong" to prosecute him, Dworkin argues, the citizen still has a "right" we should regard as absolute to disobey the law, at least as long as he doesn't engage in violence, or much violence (or otherwise interfere with the personal rights of others), and as long as he is sincere. That is, to use a terminology I prefer, the citizen has a right to disobey a law, in Dworkin's view, even though the Supreme Court has declared it constitutional, as applied to him, because in the citizen's opinion the law violates a code of natural rights which is independent of the Constitution (or the social contract, or the code of social morality) shared by the society, and even though Dworkin believes that the citizen is wrong, and the Supreme Court right, in interpreting that code in the citizen's case.

By what standard can we conclude that the citizen and Professor Dworkin are "right" or "wrong" in their respective judgments? Dworkin is clearly not applying standards which purport to be those of the code of social morality of the society; if he were doing that, he would have to be bound, though not persuaded, by the Supreme Court's conclusion that the citizen was not making a speech, but rioting. His criterion is thus necessarily a personal philosophical opinion, shared with many or a few, as the case may be—but not yet adopted by society as a principle governing its law—an opinion based on his own theory of reason, or natural rights, from which he deduces the proposition, several times repeated, that at least where rights against the state are concerned, a citizen has a "right" to decide for himself when disobedience to law is morally (and, I believe Dworkin means, legally) justified, even though for the moment the Supreme Court disagrees, and Dworkin believes the citizen is wrong in his view.

Many of Dworkin's arguments on particular points seem more like appeals to the Supreme Court than reasoning that would justify an individual in ignoring the Court: passages of utilitarian analysis, tracing the impact of an act of disobedience on the freedom or sensibility of others, or on the level of obedience to law. Perhaps his assumption that man has a "duty" to obey the voice of his conscience is a clue to his position. At several points, he remarks that both the "liberal" and the "conservative" social-contract view of rights accept the notion that society should defer to the individual's "duty" to his conscience, even if it requires the individual to disobey the law. I can find no support for this statement in the literature to which Professor Dworkin refers.

On analysis, then, Professor Dworkin's position comes down to Rawls's or Thoreau's. Dworkin asserts another version of the anarchist philosophy: that the individual must be allowed to decide for himself which valid laws he will obey, and which he will disobey, provided he is led to his decision by sincere philosophical convictions, and not by greed, avarice, pride, envy, or aggressive impulses, or by a motive even less worthy, in Professor Dworkin's code.

The objections to Dworkin's formulation of the thesis seem to me quite as weighty as those to the others. Like them, it confuses the "is" and the "ought" by assuming that his personal "ought" has been accepted as an operational rule of society.[18]

[18] Several political theorists prefer to derive the citizen's moral obligation to obey the law not from a putative contract, made at some real or imagined constituent assembly, and ratified by each individual thereafter at a ceremony of maturity—when he votes, or swears an oath, or decides not to emigrate—but from his moral assessment of the methods of social decision used by the society, and his acceptance of those methods. See, for example, Benn and Peters, *The Principles of Political Thought* (1959), pp. 385 ff. I can detect no difference between this formulation of the problem

The American community, permeated by Jefferson's ideals, can never stress enough the need to respect the autonomy of the iconoclast, or do too much to protect freedom of thought from repression at the will of the majority.

But no society of consent could live according to Thoreau's principle, and no other society would care enough about the rights of a nonconformist to consider it. It would allow each man to decree himself elect—a claim at odds with the rule of equality which is the essence of democracy.

IV. The Implication of the Major Premise: The Case for Civil Disobedience Reviewed

If the premise I have just stated is accepted—and even Thoreau conceded its moral force, although he sought to carve out an exception to it for himself—then the arguments for civil disobedience fall into place.

Manifestly, the example of Gandhi has no bearing on the moral problem of obedience to law in the United States. The laws of British India did not derive from the consent of the Indians. Gandhi's program of nonviolent resistance was planned and carried out as a device of disruption and revolution, an alternative to armed conflict. But it broke no compact voluntarily accepted by the people of India.

The philosophical point is confirmed by a comment Prime Minister Nehru once made to Ambassador J. R. Wiggins, when he was a journalist. At the time of their interview, Nehru was contending

—that is, the moral consequences of individual adherence to a system, *i.e.,* consent—and the one I have used here, nor do I believe it would lead to a different resolution of the problems which arise when the policy reaches decisions the individual believes to be wrong. The difficulty of allowing social decisions to be made in accordance with ideas which an individual considers to be the dictates of his conscience is examined by E. Van Den Haag, *op. cit.* (note 3), pp. 30 ff, and by H. A. Bedau, "On Civil Disobedience," 58 Journal of Philosophy 661 (1961).

with the fast-to-death of a Jan Sangh leader in the Punjab. Nehru was protesting against this form of civil disobedience in a democracy. Wiggins observed that it was about the same kind of thing that he and Gandhi did. Nehru said that this was so, but that the decisive and distinguishing difference was that he and Gandhi were dealing with an occupying power, and not with a self-governing country. To use civil disobedience against an occupying power, he explained, "was to act in behalf of the people; to use it in a self-governing society was to use it against the people, who themselves run the government." [19]

Arguments based on the experience of Nazi Germany stand on the same footing. Whatever obligation the German owed to his government in that period, it was hardly the proud duty of the citizen to the laws of Athens which Socrates proclaimed. Nazi Germany was a dictatorship sustained by terror. It did not even allow its citizens to leave. The state had no authority the citizen was bound to respect as legitimate.

Similarly, those among us who preach a right of civil disobedience or even of revolution often invoke the precedent of 1776. But the men of 1776 rested their case not on a universal right of revolution, but on the claim that the British government had broken its promises of local self-government made in the colonial charters. This act, they argued, breached the social contract between Britain and the American colonies, and left the colonies free.

Our tradition recognizes no general "right" of revolution. On the contrary, we rejected that claim on the battlefields of the Civil War. Like every other nation, the United States claims, possesses, and occasionally asserts an inherent right of self-defense against internal as well as external threats, a claim fully recognized as right by international law, and by the law of the Constitution. For a society of consent, there can be no claim of a "right" to revolt, unless and until the social compact itself is threatened by destruction.

Nor is the case for civil disobedience supported in any way by

[19] Letter from Hon. J. R. Wiggins. Dean Allen, *op. cit.* (note 3), discusses Gandhi's argument, and its position in India after independence, in an illuminating passage.

the experience of the civil rights movement and the philosophy of
the Reverend Martin Luther King, Jr.

By far the larger and more significant part of the struggle for
Negro equality was and is an invocation of law, and an appeal to it.
The civil rights movement did not engage in civil disobedience to a
significant extent, despite its rhetoric to the contrary, but in campaigns to require the whites to obey the law of the Constitution.
Conduct which made it possible to bring cases to test the constitutionality of state statutes or local ordinances cannot be considered
breaches of the social contract, or acts of disobedience to law.
They are, on the contrary, an exercise of one of the most precious
legal privileges of the American social order—the right of any person in an appropriate case to appeal from the positive law to the
standards of the Constitution. Such conduct is not an act of war
against society, but one of faith in its moral code, and in the law
which seeks to express and fulfill the aspirations of that code.[20]

A. *Is the Negro Bound by the Social Contract?*

There is, however, a more difficult aspect of the relation of the
black citizen to the social compact of the United States.

For nearly a century after 1868, the Negro was effectively disenfranchised in the South, and subject to harsh discrimination in most
parts of the United States. He still suffers almost everywhere from
the burden of encrusted customs which handicap him in his quest
for equality. Voting by Negroes has now been generally achieved,
under the judicial decisions and statutes of the last few years—an
immense victory for the Constitution over the long and often violent war of civil disobedience waged against it in the South. Other
gains have been made. But no one can yet say that equality for the
black—even equality before the law—is as yet a reality. Socrates
spoke of the laws of Athens as having given him "a share in every
good which . . . [they] had to give." That statement could not
come from a black man in America, without sharp qualifications.

[20] See, among other papers on this aspect of the subject, Prof. Black's
essay, referred to in note 3.

Does the burden of the past exempt the Negro from the obligations of the social compact?

This, I think, is the most difficult problem of social theory in American life, as it is the most onerous of our moral dilemmas.

Today the Negro helps, more and more genuinely, to make the laws.

We are living in the midst of a convulsive national effort to fulfill the promise of equality for the black.

But no man can say with conviction that we have yet come half, or quarter, of the way. It is true that error and the presence of injustice do not of themselves void the social compact. But when error and injustice become the rule, not the exception; when the democratic process itself is suspended; when minority rights and personal freedom are denied—then, surely, the society ceases to be one of consent; the social contract could be regarded as breached; and the power to wage war against society could be claimed as right.

I do not believe the black American today is in this position, or believes himself to be. It is apparent that society, led by its system of law, is seeking to achieve and guarantee his equality. The resistance is great. Three hundred years of experience have crystallized customs and attitudes which are hard to change. The American people are not saints. Nor are they immune from the disease of group and racial hostility which plagues every other nation on earth. But American society is trying. Before that effort, can it be said that the social compact is a nullity so far as the American Negro is concerned?

I do not believe that the American Negro can or should be regarded as exempted from the obligation to obey constitutionally valid laws. Nor do I believe that the dark history of America's treatment of the Negro justifies violence or revolution by black citizens. On the contrary, I should contend that the progress toward black equality achieved in recent years is primarily the achievement of the law, and the sense of justice of the American community which gives content to the law. It is the achievement, too, of primarily peaceful methods of political and social action which have stirred the nation to rally to the law, and attack the inertia and resistance which have for so long tolerated disobedience to the law of the Fourteenth Amendment.[21]

The moral of that conclusion, for me, is that the entire American community should redouble its efforts, through public and through private action, to vindicate its pledge of equality for the black. Nothing less could justify the conclusion I have just stated.

B. *Are Students Bound by the Social Compact?*

There are parallel contentions, though at a far less moving level, in the arguments about university rioting—that students have a right to disobey the rules of their colleges or universities, or to disrupt their operations, because they do not participate in their management. The argument has two heads—one, that no one below the legal voting age is bound to obey the laws, even under Jefferson's theory, because he hasn't "consented" to them; the second, that students are not bound by university rules because they didn't help to make them.

I, for one, cannot find either contention persuasive.

As for the first argument, every society has customary rules recognizing the moment of adult responsibility. Those rules may be unjust to precocious children like John Stuart Mill. But rules on the subject are a necessity. There is, after all, an objective difference between children and adults, and society has to establish a general line between them for many purposes. It can hardly be said that the prevailing practice, based on custom and legislative judgment, is without visible basis in reason. Here, surely, is an area where the minority is bound to accept the moral rightness of the majority's right to decide, without necessarily agreeing with the decision itself. Those deemed children under such rules have always been regarded as members of the community, protected by its laws, and bound by them as well. So were women, during the centuries without number before they were accepted legally as the equals of men.

[21] Prof. Walzer reaches the same conclusion, *op. cit.* (note 3), in Ch. 3, pp. 46–73.

The second contention—that students are not bound by university rules because they didn't help make them—I find equally unpersuasive.

Colleges and universities are established as trusts, largely under state laws, to serve important public purposes—the advancement of knowledge, and the education of young men and women. These goals are fundamental to the quality of our culture as a civilization. And they are of legitimate concern to society as a whole, and not only to the university community.

Universities and colleges are generally organized in the autonomous, self-governing pattern of the university tradition, as it has been adapted to the experience of the United States. Like other professional specialized agencies in society—those charged with licensing doctors and lawyers, for example, or those entrusted with responsibility for the banking system—colleges and universities are governed by specialists, chosen largely on the basis of professional qualifications. Custom, and the courts, have recognized a considerable zone of academic freedom and autonomy, especially in recent years, and protected universities more and more effectively from political interference, and from interference by private groups. But the authority of those who govern universities derives in a clear line from the laws under which the universities are organized, those of a state or of the nation, as the case may be.

While there is surely ground for re-examining such arrangements, and there will always be room for improving them, it can hardly be contended that the existing pattern of statutes and customs under which our institutions of higher learning are established lacks "legitimacy" in Jefferson's sense. The colleges and universities are institutions in which the community as a whole has vital interests. The laws under which they function have been passed by the state legislatures and by Congress—the institutions of society which exist to determine broad questions of public policy, especially in the field of education. Until those laws have been changed, the arrangements for the governance of our colleges and universities have democratic legitimacy.

Popular theories of "participatory democracy" would challenge this thesis. These doctrines urge that no social institutions can be truly "legitimate" unless all those affected by their functioning participate in making their rules.

The short answer to this contention, for the purposes of our problem here, is that no majority of the American people, in any state, or in the nation, has as yet adopted the theory of participatory democracy, or any variant of it, to replace or modify the statutes under which colleges and universities are administered. Without such a step there can be no claim that democratic principle requires, or perhaps even permits, the doctrine of participatory democracy to be applied as a rule for action, so long as we adhere to the principle of equality. The Constitution, Justice Holmes once said, does not embody "The Social Statics" of Herbert Spencer. One might add that it has not yet been extended to include the works of Herbert Marcuse.

Universities suffer the ailments of other institutions—bureaucracy, conservatism, timidity, and occasional failures of responsibility. Some university administrators are doubtless too weak to discharge their responsibilities for planning and initiating new ventures beyond the interests of particular schools or faculties, or for reinvigorating those which have fallen into decay. Others are too active and authoritative for the health and autonomy of their faculties.

But these are the normal problems of all organized social life. The shortcomings of a particular university at a particular moment of its history, however irritating, can hardly be put forward to justify illegal programs intended to destroy the university, or to bring about reform, or what claims to be reform, by methods of coercion rather than of democracy.

The experience of labor is sometimes invoked as a precedent in discussions of the crisis in the universities. Students are disturbed, it is contended, as workers were once disturbed—because they do not deal as equals with the faculties and administrators who fix their tasks. The normal American practice, and the basis of our labor law, is that workers bargain with their employers only about wages and working conditions. Problems of engineering, industrial method, or business policy are not submitted to the collective bargaining process. But in many colleges and universities students are seeking a voice not only in fixing the conditions under which they live and study—in dormitory rules, and the lighting of libraries—but in the curriculum appropriate to their training, in the establishment of the standards by which they are to be deemed qualified, and in the choice of those selected to instruct them. I can see no basis in labor experience to justify claims of a right to share in such professional decisions.

The difficulty with the labor analogy goes deeper. Students, after all, are men and women, or boys and girls, at an early stage of their training, seeking to acquire knowledge and skills through study under the guidance and direction of an expert faculty. In relation to their calling, they are much more like apprentices than experienced miners or steelworkers in a labor dispute.

It may be that the next few years will witness the spread and expansion of present practices of organized student participation in some aspects of university policy making. Our university systems developed, after all, in a period when students were treated paternalistically as schoolboys, and subjected to rules which no longer correspond to the mores of the community.

This is not the occasion for me to express my views about the wisdom of such developments as a matter of educational policy. I happen to sympathize with formal and informal participation by students in the governance of universities, so long as such consultative participation does not dilute the responsibility of faculties and administrators. But I should say that I can find nothing in the idea of the social compact, which in the United States requires government to be organized in accordance with the principles of representative democracy, to preclude laws which authorize the organization of specialized professional institutions under professional control. The Supreme Court and the Federal Reserve Board are not "illegitimate" because all those affected by their decisions do not participate directly in making them. Nor does democratic principle require candidates for degrees, or for the licensed professions, to share in setting the standards for their own training, or to participate in grading their own examinations. Such claims would deny the propriety of distinctions of function in the organization of soci-

ety based on distinctions of training, ability, interest, and experience. The theory of democracy doesn't support such a claim.

c. *Does the Citizen Have a Right to Disobey Laws Which Require Him to Perform Acts He Regards as Immoral?*

The last two sections dealt with the claim that blacks or students
may not be bound by the laws or regulations in a society of consent
because they do not participate fully in making them.

Now I should like to take up certain problems which arise when
citizens who do participate in the making of laws claim a right to
disobey some which they believe require them to perform acts contrary to their own religious or personal beliefs, or which they regard as otherwise immoral. This issue arises in a number of situations—in naturalization cases, for example, where the applicant
for citizenship, who under the statute must prove his attachment to
the principles of the Constitution, says that his religion, or his
deepest moral convictions, make it impossible for him to engage in
military service which requires him to kill another human being,
except perhaps in a war he himself deems just. The same issue
arises in another form in draft cases, and in the cases dealing with
statutes that require schoolchildren whose parents are Jehovah's
Witnesses to salute the flag.

It is inherent in the nature of the United States as a nation, and
as a member of the society of nations, as well as in the war powers
prescribed by the Constitution, that the national government has
authority adequate to protect the nation's security. As the Supreme
Court has remarked, the war powers of the national government
authorize it not only to wage war, but to wage war successfully—to
perform and to require whatever actions may in its judgment be
necessary and proper to that end. Chief Justice Marshall said, "The
wisdom and the discretion of Congress, their identity with the
people, and the influence which their constituents possess at elections are in this, as in many other instances . . . the sole re-

straints on which they have relied to secure them from its abuse." [22]

The military power of the United States has been used by the President from the eighteenth-century beginnings of the republic on more than one hundred and thirty occasions, and in a great variety of situations, from the Mediterranean to China, in small engagements and in large, pursuant to formal Congressional authorizations and without them, in situations which international law would classify as coming under the Law of War, and those which it would regard as hostilities in time of peace.[23] The Supreme Court decided early in its history that Congress' power to declare war was not exclusive, but that lesser hostilities could be authorized. Those decisions have governed constitutional doctrine and practice ever since. It has always been assumed, and often said, that Congress has the power to conscript men to serve in the armed forces in times of peace, of war, and of national emergency, when it decided that conscription was an appropriate means for carrying out national policy.

But the states and the Congress, and the colonies before them, have always excused from the military service those whose religious convictions oppose it. By the time of the Revolution, at least, the Quakers were a respected and accepted part of the national community. And our statutes on military service had deferred to their convictions, and to the convictions of other sects holding to pacifist principles. Chief Justice Hughes said in 1931:

> Much has been said of the paramount duty to the State, a duty to be recognized, it is urged, even though it conflicts with convictions of duty to God. Undoubtedly that duty to the State exists within

[22] Gibbons v. Ogden, 9 Wheat (U.S.) 1, pp. 195–196 (1824).

[23] This experience is reviewed in J. G. Rogers, *World Policing and the Constitution* (1945); H. W. Jones, "The President, Congress and Foreign Relations," 29 Calif. L. Rev. 565 (1941); C. Mathews, "The Constitutional Power of the President to Conclude International Agreements," 64 Yale L.J. 345 (1955); R. H. Hull and J. C. Novogrod, *Law and Vietnam* (1968); R. A. Falk, ed., *The Vietnam War and International Law,* Vol. 2 (1969); J. N. Moore, "International Law and the United States Role in Vietnam: A Reply," 76 Yale L.J. 1051 (1967), and R. A. Falk, "International Law and United States Role in Vietnam: A Response to Professor Moore," 76 Yale L.J. 1095 (1967); W. T. Reveley, "Presidential Warmaking: Courthouse Prerogative or Usurpation?" 55 Va. L. Rev. 1243 (1969); Bas v. Tingy, 4 Dallas (U.S.) 37 (1800).

the domain of power, for government may enforce obedience to laws regardless of scruples. When one's belief collides with the power of the State, the latter is supreme within its sphere and submission or punishment follows. But, in the forum of conscience, duty to a moral power higher than the State has always been maintained. The reservation of that supreme obligation, as a matter of principle, would unquestionably be made by many of our conscientious and law-abiding citizens. The essence of religion is belief in a relation to God involving duties superior to those arising from any human relation. . . .

The battle for religious liberty has been fought and won with respect to religious beliefs and practices, which are not in conflict with good order, upon the very ground of the supremacy of conscience within its proper field. What that field is, under our system of government, presents in part a question of constitutional law and also, in part, one of legislative policy in avoiding unnecessary clashes with the dictates of conscience. There is abundant room for enforcing the requisite authority of law as it is enacted and requires obedience, and for maintaining the conception of the supremacy of law as essential to orderly government, without demanding that either citizens or applicants for citizenship shall assume by oath an obligation to regard allegiance to God as subordinate to allegiance to civil power. The attempt to exact such a promise, and thus to bind one's conscience by the taking of oaths or the submission to tests, has been the cause of many deplorable conflicts. The Congress has sought to avoid such conflicts in this country by respecting our happy tradition. In no sphere of legislation has the intention to prevent such clashes been more conspicuous than in relation to the bearing of arms." [24]

The Supreme Court has ruled that the obligation to bear arms is a fundamental principle of the Constitution, and a fundamental duty of all who owe allegiance to the nation, citizen and noncitizen alike. The cases declare that the exemption of conscientious objectors from this obligation is an act of grace and prudence on the part of Congress, not a constitutional right[25]—a "happy tradition," in

[24] United States v. Macintosh, 283 U.S. 605, 633–634 (dissenting opinion) (1931).
[25] Hamilton v. Regents of the University of California, 293 U.S. 245, 266 (concurring opinion of Cardozo, J.) (1934).

Chief Justice Hughes's phrase, intended to avoid deplorable and unnecessary conflicts. But the unvarying practice of our legislatures from the beginnings of our history establishes a pattern not readily altered, even if conscientious objection be not deemed a constitutional right. That history is a fact of significance in evaluating the character and quality of our social order, and its tolerance of individual diversity, in not requiring men to commit acts which violate their own religious convictions.

The statutes now permit the naturalization and the exemption from combat service under the draft of men whose conscientious objection to war derives from religious training and belief, if they accept the obligation to perform noncombat service when called upon to do so.

The legal literature, and cases now before the courts, raise fascinating questions, whose examination I shall resist here—whether Congress can conscript men to serve in the absence of a declaration of war, or a declaration of national emergency; whether the right of exemption from the military service is constitutional or statutory in character; whether there are constitutional objections to the longstanding practice of Congress in confining the exemption to those whose scruples derive from religious training and belief; and whether men who object to the campaign in Vietnam have a constitutional right to decline to serve when conscripted.[26]

Reluctantly, I put these issues to one side. They illustrate, however, the depth and delicacy of the problem of accommodating two vital characteristics of our constitutional system—the undoubted capacity of the nation to use all means Congress and the President deem necessary and proper to protect its security and minimize the risk of nuclear war, and the equally undoubted policy of society to assure maximum freedom for individual autonomy.

The analysis from which his conclusion derives, however, does not go so far as to suggest, and far less to require, that the Constitution, or the fundamental principles which underlie it, be interpreted to reserve to the individual a right to decide whether he will

[26] See United States v. Sisson, 294 F. Supp. 511, 515, 520 (D. Mass., 1968), 297 F. Supp. 902 (D. Mass., 1969), appeal dismissed, 399 U.S. 267 (1970).

fight in a war he may not approve, or refuse to pay taxes, as Justice Cardozo wrote, "in furtherance of a war, whether for attack or for defense, or in furtherance of any other end condemned by his conscience as irreligious or immoral. The right of private judgment has never yet been so exalted above the powers and the compulsion of the agencies of government. One who is a martyr to a principle—which may turn out in the end to be a delusion or an error—does not prove by his martyrdom that he has kept within the law." [27]

D. *When the Individual Believes Valid Laws Are Immoral*
or Unjust, Does He Have a Legal or Moral
Right to Employ Civil Disobedience
as a Tactic of Protest?

Related, but different, problems arise when the citizen—confronting a law or policy he regards as immoral—contemplates tactics of opposition which go far beyond a simple refusal to obey the law as applied to himself. He has failed to persuade the majority that the law to which he objects is indeed unjust and immoral. Equally, he has failed to persuade the Supreme Court that it is unconstitutional. It may be, to recall Aristophanes' acid comment, that he has succeeded in persuading, but not in convincing, the majority.

What then? Under the circumstances, is he entitled to disobey the law as of right, and live by his own view? Is he entitled to go further, and seek to impose his views on the community not by the vigorous exercise of his constitutional rights of freedom of speech, of the press, and of peaceable assembly, but by tactics of demonstration and coercion which involve planned disobedience to valid laws, interference with the rights of others, and often violence as well? If so, by what authority? Unless one is willing to rely on Divine Revelation—and no society today can accept the idea—or on the anarchist principle, only two possible sources have been suggested for treating the individual's naked power to break the law as a right or privilege: variations on Thoreau's claim of special

[27] Hamilton v. Regents of the University of California, 293 U.S. 245, 268 (1934).

privilege for individuals of superior conscience, or of superior intellect or sensitivity; and variations on the utilitarian theme, that such conduct will, or may, or might, do more good than harm.

I shall examine some of the implications of Thoreau's thesis first.

As a matter of moral principle, as I remarked earlier, it is not compatible with the political ethics of democracy. No democratic society, and no other society based on the idea of equality, could recognize Thoreau's claim as valid, even for an aristocracy of conscience. No matter how sincerely we honor learning and wisdom, and the diversity of learned views, we have not yet made philosophers kings, nor are we likely to. If the just powers of government indeed derive from the consent of the governed, that consent can be measured and registered only in accordance with the principle of equality.

But, we have been told, the principle of the Nuremberg Trials authorizes the citizen to disobey the commands of the state—and to undertake campaigns of wider civil disobedience as well—when his own conscience, and his own conscience alone, tells him that the state is wrong.

Such a claim betrays little knowledge of the Nuremberg proceedings, which I, for one, supported at the time, and would support again.

Most of the cases conducted under the Agreement were directed to situations in which individuals accused of violating the Hague Convention and other accepted laws of war claimed as a defense that they were carrying out the orders of a superior officer.

In the first place, as I remarked earlier, Nuremberg dealt with Germans under the control of a state in which authority was utterly divorced from consent.

Secondly, with respect to the defense of superior orders, our own Code of Military Justice gives full protection to the individual soldier who refuses to obey invalid orders—for example, if his superior should order him to kill or torture prisoners, or otherwise violate the laws of war. The Supreme Court established and applied the principle as long ago as 1800.

Finally, the Nuremberg Trials examined the novel charge of

waging aggressive warfare in violation of international law—that is, of the Kellogg-Briand Treaty. This charge was confined to a few persons in positions of high responsibility in the German government—those directly associated with the decision to wage aggressive war. It was not regarded as a charge universally available, nor yet as a universal solvent of individual responsibility.

There is therefore nothing in the jurisprudence of Nuremberg to support the claim by an American that he is morally or legally entitled to disregard valid law because he disagrees with it, or regards it as immoral, in accordance with his own creed or his own interpretation of the community's creed.[28]

Such reasoning does not, of course, fully answer the question posed when an individual living in a society of consent disagrees with the wisdom or morality of a course legally adopted by the society and supported by a majority of its citizens.

An issue of this kind arose for many of us when American citizens of Japanese descent were arrested, removed from the Pacific Coast, and interned during World War II, under procedures approved by Congress and the President, and later upheld as constitutional by the Supreme Court of the United States.

Were those who remained convinced, as I was, that the Japanese-American removal programs were immoral and unconstitutional, despite the reasoning of all three branches of the government,[29] entitled to express their views through violence, or by engaging in general acts of civil disobedience, or were they required, by the ethics of responsible democratic citizenship, to engage in reasoned efforts to persuade their fellow citizens to confess error and make amends?

If you will accept for the moment the hypothesis, which I believe to be correct, that the nation did violate its own standards of justice in removing citizens of Japanese descent from the West Coast during the war, I conclude that such an act, done immediately after Pearl Harbor, under the stress of war, was not a complete breach of

[28] W. V. O'Brien reaches the same general conclusions in his article "The Nuremberg Principles" in James Finn, ed., *A Conflict of Loyalties: The Case for Selective Conscientious Objection* (1968), p. 140.

[29] See "The Japanese-American Cases—A Disaster," 54 Yale L.J. 489 (1945), reprinted in *The Sovereign Prerogative* (1962), p. 193.

the social contract, which would justify revolution, or tactics of violence which represent the same idea, but an error—a major error—which could be cured—and was cured—by the normal procedures of democratic law and politics.

In this instance, the Congress of the United States ultimately concluded that injustice had been done, and the Congress and the President sought to remedy that injustice through the payment of damages and the restoration of citizenship.

I conclude that similar considerations should govern the behavior of those who remain convinced, as many are, that the nation's course in Vietnam is illegal, immoral, and unwise.

This is not the occasion to examine the legal justification for our policies in Vietnam, either constitutionally or under international law.[30] I note, however, that our legal order provides peaceful pro-

[30] My own views on the subject are summed up in *Law, Power and the Pursuit of Peace* (1968), pp. 60–67. While it is natural for Americans to claim that whatever they dislike intensely is also unconstitutional, the constitutional base for the war in Indochina is impregnable—far stronger than the base President Truman had in Korea. The argument takes this course: (1) While it is sometimes difficult to draw the boundary between the inherent powers of the President and those of Congress in the field of foreign affairs, there are no such difficulties when the President and the Congress act together. Then the nation speaks with one voice; (2) in Indochina, Congress and the President have acted together (although some members of Congress may regret their votes): the Presidency through the successive military and diplomatic decisions of four Presidents, Congress through SEATO, the Tonkin Gulf Resolution, and many appropriation and other statutes; (3) SEATO provides that in the event of aggression by means of armed attack against any of the parties of the Treaty, or against any state or territory which the parties designate as subject to the protection of the Treaty—that is, Laos, Cambodia, and South Vietnam—each party "agrees that it *will* in that event act to meet the common danger in accordance with its constitutional processes [my italics]." Correlative provisions deal with a variety of other facts or situations that could threaten "the inviolability or the integrity of the territory or the sovereignty or the political independence" of parties to the Treaty, or states or territories under its protection; (4) what are the "constitutional processes" for an American decision to act under the SEATO treaty?

In Korea, President Truman proceeded under the United Nations Charter —a treaty ratified by the United States—without the support of a specific Congressional resolution, whether in the form of a declaration of war or otherwise. In Vietnam, the actions of three Presidents under the Treaty were ratified and reaffirmed by Congress in the Tonkin Gulf Resolution, as well as by statutes.

cedures through which these issues can be tested, both in the courts and through the possible action of Congress in repudiating the SEATO treaty and repealing the Tonkin Gulf Resolution. The availability of such procedures for determining the legality of our policy in Vietnam distinguishes the problem fundamentally from that facing a German dissenter in Hitler's Reich.

Those who disagree with the nation's policy in Vietnam have every right to employ all the methods of democratic political freedom to persuade their fellow citizens to accept their views. But, I should contend, they have no moral right to disrupt the draft; to interfere with the freedom of those who believe they are preaching national suicide; to break up universities or public meetings; to burn the files of draft boards; or to engage in other acts of violence and illegality.

The same issues arise, with far less color of right, when the ends sought in demonstrations are changes in university policies, or welfare policies, or policies with regard to the administration of educational systems. In the conflicts which have so profoundly disturbed and weakened our universities in recent years, for example,

---

Many contend that no military action can or should be taken by the United States except pursuant to a formal declaration of war, invoking all the consequences of a state of war in international law. This popular view is entirely erroneous. Armed force has been used by the United States more than one hundred and thirty times since 1789, only five times pursuant to a declaration of war. No declaration of war has been issued by any nation since 1945.

Perhaps the most clear-cut answer to the popular view that the war in Vietnam is illegal (because no "declaration" of war has been issued) arose from President John Adams' "undeclared war" with France between 1798 and 1800. In that subtle and delicate affair, Congress authorized maritime hostilities, but did not declare war against France. The constitutional validity of this procedure came before the Supreme Court several times in prize cases. The Court said Congress was wise, and entirely within its powers, in not making France "our general enemy," but in authorizing limited war to reinforce the complex American diplomacy which ultimately led to the Louisiana Purchase. Bas v. Tingy, note 23. The Congress which made these decisions, and the Supreme Court which approved them, were filled with men who had been deeply engaged in making the Constitution a few years before. Their decision—that a declaration of war is not the only means through which the Constitution authorizes the use of armed force abroad— has never been questioned or challenged. It has dominated the pattern of constitutional usage since 1800.

demonstrators have claimed a "right" to engage in tactics of disruption, the occupation of buildings, and even more extreme forms of coercion. They do not claim that the laws governing the organization of universities are unconstitutional. They undertake such tactics, and undertake to justify them, simply as means to persuade those who could not be persuaded otherwise to change policies about R.O.T.C., university research programs, and the internal organization of universities.

What is the possible source of such a right? Not the laws which establish the authority of university officials. Not the Constitution, which defines the rights of freedom of speech and of the press, and of peaceable assembly to petition for the redress of grievances. Not divine right, surely, or some impalpable right of man not articulated in the Constitution.

A number of suggestions have been made as to the legal or moral source from which the "right" to use such illegal tactics might be drawn.

Society should recognize the moral and legal propriety of such tactics, it is urged, when the violations of law are "minor" ones committed by men who are loyal to our own political and moral traditions, and who are sincerely convinced that in pursuing a particular policy the nation has not kept faith with the principles on which its legal and political system purports to rest.

But the law cannot and should not distinguish between the rights of protest of those who do and those who do not generally accept the rightness of our constitutional system. The history of attempts to condemn or to restrict the civil rights of those deemed "disloyal" or "un-American" is not a happy one, and I cannot believe it is wise or practicable for this purpose to distinguish between appeals to the conscience of the nation made by those who in their hearts are attached to the fundamental principles of the Constitution, and those who would gladly destroy it. The distinction is subjective. Ample and depressing experience attests to the difficulties of applying such a test. Our legal order has generally—and, in my view, rightly—addressed itself in large part to actions, and sought to avoid distinctions as to legal rights based on distinctions of attitude. Good men and bad men, anarchists and conservatives, men of all faiths and of no faith, are equally protected by the Constitution and its Bill of Rights, and equally bound by valid laws enacted through constitutional procedures. All are equally free to appeal to the conscience of the nation, and to its traditional values, whether their appeal is made in good faith or in bad.

This argument in behalf of men of good will echoes Thoreau's plea for the special privileges society should, he thought, be deemed to owe to an elect. It too is incompatible with the principle of equality under law, and unworkable and unsound in theory.

Three more general arguments have been put forward to justify illegal action, including some use of "minor" violence:

(1) that violating laws, and some recourse to violence, should be regarded as a permissible way to dramatize a point of view, and gain access to newspapers and television that would otherwise have been difficult to obtain; an illegal and violent act, it is urged, can shock into a state of reflection some men who would not otherwise consider the problem;

(2) that such tactics induce desirable changes in policies or institutions that might not have come, or come so soon, through democratic persuasion alone; and

(3) that violence is sometimes "forced" on militants by the stubbornness and inactivity of those who direct legitimate institutions, and who have not been persuaded by arguments in which militants passionately believe.

These contentions all rest, in effect, on the thesis that the end does justify the means, at least if the means are not "too" damaging. Convinced of the rightness of their own views, men of this outlook claim the right to seek changes in society against the will of the majority through tactics of planned disobedience which sometimes include the use of force. Thus a group of ministers in New York recently issued a statement which called for some violence if that was necessary to achieve what they regarded as justice for disadvantaged persons in our society.

But the failure to persuade a majority is hardly in itself evidence that the majority is wrong; nor is intensity of feeling sufficient proof that one is right.

I can find no justification in political philosophy, in law, or in morals for this thesis as the basis for social action in a society of consent. It is the argument which has been used to justify every tyranny in history. And it offends a principle of ethics confirmed by the experience of all men—that moral ends cannot justify the use of immoral means. Methods of civil war and of insurrection can be defended ethically in societies like that of Nazi Germany, or other tyrannies, where power rests on force alone; where the social compact of freedom has been breached, as in the America of 1776; or in situations where that compact is threatened with destruction by a *coup d'état*. But there is no ethical case for revolution in a working and effective democracy, however beset it may be with the difficult problems of social transition. In such societies, laws can be changed legitimately only by the deliberate processes of elections and of parliamentary action: by votes after hearings, reports, and debates, not by the shouts of mobs in stadiums—or on tennis courts. Recourse to illegal methods of political and social action can have the most corrosive effect on society, especially if they are employed by the well-educated and the well-established in the name of moral right. Violations of law by the leadership of a community have more impact on society than ordinary crime.

As for the thoughtless argument that tactics of violence and coercion have forced change at a more rapid pace than could have been achieved by persuasion alone, they recall the classic justifications of fascism: that Mussolini made the trains run on time.

Furthermore, those who justify acts of disruption and coercion in the name of a utilitarian theory of civil disobedience have no way of knowing, or predicting, that their behavior has a reasonable chance of achieving more good than harm. By acting on their own decision, without the backing of any majority, they necessarily function not as rational utilitarians, but on impulse and instinct. They cannot find a ground for denying the same privilege to others who feel quite as strongly about the rightness of their views. Thus they degrade the quality of public discourse, from which public opinion flows, for they necessarily reduce the level of rationality, and increase the level of passion and violence, in the process of making decisions of social policy.

The arguments used to justify illegality as a political tactic in contemporary controversies parallel those employed in the worst and most prolonged experience of the nation with civil disobedience—the resistance of the South to the enforcement of the Fourteenth Amendment for nearly a century after 1868. It is worth returning to that experience once more, in connection with the debates over the use of civil disobedience addressed to Vietnam, the crisis of the universities, and the struggle to achieve full equality for blacks in employment, education, and housing in the North.

The hardest task for law, always, is to achieve a change in custom. And the most difficult legal task our society has ever undertaken is the enforcement of the Fourteenth Amendment. There is always some difference between positive law and the living law of customary behavior. Sometimes the written law lags behind custom, as it does when laws become obsolete, like statutes proscribing contraception. Sometimes the law collides with custom and has to retreat—the case of Prohibition comes to mind. Often the law seeks to effect a change in custom. The Fourteenth Amendment is the most ambitious example of such an attempt in our history. Another is the field of labor relations, where, after years of frustration and of struggle, the law declared the right of workers to organize and bargain collectively.

The growth of the law normally reflects a complex process of interaction between behavior and the norms of law. The history of the law regarding the Negro in American life is the supreme instance of this process. Its rhythm was influenced by the persistent effort of dedicated and persuasive men, led in modern times by the Legal Defense Fund of the NAACP, and later by the Reverend Martin Luther King, Jr., as well, to persuade the law to fulfill its promise of equality for the Negro, and the slow and uneven response of the people to the urgings of the law.

I take the view that the long resistance of the South to the Fourteenth and Fifteenth Amendments was morally wrong, and I reject and repudiate the philosophy which sought to justify it as a program of civil disobedience backed by violence. As a matter of theory and of experience, I believe that the ideas represented by that campaign have no legitimate place in our national life, although, as I remarked earlier, their defenders can say, with some justice, that they "worked" pragmatically—that is, that they produced a state of policy which could not have been achieved by political means alone.

The same lesson, on a smaller but no less ominous scale, is illustrated in some of the recent experience of our universities.

In the university riots, no claim is made that illegality is undertaken to test the constitutionality of existing positive law. Nor are claims advanced that the enforcement of the law would require a man to do an act morally offensive to his religious convictions. In most cases, these episodes are not directly associated with the struggle for rights for blacks.

They are simply controversies about ordinary issues of public policy—the status of R.O.T.C. training is an example—in which men claim a right to impose their own views by force, because those entrusted by law with the responsibility for decision do not agree; that is, they assert a right to raise themselves above the law and its democratic procedures by their own ipse dixit and by the strength of their conviction of the rightness of their cause.

It is of course also true that motives other than a deep interest in the issues animate many who have organized the riots and confrontations of recent years in the universities. Some of the most active precipitators of these events are in fact revolutionaries of one sect or another. Sometimes student demonstrations have the quality of exciting student pranks, undertaken as sport, or of collective hysteria, contagious and mysterious, spreading like a frenzy around the world. Often they become more sinister, involving coercion by storm troopers, interferences with the rights of others, and procedures which resemble those of People's Courts. And it is generally forgotten that intermittent rioting, sometimes serious rioting, has been a feature of university life for many centuries. One difference between the past and the present, of course, is that a much large fraction of our youth now attends universities.

The turbulent demonstrations of recent years at many of our universities, and the cults and fads associated with them, are viewed differently by different members of the university communities. And these differences have wounded and divided faculties, and student bodies, in ways which have accomplished irreparable in-

jury. Some professors find them appealing as revolutionary activities, or as manifestations of high spirits, and of a new and vital life-
style. For others, the movement is a new name—fascism—for the
ancient social disease of tyranny. They oppose the practice of riot
as morally wrong and socially destructive. They deplore the anti-
intellectualism, and the contempt for rationality, found so often in
university disturbances. They are convinced these events have low-
ered the quality of education and scholarship. And they can no
longer respect—or often even talk to—colleagues who defend what
the rioting students have done.

Exactly the same irreparable divisions occur among students.
The condonation of tactics of disruption and riot has breached the
sense of community and trust among students in ways which will
forever color the influence of their educational experience in the
lives of this student generation.

There is a fact often ignored in the background of the university
riots. The primary responsibility for the preservation of order
within a university, and for the enforcement of university rules, is
vested in the universities themselves. At most universities today it
is well known that the normal university sanctions of suspension or
expulsion for breaches of the rules will not be applied, save in the
most extreme cases, because of the draft. Faculties and administrations are reluctant to expel or suspend students for other reasons as
well. They never lose faith in the perfectability of men. There
would be tragedy, too, in expelling some of the few black students,
whose presence represents such strenuous efforts and such high
hopes. And closing the universities before the tactics of riot would
be the greatest defeat of all for those whose trust and duty is education.

The result of this abdication of responsibility by the universities
has been a license to riot, and a transfer of the burden of preserving
order to the police. Because of the ancient tradition against having
police on university grounds, which is regarded with feeling in all
universities, although the rationale for the feeling has long since
disappeared, this step is always disturbing. And in many recent
instances it has proved disastrous.

Why have the police reacted so often to student rioters with considerable brutality, and sometimes with extreme brutality? It may well be that the motivating factors are deeper than imperfections of police training and discipline. In these cases, students and those associated with them have deliberately breached the prohibitions of the law against violent and coercive behavior. Often their defiance of law is accompanied by words and acts intended to provoke the police to violence in turn. The reaction of the police, all too often, is "If *they* can do it, why can't we?" In short, the violence of the students triggers the release of impulsive and instinctive aggression on the part of some policemen—their class feelings, their hostility, their resentment of what they regard as the privileged position of a spoiled and disturbingly radical group of different outlook, different values, and a different life-style. The effect of the invocation of violence by the students is thus to dissolve, for the moment at least, the network of restraints which the law has laboriously established to confine and contain universal impulsive forces of aggression and hostility, to guide and govern those forces, and to direct their outlet only through the agreed procedures of democracy for resolving social conflicts in peace.

In turn, very often, well-meaning and moderate students respond to the episode not by rallying to the law but to those who would destroy it. Thus they become accomplices.

These tragic consequences of illegality are among the factors which should be taken into account in evaluating the common attempts to justify such events on the ground that illegal and coercive tactics are more effective than legal ones in obtaining results the demonstrators regard as desirable.

As I have sought to show earlier, the argument does not withstand analysis as a moral justification for such conduct. It is no more than another version of the proposition that moral ends justify the use of immoral means. And even in the perspective of utilitarianism, it suffers from the vice that each man must make his own felicific calculus for society, and act on it, while conceding the same privilege to everyone else.

But I am also persuaded that at least in our recent experience with the process of social reform, the claim is not correct.*

* See Introduction to Part II.

CONCLUSION

I started by recalling the view that law was the necessary condition and predicate of individual liberty. That is a proposition which unites "liberals" and "conservatives"—that is, those who prefer somewhat more to somewhat less individual freedom from official restraint. Personal freedom within organized society is made possible, this view holds, only by law—that is, by the influence of generally accepted rules and principles which satisfy the sense of justice of the community and assure the capacity of the citizen to live and seek fulfillment without being afraid of his fellows or of the state.

I examined the case for civil disobedience against the background of the strenuous and difficult processes of social change through which we are living, and in the perspective of Jefferson's thesis that the just powers of government derive from the consent of the governed. I have tried to show that on analysis the case for recognizing a right of civil disobedience can rest on only two grounds, apart from the argument of anarchism—first, Thoreau's claim that an elite within the society is exempted from the moral sanction of majority rule, and that its members should therefore be allowed to decide for themselves which laws to obey and which to disobey; and second, that citizens are justified in conducting demonstrations which violate valid positive law in order to dramatize their cause, and to precipitate change which might not otherwise come about, or come about so soon.

Thoreau's argument denies the moral premise of democracy—that of equality among citizens as citizens.

The second set of arguments, popular at the moment, amounts to no more than the claim that it is right to seek moral ends through the use of immoral means. In any event, there can be no showing that such tactics do more good than harm. And there is a great deal of evidence that progress has come in the United States only when the community as a whole accepts both the rightness of the ends sought and the rightness of the means used to achieve them.

To accept civil disobedience as a right would make concord within society impossible. In times of stress, Thoreau's quiet war could hardly remain a limited war, confined to a few eccentrics at the fringes of society. Different groups would join him in claiming the right to dissociate themselves from society. Presumably they would be as convinced of their superior virtue as he was of his own. Competition in violence and in intimidation would become more open and more intense. The taboos with which democracy has sought to control and redirect our aggressive impulses would weaken. Despite our profound and nearly universal instinct to avoid such a course, we could all too easily find ourselves far beyond the accepted democratic limits of social conflict. As a people, we know the horror and cruelty of war among brothers, and we recoil from the idea.

Those among us who have recently pursued experiments in disorder have discovered how easy it is to paralyze a society based on consent. Such societies are not police states. They are organized on the assumption that citizens normally obey the law. It has been intoxicating for young militants to realize that, for a moment, they can paralyze cities and institutions, and provoke situations of riot and siege. But they discover too that even the most tolerant and permissive societies do not submit to their own destruction. We are slow to anger, but hardly meek. Every government and every society has an inherent right to insist on obedience to its laws, to restore order, and to assure its own survival.

Thus the idea of treating a right of civil disobedience as an aspect of personal liberty under the Constitution is at war with the moral principles on which this civilization, and any liberal civilization, rests; and it is equally at war with the possibility of social peace and of personal liberty.

Individual liberty can be respected and protected only in a society based on a shared understanding as to the broad aspirations of the law. Social concord in this sense requires a general acceptance of the citizen's moral obligation to obey valid law. Respect for the agreed limits of social conflict is essential if men are to live in liberty, and not, in Hobbes's phrase, as wolves.

The social compact of the United States is an unusual one. The power of the majority is checked and restrained in many ways, not least through the Supreme Court, enforcing a written Constitution. Our notion is that freedom is a corollary of agreed restraints on freedom; that man cannot be free, especially in a democratic society, unless the state, and the majority, are not free—unless they can be compelled to respect rights which are "subject to no vote," in Justice Jackson's vivid phrase—rights essential to the dignity of man in a free society and to the vitality of its public life.

These rules and customs, which are the glory of our Constitution and of our national life, could be destroyed, leaving not a rack behind, if we fail to insist that the citizen owes duties to the law equal to those the law owes to him. Without deference to valid law, individual liberty would always be in peril. Equality would find itself at war with freedom. And a revolt of the masses could lead, here as elsewhere, to majoritarian tyranny in one or another of its modern forms. By another path, the ideas of egalitarian anarchy could lead to the same result, by dissolving organized society into its individual atoms and inducing a war of all against all which could end only in the restoration of order by force.

Chief Justice Stone once said that the doctrine that men had a right to destroy valid and constitutional laws by tactics of planned disobedience was contrary to the most fundamental principles of the Constitution. The rule against systematic resort to the violation of law as a political tactic, he wrote, ranks in importance with "the principle of constitutional protection of civil rights and of life, liberty and property, and the principle of representative government" among the quintessential features of our social compact. "It is," he declared, "a principle of our Constitution that change in the organization of our government is to be effected by the orderly procedures ordained by the Constitution and not by force or fraud." [31]

In a society of consent, where democratic procedures of political action are open and functioning, the use of illegal means to achieve

[31] Schneiderman v. United States, 320 U.S. 118, 181 (dissenting opinion) (1943). See also Illinois v. Allen, 397 U.S. 337 (1970): "The social compact has room for tolerance, patience, and restraint, but not for sabotage and violence." (Concurring opinion of Douglas, J., p. 356.)

political ends cannot be justified, whether the ends sought be deemed major or minor, moral or political.

A prolongation of the tactics of riot, however, would have tragic consequences if fear comes to dominate the political atmosphere and if policy turns to a reliance on repression rather than on social progress as the primary method of order. Repudiating the principle of majority rule, as Jefferson said long ago, can lead only to military despotism. Violence and counterviolence, sooner or later, generate forces that demand social peace, even at the price of personal liberty.

It could happen here. We cannot expect to be immune from the experience of all mankind if we defy the principle of democratic consent, which thus far has been the essence of our destiny, and of our freedom.

COMMENT

by Christopher D. Stone

Professor Rostow's concern is that we have not only found ourselves swept up in disturbances and unrest but, more specifically, that so much of the lawbreaking has come to be defended on insistent ethical grounds. Many persons who occupy positions of moral leadership, who in ordinary times we would expect to stand firm against lawbreaking, are either indecisive or giving support to the disobedients.

Rostow's aim is to get the moral critics to put their own actions under as scrupulous ethical review as they put the state's. If they do so, he sets out to demonstrate, they will find that while there is a right —perhaps even a duty—to vent the strongest criticisms of government policy, one cannot make a case for the "rightness" of violating any valid law[1] "as long as the state remains faithful to the fundamental rules."

[1] Rostow makes specific allowance for orderly breaches of law undertaken, in good faith, to set in motion a test of constitutionality.

One should keep firmly in mind what Rostow is *not* saying. He is not saying, merely, that there is a presumptive moral quality to the law, which anyone who is contemplating a violation of the law is under an obligation to take into account before he goes ahead with his actions. Nor do I understand him to be saying merely that the morality of the law should prima facie dominate over other moral tugs that the actor might feel, so that only the very strongest countervailing moral consideration can make a violation of a democracy's laws "right." He is saying, beyond this, that in *no case* has a citizen in a "society of consent" a right to violate the law, no matter how non-violent he may be, and no matter how earnestly he may feel that his actions are destined to further the common good, moral or otherwise.

Now, it should be obvious that Rostow has carved out for himself the hardest of these positions to maintain. It is not, I think, because he feels that the social compact leaves him, as a matter of abstract logic, no choice but to defend that particular interpretation. His is distinctly an interpretation of the social compact read (as it must be) against the author's views—of life, of history, of the capacities and limitations of competing ways of organizing our lives. Much of his paper speaks from this level, and what it comes down to, in sum, is the strong doubt that a society can hold together upon a citizenry of Thoreaus, each opting to follow or disregard the society's commands as he chooses.

There are thus two separate problems to explore and then tie together: First, how far can the argument from social compact go, on its own terms, in convincing the potential dissident that he has a moral duty to obey all laws? Second, when we have those limits in better perspective, what additional empirical and historical judgments does one have to agree with to sustain Rostow's position?

In answering the first question, one ought to recognize that Rostow's argument from social compact does not have to stand or fall depending on whether it can persuade everybody to obey the law in every situation. Some people—cultists, madmen, extreme dissidents—are going to disobey some laws, and perhaps the law in general, no matter what moral arguments we present to them; just as others, through their unquestioningly positive attitudes toward authority, are going sheepishly to obey the law no matter what it tells them to do and what sort of government has issued it. Neither of these two extremes is within the reach of moral suasion, and we cannot expect Rostow's efforts to apply to either of them.

What we have got to test Rostow's position against involves the vast majority of others, those who lie somewhere between these extremes, who find themselves in situations where they (a) more or less consciously feel a dilemma of whether to obey the law; (b) perceive, or can be made to perceive, their dilemma as a moral one (that is, one the solution of which can be advanced by the application of moral terms); and (c) are genuinely willing to apply the intellectual energy that the working out of a moral conclusion demands.

These people can be divided into three groups so far as they help us isolate the problems that Rostow's position faces. First, there will be a group which (a) thinks that the compact model, with its constellation of contract terminology, is the best possible guide to determining political obligation, and (b) also feels that it is applicable to our present society; second, a group which, like the first group, believes in the compact analysis as a way of ordering people's choices in the best of all possible worlds, but is not convinced that it is appropriate to our present circumstances; and, third, a group of people who are principled, in the sense that they genuinely want to orient their impulses in accordance with some moral principles, but for whom the compact model and its elaborate metaphors hold no attraction.

The first group, composed of persons who by definition both subscribe to the compact metaphor as an ideal guide *and* feel it is presently applicable, are those to whom Rostow's argument is going to have the most success. They are committed to accept the relevance of the questions that the model brings with it: Have you not made a *promise* to do such and such? Has not someone else, or the entire society, *relied* on your *implied agreement?* Have you not signified *consent* by *accepting* such and such *benefits?* What Rostow is able to do for these people is to clarify the nature of their commitment by dispelling a number of misconceptions about what the model entails and what it does not. He explains, for example, that when one agrees to a contract, one is accepting a total package, and has not retained the "right" to breach without liability because he would prefer not to have had one or two of the clauses that went along with the whole bargain—or because some of the terms are turning out badly for him.

But ultimately, is there anything in the principles of these people's commitment that entails what Rostow wants finally to convince them of: that they have no "right" to disobey *any* law that has been enacted and sanctioned by the processes "agreed upon," that is, which has been passed by a constitutionally apportioned Congress, signed by the President, upheld by the judges, and so on? Rostow can show them—and does show them—that when they breach such a law, they are breaching "a covenant with moral dimensions, and . . . not committing a purely technical offense" because their obligation to the law is "rooted in [their] own promises." But even supposing this, and supposing that we are now addressing people who give large moral weight to promise-keeping, where does that leave us? Do we not sometimes think it "moral" that we break some promises, "promises" usually of a more specific and considered kind than our "promise" to the state? This is an especially telling point when we observe that our lives are full of countervailing promises, some to the state (say) and some to our family, friends, and colleagues. Even if we accept an obligation to keep promises, and agree to regard our obligations to the state as rooted in a very important promise, it is not to tell us which of the promises is to prevail in any concrete case.

Take, for example, the case Rostow cites of the internment, during the war, of the Japanese Americans. Rostow says that the nation's act was wrong but that it "was not a complete breach of the social contract, which would justify revolution, or tactics of violence that represent the same idea." Maybe. But Rostow has cut out for himself a much harder task than to argue against *revolution* or even *violence;* he wants to argue against even nonviolent disobedience to law.[2] The real case to test Rostow's position demands, we suppose, a citizen of Japanese descent who is faced with the choice of turning himself and his family in to a "relocation center," as per the law, or hiding out. Has he not made "promises" to his family? Have they not "relied" on him? The set of obligations to his children and to his nation came

[2] This distinction is explored with especial cogency in Wasserstrom, "The Obligation to Obey the Law," 10 UCLA Law Review 780 (1963).

about in much the same way—in a hospital room. What is there about keeping promises, per se, which tells him that his violating the law by hiding out and protecting his family is immoral, rather than the contrary? There are arguments both ways; but the further one tracks them, the less he finds himself arguing about simple promise-keeping.

Rostow evidently bases his compact argument not merely on the obligation to keep promises, but on the supportive position that, in conditions of democracy, we are bound to assume that the machinery of state—not the various conjectures of various dissidents—expresses the will of the majority and the community's sense of justice. Here, too, however, we are not apt to dissuade from civil disobedience even those who agree with the premise. Most civil disobedients do not doubt to start with that the laws are expressive of the community's will. They may think, however, that the community's sense of justice is both *wrong* (its increasing discredit is a factor that compact theorists will have to contend with) and intruding into areas in which they never "agreed" that the larger community's sense of justice ought to prevail; for example, in tolerating segregation. If the disobedient feels strongly, then he is not apt to find anything in the assumption that the majority's will is prevailing to dissuade him from committing some technically illegal but nonviolent protest to stir the majority to reconsider its views more rapidly than could be accomplished through lawful channels. There are arguments to be made, of course, for his exercising restraint. The point is that the social compact, so far as it is predicated on either the obligation to keep promises or on the presumption that the majority's sense of justice will be effectuated in a democracy, stops far short of—indeed, is quite indecisive with respect to—convincing anyone in a real dilemma.

The problem is, in more general terms, that there is simply nothing odd or striking about people believing in the compact metaphor, but only insofar as they are deemed bound by decisions which affect all parties in a pretty much nondiscriminatory way (say, when Congress decides how much money is to go to the highway trust fund and how much to foreign aid). But it is far harder to convince anyone that he has so "promised" to abide by the laws that he is morally bound not to disobey an order which singles him out for concentration camp because of his race. Certainly no judge, in interpreting the humdrum contracts that are his daily fare, would impute such unlikely intentions to the parties before him.[3]

Rostow acknowledges the difficulty that countervailing moral tugs pose for the compact analysis, but seems to suggest, as a way around them, what appears at first blush a compromise position: that the actor who feels overwhelmed by his other moral commitments and breaks the law "should at least respect his duty to the law he has helped make by accepting its penalties." This is, however, considerably less than the solution one wanted. The whole aim of a moral model is to offer a framework people can use to resolve their obligations by moral analysis and suasion—that is, before force (the individual's or the state's) is the only recourse that remains. Thus, what the potential disobedient wants from the moral model is guidance as to whether it is "right" to break the law in the first place. Once he has chosen to do so, whether he "accepts" the law's penalties is beside the point of the social compact as a moral model, because he has made the basic *moral choice* we were concerned with, and it is only in limited cases that he still is the object of a *moral argument*.[4] Once he is in the hands of the state, the choices are those of the state, and whether he "accepts" what the state does to him is more a matter of psychological interest than a moral dilemma on the same order as that which the disobedient faced originally.[5]

---

[3] It is worth remembering in this regard that part of the reason why contract law works as well as it does is that the parties are implicitly agreeing that the courts may render certain binding interpretations. But the civil disobedient will not recognize any such machinery of state for interpreting the compact obligations he feels strongly about because—in contract terms —the state is the other party.

[4] For example, if he is asking himself, "Ought I to resist arrest?" or, not apropos the typical disobedient, "Ought I—a fugitive—to turn myself in?"

[5] Note that vis-à-vis the prosecutor, there still is a quasi-moral choice in the case: *"Ought* I to prosecute the lawbreaker?" In deciding whether to use his discretion to prosecute, the considerations of whatever ethical model the prosecutor subscribes to are still alive and effective; that is, he is the one now open to appeal on moral principle, and among other questions he may well ask himself, "Had the civil disobedient a 'right' (in the moral sense) to disobey the law?" (Rostow's answer, as noted, would be in the negative.)

By calling the matter of "acceptance" one of "psychological interest" I do not intend to demean it in the least. There undoubtedly runs throughout societies the strongest desire that law violators—subversives, cutpurses or witches

The second group of people present to Rostow's position all these problems and an additional one. While they are (unlike the next group) attracted by the compact metaphor as a guide for ordering one's obligations, they feel that, given the structure of our present society, with, for example, the present maldistribution of effective participation, the compact simply is not applicable *now*. Their position might be likened to that of the industrial workers in the early part of the century, who wanted to organize their relations with their employers on the basis of contract, but who felt that until bargaining power was equalized by changes in the negotiating structure, contract negotiations should not bind—or even be entered into. Rostow is, I take it, acknowledging argument of this sort in his special efforts to respond to the Negroes and students. But throughout his paper as a whole, there is not the sort of support that many readers will demand of his repeated assertions that ours is "a society of consent," that our government's powers are legitimate "because authorized and renewed by procedures all must respect," and that ours is "a society of liberty and equality." These are grand claims, but nonetheless they are very much in question today by people who are not in bad faith, and whose attitude toward the arguments from compact are influenced accordingly.

The third group is the most difficult of all to deal with, and, again, I do not think that they can be dismissed as of bad faith. Many people want keenly to keep some set of obligations to the state and to their fellow citizens, but simply find the compact unacceptable as a strategy of argument for anyone who is not already convinced.

Rostow, anticipating them, speaks of Locke's social-compact model as "the only modern rival to the doctrine that power proceeds from the barrel of a gun," and the truth of this negative, alone, may be seen as shifting the burden back on his critics. Certainly no one can have much taste for positivism after what we saw in Europe in the thirties—and since—and arguments, like Plato's, from the healthy body, or, like Filmer's, from the divine right of kings, are no less unsupportably fic-

—confess and apologize and therefore ratify the system and its presuppositions. Their decision as to whether or not to give in this way does involve moral elements (*cf.* Koestler, *Darkness at Noon*), and Rostow may be suggesting that the lawbreaker's compact commitments entail his at least giving society this gratification. But the disobedient's major problem—and ours— is still: Ought I to break the law in the first place?

tive than the compact. These objectors ought to recognize, too, how hard it is to think of a model that promises to fulfill as many goals as does the compact. Its terms encompass in one set of shared symbols reminders (a) to the governors as to their obligations to the governed; (b) to the governed as to their duty to obey laws; and (c) to the governed as to their duty when not to obey, or perhaps even affirmatively to disobey, the laws. Further, on a less tangible but at least equally important level, it develops and reinforces a broad range of attitudes toward life that we attach high importance to—senses of our freedom, dignity, autonomy, and choice.

These are all, I feel, strong arguments. But we have to recognize, as a fact, that notwithstanding them the compact model does not seem to have a great deal of attraction as a model. And the real *sine qua non* of a model of political obligation is not its abstract intellectual appeal (as a matter of its coherence with other beliefs the society deems acceptable) but its capacity to exercise influence over real people.

What is the reason for the compact model's lack of drawing power?

For one thing, as observed already, even on its premises it does not seem to give much guidance in most of the very cases one feels strongly enough about to want to think through morally. An argument that is based on promise, reliance, and so forth, is always going to turn up counter-promises and counter-reliances, usually of a more immediate and tangible sort than those to the state.

Secondly, I think we ought to recognize too that people today have associations toward contractual obligation different than they had in Locke's time. In Locke's time, for example, the prevalent epistemology and psychology were of a much simpler sort—everyone was assumed to know the world, and know his wants, by simply inspecting and inventorying basic concepts and perceptions. A neo-Kantian, neo-Freudian era in theories of knowledge lends itself to increased doubts that "the facts" people have to go on are really so simple, or that people "really" know what they want. Many of the avant-garde skeptics of compact obligations can be read as saying, from this perspective, that our knowledge and wants are so inadequate and manipulable that we do not have, in contract terminology, contractual capacity in our political lives; in all events, the fiction seems just that much more fictive.

The political model cannot but suffer, too, from the fact that the contracts people today really know of—those with their insurance agent and telephone company—seem so imposed on them and so unwilled. The bills are paid, but the feeling of moral commitment to one's contracts must be minimal.

There is a deeper level of problem, as well. In Locke's day the contract had the attractiveness of an instrument that liberated people (from status) and was (like promise-keeping) fundamental to long-term, orderly planning; an age that is putting more and more emphasis on spontaneity and the present is apt to regard a contract as less desirable and understandable, as "binding." [6] This lost luster carries down to the very level of promise-keeping, on which the contract's obligatoriness is rested. In the age into which we are entering, the keeping of a promise tends to seem more and more *immoral*. It is viewed as if the speaker said "I will carry out some action because of the person that I was when I made the promise." New senses of change and speed are tending to replace that thinking with a morality which demands that appeals for moral support be addressed to one's present commitments; that is, "I love you," not "I promised to love you." In such times the compact model, along with promises, contracts, and loyalty oaths, is going to have lessened moral appeal.

None of this is to say that Rostow is wrong in his basic position. But the objections that these three groups of people present place for us in clearer perspective the difficulties that the compact model faces in arresting the centrifugal forces that are pulling us apart.

My sense is that we will not resolve these problems until we have a deeper understanding than we now have of how important it is for a society to have *any single shared model of obligation at all*. The persuasiveness of all the steps of Rostow's argument—the defense of the social compact as an ideal model of obligation, the judgment that the model is applicable to our present society, the interpretation that it admits of no exceptions by appeal to "higher" moral claims—are all in some ways responsive to that one problem.

I say this because, when we get right down to it, whether we deem the compact model applicable to our society is not a pure empirical

[6] An interesting circle of events considering the etymology of "bound by contract."

question about "the facts" of our daily lives—for example, whether the distribution of effective voting power is "really" equal—but a decision of degree that is very much influenced by theoretical and pragmatic considerations about what will happen to us if we act *as though* there is no compact. People who feel that there are large values in having *some* shared model of obligation to guide us will be that much less hasty to throw over whatever we do have because they spot (who could not spot?) some structural inequities. And similarly with respect to whether we should admit of exceptions. We cannot answer that without having a good sense of what it is, exactly, we can hope a firm set of guidelines to do for us. For the higher our expectations of what unyielding fidelity to law can bring, the less prone we will be to undermine it with special allowances for "good faith" lawbreakers.

Rostow's answer to this underlying question is to be found most importantly in the one phrase, "no society of consent could live according to Thoreau's principle." He regards, in sum, a society that lacked a firm model as a historically impossible one; he sees the social compact as the only real choice we have; and he does not think it can remain in force at all if even the limited amount of concrete direction we can draw from it is regarded as exhortatory only.

This judgment is not self-evident, but no historical judgment is. Does disregard for law become a habit and spread? To the extent that a society's capacity to command order by moral suasion suffers, how much of the "slack" may have to be (or will be) taken up by repressive state action and how much—no less insidiously—by internalized means of control? Is a society better off, in the long term, by tolerating some short-run wrongs in the interests of preserving a viable system? Does habitual obedience to any law the state offers up deprive people of their moral timbre and lay them open for dictators? Are the actions of a self-styled moral "elite," working outside the most dissenter-oriented system the world has ever seen, going to bring it all tumbling down around their—and our—feet?

These are, none of them, easy judgments. They are, however, the most important that a citizen can come forward to make. In making them as he does, Rostow brings to this paper a distinguished career of troubling over what they mean—in academic theory and in public practice.

His conclusions will cause many—as they cause this commentator—to give a sober second look to what is going on around us.

COMMENT
by Patricia Roberts Harris

I welcome the opportunity to make public a longtime private disagreement between Dean Rostow and me on the subject of his paper. There are only two points in either the explicit statements or the necessary inferences to be drawn from Dean Rostow's paper with which I agree.

The first is that there is no "right" to be civilly disobedient in any society that has any expectation of maintaining itself, whether that society be a democratic society or a totalitarian society. By their very nature, governments must exercise their powers as though they were legitimate. Civil disobedience raises the question of the legitimacy of the operation of some or all parts of that government. Therefore, I do not wish to suggest in any of the remarks that follow that civil disobedients have a right to be exempted from punishment because of the moral claims they make as they refuse to obey the law that others would impose upon them.

The second point on which I agree with Dean Rostow is that violence is very dangerous. It is dangerous for those who are its users, and it is dangerous for those of us who are its targets (or caught in between). Save for those two specific matters there is little else in the paper with which I agree, and I want to say why as briefly as I can.

Each of us believes in the democratic procedure by which citizens by a show of hands choose among competing but equally feasible courses of action. However, when many support a particular course of action which is defeated in the show of hands, the winning side has exercised a veto over the perceived interest of the losing side. If the issue is whether to build a supersonic transport, losing the vote may be costly to major interests. However, one wonders whether the failure to fund food programs for hungry children, although determined by the same decision method as the SST result, is not significantly different and if the reaction to the no-food-money decision might not legitimately differ from the reaction to loss of the SST.

Under Dean Rostow's acceptance of the "will of the majority theory" the minority continues its efforts to persuade enough members of the majority to the minority cause to convert the minority into an effective political majority. This theory (to which I subscribe operationally) ignores the dilemma faced by a minority unable to persuade the majority to change for reasons having little to do with the reasonableness of the minority goals. The majority may be able to grant the demands of the minority, but may choose not to do so because the *status quo* is so comfortable for the majority.

The result of such majority intransigence is to place upon the minority the full burden of the majority's refusal to change the *status quo*. Regardless of the merit of the minority's call for change, and regardless of the ease or difficulty of achieving the change, in a democracy the minority, outvoted, is impotent unless it can convert itself into a majority. Until that conversion takes place, the burden of failure to change falls upon the minority. Therefore, if one examines the consequences of Dean Rostow's "drink-the-hemlock" theory of acceptance of the decision of the majority regardless of the discomfort that the decision occasions the unsuccessful minority, one comes to understand the possibility that a losing minority may decide not to bear the burden of loss of a vote alone, but may decide to find ways in which to spread the social cost of inaction by the majority.

Civil disobedience and violence have two things in common. First, each commands the attention of the public. Second, each spreads the cost of social neglect of the expressed needs of a minority. However, it is grossly unfair and highly inaccurate to suggest any other necessary linkage between civil disobedience and violence. In fact, the major twentieth-century proponents of civil disobedience, Gandhi and Martin Luther King, insisted upon the absence of violence as part of the moral force of civil disobedience.

Civil disobedience, which Dean Rostow seems to believe is in derogation of the tenets of democracy, is in fact a rational and often essential extension of that democracy. Unlike violence, which frightens us all because of the irreversible damage it can do to individuals and objects, nonviolent civil disobedience seldom harms anyone. However, civil disobedience can make large numbers of people very uncomfortable, physically and psychologically, because they must face a reality in which significant numbers of people peaceably refuse to accept the requirements of the society in which they live. When, as is usually the case, the civil disobedient accepts punishment and ostracism rather than obey the law, observers become uncomfortable and search for an explanation and an end to the discomfort.

The invocation of civil disobedience makes the community decide whether it is willing to accept the social turmoil inherent in the continued refusal of significant groups to obey what appears to be the valid law of the community, or whether it is easier to secure "domestic tranquility" by granting what the minority strongly believes are just demands. Civil disobedience, by making the majority uncomfortable, spreads the social cost of the refusal of the majority to act, and puts some of the burden on the majority.

That social cost is further spread from the minority to the majority when the acts of civil disobedience are those which inconvenience the majority, such as sit-ins, refusals of teachers to teach despite no-strike laws, and so on.

In the United States political civil disobedience has been used more often than has political violence. In fact, deliberate political use of violence has been rare in American political life.

Whenever a minority group has threatened in advance to use violence for political purposes, the tendency of the society has been to repress the group threatening violence, as witness the attitude toward anarchists and Communists, and now, toward the Black Panthers. However, violence for political ends has not always been repressed. When the violent group is a local majority arrayed against a minority, as was the case in the South, or when powerful interests have used violence against nascent interest groups, as with the early labor movement, violence has been repressed only after the victims gained some political power.

Threats of violence by a minority, however, are very likely to lead to early repressive acts by the majority because violence is dangerous to those who are its announced targets. Despite such repressive action, threats of violence and actual acts of violence by those seeking change, but consistently denied it, tend to continue because both threats and actual violence give a high level of visibility to the perpetrators. Despite moralistic statements to the contrary, violence or the threat thereof has often had the utility of raising submerged groups to the level of the conscious attention of society where that society has otherwise ignored them.

For example, the threat of violence by the Deacons for Defense and Justice in Louisiana is acknowledged by all to have been a threat necessary to impress upon violence-wielding whites the fact of an end to black submission to terror. When the threats escalated to actual use of violence in a few shotgun blasts, the Deacons convinced the whites that they meant business.

The threats and violence of the Deacons brought to the attention of the community the existence of a group that intended no longer to accept the depredations of the majority violent community. The threat and use of violence made it clear that a new black force existed and that it was dangerous to use violence against them.

Few suggest that the use of violence by the Deacons for Defense and Justice was either wrong or an exercise in futility, probably because most people disagreed with the behavior of the whites and sympathized with the defensive role of the Deacons.

I would submit that absence of agreement and sympathy with the goals of perpetrators of violence should not blind us to the possibility that their use of violence may not be futile.

Putting aside the use of violence in the revolutionary displacement of existing governmental authority, political violence is being used today and has been used in the past for a purpose that has revolutionary aspects but is not in fact revolutionary.

Much of today's violence, particularly that by black and white youth, appears to have as its goal the spreading of the social cost of social neglect.

Today the violent minority does not seek revolutionary change through the use of violence nor does it wish to create a new majority to wreak its will at the ballot box. The minority uses violence as a harassing tactic to create discomfort for the majority.

The discomforting violence is usually accompanied by reiteration of the demands for change and of the identification of the demanding group, so that the relationship between the violence and the demand is apparent.

Of course, those who use violence in this way are playing Russian roulette because the targets immediately begin to search for ways to get rid of the violence-perpetrators, and are not averse to a counter-application of violence for the purpose of defense and self-preservation.

Nonetheless, the existence of violence and the need to provide resources to prevent it place a burden upon the violence targets. The purpose of the violence-perpetrators in announcing themselves as responsible for the violence is to inform the targets that the burden of violence or violence prevention can be avoided if the demands of the minority are met.

Although we would all respond with rhetoric and initial activity denying any intent to give in to force, the reality is that changes are likely to be made when the demands of the perpetrators of violence are demands which fair men recognize as deserving attention.

Ghetto violence, whether the unplanned emotional outpouring of Watts, or the cold-blooded snipings of Chicago, has led to action at diverse levels on problems such as housing and employment for blacks, improving police community relations, electing black officials, and many more.

Acknowledging the fact that such violence has increased anger and even hatred directed to blacks, there has been, nonetheless, a consistent attempt by large segments of the community to meet legitimate black demands, with hope of thereby avoiding further violence.

Of course, the Russian roulette aspect of such use of violence is demonstrated by the other responses to black violence. Some police are today even more likely to shoot into Black Panther headquarters than they were when sniping began. White voters who resented the attention paid to the needs of blacks in the past are freed by knowledge of ghetto violence from any sense of guilt when they oppose social change. Nonetheless, there is consistent evidence that attempts are being made to meet the justified demands of blacks in an effort to avoid the continuation or extension of violence.

Another example of demonstrative violence that spreads the cost of social neglect by requiring the majority to consider the likelihood that violence will increase if there is no change is the opposition to the war in Vietnam. The often expressed sentiment that the war is "tearing the country apart" refers to both psychic and physical phenomena. Attacks on draft boards and bombed buildings must be severely punished, but few will deny the hope that the end of the war would end war-related violence. The growing consensus that the war should end is in no small part a reflection of this hope. The social turmoil accompanying the war, as well as the violence, has spread the social cost of the war from the drafted young and the uncared-for poor to the essentially neutral majority. The social turmoil—first, of civil disobedience, and later, of violence—has increased the willingness to consider an end to a venture opposed by what is still probably only a minority.

Therefore, we delude ourselves when we insist that the use of violence only leads to repression. When the demands of the violence perpetrators are perceived by the targets of the violence to be demands that should have been met, the targets of the violence are more rational than the violence-perpetrators and seek to do justice.

The consequence of this perception ought to be clear. The rational among us (and I still believe such exist) must come to understand that patience is a virtue that can be adopted, but cannot be demanded. People who have some pieces of power must learn to use that power before the explosion by those who have been asked, unfairly, to be patient with majority failure to change.

A good deal of black violence could have been prevented, and can still be stemmed, by increase of efforts to change the conditions of black citizens. The Black Panthers need the hatred of the police in order to survive. When police hatred becomes police compassion, Black Panther recruiting suffers. This does not mean that Panther rhetoric becomes less violent, but action on the ills they continually describe makes potential Panthers unwilling to act out the violent rhetoric.

What is true of violent black rhetoric and action may well be true of the violent words and actions of other youths. We still have a chance to head off Chicano violence, if we do not wait for the Mexican Americans to force themselves upon our consciousness by some guns and bombs. And Alcatraz may be a harbinger of danger from our long-quiescent red brothers.

We are not now concerned with the demands of Chicano and Indian, as most whites ten years ago were not concerned with blacks. Few today are unaware of black demands. We can debate whether violence has helped the achievement of black demands, but every riot-torn community has paid a high price for complacency and indifference. The cost of that complacency no longer rested in those communities with blacks alone, but was shared in some measure in money, fear, and anger, by all. Other groups have learned that whatever violence may not achieve, it does mean that everybody, minority and majority, loses. For a minority used to losing, it does not matter. What does matter to the minority is that for a change the majority loses too.

Until we understand that such a loss to the majority, in and of itself, provides comfort to the ignored and unhappy minority, we will continue to insist that violence is futile, and will continue to be shocked when it occurs; even though circumstances are such that we should all expect it.

A democratic system that does not voluntarily adjust majority comfort to make certain that the system's minorities feel accommodated can expect both civil disobedience and violence, because they are surefire ways of reminding the majority that the minority is unhappy. With that knowledge the majority is free to choose between acting to minimize the unhappiness of the minority or repressing the minority. Whichever course the majority takes, it has been forced by the minority to alter the *status quo*. Change by such methods is a perversion of democratic procedures, but it flows from the essence of democracy itself, which rests upon consent, but cannot compel consent.

Dean Rostow's social compact can be breached successfully, and to deny it is to deny a present-day reality understood only too well by today's dissidents.

Therefore, cooperation of dissidents to avoid violence is essential if democracy is to survive. The ultimate futility for our system is to assert the futility of violence, which admittedly may not succeed in achieving its goals, but which almost always succeeds in altering the society it infects.

CHAPTER 3

IN DEFENSE OF ANARCHISM

by Robert Paul Wolff

Does a citizen have a moral obligation to obey the law? Are there any limits to the extent or force of his obligation? Are there circumstances in which he is relieved of any duty of obedience? What are those circumstances, and why?

These questions express, at one and the same time, the most fundamental issues of political philosophy and the most immediate personal choices facing young American men today. Indeed this congruence of abstract philosophy with practical life-decisions is a mark of the crisis of our age, for the theoretical and the practical come together most urgently when the underlying rationale of a social order is called into question. So it was that ordinary men in sixteenth-century Germany debated the theological questions which set Protestant against Catholic; and so it is that ordinary men today debate the authority and legitimacy of the secular political order.

Because of the complexity of the issues surrounding the citizen's relation to the law, I have cast about for some device which might organize and focus our discussion. Let us imagine, then, that we have before us a young man who faces the terrible decision whether to obey an order of induction into the United States Army. Like many of his friends, Stephen—as we may call him—is deeply troubled by the conflicting moral demands which he feels are being made upon him. He is an American born and bred, and he identifies very powerfully with the history, culture, institutions, and government of his native land. Stephen is no alienated youth, projecting his allegiance onto the imagined virtues of distant and unfamiliar lands. But Stephen has come, after troubled reflection, to believe that the American cause in Southeast Asia is immoral—not simply imprudent, or shortsighted, or unpolitic, or on balance a mistake, but immoral, in just the way that the Soviet invasion of Czechoslovakia, and the French repression of Algeria, and the German invasion of the Low Countries were immoral.

We must imagine that Stephen is debating with himself and his friends what response he shall make to the induction order. One by one, arguments are brought forward to persuade him that he should comply with the legal command. As he replies to the arguments, he is drawn more and more deeply into the heart of the problem of political obligation, until finally he confronts directly the pure theory of democratic society. For it is my intention to strike at the very foundations of the myth of legitimate authority, not merely to dispose of the superficial defenses which are thrown up from time to time when that authority is challenged.

PART ONE: THE PRELIMINARY DEFENSES

The first argument that Stephen's distraught parents bring forward is purely prudential: Refusal to serve will mean trial, conviction, and imprisonment. A promising career halted, perhaps forever. Three, four, or five years in a miserable jail with hardened criminals. Is there no way to avoid such a fate without actually fighting in Vietnam? Perhaps a petition for conscientious objector status. Even if it fails, the procedure can be prolonged for a year or more, and by then President Nixon may have withdrawn all combat troops from the war zone. Or enlistment in some safer branch of service. With Stephen's education, a commission in the navy might be possible.

These are powerful arguments; I for one would be strongly persuaded by them if I were in Stephen's place. Each of us has a right to assign a high value to his own safety and interest. There is no virtue in fruitless martyrdom, and the man who seeks legal punishment for an action which he believes to be right is better suited for psychoanalysis than sainthood.

But Stephen's parents are not arguing that he has a moral duty to obey the induction order. They merely want him to avoid the legal penalties if he can. Many of us abide by the law principally out of fear of, or distaste for, the penalties. Sometimes we even calculate just how far we can risk bucking the law without too great a danger of punishment. However, conformity to law out of fear of punishment is not what most of us mean by "duty." When I posed the question whether a citizen had a moral obligation to obey the law, I was not merely asking whether, as a matter of prudential fact, lawbreakers would be punished. That is an issue for the sociologists and statisticians. I wished to know whether a man like Stephen had a duty to conform to the law's demands *whether he could reasonably expect punishment or not.*

I am quite willing to grant that only a relatively few persons in any society base their response to the commands of the law on self-consciously reasoned moral considerations. Nevertheless, the number appears to be growing in America today, and it is well worth determining the precise grounds and limits of the citizen's *moral* relationship to the law. Later on, we shall have to consider whether it is a good thing for men to discuss that relationship publicly and honestly.

So putting aside considerations of personal safety and private interest, what argument can be advanced for the proposition that Stephen morally *ought* to report for induction?

At this point, a supporter of our Vietnam policy may step forward to offer the simplest of all arguments: The war is just, the policy is morally right, and therefore all men of conscience should support it in whatever way the government requires. Just such an argument, after all, persuaded thousands of Americans to enlist in the Canadian or British armed forces in the opening years of World War II and the Abraham Lincoln Brigade during the Spanish Civil War.

This is not the place to debate the rights and wrongs of Vietnam yet again. Perhaps it is a just war, perhaps not. But remember that Stephen, our hypothetical young man, has been assumed to be opposed to the war on moral grounds. We may take it for granted that he would feel no conflict about the induction order if he could convince himself of the justice of America's cause. He might feel fear or reluctance, to be sure; but he would face no *moral* dilemma. The problem of obedience and conscience only arises with any urgency when the law commands what the individual believes to be wrong.

To put this point somewhat differently, we are concerned with the formal or procedural issue of the citizen's relationship to the laws of the state; we are not here debating the substantive merits of this or that particular law. The defenders of the authority of the law, such as Justice Fortas in his essay "Concerning Dissent and Civil Disobedience," specifically reject the notion that the citizen is obliged to obey only those laws of which he approves. Such a position, they quite correctly insist, is tantamount to denying the authority of the law entirely.

The second argument that might be offered to Stephen is the exact opposite of the first: not that the war is just or right, but simply that the law is the law and ought to be obeyed. Respect for law as such is so strong in most men that they really need no more elaborate rationale for obedience. Cultures vary in this regard, of course. Northern Europeans are rather more prone than their southern neighbors to strict law-abidance, at least according to the folklore of national character. But as Max Weber pointed out half a century ago, unquestioning acceptance of state authority is the norm in human affairs. Only under special, and usually temporary, circumstances do men question the right of their government to command and the duty of citizens to obey. In a gathering of legal personages as distinguished as those here today, we may assume a very high degree of respect for the authority of the law. Even so, no one among us would wish to claim that *every* law, whatever its source and content, deserves to be obeyed. We may balk at different points, of course. Some of us may refuse to acknowledge the moral authority of any law promulgated by a dictatorship. Others will draw the line at a law that commands us to murder our neighbors. Still others will refuse to sacrifice our children. But surely no sane man can have so slavish a respect for all law *as such* that he would argue for submission to any *de facto* legal command, irrespective of the circumstances. Later on, we shall have to consider whether such absolute obedience *is* reasonable in the special case of laws issuing from a genuinely democratic legislature.

Thus far, the arguments have been easy to handle. We have re-hearsed them more for the purpose of clarifying certain elementary matters than because a young man like Stephen would be per-suaded by them. But now the first serious challenge is thrown at Stephen's act of conscience. You choose to refuse a legal induction order because you have adjudged the Vietnam war immoral. (This, we may imagine, from Stephen's rather proper uncle.) But have you given any thought to the consequences of your own defiant act? To be sure, you will avoid complicity in what you believe to be an evil policy, but that will not be the end of it. Your act will inspire others. As you and your fellow "men of conscience" publicly deny the authority of the law, an atmosphere of disrespect for law itself will spread throughout society. Others will imitate you, and not always for purposes that you would approve. You cheered when the Supreme Court struck down discriminatory practices in school-ing and housing. But what use are court decisions to Black Amer-ica if growing numbers of white men and women are prepared to defy the law? Do you imagine that you can quarantine your disobe-dience so that it will not infect others in this society? Disrespect for law is a plague as virulent to social health as the Black Death. Social order is like an old, majestic tree; it can be killed by a simple, wanton act of thoughtless destruction, but many genera-tions are required to create it anew.

Nor should you shield yourself from this charge by pleading your unimportance in the larger social scheme. If you weigh so heavily the responsibility you would bear as one single soldier in a force of nearly half a million Americans, then you must take with equal seriousness your possible effect on the internal order of your own country.

These are weighty arguments indeed, and Stephen must find very strong counterarguments if he is to justify his continued refusal to obey the law. One need not have the dark vision of a Thomas Hobbes to appreciate the social value of universal respect for the processes of the law. But there are two questions which must be answered before we can properly measure goods against goods, and evils against evils, in the situation confronting Stephen.

First, how bad is the evil which the dissenter seeks to deter by his refusal to observe the law? Even if social disruption is a by-product of resistance to law, we must still ask whether that disruption is not the lesser evil. For example, suppose that Germans opposed to the extermination of the Jews had managed to thwart that policy by widespread resistance to the legal authority of the Nazi government. Let us even suppose that the resultant social disorder caused a breakdown in health services and food distribution. Innocent Germans would have been hurt by such a train of events, but many equally innocent persons would have been saved from the gas chambers. Can anyone—*even* Thomas Hobbes—deny that the harmful consequences of social disorder would in this case have been a reasonable price to pay for the end accomplished?

When we try to make an analogous calculation in the case of the Vietnam war, we immediately come to an impasse. Defenders of the authority of the state—whether or not they are also defenders of the war—insist that there is no legitimate analogy between the extermination of the Jews and the Vietnam war. The fate of the six million Jews has too often been used in the last twenty years as a club to beat down any reasoned criticism of extralegal political tactics. Self-righteous moralists wrap themselves in the winding-sheets of those slaughtered innocents as if to dare anyone to utter a word against them. And too often their opponents, embarrassed into silence by the memory of such appalling suffering, retire from the debate in confusion. So let us not hear of the Nazi atrocities, Stephen's critics will say. Nor confuse the issue with easy appeals to the trials at Nuremberg. Vietnam is not Buchenwald, and Nixon is not Hitler.

But the issue is not so quickly settled, for it is *precisely* the depraved brutality of America's actions in Vietnam that has driven normally law-abiding citizens into defiant postures of deliberate disobedience. The decision to set oneself against the state is not taken easily by young men like Stephen. The habit of obedience, reinforced by a prudential concern for personal safety, effectively binds most men to the law under ordinary circumstances. We do not find them risking their future over a disputed trade policy or the unwarranted recognition of a dictatorial regime. The war resisters may be wrong in their evaluation of the actions of our government;

that is not an issue to be debated here. But one can hardly persuade them to obey the law merely by pointing to the danger of social disorder. They have, so to speak, already discounted that side effect, in their calculation of moral costs.

To the first question—How grave is the evil which they oppose by their breach of the law?—Stephen and his fellows reply, "Grave enough to justify even a decline of the respect for law itself, if that should indeed be a consequence of our action."

However, a second question must be asked: Is it in fact plausible to suppose that the open defiance of war resisters will weaken the general respect for law in the society as a whole? Can one really trace a causal link between draft resistance, on the one hand, and southern defiance of integration orders, or illegal strikes by public employees, or a rise in violent crime, on the other?

This question is too large to be treated adequately here, but I should like to suggest that such a claim betrays a fatally simple-minded conception of social causation. Medical metaphors to the contrary notwithstanding, disrespect for law is not a contagious disease which spreads through a society by contact. If one wishes to explain the readiness of southern communities to defy the lawful orders of Federal courts, one must look to the social pressures and conflicts indigenous to the community; to the historical conse-quences of the Civil War; to the calculations of politicians willing to exploit explosive feelings; but surely *not* to the refusal of young men to serve in Vietnam. The reaction by striking postal workers in New York to the offers of support from SDS activists shows—if anyone doubted it—that their willingness to break the law does not derive from the example of draft evaders. As for the claim that such a connection exists with the general rise in street crime, I take it that no one would be so foolish as to look for correlations be-tween muggings and conscientious objection.

Perhaps I should add—though it hardly seems necessary—that the more socially harmful forms of disrespect for the law can also not be blamed upon the writings of academic intellectuals or left-wing pamphleteers. I am sometimes astonished at the degree of influence which defenders of the established order are willing to impute to my friend and colleague, Herbert Marcuse. To hear them tell it, Marcuse has the power, merely by a flourish of his Hegelian prose, to set the Four Horsemen of the Apocalypse riding across the face of America. In this, as in so much else, Marx was quite correct. Ideas may shape a social movement, but they do not give rise to it. If there is indeed a breakdown in respect for law in America, we must look farther than the periodical reading room of the local library for its causes.

At this point, a philosophical question intrudes on our deliberations—not a question, perhaps, that would arise most naturally in a debate of the sort we have imagined, but still a question worth posing to a man who claims to act out of moral conviction. Granted there is very little *causal* connection between Stephen's defiance and other acts of deliberate illegality in American society; still we may fairly ask Stephen: What would happen if *everyone* were to act as you are acting? *Universalizability* of one's principles, as philosophers call it, is widely regarded as a test of the rightness of a course of action. The point is that a man should not make an exception of himself when he chooses how to act. He should only adopt a policy which he would be prepared to have everyone adopt. So, for example, he ought not to cheat on his income tax while still expecting others to provide the tax revenues for the government programs he favors.

To Stephen we can say, Are you not making an exception of yourself? Do you not secretly count on the law-abiding habits of the great majority of your fellow countrymen? Can you honestly defend the right of *every* American to decide for himself when the law is to be obeyed and when it is to be disregarded? Or are you reassuring yourself with the thought that most people will reject your anti-authoritarian example? What an irony it would be if, in the name of morality, you were to set yourself up as an elite to whom the moral rules of the common man did not apply!

We shall return to this issue at the very end of our discussion, but a preliminary answer can be given here. What principle is it that Stephen is being asked to measure against the standard of universalizability? *Not* a principle of licentious self-indulgence or willful amorality. Stephen is hardly to be confused with the sort of selfish sneak who ignores the rights of others and looks out only for his own interests. He is not a stock manipulator foisting watered securities on unsuspecting widows, nor is he a soulless drug peddler exploiting the misery of addiction. In every way except one, Stephen is exhibiting the marks of the highest form of conscientious responsibility. His concern is entirely for those who will suffer the consequences of whatever course of action he may choose. The sole difference between Stephen and the most dedicated public servant is that Stephen believes that he must defy the law in order to do what is right.

Now seriously—would America really be a worse place to live if everyone were like Stephen? To be sure, there would be bitter conflict between men of opposed moral dedication. But the whole level of private and public life would be raised to a new level of personal responsibility. Exploitation, crime, the callous neglect of the poor and needy, would cease. The horror of My Lai, the degradation of the ghetto, the mindless destruction of the environment, would cease. For a society thus transformed, the intransigence of committed conscience would be a small price to pay.

The discussion now shifts from the abstractly philosophical to the directly personal. Stephen finds himself confronted by an argument as old as Plato's dialogue, the *Crito,* but still capable of moving men of conscience. Put to one side for the moment your private moral convictions, Stephen is urged. You are a member of this society. For nearly twenty-two years you have lived in its midst, benefiting from the peace and abundance which it offers. Do you not owe a debt of gratitude to America which requires that you perform the task it now calls you to? Can you now turn your back on your country, ignoring the benefits it has conferred upon you? You may protest that you did not ask to be so cared for and protected; but you would hardly hide behind such an argument to evade your debt to your parents! Why can you not acknowledge a similar debt to the nation as a whole?

Like the argument concerning the dangers of social disorder, the appeal to gratitude is a legitimate move in general, but irrelevant in regard to the decision facing Stephen. First of all, let us be clear about the nature of Stephen's debt. He owes nothing to the *government* of the United States. It is the American *people* whose collective efforts have sustained and protected him throughout his life. Governments like to identify themselves with the nations they rule, and democratic governments insist upon the identification as a matter of philosophic principle; but Stephen's debt is to the farmers who grew his food, to the workers who made his clothes, to the policemen who stood ready to protect his life, not to the legislators who made the laws under which he lived.

All that is irrelevant, however, in the case of Vietnam, for no debt of gratitude to one group of men and women can possibly oblige me to go forth and kill a different group of men and women. Stephen may owe his life to the productive activities of his fellow Americans, but how can that give them the right to insist that he take part in the killing of Vietnamese?

I suppose a case could be made in a genuine instance of national self-defense. A Russian who truly believed in the ideals of Nazism might still have an obligation to fight against the German invaders, in payment of his debt to his fellow countrymen. But it would take a Strausz-Hupé to claim that the North Vietnamese posed a genuine danger to America's security. So Stephen can reject this latest appeal with immunity. There are limits to the claim that a nation can make on the gratitude of its citizens, and wherever they may precisely be drawn, Vietnam does not fall within them.

At this point, we can imagine Professor Rostow breaking into the discussion impatiently: "You are completely neglecting the central issue," he will insist. "With all your talk of social order, debts of gratitude, and the like, you have simply ignored the crucial fact that Stephen lives, as do we all, in a democratic society based upon the principle of consent. No one imagines that the citizen's responsibilities to the law are identically the same in a monarchy, a dictatorship, a democracy, and heaven knows what other sorts of political order. Stephen is not a subject of the Nazi regime, or a student in Stalin's Russia. He is a free, adult, voting member of a functioning—though to be sure imperfect—democracy, and it is that fact which lays upon him an absolutely binding moral duty to abide by the valid laws enacted by a duly elected Congress."

This criticism of our discussion thus far is perfectly valid. I have deliberately put off until this point all consideration of the distinctively *democratic* argument for obedience to law, because I wished to impress upon your attention a fact that is frequently overlooked. None of the arguments brought forward thus far in Stephen's imaginary debate makes the slightest reference to the nature of the political arrangements in Stephen's society. Consequently, if you believe that those arguments have any merit, then in all consistency you must admit that they would have equal merit in Franco's Spain, Castro's Cuba, Mao's China, or Imperial British India. The danger of social disorder, the universalizability of one's principle, the debt of gratitude—all these are considerations which apply to *every* state, although of course their weight varies with the circumstances. So if you feel sympathy for arguments of this sort—if, indeed, you have used some such arguments with your own sons or nephews—do not suppose that you were in any way defending obedience to *democratic* laws. If you wish to claim that Stephen's situation is a special one because he lives in a democracy, then arguments of a very different sort must be advanced.

Since our analysis will now become theoretical and abstract, permit me to drop the fiction of Stephen and his friends, and speak in a more directly formal way. I confess that this feeble effort at a Platonic mode of exposition was already exhausting my meager literary talents.

PART TWO: POLITICAL OBLIGATION IN A SOCIETY OF CONSENT

In his extremely effective presentation, Professor Rostow devotes considerable effort to rebutting those defenders of disobedience who base their case upon the supposedly nondemocratic nature of the American political system. He considers, for example, the claim that black Americans are released from any duty to obey the law because of their past—and present—exclusion from the political process itself. He rejects the analogy with Gandhi's India or Hitler's Germany on the grounds that those societies were not ruled by the consent of the governed. He traces the right of rebellion of the American colonies to the British Crown's breach of its agreements with them. In short, throughout his paper, Professor Rostow

takes it as beyond question that the citizens of a genuinely democratic state are morally obliged to abide by its laws. His principal
aim is to show that, within the reasonable limits imposed by the
imperfection of man and nature, the United States is such a democracy.

Professor Rostow is not alone in his failure to examine the theoretical justification of the legitimacy of the democratic state. Most
proponents of war resistance and other forms of law defiance share
his unreflective attitude toward democracy. Some of them try to
show that the United States does not adequately meet the criteria
for a true democracy; others plead a religious or quasi-religious
privilege of private conscience while nevertheless implicitly granting the moral claims for the democratic state. Indeed it is very
difficult even in the history of political theory to find a straightforward defense of the proposition that citizens of a democracy have a
moral obligation to obey the law. Only Rousseau, among the great
philosophers of democracy, attempts an explicit justification of the
majority's authority over the members of the society.

All states claim legitimate authority, of course; and all *de facto*
states succeed in imposing their claim on those who live within
their borders. That, indeed, is all we mean when we accord *de facto*
recognition to a regime. But the theory of democracy asserts that
only one sort of state has a genuine moral *right* to claim legitimate
authority. If we may borrow a term from the language of international law, we may express the theory of democracy in the proposition that only a state founded upon the consent of the governed has
de jure legitimate authority. Or, to put the same point in the language of ethics, only the citizens of a democracy have an absolute
moral obligation to obey the valid laws enacted by a genuinely representative legislature.

After long reflection, I have come to the conclusion that the
theory of democracy is wrong. No one, not even a citizen of a true
democracy, has an obligation to obey the law, save under conditions so special and difficult of fulfillment as hardly to constitute an
exception at all. In short, I have come to believe that the doctrine
known as philosophical anarchism is true. There are no circumstances, real or hypothetical, under which a state can validly de-

mand the obedience of its subjects. Not even a state actually founded upon a real, historical social contract would have what I have called *de jure* legitimate authority.

This is a strong assertion, and I am well aware that I shall have difficulty persuading you of its truth in the brief time remaining here. I have attempted to set forth my argument more fully in a book entitled *In Defense of Anarchism,* published in the summer of 1970, but even that work is incomplete, and will require further argument to support its conclusions. What I should like to do here is to sketch the outlines of my argument, so that you can form at least a preliminary opinion of its cogency.

The theory of government by consent of the governed was advanced as the solution to a conflict which seems on first examination to be utterly irresoluble. On the one hand, morality demands that each man freely and autonomously determine the guiding principles of his life, and take full responsibility for the consequences of his own actions. To the men of the Enlightenment, who brought to its highest expression the doctrine of moral autonomy, subservience to authority of any sort was anathema. They refused to bend their minds to Aristotle, their souls to the church, or their bodies to a royal monarch. They insisted upon being their own men, free, upright, and individually responsible. Rousseau's *Social Contract* and Kant's *Foundations of the Metaphysics of Morals* are the finest statements of this philosophy, to which—I freely admit—I wholeheartedly subscribe.

Standing over against this principle of autonomy is the authority claimed by the state. If autonomy means anything at all, it means making one's own decisions, being no man's servant. But if authority means anything at all, it means the right to command, which is to say, the right to be obeyed. Authoritative commands are not mere threats, although they may be enforced by sanctions. Nor are they suggestions, even though the sovereign may choose to explain the reasons for his commands. When the state issues laws, it *claims* to have a right to expect obedience. That, indeed, is what distinguishes a state from a mere occupying army.

The problem faced by the early theorists of democracy was quite simply this: How can free and autonomous men submit to the authority of any state without truly losing their freedom? Rousseau put the problem sharply and directly in this way:

> Where shall we find a form of association which will defend and protect with the whole common force the person and the property of each associate, and by which every person, while uniting himself with all, shall obey only himself and remain as free as before? [1]

The solution lies in the nature of moral autonomy. To be free is not at all to be irresponsible, or licentious, or capricious. As Kant demonstrated, moral freedom consists in conforming one's behavior to principles which one lays down for oneself. The word "autonomous" literally means "giving laws to oneself," and so Kant argued that the truly moral man was simultaneously a lawgiver and a law obeyer. To obey the laws handed down by another is slavish servility—what Kant called heteronomy. To obey no law at all is irrational and irresponsible caprice. But to obey laws which one has legislated for oneself is the highest manifestation of human dignity. By the exercise of such autonomy, Kant said, men earned the right to be treated not as mere means or instruments, but as ends in themselves.

The extension of this doctrine to the political sphere is immediately obvious. When men submit to the commands of a ruler, they forfeit their freedom and become heteronomous slaves. When they submit to no laws at all, they sink into the caprice and chaos of anarchy. But when men submit to laws they have themselves made, then they are autonomous. Rule *of* the people is tyranny; rule *for* the people is at best benevolent tyranny. But rule *by* the people is *liberty,* which is to say, the union of individual autonomy with legitimate state authority.

This is a good argument. Indeed I think it can fairly be described as the *only* good argument in the entire history of Western political theory. It faces squarely the conflict between conscience and state authority, and provides a coherent account of the way in which democracy is supposed to differ morally from all other forms of political society. What is more, it makes no spurious appeals to

[1] *The Social Contract,* Bk. I, Ch. 6.

religious sanction, utilitarian consequences, or other irrelevant matters. Unfortunately, although it is the best justification that has ever been offered for the authority claims of any form of political society, it is nonetheless—in my opinion—wrong. Save under very special circumstances, rule *by* the people violates the moral autonomy of the individual, just as rule *of* and rule *for* the people do.

Consider the original argument. If freedom requires that each man submit only to laws which he himself has legislated, then obviously unanimous consent must be obtained before any law can be put in force. Under these stringent constraints, it would literally be true that each man would obey only himself and remain as free as before. Unanimous direct democracy—the system in which every citizen votes on all the laws and a single negative vote defeats any measure—is thus a theoretical solution to the conflict between individual autonomy and the state's claim to authority.

I shall not try your patience by launching into a technical digression on the highly abstract investigations of unanimous decision-making which have appeared in the past few years in the literature of mathematical economics and political philosophy. I hope you will accept my judgment that this work, although quite interesting to anyone of a logical turn of mind, has not seriously overcome the obvious impracticality of a form of democracy based upon unanimity. When we raise questions about the citizen's obligation to obey the law in a society of consent, we are *not* restricting our discussion to *unanimous* consent.

Nevertheless, it is worth pointing out that all classical democratic theorists base their justification of democracy on unanimity. It is always assumed that the original social contract, by which the authority of the state is first established, is signed by *all* the members of the society. And how could it be otherwise, after all? If a community collectively agrees upon a form of political association which I reject, why should I consider myself morally bound by its decision? If I enter the original compact, and later find myself at odds with the rest, then perhaps I can truly be said to be bound by their will. But at the outset, only those who give their consent to the establishment of the state have any moral obligation to obey its commands.

How are we to handle those situations in which a unanimous consensus does not miraculously emerge from the debate? The answer springs unbidden to every mind: Take a vote, of course, and let the state be guided by the will of the majority! We are, all of us, so accustomed to majority rule that it is very difficult for us even to notice that it is one distinctive way among many for settling disputes, and not the inevitable, natural, unquestionably obvious way. In the United States particularly, we are raised from the cradle as majoritarians. As soon as little children can count, they are taking votes. First-grade boys and girls in our public schools dutifully elect a class president, vice-president, and secretary-treasurer before they are old enough to write or carry money. I realize, therefore, that it will be difficult for me to persuade you to question the legitimacy of majority voting. Nevertheless, I must ask your indulgence, for this familiar rule is in fact the Achilles' heel of the defense of democracy. The entire theory of government by consent of the governed rests upon the principle of majority rule, and that principle is utterly without justification.

Let us remember the original purpose for which the theory of democracy was advanced. The problem was to find a form of political association that *free* men could join without losing their freedom. Government by unanimous consent met that requirement, and majority rule was then put forward to handle the situations in which unanimity could not be obtained. So the crucial question is this: Does majority rule provide a way of making collective decisions which preserves the moral autonomy, or liberty, of each member of the society?

Nobody denies that we *can* make decisions by majority rule. We can also make decisions by dictatorial rule of one man, or by rule of an elite minority, or even by putting all the alternatives in a fishbowl and pulling one out at random. The question is whether majority rule can preserve the union of individual freedom and state authority which unanimous democracy achieves.

Needless to say, the problem is with those persons who are in the minority. When a vote is taken, the majority are clearly bound by the outcome because they have directly willed the law which has been enacted. To put the point rather simplemindedly, no senator who votes to go to war has any moral right to refuse induction, no matter what his conscience may tell him. But the minority have voted *against* the law, presumably because they believed it to be unwise, or immoral, or contrary to the interests of the nation. If the theory of democracy is to have any plausibility at all—and if young men like Stephen are to be morally obligated to obey laws of which they disapprove—then a proof must be found for the paradoxical proposition that in a majoritarian democracy, the minority have a moral obligation to obey the majority. What is more, we must show that a member of the minority, in submitting to the majority, is not merely forfeiting his freedom and bowing his knee to tyranny.

Once again, permit me to quote Rousseau, who exhibits a vivid awareness of the force of the problem:

> Except in the original contract, a majority of votes is sufficient to bind all the others. This is a consequence of the contract itself. But it may be asked how a man can be free and yet forced to conform to the will of others. How are the opposers free when they are in submission to laws to which they have never consented? [2]

The traditional answer, to which Rousseau himself alludes, is that majority rule is built into the original contract. When everyone first agrees to establish the state and submit to its laws, there is a clause in the agreement to the effect that henceforward a majority shall bind or oblige the whole. But this is not really any answer at all to the question we asked. No one denies that a man can bind himself by a promise; and he can quite obviously promise to obey the majority, just as he can promise to obey a king, or a priest, or a slave-master. The promise is equally binding in every instance. The question is whether a free man can promise to obey the majority without thereby forfeiting his freedom. We have already seen that he can make such a commitment to *unanimous* decision, because his consent is included in the collective will by which each law is enacted. He literally obeys only himself and "remains as free as before." Is there anything about majority rule which distinguishes it from all the various authoritarian or heteronomous forms of de-

[2] *Op. cit.,* Bk. IV, Ch. 2.

cision making, so that the moral liberty of the minority is preserved even though they, like the majority, have an absolute duty to obey validly enacted laws?

In the book which I mentioned earlier, I have canvassed the more prominent attempts to demonstrate the liberty-preserving character of majority rule. John Locke has a sketch of an argument; Rousseau offers a rather tricky "proof." But the result of my search has been completely negative. I can neither find nor think of a way of making majority rule compatible with the moral autonomy of the individual. The problem is always the same: Either the minority submit to the majority, thereby conforming to laws which they think are bad and against which they voted; or else the minority reserve to themselves the right to defy those laws which they consider too evil, in which case the fundamental authority of the state is negated.

Now, it goes without saying that a member of the minority may *choose* to go along with the majority on certain occasions, perhaps because he judges that the bad consequences of his acquiescence in an evil law are less serious than the general harm that would be caused by his defiance. In other words, the minority may in some cases be swayed by the sorts of arguments we examined in the first part of this discussion. But once they begin to reason in that manner, they have rejected the special claims of the democratic state, and are reduced to making their political decisions on the basis of considerations which would arise in any state, democratic or otherwise.

Since the analysis has by this time become rather intricate, let me recapitulate the principal steps that have been taken thus far. I began by posing the hypothetical problem of Stephen, who must decide whether to obey an order to report for induction into the armed forces. One by one, I reviewed a number of arguments that might be put forward to persuade Stephen that he has a moral duty to obey. In each case, I tried to show that the argument had limited force at best, and insufficient force in the case actually facing Stephen.

Then a different sort of argument was offered, one which rested on the special nature of democratic society. This argument claimed to show that Stephen had an absolute or unconditional obligation to obey the valid laws of a state based upon the consent of the governed. Leaving to one side all consideration of the controversial question whether America today really is a society based on consent, I went directly to the theory of popular democracy, and tried to show that *even as a pure theory* it is invalid.

If all of this is correct—though I do not dare to hope that I have won you to my way of thinking—then Stephen has no obligation whatsoever to submit to the induction order. Speaking more generally, if a man has not signed his freedom away by a rash promise to obey the commands of the majority, whatever they may be; and if he has not directly voted for the laws which have been enacted; then he does not stand under any moral obligation to obey those laws *as such*. As a moral agent, he is of course responsible for the consequences of his actions, and he must therefore consider what will result *both* from his conformity to the law *and* from his defiance of it. But after he has weighed the goods and evils to the best of his ability, no one can say to him, "This is a democracy, and therefore irrespective of consequences you have a duty to obey the laws."

The doctrine which I have been expounding is properly called *anarchism*. Unfortunately, that term has come to be associated with the pointless destructiveness of sick young people in this and other societies. I do not wish to talk about the phenomenon of bomb throwing, which is in my judgment more properly left to the psychiatrist than to the political scientist or philosopher. But I must insist that it makes no more sense to blame a rash of bombings on the doctrine of philosophical anarchism than it does to blame the My Lai massacre on the theory of democracy or the Moscow trials on the theory of socialism. No doctrine is to be judged by the deeds of those who *claim* to act in its name, irrespective of any actual connection between their action and the tenets of the doctrine.

PART THREE: SOME TROUBLING AFTERTHOUGHTS

My argument is concluded. From a philosophical point of view, there is nothing further to be said. But I am not comfortable about allowing the matter to rest with the enunciation of a theory of anarchism. I seem to hear voices—sober, troubled, responsible voices —telling me that the theory is too clever by half, too much a philosopher's construction and too little relevant to the reality of human experience. The theory of legitimate authority may indeed be a myth, but if so, then it is a myth which men cannot easily do without. Men are not creatures of pure rationality and perfect moral responsibility! If they were, who would imagine that governments and laws were necessary? Men are fallible, brutal, irrational, contentious—sometimes noble, but more often base. Men live by symbols, by faith, by the patriotic songs which move their hearts, as well as by the syllogisms that fitfully persuade their imperfect minds. Destroy their belief in the sanctity of law and you deprive them of their principal defense against the darkness within them. Even those ultimate ideologues of rationality, the Jacobins, felt the need of a state religion to take the place of the church they were so eager to tear down! Dostoevsky's Grand Inquisitor understood the matter. The liberty of individual conscience is a burden too heavy for most men to bear. Better that the truth be hidden beneath ritual, miracle, and mystery. Plato too perceived the dangers of truth. Let the philosophers know the real foundations of their aristocratic authority, he said. The others can be told a "noble lie" to reconcile them to their station.

Do these voices speak the truth? Is this a time to celebrate the theory of democracy, even though it may be false? Should all of our social criticism be focused upon the ways in which America fails to achieve the democratic ideal, despite the illegitimacy of that ideal itself?

I do not know. It would be easy, but dishonest, to brush these doubts aside and end with a ringing affirmation of the liberty of individual conscience. Strange as it may seem, I am more confident that Stephen ought not to report for induction than I am that I ought to explain why. So I shall end on this note of uncertainty, and look to our discussion for enlightenment.

COMMENT

by Carl A. Auerbach

Professor Wolff's attempt to strike "at the very foundations of the myth of legitimate authority" in a democratic state is an exegesis of anarchist utopian thought which is absurdly irrelevant to any discussion of the adequacy of our legal system to cope with the urgent problems of our day. If law as we know it in our democracy should "die," the cause of death will not be the onslaughts of philosophical anarchism or the coming into being of a human society without any government, without any law, and without any coercion.

The two separate parts of Wolff's paper are not really interdependent, because Wolff misuses Stephen's case.

Stephen is an attractive young man who is not a conscientious objector to all wars but who disobeys an order of induction into the army because he believes America's cause in Southeast Asia is immoral. He does not claim he has a "legal right" to disobey the law and escape legal punishment; he seeks such punishment. If the legal system recognized such a right, Stephen's act of civil disobedience would lose its character. It would become an act in accordance with law. Stephen also weighed the possibility that general respect for law might decline as a result of his action and concluded that the evil he was opposing was greater than the evil that would result if this possibility materialized.

I have no great quarrel with Stephen and no wish to chide him for not behaving as I would in his place. Stephen followed the dictates of his conscience, but only after examining the reasons for and against his action and deciding, in the light thereof, that his conscience was clear. I wish he had appreciated more that there are moral considerations underlying the law he violated, apart from the justification of the war in Vietnam and the social interest in respect for law—the fair allocation of the burden of bearing arms—and that his decision will shift his share of this burden to others and to some with his views about the Vietnam war but not his intransigence about disobeying a lawful induction order. I wish, too, he had entertained the possibility that he might be wrong about Vietnam; that the voice of individual conscience might not always be right.

My quarrel is with the generalizations Wolff draws from Stephen's case which, taken by itself, cannot reasonably be used to defend philosophical anarchism, the doctrine, in Wolff's words, that "[t]here are no circumstances, real or hypothetical, under which a state [even a truly democratic one] can validly demand the obedience of its subjects." In the first place, I do not maintain that a citizen in a democracy has an absolute or unconditional moral obligation always to obey every law passed by a democratic legislature. Nor does the theory of democracy or the principle of majority rule, as Wolff supposes, impose such an absolute or unconditional moral obligation upon those morally opposed to validly enacted laws. This does not mean there is no general moral obligation to obey law. This obligation arises from consideration of the general social consequences of disobedience. The legal system, not the "intransigence of the committed conscience," will have to be relied upon to effectuate the social changes Wolff favors. To this end, it is vital that the habit of obedience to law not be weakened. So the effectiveness of the legal system as a whole is a moral consideration not to be minimized by an individual citizen in deciding whether to disobey a specific law he thinks is unjust. Recent national experience should also make us more receptive than is Wolff to the possibility that disobedience to law might be contagious.

In asking whether America would "really be a worse place to live if everyone were like Stephen," Wolff implies his agreement with Stephen's conclusions as to the "depraved brutality of America's actions in Vietnam." But he does not rest his case on the assumed injustice of America's cause in Vietnam. To do so would not constitute a defense of anarchist doctrine. For the same reason, Wolff does not argue, as it may be reasonable to do, that disobedience to a specific law or application of law is morally justified not because it is consonant with the moral code of the individual violator, but only if it is impelled by reasons which must be regarded as good in the light of a rational, objective analysis.

To Wolff, the crucial aspect of Stephen's case is that Stephen disobeyed the law because *he, Stephen,* believed that what the law commanded was wrong. It is this "moral autonomy of the individual" which Wolff posits as an absolute value. He is dissatisfied with the principle of majority rule which underlies democratic theory because it is incompatible with this autonomy. Here, it seems to me, Wolff reveals his myopia.

In the first place, it is doubtful whether even the unanimous consent Wolff would require as a condition of legitimate government would be sufficient to preserve the moral autonomy of the individual, in Kant's sense. It would not be sufficient, for example, if unanimous consent were obtained because individuals followed a leader in sheeplike fashion. We need not go to this extreme. At times, it is safe to say, the subjective moral conviction of the individual is itself the product of habit, custom, tradition, group affiliation—even law—and is an obstacle to social change. Furthermore, the moral autonomy of the individual is preserved, in Kant's sense, so long as he acts in accordance with the categorical imperative, even if his act is socially inefficacious.

But more important for present purposes than whether Wolff is correctly reading Kant is the question: Why should the subjective moral conviction of the individual always be society's paramount concern? If, for example, Stephen is morally justified in disobeying a law simply because *he* believes it to be wrong, so is a racist who disobeys an anti-discrimination law, a heroin peddler who disobeys a law prohibiting its sale, and a taxpayer who refuses to pay taxes to support the welfare state, so long as their private moral convictions tell them that the laws they are violating are wrong. Bertrand Russell described this "extreme of subjectivism" which is anarchism as "a form of madness." [1]

Who is to decide the issue of moral justification when there is "bitter conflict," as Wolff acknowledges there may be, "between men of opposed moral dedication"? Suppose some intransigent, committed consciences told their possessors that Stephen was a traitor to his country and should be lynched for what he did? Must not the legal system—and the habit of obedience upon which it rests—be called upon to

[1] Russell, *A History of Western Philosophy* (1946), p. 514.

restrain them from acting in accordance with their moral convictions to harm Stephen for acting upon his? Is it not the function of the legal system in our society to resolve such conflicts and, in the process, inevitably, to inhibit the freedom of some so as to enlarge the freedom of others?

If men were angels, social harmony without the constraint of law might be conceivable. But men are not angels; neither their interests nor their ethical convictions are identical. Wolff ignores the problem of how the conflicting claims of different individuals and groups in a complex, industrial society of 200,000,000 people are to be adjusted peacefully and common interests advanced—how, in short, if every individual refuses to obey every law that seems to him immoral, any framework of social order can be established for carrying on individual and group life.

For these tasks, we have created a particular kind of political organization, a government which depends upon the freely given consent of the governed, acts by majority rule, under law, and is backed, if necessary, by legal force. Furthermore, by placing fundamental individual rights beyond the reach of majoritarian decisions, by guaranteeing freedom of speech, the press, association and political participation, our democracy does not permit a particular coalition of minorities which may constitute a temporary majority to crush other minorities. New coalitions may form new majorities and expect obedience to the new laws they enact. Because our democracy is an instrument of collective life which thus keeps open the possibility of peaceful change and relies upon the legal system to effectuate such change, its citizens have a special moral obligation which, again, is not absolute or unconditional, to obey its laws, even those they may find unjust. Without such general obedience, neither social justice nor individual freedom will be possible.

CHAPTER 4

FREEDOM, CONSENT, AND THE COSTS OF INTERACTION

by Charles Dyke

That man is free who lives as he wishes, who is proof against compulsion and hindrance and violence, whose impulses are untrammeled, who gets what he wills to get and avoids what he wills to avoid.

(*Discourses of Epictetus,* Bk. IV, Ch. 1)

Freedom is one of the three or four key concepts in political thought since the Reformation. This means that it has been the subject of more words of explication, exhortation, and analysis than almost any other political concept. But new words are continually being found, and new analyses adduced. Among the many reasons for all the words about freedom is that in the last analysis the words are of only secondary importance. First in importance is the fact of freedom. But we find that the fact of our own freedom depends in pervasive and complex ways on the freedom of others. And we find that our own conception of freedom must be shared by many others if our own freedom is to be a fact. So we talk about freedom in an attempt to create the shared conception that is necessary. We must be careful, or we will end up with all talk—and the fact of freedom will get lost, as it has time and again in the history of political theorizing. If we end up with mere words, we will have failed.

What follows is an attempt to get at the fact of freedom as it has a concrete meaning for people whose freedom is threatened or absent. Partially, it is an attempt to make use of some notions developed in welfare economics—and the jargon which goes with them. Whether this attempt is a success depends on the contribution that it makes toward promoting freedom in fact. No jargon or conceptual scheme has a life of its own independent of such aims.

A Conception of Freedom

In a recent paper called "Freedom as a Problem of Allocating Choice," Professor Lon Fuller argues that freedom is a scarcity; hence we must be extremely careful how, and to whom, it is allocated.[1] I think that he is right about this, and that freedom as it is important to us in our day-to-day lives can be better understood than it now is if we follow out the implications of Professor Fuller's important suggestion.

When we talk about scarcities we immediately think of goods, raw materials, and, in short, the stuff of economic exchange. Freedom is not a good in the usual sense, but it is like a good in that it is valued, and subject to comparisons of more or less. It differs from usual goods in that it is a necessary condition for the attainment of other goods, hence a second-order good. Of course it is not unique in this, since food, for example, is a good which, in normal circumstances, is a necessary condition for the attainment of other goods, since it is a necessary condition for survival. But freedom differs from other goods in that it has no independent substantive existence. That is, in order to talk of freedom we must make reference to the activities that one is free to pursue, or the goods that one is free to obtain.

There are many facets to the concept of freedom. In addition to its political aspects there are metaphysical aspects to the concept, and even physicists have a use for the word "freedom" which is not quite far enough from the political sense of the word to be called metaphorical. We may begin, though, with the following observations: If I can't do something, then I am clearly not free to do it.

[1] "Freedom as a Problem of Allocating Choice" in *Proceedings of the American Philosophical Society*, Vol. 112, No. 2, April 1968.

For anything that I might want to do, there may be a number of reasons why I can't do it: My abilities may be limited; physical circumstances may not allow it; others may prevent me from doing it. From a political point of view these are the important sorts of limitations upon me. In order to see more clearly the limitations on freedom, and hopefully, to see what political freedom is, let us look at what is involved when we decide what we would prefer to do.

Human beings are valuing beings who make judgments about better and worse. The grounds upon which they make these judgments will concern us only peripherally. For our immediate purposes it is immaterial whether people make judgments of better and worse on utilitarian grounds, casuistically on the basis of a set of principles, by consulting an oracle, or in any other way. The important thing is that they do make judgments of value, and rank what they value along a scale of better and worse.

Furthermore, people make decisions on the basis of their values, on what they think best, and when they can manage to do so, they do what they think is best.

There are two major sets of determinants in any decisions: the values involved, and the conditions under which the values are to be pursued. The values pursued may be activities engaged in for their own sake or substantive goods to be obtained by a course of activity. A man's success in attaining his values depends on the conditions under which he has to pursue them. These conditions impose limitations on his pursuit of values in two ways: First, conditions might simply prevent him from attaining some value. This is clear enough. Second, conditions might alter the circumstances in which the value can be attained in such a way that the value is no longer as attractive as it was, and in fact may no longer be worth pursuing. For example, if I am free of an evening and decide that what I most want to do is go for a walk, I might well decide against it if I find that it is raining. Again, I may want to go to a particular movie, but if I find that the theater is going to be very crowded I might decide not to go.[2] Obviously, if I have ranked a number of

---

[2] The more usual way to deal with these situations is to talk of choosing between complex states of affairs made up of the situation originally valued

values to be pursued in order of preference, then my recognition of one condition or other might well lead me to reorder the values in a new ranking. It might be mentioned here that certain conditions might lead to the enhancement of some values. For example, I might regard a visit to the local bawdy house rather tepidly, but if I find out that Flossie will be available . . .

In order to be more precise about the conditions for the attainment of values as they relate to problems of freedom, I will adapt a terminology which has held a key place in welfare economics for a number of years, namely, the terminology of positive and negative externalities: external benefits and external costs. Let me emphasize that I consider my discussion to be an adaptation and an extension of the concept as it occurs in the literature of welfare economics. The extension may well not meet with the approval of the theorists who have contributed to the development and precision of the concept in strictly economic contexts.[3]

An externality is a condition of an activity which is not necessarily connected with that activity; which modifies the possibility or

---

plus the conditions under which it can be attained. Thus I would be said to choose walking-with-no-rain, and decide against walking-in-the-rain. The points that I want to make could be made using that terminology too. I choose to do it the way I do because I can bring out the nature of constraints more easily.

[3] Probably the most rigorous definition of externality is that of Buchanan and Stublebine in "Externality," reprinted in *Readings in Welfare Economics,* edited by Arrow and Scitovsky, London: 1969, p. 200.

"We define an externality to be present when $u^A = u^A$ $(X_1, X_2, \ldots, X_m, Y_1)$. This states that the utility of an individual, A^2, is dependent upon the 'activities,' $(X_1, X_2, \ldots X_m)$ that are exclusively under his own control or authority, but also upon another single activity, Y_1, which is, by definition, under the control of a second individual, B, who is presumed to be a member of the same social group. We define an *activity* here as any distinguishable human action that may be measured, such as eating bread, drinking milk, spewing smoke into the air, dumping litter on the highways, giving to the poor, etc."

I am fairly confident that this definition is equivalent to the one I give for interaction costs and benefits. My extension to personal inabilities and physical conditions does nothing more than emphasize the distinction, implicit in the notion of an externality, between what is in my control and what is not—the distinction which provides the relation between freedom and externality.

the value of the activity; and about which, in a particular instance, the actor can do nothing.[4]

An externality, if it makes the attainment of a value impossible or less attractive, is called an external cost; if it makes the attainment of a value possible where it was not, or more attractive, it is called an external benefit. This is merely a generalization of a narrower conception in which external costs are conditions which I would be willing to pay to get rid of if I could; and external benefits are conditions I would pay to obtain.

An excellent set of cases illustrating the distinction between values sought and external costs and benefits is provided by an examination of simple bargaining situations. When people are bargaining they are each trying to obtain an optimal mix of the commodities being traded. But they must be careful that they do not haggle so long that the benefits of additional haggling are outweighed by the time and energy expended on haggling.

Haggling need not impose external costs, as anyone who has bargained for an antique Oriental rug knows. In such bargaining, what is known as the Yuldoosian effect comes into play, and the excitement and one-upmanship of haggling yield external benefits. In this special case the primary values pursued in the buying and selling of the rug are enhanced by the pleasures of haggling. Another case illustrating external costs is the following: A person may come to feel that his values are more likely to be attained if he is a member of a committee set up to decide certain issues important to him. But he must be careful that the time and energy that he spends in committee work does not involve a cost greater than the incremental increase in his value attainment.

As I said, in most of this paper I will take persons' values to be given, although at some stages I will discuss some features of the process by which people come to have values. But let me forestall

4 Externalities in my sense could be defined marginally only if the continuity conditions necessary for such a definition could be realistically assumed to hold. The first conjunct would have to be dropped if we adopted the suggestion of footnote 1, and we would then have to define externalities by making distinctions between central and accidental features of the complex descriptions which constituted the domain of alternatives. The logical apparatus is available for doing so.

two common objections. It is sometimes said that anyone engaging in the (basically "utilitarian") sort of analysis that I am engaging in here is making the implicit assumption that the consumption of commodities is of primary importance. This is nonsense. I myself think that what a man *does* is more important than what he *has;* but the analysis in this paper is indifferent with respect to most views of what values are, or what they should be.

In the pursuit of his values, a person will be faced with externalities of basically three kinds: those that are the result of limitations of his own abilities, those that are the result of natural circumstances, and those that are the result of the activity of other people. The last-mentioned externalities I will call interaction costs and benefits. It will clearly be to a person's advantage to minimize external costs, and maximize external benefits. The way to do this is to bring as many of the conditions of one's activities under control as is possible. One brings one's own abilities under control by improving the condition of one's mind and body. Nature is brought under control by technological advance. And the conditions of one's interaction with other people are controlled by a number of devices to be discussed as we go along, the chief of which are the establishment of agreements and the passage of laws.

When an externality has been brought under control, it is said to have been internalized, which is to say that it is no longer a *given* condition of our activity, but a value component of an activity in its own right. It is apparent that there are very few conditions of our activity which are *necessarily* externalities. Most conditions can be somehow brought under control by the right people in the right circumstances. Of course there are physical circumstances that we can do nothing about, but technological advance pushes back the limits imposed by nature, or at least allows us to maneuver around those conditions which prove intractable. Whether there are interaction costs which are not internalizable is almost entirely up to us as rational agents—insofar as we *are* rational agents.

I should like, then, to put forward a working conception of freedom. It may not capture everything that anyone has wanted to say about freedom, but as we go along I think I can show that many of the important questions we have about freedom can be discussed in terms of what is in fact a comparative notion. Very simply, a man is freer the lower the level of external costs that are imposed upon him, and less free the higher the level of extreme costs.

When is a man free in a non-comparative sense? I am not sure that anyone has ever said with any certainty. For certain purposes and certain key contrasts, we might try to define freedom in terms of a particular set of externalities. For example, we can contrast the free man and the slave in terms of the presence or absence of the externalities of the master–slave relationship.[5] But this is clearly only a special case of the comparative sense of freedom, and will be useless in cases where freedom is an issue but slavery is not.

The notion of freedom that I am putting forward also captures the connection between freedom and self-conscious rational control, since what it is to internalize an externality is to bring it under one's control. In addition, this notion seems to me to be a generalization of the classic conception that Mill puts forward in *On Liberty*. In the first chapter, Mill's problem is that of showing how freedom or liberty can be maximized in circumstances in which perfection is a forlorn dream. His claim is that a man is antecedently assumed to be free to do anything he wants to do that contributes to his development as an individual. His fellow men have the right to constrain his activities only when they impinge upon the lives of others in a harmful way, that is, impose interaction costs. But, as is well known, Mill's formula, expressed in Chapter 1 of *On Liberty,* is inadequate in that it gives no practical guide to the kinds and extent of controls we may legitimately apply. In particular, when there are many of us involved, the imposition of interaction costs will be relatively symmetrical, and some mutual adjustment of these costs will be necessary. Mill's discussion is important insofar as it leads us to acknowledge that issues of freedom are issues susceptible to the calculation of more or less. Interaction costs are always present; hence we will be faced with a double-faceted task at every stage of our quest for freedom: We will have the aggregative task of maximizing freedom (minimizing external

---

[5] But remember Hegel's doubts as to who was free in this relationship.

costs), and the distributive task of protecting the freedom of everyone (spreading evenly the external costs that remain).

Suppose, for example, that a neighbor is dumping garbage on my back lot, and this is an annoyance to me, since it makes activity on my back lot less enjoyable. I can remove this annoyance in a number of ways. The most attractive way is to talk to my neighbor and point out the costs that he is imposing on me. If I can persuade him to stop emptying his garbage in my yard, then the externality can be eliminated without the creation of ill will or new externalities. However, if he persists in spite of my efforts at amicable resolution, I may have to invoke the resources of the law. Of course, when this happens, the externalities represented by the garbage dumping will be eliminated only at the expense of externalities imposed upon my neighbor by the legal system. Notice that if I am concerned with distributing freedom justly between myself and my neighbor, there might be some courses of action open to me which would eliminate the interaction costs, but which I would not want to pursue. The costs to be imposed upon him might strike me as excessively high. As soon as I move from an entirely self-interested position, I open the possibility that I may have to accept the presence of some interaction costs which I could remove if I wanted to.

Again, suppose that a relatively long-established urban university decides that it must expand in order to provide gymnasium facilities. These facilities are required so that nubile young coeds may have the opportunity to prance around in leotards, and so that virile young men may have the opportunity to engage in complementary pursuits. A noble enterprise: In providing the gym facilities the university is increasing the freedom of the students since it is making activities possible which were not possible before.

Now suppose that in building the gym the university has to expand into the surrounding neighborhood. In this case, the people who are dispossessed will be made less free to pursue the life that they would like to live in the place where they would like to live it. Here is a case in which each of two parties is imposing or threatening to impose interaction costs on the other. An equitable solution is likely to require a complex bargaining process in which the level of costs (advantages, hardships, and so on) is assessed, and a mutual adjustment attempted. While the freedom of each party to pursue its chosen activity is at stake, there is no question of "absolute freedom" being attained; nor should there be. However the dispute is resolved, reference should be made to the relative claims of each party to be free to pursue its most valued activities.

In cases of urban universities expanding into surrounding (usually black) communities, only recently has it been acknowledged that the freedom of the people of the community is at stake. Hence, only recently have any equitable adjustments been attempted which take their freedom into account.

Any satisfactory mutual adjustment of freedom will have to conform to the principles of aggregative and distributive adequacy which we choose to hold. It will be impossible to compare two societies with respect to freedom without making these aggregative and distributive principles absolutely explicit.

It is not my intention here to suggest any aggregative and distributive principles, but I would like to mention an oddity in our usual thinking about them. There seems to be a relatively widespread belief in the egalitarian distribution of freedom. Except when explicit reference is made to criminals (of whom more later), it is very odd indeed to think of someone arguing that some people ought to have more freedom than others. There is a much broader consensus on this than there is on the corresponding issue of the distribution of wealth. The oddity is that there is a fundamental connection between the two issues. For there never was a time, and never could be a time, in which our sphere of chosen activity was not a function of the geographical and material resources at our disposal. And if geographical and material resources are scarce, as they always are, then the manner in which they are distributed is of crucial importance for the distribution of freedom. It would clearly be a mistake, however, to conclude that equality of freedom demanded equality of material resources. The operative question is "At what distribution of wealth do externalities appear which are inadjustable at satisfactory levels, and at what distributions are they absent?" This is an empirical question, which means, in effect, that arguments a priori for the equal distribution of wealth on grounds of freedom are not to be taken seriously. It also means, however, that the complacent belief that a satisfactory distribution of freedom is independent of the distribution of wealth is also not to be taken seriously.

An extremely important question which must now be faced is this: How are we to solve the aggregative and distributive problems of freedom as they arise in actual societies? How are we to minimize externalities, and distribute those that remain in a satisfactory way? It might appear that we could make a promising beginning by leaving aside interaction costs and concentrating on the elimination of the external costs imposed by the environment. This seems to have been the view of advocates of technological progress since the onset of the industrial revolution. And who can deny that they have pushed back the limitations on human capabilities? But a measure of their achievement can be discerned in the fact that the classic example in economic literature of a negative externality is the smoke and soot which are produced by a factory and which pollute the atmosphere, soil clothes, and so on. In fact the cases in which attempts to remove one externality introduce another externality are more numerous than cases in which an externality can be removed at no cost at all. Thus even at the level of environmental externalities we are plunged into the calculation of more and less.[6]

But, as Mill saw, the most important externalities from the point of view of our freedom are interaction costs. We must deal with them in a satisfactory way. There are relatively few techniques available to us, the central ones being bargaining and negotiation.[7]

When we talk about trading and bargaining, we have in mind a process in which two people who have interlocking interests effect a

[6] Another classic case is that of population increase. As we master our environment, we create the conditions for overpopulation, which in some cases impairs the quality of our lives. In order to remove this (created) externality, we have to institute controls which in their turn create more externalities.

[7] Charles E. Lindblom lists twelve in *The Intelligence of Democracy* (New York, 1965). Not all of them are independent. But the exact number is less important than the clear understanding of the most common techniques and the results we can hope to attain with them. Lindblom contributes significantly to that understanding.

redistribution of certain goods, services, and so on. We usually assume that the bargaining results in mutual benefit, and indeed most often it does, or it wouldn't take place. The possibility for bargaining is present between two people whenever a simultaneous modification of their activity would be mutually beneficial. Thus the mutual elimination of externalities is an obvious field for bargaining, and, from an aggregative point of view, bargaining can be a device for increasing our freedom by removing interaction costs. As has been mentioned, new costs may be introduced in the bargaining itself, but we can assume that they would be recognized and incorporated in the overall calculation of mutual benefit. In the ideal case we will be able to adjust our behavior in such a way that we no longer impose interaction costs upon one another, but there is no guarantee that bargaining will take us to this ideal. It goes without saying that as the societies in which we are attempting to adjust interaction costs become larger and larger, the problems of adjustment will increase, and the chances of reaching any ideal or optimum will decrease.

The last observation suggests that the question of the optimum size of a polity ought to be reopened. Of course the discussion of this issue is inhibited by the petrification of modern nation-states in their present form. But questions of optimum size might well be discussed in terms of centralization versus decentralization. If in a large social unit the process of adjusting interaction costs does not result in an acceptable aggregative or distributive level of freedom, then the possibility that mutual adjustment be attempted within the confines of a smaller social unit, and then the units adjusted to one another, ought to be explored. This should be familiar as one of the key ideas behind the notion of federalism. Federalism, so conceived, must be distinguished from another species of decentralization, which I shall call pluralism. The pluralist holds that while mutual adjustment should take place over the range of the whole society, no central agency should impose the adjustment, which should be the result of bargaining between various groups in the society trying to do the best they can for themselves. The federalist holds that there should be a two-stage process of mutual adjustment, the primary stage taking place entirely at the level of small social units which are later to be federated. This is theoretically consistent with the presence of central control at every level of mutual adjustment. For example, each federated unit could be an absolute dictatorship.

The decision on whether we want to be federalists in a given context, or opt for mutual adjustment in one stage over the society at large, involves another process of calculating more and less. We ought to consider federalism when the only possible adjustments of interaction costs in the society at large leave us with an intolerably low level of freedom, or distribute this freedom in unacceptable ways. But resorting to federalism may itself introduce externalities. For example, the small units may be cohesive enough to attain satisfactory mutual adjustment internally, but this very cohesiveness may make them intransigent to any attempt to reach a mutual adjustment externally with relation to other small units. This could be called the general problem of "us" and "them," and reminds us that any attempt to establish small federal units is likely to generate centrifugal forces counter to mutual adjustment as well as centripetal forces which serve mutual adjustment.

An additional problem with federalization is that some of the small units may find that other units have come to an internal adjustment of freedom which is unacceptable to them. For example, some states in a federation may decide that slavery is an acceptable institution, and this may be abhorrent to other states in the federation who may decide that federalism must be abandoned. In this case, war might become a substitute for the mutual adjustment of interaction costs. While the previous example is an obvious reference to our own history, the same considerations apply to our attitudes toward, say, the developing nations of Africa and Asia where the temptation to meddle might become uncontrollable, especially if we have strong a priori notions as to what an acceptable mutual adjustment of freedom must be. The issues involved are tortuous and difficult ones, and if we conceive them as I think they ought to be conceived—namely, as issues involving the balancing, weighing, and bargaining of interaction costs—some of our cherished dogmas might have to be abandoned, and our feeling of moral rectitude muted.

In the remainder of this paper I will discuss some specific concepts traditionally associated with the concept of freedom. I will try to show how the discussion of freedom which I have presented so far can contribute to our understanding of these concepts. Before I do this, there are two more facets of the mutual adjustment of externalities which must be mentioned.

First, in eliminating externalities we may be inclined to concentrate on establishing the conditions for the activities which we presently value. But if we have any conception of ourselves as developing individuals, such as the concept which Mill puts forth in Chapter 3 of *On Liberty,* then we know that in the future we may come to value activities which we do not now value. Since the values we are likely to have at a later time are a function of a course of personal development which we cannot entirely predict, we will be in doubt about just exactly which externalities it is most important to eliminate. In fact, insofar as we do not know what we will value at a later time, we cannot even say what activities of other people at that time will generate external costs (or benefits, for that matter). Among the many things to be said about this problem are the following: (A) Our development of new interests must fall short of fickleness, for it is likely that if people are limitlessly changeable there is just no way in which they can keep out of each other's way, no matter how hard they try. (B) We do not develop as individuals in isolation, but in the context of the growth of others around us; hence it may be possible to come to adjustments which reflect the personal development of those who have contributed to our change, and to whose change we have contributed. (C) We will be more concerned with the establishment of general conditions for the elimination of interaction costs than with *ad hoc* accommodations directed at the whim of the moment. And (D), we will want to leave room for the review at frequent intervals of the arrangements and mutual adjustments that we have made.[8]

[8] The problem of mutual adjustment for the optimization of freedom may be more difficult with respect to this issue than the parallel problem in economics of the optimization of want satisfaction—although that remains to be seen. In the economic parallel, what this point tells us is that the utility-possibility surface can be expected to change its shape for reasons which are exogenous to the main determinants; namely, the increase in

Second, to talk of freedom as an aggregation-distribution problem, or as a problem of allocating choice, seems to run counter to our feeling that freedom is inviolate, and not subject to the nice calculation of more or less. It commits us to thinking of freedom as negotiable. But are not certain freedoms nonnegotiable—what old-time philosophers would have called natural rights?

To say that some freedoms *should* not be negotiable is to say that there is some externality or externalities which should be prohibited a priori; or (more interestingly) that there is some technique for internalizing externalities which ought to be available to everybody. Although I am sympathetic to such views, I am not sure what an absolutely successful argument to either of these conclusions would look like. One might try to show that the absence of certain externalities is a necessary condition for any sort of tolerable life, or for a "truly human life." Arguments of this sort are notoriously inconclusive, since the conception of human life upon which the argument rests is usually at least as controversial as the conclusion to be reached. Arguments to the effect that a certain technique for controlling interaction costs must be available if there is to be any freedom at all are dubious, since so many techniques have grown up in various cultures and societies. The claim that *some* technique for controlling interaction costs must be available to every social being if he is to have any freedom is trivially true.

One freedom which is often thought to be necessary and nonnegotiable is the freedom to vote, the so-called cornerstone of democratic theory.

The freedom to vote, like all constitutional freedoms, is a second-order freedom specifying how externalities are to be adjusted at the operational day-to-day level. Voting is usually defended on grounds of personal autonomy; that is, on the grounds that a man ought to be self-legislating. This fits in perfectly well with what I have been saying about freedom and the elimination of externalities. We might notice, however, that if autonomy is pushed as the

---

productivity. In general it will not be possible to state the function according to which the utility-possibility surface changes. In fact, there is no reason to believe that there is any continuous function involved.

single principle that we are prepared to accept, then we will be satisfied with nothing short of anarchy. For in any other circumstance, others will be involved in deciding what mutual adjustments will take place.[9]

But important as voting is from the point of view of autonomy, it in itself does not offer a guarantee of freedom in any concrete sense. A full-blooded analysis of voting, voting rules, and their consequences is beyond my purview. However, I will allude to one feature of voting which is of crucial importance for the understanding of the freedom involved in the right to vote.

Every voting procedure has two stages: the specification of alternatives, and the actual vote on the alternatives specified. If the specification of alternatives is unsatisfactory, then the freedom implied in the right to vote is a sham. To take an extreme example: The inmates of a concentration camp might be asked to choose between dying of starvation and dying in the gas chambers. The right to vote would be unequivocally extended to them, yet clearly they would be prevented from reaching a satisfactory aggregative and distributional level of freedom. This example indicates that the right to vote is not by itself sufficient to provide a decent level of

[9] It seems to me that the anarchist has two alternatives. He might simply take the hero's course, let everybody have complete control over his life, and let the chips fall where they may. The chips would fall in such a way that the notion of control over one's own life would be an entirely Pickwickian one. Alternatively the anarchist could resort to an argument involving a set of complicated judgments about human motivation. If human beings could somehow be made such that they did not impose external costs on one another, then no techniques for mutual adjustment would be necessary, since, in effect, mutual adjustment would be achieved automatically. In such circumstances, everything that anyone did would be either neutral or beneficial with respect to anyone else. It is far from clear how such men could be produced, and what circumstances could produce them. The theory of perfect market equilibrium assumes that it could happen. The classic discussion seems to me to be that between Godwin and Malthus. Godwin argues (as have others, including Marx at some stages) that in the absence of positive institutions the motivation for behavior of the sort which will tend to impose external costs will be absent, or gradually disappear. In other words, government as such is the ultimate cause of all interaction costs. Malthus replies that there are natural sources of interaction costs, including, of course, population pressure. I tend to think that Malthus is right, but the issue need not be decided here since there is not the remotest chance that we will ever have the choice that it presents us.

freedom. It must be supplemented by certain freedoms with respect to the specification of alternatives.

In this country, the main device for specifying alternatives is the two-party system. This is supposed to be a method which places alternative specification as well as actual choice in the hands of the people. Well, it certainly places the power of alternative specification somewhere; but to know where it places it requires accurate empirical analysis of such matters as how candidates become available and get chosen, how platforms are chosen, the relation of party finance to party program, the dynamics of coalition formation, and the like. Until we have all this information, we do not know how free we are. For we do not know how decisions are made with respect to the retention, elimination, and generation of externalities. For example, what sort of political action would it *in fact* take to adjust the external costs imposed upon us by the petroleum industry or the public disutilities to a satisfactory distributive level?

When all this has been said, it could still be true that voting or something very much like it is indispensable for the preservation of a tolerable level of freedom under normal conditions. And if we found ourselves under those conditions, then we might want to argue that the freedom to voice was, to us, nonnegotiable. But we must be careful to specify the exact sense in which voting is nonnegotiable—or ought to be made so. For in a system in which coalition formation is necessary for the passage of a measure, one of the ways in which we might eliminate externalities is by a system of vote trading, or logrolling. If the right to vote is taken to imply that a man must express his opinion on the rightness or wrongness of an alternative when he votes (as Rousseau maintained), then clearly logrolling is inconsistent with the right to vote. But contrary to this, and in the interest of mutually adjusting interaction costs, we can think of the right to vote as the possession of a negotiable good. In this case to prohibit logrolling would be to limit the negotiability of the vote, thus making it impossible for the voter to minimize interaction costs. Looked at in this way, the claim that a man ought to have the right to vote is tantamount to the claim that he should be given the wherewithal to negotiate with others with respect to the social conditions of his action; and the right to this negotiating power is what he ought to consider nonnegotiable.

Further, if this is the correct way to look at the right to vote, voting rights will be worth having only if votes have a real value, which is to say that they must be scarce. In the context of coalitional politics, where to permanent majority coalition exists, votes will tend to be scarce. Where permanent disciplined majorities are present, votes will not, in general, be scarce. A general statement of the conditions which must be present if votes are to be scarce is a problem for political analysis, and again, we must have the results of such an analysis if we are to be able to assess the relationship between our right to vote and our freedom.[10]

This analysis of voting has a clear moral. Voting is a contribution to freedom only insofar as it embodies the power to affect the social environment. For any given political system it is a matter for empirical investigation whether, in what ways, and to what degree a vote constitutes power. Consequently, it is a matter for empirical investigation whether in given circumstances we can claim that a man is free because he has the right to vote. Does a man's right to vote materially affect the mutual adjustment of his aspirations and the aspirations of others? If we know what to look for, we ought to be able to answer that question rather precisely. Clearly, if a man finds that his right to vote is worthless, then it is only rational for him to turn to other techniques to affect the pattern of adjustment of interaction costs.

Freedom and Community

In the first chapter of *On Liberty,* Mill focuses on the external costs that we impose on one another, and on the necessary task of minimizing these costs. But by the time he gets to the third chapter it is clear that he feels that ideally we ought to be positively related

[10] Among the many important contributions to an understanding of these problems are: James Buchanan and Gordon Tullock, *The Calculus of Consent* (Ann Arbor, 1962); William Riker, *The Theory of Political Coalitions* (New Haven, 1962); and the journal literature which they have occasioned. This is hardly the place for a detailed discussion of these issues.

to one another. That is, our presence in the world ought to yield external benefits to others, as well as external costs. I should now like to say a few words about the conditions which make such relationships possible.

The first set of circumstances in which mutual benefit is possible is that in which productivity can be increased and life made more secure by the formation of associations directed toward these goals. A study of mutual benefit associations at this stage would add nothing to what we have said about freedom. In fact, mutual benefit associations are analyzable in just the sort of cost-benefit terms that have been used throughout the paper. But mutual benefit associations must be contrasted with other social systems whose cohesion does not lie in their ability to aggregate and distribute want satisfaction. I shall call such social systems communities, adopting a long-standing usage.

Max Weber said that people were in community when they felt that they belonged together. The psychological and ideological components of this feeling of belonging are subject to debate and dispute, and I shall not go into them here. In order to show the relevance of community for the understanding of freedom I shall focus on three features of community which might be said to be consequences of the feeling of belonging: namely, the fact that people in community are mutually supportive; the fact that when community is present, the continuance of the community is a good in itself not reducible to the ability of the community to provide mutual benefit; and the fact that the members of the community share a common style of life.

The fact that the members of the community share a common life-style makes it possible for them to formulate limits upon permissible activity which do not conflict with individual value attainment. The toleration of modes of activity which are not characteristic of the common life-style is not an issue. Consequently, mutual adjustment is not difficult and, in most cases, can be achieved by means of the enunciation of principles adhered to by all right-thinking members of the community. It is important to note that a community has the ability to achieve mutual adjustment at a high level of freedom partially as a consequence of the shared style of life. For in such a situation principles can easily be enunciated which impose no costs upon those who conform to the standard pattern. If the socialization process in the community has been successful, then the members will define their values in such a way that the standard prohibitions and controls will not be perceived as restrictions on their freedom. The standard prohibitions and controls will fall heavily only on those who are marginal to the community, in the sense that they do not conceive their values in the standard ways, and in consequence do not contribute to the cohesion of the community. From a sociological point of view, these marginal people can be described as having a high degree of functional autonomy, which means simply that they and the community have a limited degree of interdependence.

This has consequences both from the point of view of the individual and from the point of view of the community. If the individual has a high degree of functional autonomy, then we can expect him to be relatively immune to the normal, informal social sanctions which keep more conforming individuals in line. For he will find little or no need to seek out the other members of the community for recognition or confirmation. His sense of his own worth will have developed independently. In fact he will find that adherence to the normal pattern of life of the community will impose external costs upon him, and that the more conforming members of the community are related negatively to him. From the community's point of view the functionally autonomous individual will be looked upon as a deviant, a rebel, or an outlaw; and they will feel justified in applying sanctions in an attempt to modify his behavior. The stronger threat an individual is to the cohesion of the community, the stronger sanctions will seem to them to be justified in regulating his activity. This situation is particularly interesting, for if the community wishes to tolerate the functionally autonomous individual because, for example, they believe strongly that anyone born among them has a worth which must be respected, they must weaken the cohesiveness of the community. This will happen in two ways: First, they will allow in their midst an example of a style of life foreign to their own standard, and this will make socialization more difficult; and second, they will have to relax the principles and sanctions which have secured their way of life against minor deviance.

The upshot of all this from the point of freedom is the following: If the members of the community retain their traditional values, and if they make a place for functionally autonomous individuals, then they will find that they must adjust external costs at a higher level than they had previously found necessary; on the other hand, a fragmentation of traditional values will move them closer to the kind of social system grounded on mutual benefit, in which case the standard forms of bargaining and negotiation will emerge in order to adjust a plurality of ways of life. But insofar as there is a plurality of ways of life it will no longer be possible to think of persons who do not share values as deviants or outlaws; and it will become increasingly difficult to fashion a set of principles and laws which merely regulate marginal behavior of marginal individuals. For once the standard style of life of the old community has broken down, it is impossible to say with any certainty which individuals and activities are marginal. It is most probable that any prohibitions and controls which are introduced will simply reflect the distribution of power present in the system for legitimizing these controls, and the very best that can be hoped for is that the burden of prohibitions can be kept relatively low and relatively well distributed.

I can cite one more advantage that a cohesive community can have from the point of view of stability. Since the maintenance of the community is seen as good in itself, it is probable that the members of a community will tolerate a mutual adjustment of interaction costs at a much higher level than the members of an association for mutual benefit. For example, the tolerable level of mutual annoyance within a household composed of a family with close ties is likely to be greater than that in a cooperative living situation in which the participants have gotten together merely to save rent. In general, closely knit communities tolerate a great deal of misery and adversity before the dissolution of the community comes into question. Perhaps this is, operationally, a tautology, since one of the ways in which we test the cohesiveness of a social system is to determine the amount of adversity it can withstand without falling apart.

The foregoing analysis of freedom and community is sketchy. But from it can be drawn two consequences of extreme present-day importance.

First is a point in regard to neo-anarchism. The neo-anarchist creed, at least in the circles with which I am familiar, is "Form genuine communities and let everyone do his own thing." I would like to suggest, on the basis of the foregoing analysis, that this is utter nonsense. For it requires close social cohesion in an entire society of functionally autonomous individuals. Or it may be that the neo-anarchists mean to be saying that while the individuals will be doing their own thing they will both want the recognition of the others in the community and want to contribute to others' ability to do *their* own thing. But if scarcities are present, this high degree of cooperation will require constant delicate allocational decisions. Furthermore, externalities are sure to emerge, and even if the members of the community have the finest of motives, some institution for making allocational decisions will have to emerge. If participatory democracy is the favored institution, then the communities will have to be careful that they remain very small, for otherwise decision-making costs will become prohibitively high. It goes without saying that factionalization must not be allowed to take place.

The second point is of more far-reaching importance. Modern nation-states, including our own, like to think of themselves as communities: cohesive and homogeneous. This provides grounds for considering those who find their freedom severely limited by the pattern of laws and customs to be deviants and outlaws. But in fact, and it hardly needs arguing, our country, for one, is not a community in the sense necessary for that judgment to be true. There is no common shared way of life in terms of which we can define marginal behavior. So the claim that we are a community is a sham, and can only serve to mask the fact that in our mutual adjustment of interaction costs we regularly exclude certain groups from participation. As we now know, this can be true even though everyone has the right to vote. How freedom is distributed is a matter for empirical investigation. If such an investigation should show that freedom is wrongly distributed, then it seems to me that we ought to embark on a program of readjustment of interaction costs which would distribute freedom rightly.

Freedom and Consent

As my last major discussion of freedom, I should like to say a few words about the concept of consent. The apologists for Western liberal democracies are fond of taking pride in the fact that their societies are legitimized on the basis of the free consent of the governed. Thus the question arises: In what does this consent consist?

Let us make the assumption, almost universally accepted, that people try to act in such a way that they attain their values. We may note that this is perfectly consistent with the belief that people are solicitous of the values of others, and want the possibility of value attainment to be justly distributed. Furthermore, let us remind ourselves that the word *value* is being used in a sense broad enough to include anything thought to be worth achieving. Thus, if we assume that people are smart enough to be able to see where their path of maximal value attainment lies, we should expect that they would make calculations about better and worse courses of action; and we should expect them to choose the better. If one of the conditions under which they must make these choices is the presence of a powerful firmly established governmental apparatus, then we should expect them to take the presence of this apparatus into account when they make their choices. Taking the governmental apparatus into account may be very complicated, for not only does it embody prohibitions, with sanctions to enforce them, but it also is the source of certain opportunities which would otherwise be unavailable. Furthermore, it is possible that individuals might have some chance to modify the conditions for action that the governmental apparatus imposes.

It seems to me that given these circumstances, to say that a man consents to being governed by a particular apparatus is to say that he calculates that his path to maximum value attainment lies with the acceptance of the conditions imposed by the government rather than with the attempt to modify those conditions by methods not sanctioned by the government itself.[11] If this conception of consent is correct, then consent simply comes to this: To consent is to calculate that it would be more expensive not to conform to the requirements placed upon your behavior by government than it would be to conform. Thus consent ranges from a total belief in the sanctity and perfection of the governmental system on the one hand, to a detestation and revulsion coupled with the belief that failure to conform would be worse on the other. Hence the only people who would fail to consent would be those who felt that they were worse off with the government than they would be without it.

In an age where the state commands a virtual monopoly of force, it will always be able to regulate the level of conformity, hence consent, if it wishes to do so. Thus, on the model of behavior we have been using, there is a continuum of consent ranging from situations in which no force needs to be applied by the state in order for a satisfactory level of mutual adjustment to be maintained, to the other extreme, in which the full pressure of the police state must be applied in order for even a minimal mutual adjustment to take place.

But it might appear that within the range of those who consent we might distinguish between those who consent willingly and those who consent against their will—or we might distinguish between free consent and forced consent. This would be important to us insofar as we felt that those who consented willingly were free within that order, whereas those who consented against their will were in bondage. Further, it might seem strange to say that a slave consents to his servitude if he fails to rebel. The question is

[11] Since some people never bother to consider the possibility of modifying conditions which a government imposes, but think these conditions to be given, rather like the weather or any other natural condition beyond their control, it is difficult to see how they could be said to consent to the government.

whether a non-arbitrary distinction of the required type can be made.

I think that it can, but only if we fall back on the previously discussed notion of the satisfactory aggregative and distributive level of freedom. For if we use that notion we can say that people freely consent to their government when there is a satisfactory aggregative and distributive level of freedom and they choose to conform to the behavior patterns required of them. Whether any modern state conforms to this standard remains an open question, for the satisfactory level of freedom remains to be specified.

As a consequence of the features of consent that I have been presenting, it is very difficult to make any talk of "government by consent" sound convincing when applied to a political system of long standing—especially one in which disharmony and discord are present. Under such conditions, the concept of consent, and its evocation in defense of long-established institutions are part of a flimflam designed to divert attention from the actual distribution of power and opportunity for advantages which is at the heart of the distribution of freedom.

But the conditions of freedom and consent can be brought out into the open and examined. Judgments about aggregative and distributive levels can be made. So there is no reason why we cannot discuss and determine the state of our freedom—and only then the meaning of our "consent." [12]

[12] There seems to be another notion of consent traveling in current jurisprudential circles: namely, one deriving from the later thought of Wittgenstein. In a discussion of following rules in the *Philosophical Investigations,* the question of the necessity for having a rule for applying a rule arises. This obviously threatens an infinite regress. Since we somehow do follow rules, the regress seems to have to end at a stage of rule-following which is not governed by rules in the same way as the rule-following of the earlier stages. Similarly any mutual act of consent presumably requires agreement or consent on the criteria for what will constitute consent—threatening a regress. It is tempting to think that this potential regress ends at a kind of consent which is like all consent except that it requires no prior consent in any way.

This whole area contains some of the most difficult problems in all philosophy, but we can say with some certainty that if some such notion of Ur-consent were established, it could not be the concept of consent which

CONCLUSION

Emphasis on the calculation of more or less with respect to our freedom has the salutary effect of making it possible for us to make accurate judgments about our freedom, and do something about any deficiencies. It shows us what we ought already to have known —namely, that our freedom is a political problem, not an ideological or rhetorical one. Political problems are solved by the real activity of real people in a real world. So we should not be surprised if we find ourselves acting as we feel we must in order to move the mutual adjustment of freedom to a satisfactory aggregative and distributive level. It would be irrational for us to do otherwise. And whether or not the prevailing rhetoric of freedom and consent sanctions our activity is irrelevant. If it does, then it proves itself to be practical wisdom. If it does not, then so much for it.

When we finally give up our superstitious belief in the magical power of words—even old and venerated words like freedom and consent—then we will begin to be able to control our own lives. The black man does not gain entry into the halls of justice by standing at the door saying "Open sesame." He gains entry by forcing us to take his freedom into account when we establish the mutual adjustment of freedom in the society which he shares with us. How he does this is irrelevant, except insofar as he has made an accurate calculation of more or less, has accurately assessed our response, and has contributed materially to an improvement in the aggregative and distributive level of freedom.[13]

---

was needed in the context of "government by consent" for two reasons: First, Ur-consent would have to be nonrational—far from the "consent freely given as the result of rational choice" which we associate with "government by consent"; and second, if there were such an Ur-consent, it would lie at the base of *all* human activities involving the cooperating (mutual understanding) of two or more people, hence would do us no good in distinguishing societies of consent from others.

[13] In connection with some of the points that I have been trying to make, it might be instructive to read Eldridge Cleaver's "Stanford Speech" contained in Eldridge Cleaver, *Post-prison Writings and Speeches*, New York, 1969; especially see pp. 130–133.

COMMENT

by Christopher D. Stone

Professor Dyke does well to make us rethink the problem of freedom. It is one of the few philosophical concepts that ordinary people connect with their lives (no one, Camus observed, ever died for the ontological argument). Yet, if we put ourselves to the discipline of explaining what we mean by it, we find we are hard pressed to come up with any definition that is adequate. And when we consider that we are in this muddle after centuries of groping with the problem, it gives us all the more reason to presume that something is askew about the way we have been putting it to ourselves. We should be open to those, like Dyke, who offer us new ways of thinking it through.

Dyke suggests that a good deal of the confusion arises from our wanting a theory of freedom that justifies there being something absolute and uncompromisable about it. This, Dyke says, is simply not a realistic way to begin, given that in our political and social lives we are continually finding that in order to preserve or advance one man's freedom, we have to diminish someone else's. Thus, a theory of freedom ought to allow for the fact that we are inevitably going to wind up compromising and negotiating some freedom, just as a theory of economics has to start with a sense of the limitations on our wealth. The point to focus on is not whether we should allocate freedom, but how to do so best.

Obviously, to work this into a coherent theory is an ambitious project. But the analogy of freedom to a scarce resource[1] holds some promise as to a general direction. For it suggests the possibility of clarifying our freedom dilemmas by reference to the terminology of welfare economics. Specifically, if what we mean by freedom can be explained in terms of measurable states of affairs, then we may be able

[1] Professor Dyke credits the suggestion to Lon Fuller, "Freedom as a Problem of Allocating Choice," 112 *Proceedings of the American Philosophical Society* 101 (1968).

to call on the economic model as a guide for calculating what compromises in some freedoms will yield what increases in others, and
what solutions to inconsistent demands on freedom will optimize the
freedom of everyone involved.

This may sound strange, given that we are not used to thinking of
our freedoms as tradable commodities. But the possibility of such a
fruitful cross-pollination of freedom and economics gets off to a promising start. Dyke shows that a good deal of what we want to say when
we speak of freedom lends itself to expression in basic welfare economics terms, specifically those of "externality" and "internality." Suppose, for example, I want to cure leaf tobacco on my farm. I am not
free to do so if it rains. Dyke is pointing out that to have this freedom,
I have to bring the rain under my control (as by seeding clouds) so
that if and when it rains it is because I want it to rain: in Dyke's
terminology, to "internalize" the conditions that bring rain.

Dyke's aim, however, is not merely to give us another way of looking at an important term. His larger purpose is to fit our conception
of freedom into the welfare economics rubric so as to give us the
capacity to make the relationship "have more freedom than" useful as
a cornerstone of comparison and measurement, something we can do
now only in the roughest way. What he suggests toward this end is
that *"a man is freer the fewer negative externalities are imposed upon
him; and less free the more negative externalities are imposed upon
him."* [2]

What I want to point out in the balance of my comments is (1)
why I do not believe that such a definition advances us toward a true
measurement of freedom (that is, why the relationship "having more
freedom" cannot be treated analogously to "having more of a resource"), and (2) what I think Professor Dyke *is* contributing to our
understanding, a contribution I do not think really depends upon

---

[2] After these comments were written and delivered, Professor Dyke saw
fit to adjust his definition of freedom. In the final manuscript he speaks in
terms of the level of external costs, rather than the number of negative
externalities. I am pleased that some of my specific objections are thereby
met. But the thrust of the criticisms remains. As far as I can judge, the basic
problems illustrated with respect to counting externalities apply with equal
force to measuring their level.

whether the analogy of freedom to a scarce resource carries us as far as we might have hoped.

As for the first point, I do not think that there is much hope in expressing statements like "John has more freedom than Mary" or "The United States has more freedom today than it had twenty years ago" in terms of a number of negative externalities.[3]

To begin with, there is a serious difficulty inherent in speaking of the *number* of negative externalities at all. Our "count" will always depend too much on our subjective desires and conceptual abilities to serve the purpose Dyke wants of it. How many negative externalities is a man who is forbidden from driving subjected to? One (each day, hour, minute)? Or the number of activities that he wants to use the driving as a means to achieve and is frustrated from? Or the number of activities that driving *could* be a means to achieve, whether he knows of them (or even wants them) or not? Any negative externality prohibits something like an infinity of choices and is therefore something like an infinity of negative externalities.

What I think Dyke wants to talk about is not the absolute number of negative externalities, anyway—despite what he says in his definition—but that number as a function relative somehow to one's preferences. That, at least, is the thrust of his remark that people "make

---

[3] One ought to note that to lend itself to true measurement, a quality (for example, weight) must be expressible in a relationship ("is heavier than") which, in turn, is capable of meeting two tests: It must be *comparative* and it must be *transitive*. A science of weighing is possible, because we cannot only arrange agreed-upon tests for determining (comparatively) whether A is heavier than B, but (transitively) we discover in all cases that if A is heavier than B and B is heavier than C, then A is heavier than C. (It is possible for a quality to lend itself to comparative relationships, but not transitive relationships, and if so the quality is not measurable. One way in which people want to explicate the relationship "is harder than," for example, is in terms of whether A can scratch B, or vice versa. This comparative judgment can be easily performed; but it turns out, empirically, that A's capacity to scratch B and B's capacity to scratch C does not entail A's capacity to scratch C.)

I do not think that Dyke's definition meets even the first criterion (comparativeness) in an adequate way; that is, I do not think it can satisfactorily handle even comparative statements like "John has more freedom than Mary." If I am right, we do not even have to go on to demonstrate that "has more freedom than" is inadequate to establish transitive relations.

judgments of value, and rank what they value along a scale of better or worse." And, indeed, one does expect a theory of freedom to take into account that some limitations on our choices seem to be more intrusive—make us "less free"—than others.

But it is one thing to suppose we have rough preferences and quite another thing to suppose that we systematize our feelings by carrying around with us elaborate rankings that we can make calculations upon. The latter assumption simplifies model building, but it also simplifies some of the major problems of life out of existence.[4] What is more, if we simply accept such rankings as a starting point for analysis, I do not think the difficulties Dyke faces are solved.

Let us take, for example, a freedom dilemma from the point of two men, A and B. We will assume them to have fixed preferences and, at the start, equal freedom. A knows how to read books in ten languages and B knows how to read books in only two languages.[5] Suppose, now, that the state passes a law prohibiting the reading of books. What has happened to the relative freedoms that they have? If we look upon the state's act as one negative externality—a prohibition from reading books—one would be inclined to say they have been deprived of equal amounts of freedom, and so are still equally free. But if we look upon the law as prohibiting A from reading all the books in ten languages and B all the books in only two languages (some lesser number of books), then there is reason to say that A has less freedom than B, even though they are still presumptively equal in what they *can* do.

---

[4] Even if we assume that people have such rankings, we should still want to know how they got them: Is it possible that anyone's "rankings" can be separated out from the web of social and personal threats—negative externalities, as Dyke would call them—in which we are all inextricably enmeshed? Why does one want (or: say that he wants) *most of all* to design a great city? Has it not something to do with there being less serious threats associated—through "guilt" or "the generalized other"—with that choice than with the choices lower on his ranking?

Not only are such questions interesting but it seems to me that the answering of them is very much a part of what people are looking for in an analysis of *freedom:* an understanding of the "negative externalities" that are imposed upon us through internalized controls.

[5] Dyke would not count a discrepancy in capabilities as a difference in freedom, on the view that negative externalities—limitations imposed by others—are not immediately involved.

But what, now, if B, though he can read fewer books than A, enjoys reading books more than A does? This introduces the problem of priorities. If instead of counting negative externalities (the way Dyke's definition suggests) we take rankings and intensities of feeling into account, we will make some further advances toward understanding "freedom." But we will still be a long way from Dyke's goal.

By recognizing priorities, we would be keeping ourselves aware that, because book reading was lower on A's ranking of priorities than on B's, at some point of their relative capacities to read books, the law caused B to have less freedom than A.

But at what point? How can we possibly make the interpersonal comparisons that are involved? Just consider the difficulties inherent in the different "negative externalities" they may face. On this score, Dyke does not take into account that the limits others impose on our actions are not absolute but at some cost. Suppose, for example, that the law prohibiting the reading of books was unequal in its sanction, laying down a penalty of death for A but only a five-dollar fine for each violation by B. Would we not now be inclined to say that A had less freedom than B? But what if B is a tightwad, or painfully poor, and A has a death wish, or is indifferent to dying? And will not these subjective differences dog us even if A and B face the same (objective) sanction? That is, would they regard a year in jail as equally intrusive—as the "same" negative externality?

These examples could be multiplied, but I think they indicate enough of the difficulties. Ultimately, any attempt to reduce the concept of "having more freedom" to numbers of physical possibilities available, physical possibilities denied, or either of those relative to a ranking of desires, is doomed to be unsatisfactory. The whole attempt, indeed, has about it the aspect of a philosophical goose chase, one which I think owes in part to a happenstance of the English language that allows us to speak of our relationship to freedom with the possessive, and so encourages us to think of it as a possessable *thing*. A contrast may make this clearer: We do not say, as the French do, that "I have fear" (*j'ai peur*), but rather, "I am afraid." The verb form reminds us that we are speaking about a state of mind, rather than a physical possession. On the other hand, we can say "I have freedom" (as well as "I am free") and our minds, as Wittgenstein suggests, "become captive of the picture" that this language "paints for us." The "picture" of *having* freedom encourages us first to reify freedom, and then—accepting the reification all too unquestioningly—to speak of it as though it could be treated literally like a scarce good or resource.

But the real uses of "having freedom" are too rich and varied to be captured and explained the way in which we can explain the United States' having more timber than France. When we say, even in a case that seems as forthright as "If you go to prison you will not have the freedom you now have," what we are saying is infused with social judgments and personal exhortations, akin to "Stay out of prison" and "Looking at a wall is not as satisfying as watching a ball game"; and these judgments and exhortations are inseparably a part of the job we want the expression to do—to instruct people in the society's way of looking at the world. Again, when we say, "You have more freedom than that," we *mean*—in a way too important to be stripped from the words—something like "Don't do that" or "Think it through again" or "You have not such limited discretion as you think." In like vein, so far as we are inclined to speak of political freedoms as though they were absolute and nonnegotiable, it is not because we are naïve but because one of the functions of a symbol like freedom is to exhort and to organize, and we exhort and organize more effectively if we keep up what Dyke would call, I expect, a "fiction." It is, in all events, a fiction not to be dropped on the hope that by doing so the welfare economists can give us something better. (We ought to wait at least until welfare economics shows its ability to help us calculate real problems of economics.)

These are only some of the difficulties that suggest why, on balance, the analogy between "having freedom" and "having a resource" cannot be carried very far. But as I indicated earlier, I do not think that the difficulties of carrying through that analogy are fatal to the basic point Dyke has to make in the second part of his paper.

What Dyke wants us to see can best be illustrated by the example of a simple community. Take an island with 100,000 square feet of space and 100 people who have divided the land equally among themselves. Each person occupies, at the start, a 1,000-foot square. Let us suppose further that all their values have to do with listening to music, but they have different tastes. Some want to hear acid rock played full blast, and do not mind too much if it is blended a bit with their neighbors' Bartók; others strongly want to hear Beethoven and hear it uninterfered with. The problems that will thus arise are much the problems of any society. Some procedure for give-and-take bargaining will have to be arranged, in accordance with the intensities of various people's desires. Some person, B, will want to contract with his four adjacent neighbors so that his Beethoven gets no interference from any direction for three prime listening hours, in exchange for B's agreement not to play anything himself for the remaining twenty-one hours, and so forth. The "government's" role might well be to serve as mediator and enforcer in the negotiations that will ensue.

The crux of Dyke's position can be illustrated this way. The four corners of the island will be the best living quarters in the eyes of many people, because there they will be subject to interference from two directions at the most. People will thus "pay" a good deal to obtain these corners. Suppose now that someone wants to include among these things he has to trade off one of his "freedoms" (as we regard them). For example, suppose that to obtain a prime position he offers in return to surrender his "rights" to vote and to express opinions on public matters. (This might be received as a "gain" by the others inasmuch as it proportionately increases everyone else's influence.) What Dyke is pointing out is that there is no reason to suppose that such a trade-off will not increase the welfare of the person surrendering those rights. He simply might value the relative freedom from extraneous noise more than the relative political participation. And others in the society might prefer the concentrated voting power to other values that could be received from auctioning the corners. Furthermore, it would seem to be in the interest of any man's freedom (not just his welfare) to allow him this choice of having the freedom *to trade* freedom rather than to be subject to a "negative externality" *prohibiting that option.*[6]

[6] Indeed, the most solid case for Dyke's explication of "have more freedom than" would seem to be applicable here. Suppose a single individual who wanted (in any ranking) to A, B, C, D, V (vote) and T (trade his right to vote for something else). Compare one state of affairs in which he is not forbidden from T trading his right to vote) with another state of af-

Dyke can thus be read as making the interesting observation that any person might be happier and freer if he were at least allowed the choice of trading off for some other value what we tend to regard as the most basic and nonnegotiable freedoms.[7]

This is true, but it is somewhat like pointing out that any given person might be happier and freer if he had, in addition to his present "rights," the right to contract with C to murder D. The problem the society has is not to increase the happiness and freedom of each individual viewed separately, but, as Dyke is emphasizing throughout, to find compromises that maximize everybody's position. Thus, a society might well find that although each person separately would prefer to have the right to contract for murder, considered as a society they would prefer a rule denying everybody that option as best on the whole. They would say that although such a law was a limit on each man's choices, it inured to their mutual welfare and freedom.

Now, the thing to note is that an individual's contracting away his basic rights is more like contracting for murder than one might first suppose. A man who negotiated with his neighbors never to vote or speak out is exerting some negative influence on the entire society as third parties. Furthermore, to the rest of the society, as to any negotiant, there will be a considerable cost just to getting the information necessary to determining value—how much the freedoms traded off really "cost." For example, how "bad" it was for everybody else if B agreed with C never to vote would depend on how many other people had traded away their right to vote, so that we knew whether B was putting on the block $\frac{1}{100}$, $\frac{1}{50}$, $\frac{1}{24}$ of the effective voice in the community, or what.

But these problems, Dyke would point out, I think, are problems inherent in the negotiation of any value: Should we let people deal in real estate? There are the same uncertainties there. The difference between negotiating our political freedom and negotiating our other

fairs in which he has V but not T. I do not think we can quibble here with the appropriateness of saying he has "more freedom" in the first case than in the second.

[7] I take it Dyke is referring not just to passing up his chance to vote now, or bartering it off in a logroll, but contracting not to exercise it for a period —for life, perhaps.

bases of power and well-being are matters, Dyke is showing us, of degree. It is support for Dyke that those who most clearly regard free speech and the vote as "nonnegotiable" have been people with other forms of power to negotiate. History shows us how often people who have nothing but the vote are apt to regard its nonnegotiability as a luxury and trade it for whatever other values they can get for it. And similarly, a person whose vote carries concentrated power—say, a high public official's—will find himself the target of high offers by those with more tangible value to exchange. Such negotiations, Dyke points out, are taking place all the time, not merely in the form of bribes but in sanctioned forms of logrolling. Indeed, on some level, every vote is a sale of choice for some reason, for example, the likelihood of a defense contract for one's home state.

But it is one thing to "sell" (in this sense) one's vote—which is the essence of voting—and quite another to sell one's right to vote. The latter supposes a long-term agreement enforced, if necessary, by state machinery.

It is not impossible to imagine a society which would allow such agreements to be enforced. (Nor is it impossible to imagine a society in which the people decided that, on net, it would be best to enforce contracts for murder.) But I do not think that a society is likely to enact such a rule of its own accord, given the small gain that any citizen might realize (what would he be paid for $\dfrac{1}{100,000,000}$ of the voting power in the next five Presidential elections?) and given the large losses, practically and morally, that the legitimation of such a practice would threaten.

CHAPTER 5

TAKING RIGHTS SERIOUSLY

---

by Ronald Dworkin

I

The language of rights now dominates political debate. Does our government respect the moral and political rights of its citizens? Or does the government's war policy, or its race policy, fly in the face of these rights? Do the minorities whose rights have been violated have the right to violate the law in return? Or does the silent majority itself have rights, including the right that those who break the law be punished? It is not surprising that these questions are now prominent. The concept of rights, and particularly the concept of rights against the government, has its most natural use when a political society is divided, and appeals to cooperation or a common goal are pointless.

The debate does not include the issue of whether citizens have *some* moral rights against their government. It seems accepted on all sides that they have. Conventional lawyers and politicians take it as a point of pride that our legal system recognizes, for example, individual rights of free speech, equality, and due process. They base their claim that our law deserves respect, at least in part, on that fact, for they would not claim that totalitarian systems deserve the same loyalty. Some philosophers, of course, reject the idea that citizens have rights apart from what the law happens to give them. Bentham thought that the idea of moral rights was "nonsense on stilts." But that view has never been part of our orthodox political theory, and politicians of both parties appeal to the rights of the people to justify a great part of what they want to do. I shall not be concerned, in this essay, to defend the thesis that citizens have moral rights against their governments; I want instead to explore the implications of that thesis for those, including our present government, who profess to accept it.

It is much in dispute, of course, what *particular* rights citizens have. Does the acknowledged right to free speech, for example, include the right to participate in nuisance demonstrations? In practice the government will have the last word on what an individual's rights are, because its police will do what its officials and courts say. But that does not mean that the government's view is necessarily the correct view; anyone who thinks it does must believe that men have only such moral rights as government chooses to grant, which means that they have no moral rights at all.

All this is sometimes obscured in the United States by our constitutional system. The Constitution provides a set of individual *legal* rights in the First Amendment, and in the due process, equal protection, and similar clauses. Under present legal practice the Supreme Court has the power to declare an act of Congress or of a state legislature void if the Court finds that the act offends these provisions. This practice has led some commentators to suppose that individual moral rights are fully protected by our system, but that is hardly so, nor could it be so.

The Constitution fuses legal and moral issues, by making the validity of a law depend on the answer to complex moral problems, like the problem of whether a particular statute respects the inherent equality of all men. This fusion has important consequences for the debates about civil disobedience; I have described these elsewhere,[1] and I shall refer to them later. But it leaves open two prominent questions. It does not tell us whether the Constitution, even properly interpreted, recognizes all the moral rights our citizens have, and it does not tell us whether, as many suppose, citizens would have a duty to obey the law even if it did invade their moral rights. Both questions become crucial when some minority claims moral rights which the law denies, like the right to run its local school system, and which lawyers agree are not protected by the

[1] "On Not Prosecuting Civil Disobedience," *New York Review of Books,* June 6, 1968.

Constitution. The second question becomes crucial when, as now, the majority is sufficiently aroused so that constitutional amendments to eliminate rights, like the right against self-incrimination, are seriously proposed. It is also crucial in nations, like England, that have no constitution of our form.

Even if the Constitution were perfect, of course, and the majority left it alone, it would not follow that the Supreme Court could guarantee the individual rights of citizens. A Supreme Court decision is still a legal decision, and it must take into account precedent, and institutional considerations like relations between the Court and Congress, as well as morality. And no judicial decision is necessarily the right decision. Judges stand for different positions on controversial issues of law and morals, and, as the recent fights over Nixon's Supreme Court nomination showed, a President is entitled to appoint judges of his own persuasion, provided they are honest and capable.

So, though the constitutional system adds something to the protection of moral rights against the government, it falls far short of guaranteeing these rights, or even establishing what they are. It means that, on some occasions, a department other than the legislative has the last word on these issues, which can hardly satisfy someone who thinks such a department profoundly wrong.

It is of course inevitable that some department of government will have the final say on what law will be enforced. When men disagree about moral rights, there will be no way for either side to prove its case, and some decision must stand if there is not to be anarchy. But that piece of orthodox wisdom must be the beginning and not the end of a philosophy of legislation and enforcement. If we cannot insist that the government reach the right answers about the rights of its citizens, we can insist at least that it try. We can insist that it take rights seriously, follow a coherent theory of what these rights are, and act consistently with its own professions. I shall try to show what that means, and how it bears on the present political debates.

II

I shall start with the most violently argued issue. Does an American ever have the moral right to break a law? Suppose someone admits a law is valid; does he therefore have a duty to obey it? Those who try to give an answer seem to fall into two camps. The conservatives, as I shall call them, seem to disapprove of any act of disobedience; they appear satisfied when such acts are prosecuted, and disappointed when convictions are reversed. The other group, the liberals, are much more sympathetic to at least some cases of disobedience; they sometimes disapprove of prosecutions and celebrate acquittals. If we look beyond these emotional reactions, however, and pay attention to the arguments the two parties use, we discover an astounding fact. Both groups give essentially the same answer to the question of principle that supposedly divides them.

The answer that both parties give is this. In a democracy, or at least a democracy that in principle respects individual rights, each citizen has a general moral duty to obey all the laws, even though he would like some of them changed. He owes that duty to his fellow citizens, who obey laws that they do not like, to his benefit. But this general duty cannot be an absolute duty, because even a society that is in principle just may produce unjust laws and policies, and a man has duties other than his duties to the state. A man must honor his duties to his God and to his conscience, and if these conflict with his duty to the state, then he is entitled, in the end, to do what he judges to be right. If he decides that he must break the law, however, then he must submit to the judgment and punishment that the state imposes, in recognition of the fact that his duty to his fellow citizens was overwhelmed but not extinguished by his religious or moral obligation.

Of course this common answer can be elaborated in very different ways. Some would describe the duty to the state as fundamental, and picture the dissenter as a religious or moral fanatic. Others would describe the duty to the state in grudging terms, and picture those who oppose it as moral heroes. But these are differences in tone, and the position I describe represents, I think, the view of most of those who find themselves arguing either for or against civil disobedience in particular cases. I do not claim that it is everyone's view. There must be some who put the duty to the state so high that they do not grant that it can ever be overcome. There are certainly some who would deny that a man ever has a moral duty to obey the law, at least in the United States today. But these two extreme positions are the slender tails of a bell curve, and all those who fall in between hold the orthodox position I described —that men have a duty to obey the law but have the right to follow their conscience when it conflicts with that duty.

But if that is so, then we have a paradox in the fact that men who give the same answer to a question of principle should seem to disagree so much, and to divide so fiercely, in particular cases. The paradox goes even deeper, for each party, in at least some cases, takes a position that seems flatly inconsistent with the theoretical position they both accept. This position is tested, for example, when someone evades the draft on grounds of conscience, or encourages others to commit this crime. Conservatives argue that such men must be prosecuted, even though they are sincere. Why must they be prosecuted? Because society cannot tolerate the decline in respect for the law that their act constitutes and encourages. They must be prosecuted, in short, to discourage them and others like them from doing what they have done. But there seems to be a monstrous contradiction here. If a man has a right to do what his conscience tells him he must, then how can the state be justified in discouraging him from doing it? Is it not wicked for a state to forbid and punish what it acknowledges that men have a right to do?

Moreover, it is not just conservatives who argue that those who break the law out of moral conviction should be prosecuted. The liberal is notoriously opposed to allowing southern school officials to go slow on segregation, even though he acknowledges that these school officials think they have a moral right to do what the law forbids. The liberal does not often argue, it is true, that the desegregation laws must be enforced to encourage general respect for law. He argues instead that the desegregation laws must be en-

forced because they are right. But his position also seems inconsistent: Can it be right to prosecute men for doing what their conscience requires, when we acknowledge their right to follow their
conscience?

We are therefore left with two puzzles. How can two parties to
an issue of principle, each of which thinks it is in profound disagreement with the other, embrace the same position on that issue?
How can it be that each side urges solutions to particular problems
which seem flatly to contradict the position of principle that both
accept? One possible answer is that some or all of those who accept
the common position are hypocrites, paying lip service to rights of
conscience which in fact they do not grant. There is some plausibility to this charge. A sort of hypocrisy must be involved when public
officials who claim to respect conscience denied Muhammad Ali the
right to box in their states. If Muhammad Ali, in spite of his religious scruples, had joined the army, he would have been allowed to
box even though, on the principles these officials say they honor, he
would have been a worse human being for having done so. But
there are few cases that seem so straightforward as this one, and
even here the officials do not seem even to recognize the contradiction between their acts and their principles. So we must search for
some explanation beyond the truth that men often do not mean
what they say.

The deeper explanation lies in a set of confusions that often
embarrass arguments about rights. These confusions have clouded
all the issues I mentioned at the outset, and have crippled attempts
to develop a coherent theory of how a government that respects
rights must behave.

In order to explain this, I must call attention to the fact, familiar
to philosophers but often ignored in political debate, that the word
"right" has different force in different contexts. In most cases, when
we say that someone has a "right" to do something, we mean that it
would be wrong to interfere with his doing it, or at least that some
special grounds are needed for justifying any interference. I use this
strong sense of "right" when I say that you have the right to spend
your money gambling, if you wish, though you ought to spend it in

a more worthwhile way. I mean that it would be wrong for anyone to interfere with you even though you propose to spend your money in a way that I think is wrong.

There is a clear difference between saying that someone has a right to do something in this sense, and saying that it is the "right" thing for him to do or that he does no wrong in doing it. Someone may have the right to do something that is the wrong thing for him to do, as might be the case with gambling. Conversely, something may be the right thing for him to do and yet he may have no right to do it, in the sense that it would not be wrong for someone to interfere with his trying. If our army captures an enemy soldier, we might say that the right thing for him to do is to try to escape, but it would not follow that it is wrong of us to try to stop him. We might admire him for trying to escape, and perhaps even think less of him if he did not. But there is no suggestion here that it is wrong of us to stand in his way; on the contrary, if we think our cause is just, we think it right for us to do all we can to stop him.

Ordinarily this distinction, between the issues of whether a man has a right to do something and whether it is the right thing for him to do, causes no trouble. But sometimes it does, because sometimes we say that a man has a right to do something when we mean only to deny that it is the wrong thing for him to do. Thus we say that the captured soldier has a "right" to try to escape when we mean, not that we do wrong to stop him, but that he has no duty not to make the attempt. We also use "right" this way when we speak of someone having the "right" to act on his own principles, or the "right" to follow his own conscience. We mean that he does no wrong to proceed on his honest convictions, even though we disagree with these convictions, and even though, for policy or other reasons, we must force him to act contrary to them.

Suppose a man believes that welfare payments to the poor are profoundly wrong, because they sap enterprise, and so declares his full income tax each year but declines to pay half of it. We might say that he has a right to refuse to pay, if he wishes, but that the government has a right to proceed against him for the full tax, and to fine or jail him for late payment if that is necessary to keep the collection system working efficiently. We do not take this line in most cases; we do not say that the ordinary thief has a right to steal, if he wishes, so long as he pays the penalty. We say a man has the right to break the law, even though the state has a right to punish him, only when we think that, because of his convictions, he does no wrong in doing so.[2]

These distinctions enable us to see an ambiguity in the orthodox question: Does a man ever have a right to break the law? Does that question mean to ask whether he ever has a right to break the law in the strong sense, so that the government would do wrong to stop him, by arresting and prosecuting him? Or does it mean to ask whether he ever does the right thing to break the law, so that we should all respect him even though the government should jail him?

If we take the orthodox position to be an answer to the first— and most important—question, then the paradoxes I described arise. But if we take it as an answer to the second, they do not. Conservatives and liberals do agree that sometimes a man does not do the wrong thing to break a law, when his conscience so requires. They disagree, when they do, over the different issue of what the state's response should be. Both parties do think that sometimes the state should prosecute. But this is not inconsistent with the proposition that the man prosecuted did the right thing in breaking the law.

The paradoxes seem genuine because the two questions are not usually distinguished, and the orthodox position is presented as a general solution to the problem of civil disobedience. But once the distinction is made, it is apparent that the position has been so widely accepted that only because, when it is applied, it is treated as an answer to the second question but not the first. The crucial

[2] It is not suprising that we sometimes use the concept of having a right to say that others must not interfere with an act and sometimes to say that the act is not the wrong thing to do. Often, when someone has *no* right to do something, like attacking another man physically, it is true *both* that it is the wrong thing to do and that others are entitled to stop it, by demand, if not by force. It is therefore natural to say that someone has a right when we mean to deny *either* of these consequences, as well as when we mean to deny both.

distinction is obscured by the troublesome idea of a right to conscience; this idea has been at the center of most recent discussions of political obligation, but it is a red herring drawing us away from the crucial political questions. The state of a man's conscience may be decisive, or central, when the issue is whether he does something morally wrong in breaking the law; but it need not be decisive or even central when the issue is whether he has a right, in the strong sense of that term, to do so. A man does not have the right, in that sense, to do whatever his conscience demands, but he may have the right, in that sense, to do something even though his conscience does not demand it.

If that is true, then there has been almost no serious attempt to answer the questions that almost everyone means to ask. We can make a fresh start by stating these questions more clearly. Does an American ever have the right, in a strong sense, to do something which is against the law? If so, when? In order to answer these questions put in that way, we must try to become clearer about the implications of the idea, mentioned earlier, that citizens have at least some rights against their government.

I said that in the United States citizens are supposed to have certain fundamental rights against their government, certain moral rights made into legal rights by the Constitution. If this idea is significant, and worth bragging about, then these rights must be rights in the strong sense I just described. The claim that citizens have a right to free speech must imply that it would be wrong for the government to stop them from speaking, even when the government believes that what they will say will cause more harm than good. The claim cannot mean, on the prisoner-of-war analogy, only that citizens do no wrong in speaking their minds, though the government reserves the right to prevent them from doing so.

This is a crucial point, and I want to labor it. Of course a responsible government must be ready to justify anything it does, particularly when it limits the liberty of its citizens. But normally it is a sufficient justification, even for an act that limits liberty, that the act is calculated to increase what the philosophers call general utility—that it is calculated to produce more over-all benefit than harm. So, though the New York City government needs a justification for forbidding motorists to drive up Lexington Avenue, it is sufficient justification if the proper officials believe, on sound evidence, that the gain to the many will outweigh the inconvenience to the few. When individual citizens are said to have rights against the government, however, like the right of free speech, that must mean that this sort of justification is not enough. Otherwise the claim would not argue that individuals have special protection against the law when their rights are in play, and that is just the point of the claim.

Not all legal rights, or even Constitutional rights, represent moral rights against the government. I now have the legal right to drive either way on Fifty-seventh Street, but the government would do no wrong to make that street one-way, if it thought it in the general interest to do so. I have a Constitutional right to vote for a congressman every two years, but the national and state governments would do no wrong if, following the amendment procedure, they made a congressman's term four years instead of two, again on the basis of a judgment that this would be for the general good.

But those Constitutional rights that we call fundamental, like the right of free speech, are supposed to represent rights against the government in the strong sense; that is the point of the boast that our legal system respects the fundamental rights of the citizen. If citizens have a moral right of free speech, then governments would do wrong to repeal the First Amendment that guarantees it, even if they were persuaded that the majority would be better off if speech were curtailed.

I must not overstate the point. Someone who claims that citizens have a right against the government need not go so far as to say that the state is *never* justified in overriding that right. He might say, for example, that although citizens have a right to free speech, the government may override that right when necessary to protect the rights of others, or to prevent a catastrophe, or even to obtain a clear and major public benefit (though if he acknowledged this last as a possible justification, he would be treating the right in question as not among the most important or fundamental). What he cannot do is to say that the government is justified in overriding a right on the minimal grounds that would be sufficient if

no such right existed. He cannot say that the government is entitled to act on no more than a judgment that its act is likely to
produce, overall, a benefit to the community. That admission would
make his claim of a right pointless, and would show him to be
using some sense of "right" other than the strong sense necessary
to give his claim the political importance it is normally taken to
have.

But then the answers to our two questions about disobedience
seem plain, if unorthodox. In our society a man does sometimes
have the right, in the strong sense, to disobey a law. He has that
right whenever that law wrongly invades his rights against the government. If he has a moral right to free speech, that is, then he has
a moral right to break any law that the government, by virtue of
his right, had no right to adopt. The right to disobey the law is
not a separate right, having something to do with conscience, additional to other rights against the government. It is simply a feature of these rights against the government, and it cannot be denied
in principle without denying that any such rights exist.

These answers seem obvious once we take rights against the
government in the strong sense I described. If I have a right to
speak my mind on political issues, then the government does wrong
to make it illegal for me to do so, even if it thinks this is in the
general interest. If, nevertheless, the government does make my
act illegal, then it does a further wrong to enforce that law against
me. My right against the government means that it is wrong for the
government to stop me from speaking; the government cannot make
it right to stop me just by taking the first step.

This does not, of course, tell us exactly what rights men do have
against the government. It does not tell us whether the right of free
speech includes the right of demonstration. But it does mean that
passing a law cannot affect such rights as men do have, and that
is of crucial importance, because it dictates the attitude that an individual is entitled to take toward his personal decision when civil
disobedience is in question. Both conservatives and liberals suppose
that in a society which is generally decent everyone has a duty to
obey the law, whatever it is. That is the source of the "general
duty" clause in the orthodox position, and though liberals believe

that his duty can sometimes be "overridden," even they suppose, as the orthodox position maintains, that the duty of obedience remains in some submerged form, so that a man does well to accept punishment in recognition of that duty. But this general duty is almost incoherent in a society that recognizes rights. If a man believes he has a right to demonstrate, then he must believe that it would be wrong for the government to stop him, with or without benefit of a law. If he is entitled to believe that, then it is silly to speak of a duty to obey the law as such, or of a duty to accept the punishment that the state has no right to give.

Conservatives will object to the short work I have made of their point. They will argue that even if the government was wrong to adopt some law, like a law limiting speech, there are independent reasons why the government is justified in enforcing the law once adopted. When the law forbids demonstration, then, so they argue, some principle more important than the individual's right to speak is brought into play; namely, the principle of respect for law. If a law, even a bad law, is left unenforced, then respect for law is weakened, and society as a whole suffers. So an individual loses his moral right to speak when speech is made criminal, and the government must, for the common good and for the general benefit, enforce the law against him.

But this argument, though popular, is plausible only if we forget what it means to say that an individual has a right against the state. It is far from plain that civil disobedience lowers respect for law, but even if we suppose that it does, this fact is irrelevant. The prospect of utilitarian gains cannot justify preventing a man from doing what he has a right to do, and the supposed gains in respect for law are simply utilitarian gains. There would be no point in the boast that we respect individual rights unless that involved some sacrifice, and the sacrifice in question must be that we give up whatever marginal benefits our country would receive from overriding these rights when they prove inconvenient. So the general benefit cannot be a good ground for abridging rights, even when the benefit in question is a heightened respect for law.

But perhaps I do wrong to assume that the argument about respect for law is only an appeal to general utility. I said that a state may be justified in overriding or limiting rights on other grounds, and we must ask, before rejecting the conservative position, whether any of these apply. The most important—and least well understood—of these other grounds invokes the notion of *competing rights* that would be jeopardized if the right in question were not limited. Citizens have personal rights to the state's protection as well as personal rights to be free from the state's interference, and it may be necessary for the government to choose between these two sorts of rights. The law of defamation, for example, limits the personal right of any man to say what he thinks, because it requires him to have good grounds for what he says. But this law is justified, even for those who think that it does invade a personal right, by the fact that it protects the right of others not to have their reputations ruined by a careless statement. The individual rights that our society acknowledges often conflict in this way, and when they do it is the job of government to discriminate. If the government makes the right choice, and protects the more important at the cost of the less, then it has not weakened or cheapened the notion of a right; on the contrary, it would have done so had it failed to protect the more imporant of the two. So we must acknowledge that the government has a reason for limiting rights if it plausibly believes that a competing right is more important.

May the conservative seize on this fact? He might argue that I did wrong to characterize his argument as one that appeals to the general benefit, because it appeals instead to competing rights; namely, the moral right of the majority to have its laws enforced or the right of society to maintain the degree of order and security it wishes. These are the rights, he would say, that must be weighed against the individual's right to do what the wrongful law prohibits.

But this argument is confused, because it depends on yet another ambiguity in the language of rights. It is true that we speak of the "right" of society to do what it wants, but this cannot be a "competing right" of the sort that might justify the invasion of a right against the government. The existence of rights against the government would be jeopardized if the government were able to defeat such a right by appealing to the right of a democratic majority to work its will. A right against the government must be a right to do something even when the majority thinks it would be wrong to do it, and even when the majority would be worse off for having it done. If we now say that society has a right to do whatever is in the general benefit, or the right to preserve whatever sort of environment the majority wishes to live in—and we mean that these are the sort of rights that provide justification for overruling any rights against the government that may conflict—then we have annihilated the latter rights.

In order to save them, we must recognize as competing rights only the rights of other members of the society as individuals. We must distinguish the "rights" of the majority as such, which cannot count as a justification for overruling individual rights, and the personal rights of members of a majority, which might well count. The test we must use is this. Someone has a competing right to protection, which must be weighed against an individual right to act, if that person would be entitled to demand that protection from his government on his own title, as an individual, without regard to whether a majority of his fellow citizens joined in the demand.

It cannot be true, on this test, that anyone has a right to have all the laws of the nation enforced. He has a right to have enforced only those criminal laws that he would have a right to have enacted if they were not already law. The laws against personal assault may well fall into that class. If the physically vulnerable members of the community—those who need police protection against personal violence—were only a small minority, it would still seem plausible to say that they were entitled to that protection. But the laws that provide a certain level of quiet in public places, or that authorize and finance a foreign war, cannot be thought to rest on individual rights. The timid lady on the streets of Chicago is not entitled to just the degree of quiet that now obtains, nor is she entitled to have boys drafted to fight in wars she approves. There are laws—perhaps desirable laws—that provide these advantages for her, but the justification for these laws, if they can be justified at all, is the common desire of a large majority, not her personal right. If, therefore, these laws do abridge someone else's moral right to protest, or his right to personal security, she cannot urge a competing right to justify the abridgment. She has no personal right to have such laws passed, and she has no competing right to have them enforced either.

So the conservative cannot advance his argument much on the ground of competing rights, but he may want to use another ground. A government, he may argue, may be justified in abridging the personal rights of its citizens in an emergency, or when a very great loss may be prevented, or perhaps when some major benefit may clearly be secured. If the nation is at war, a policy of censorship may be justified even though it invades the right to say what one thinks on matters of political controversy. But the emergency must be genuine. There must be what Oliver Wendell Holmes described as a clear and present danger, and the danger must be one of magnitude.

Can the conservative argue that when any law is passed, even a wrongful law, this sort of justification is available for enforcing it? His argument might be something of this sort. If the government once acknowledges that it may be wrong—that the legislature might have adopted, the executive approved, and the courts left standing a law that in fact abridges important rights—then this admission will lead not simply to a marginal decline in respect for law, but to a crisis of order. Citizens may decide to obey only those laws they personally approve, and that is anarchy. So the government must insist that whatever a citizen's rights may be before a law is passed and upheld by the courts, his rights thereafter are determined by that law.

But this argument ignores the primitive distinction between what may happen and what will happen. If we allow speculation to support the justification of emergency or decisive benefit, then, again, we have annihilated rights. We must, as Learned Hand said, discount the gravity of the evil threatened by the likelihood of reaching that evil. I know of no genuine evidence to the effect that tolerating some civil disobedience, out of respect for the moral position of its authors, will increase such disobedience, let alone crime in general. The case that it will must be based on vague assumptions about the contagion of ordinary crimes, assumptions that are themselves unproved, and that are in any event largely irrelevant. It seems at least as plausible to argue that tolerance will increase respect for officials and for the bulk of the laws they promulgate, or at least retard the rate of growing disrespect.

If the issue were simply the question whether the community would be marginally better off under strict law enforcement, then the government would have to decide on the evidence we have, and it might not be unreasonable to decide, on balance, that it would. But since rights are at stake, the issue is the very different one of whether tolerance would destroy the community or threaten it with great harm, and it seems to me simply mindless to suppose that the evidence makes that probable or even conceivable.

The argument from emergency is confused in another way as well. It assumes that the government must take the position either that a man never has the right to break the law, or that he always does. I said that any society that claims to recognize rights at all must abandon the notion of a general duty to obey the law that holds in all cases. This is important, because it shows that there are no shortcuts to meeting a citizen's claim of right. If a citizen argues that he has a moral right not to serve in the army, or to protest in a way he finds effective, then an official who wants to answer him, and not simply bludgeon him into obedience, must respond to the particular points he makes, and cannot point to the draft law or a Supreme Court decision as having even special, let alone decisive, weight. Sometimes an official who considers the citizen's moral arguments in good faith will be persuaded that the citizen's claim is plausible, or even right. It does not follow, however, that he will always be persuaded or that he always should be.

I must emphasize that all these propositions concern the strong sense of right, and they therefore leave open important questions about the right to do so. If a man believes he has the right to break the law, he must then ask whether he does the right thing to exercise that right. He must remember that reasonable men can differ about whether he has a right against the government, and therefore a right to break the law, that he thinks he has; and therefore that reasonable men can oppose him in good faith. He must take into account the various consequences his acts will have, whether they involve violence, and such other considerations as the context makes relevant. He must not go beyond the rights he can in good faith claim to acts that violate the rights of others. On the other hand, if some official, like a prosecutor, believes that the citizen does *not* have the right to break the law, then *he* must ask whether he does the right thing to enforce it. In the article I mentioned earlier, I argued that certain features of our legal system, and in particular the fusion of legal and moral issues in our Constitution, mean that citizens often do the right thing in exercising what they take to be moral rights to break the law, and that prosecutors often do the right thing in failing to prosecute them for it. I will not repeat those arguments here; instead I want to ask whether the requirement that government take its citizens' rights seriously has anything to do with the crucial question of what these rights are.

III

The argument so far has been hypothetical: If a man has a particular moral right against the government, that right survives contrary legislation or adjudication. But this does not tell us what rights he has, and it is notorious that reasonable men disagree about that. There is wide agreement on certain clearcut cases. Almost everyone who believes in rights at all would admit, for example, that a man has a moral right to speak his mind in a non-provocative way on matters of political concern, and that this is an important right, that the state must go to great pains to protect. But there is great controversy as to the limits of such paradigm rights, and the so-called "anti-riot" law involved in the Chicago Seven trial is a case in point.

The defendants were accused of conspiring to cross state lines with the intention of causing a riot. This charge is vague—perhaps unconstitutionally vague—but the law apparently defines as criminal emotional speeches which argue that violence is justified in order to secure political equality. Does the right of free speech protect this sort of speech? That, of course, is a legal issue, because it invokes the free-speech clause of the First Amendment of the Constitution. But it is also a moral issue, because, as I said, we must treat the First Amendment as an attempt to protect a moral right. It is part of the job of governing to "define" moral rights through statutes and judicial decisions; that is, to declare officially the extent that moral rights will be taken to have in law. Congress faced this task in voting on the anti-riot bill, and the Supreme Court will face it if the Chicago Seven case goes that far. How should the different departments of government go about defining moral rights?

They should begin with a sense that whatever they decide might be wrong. History and their descendants may judge that they acted unjustly when they thought they were right. If they take their duty seriously, they must try to limit their mistakes, and they must therefore try to discover where the dangers of mistake lie.

They might choose one of two very different models for this purpose. The first model recommends striking a balance between the rights of the individual and the demands of society at large. If the government *infringes* a moral right (for example, by defining the right of free speech more narrowly than justice requires), then it has done the individual a wrong. On the other hand, if the government *inflates* a right (by defining it more broadly than justice requires), then it cheats society of some general benefit, like safe streets, that it is perfectly entitled to have. So a mistake on one side is as serious as a mistake on the other. The course of government is to steer to the middle, to balance the general good and personal rights, giving to each its due.

When the government, or any branch, defines a right, it must bear in mind, according to the first model, the social cost of different proposals and make the necessary adjustments. It must not grant the same freedom to noisy demonstrations as it grants to calm political discussion, for example, because the former causes much more trouble than the latter. Once it decides how much of a right to recognize, it must enforce its decision to the full. That means permitting an individual to act within his rights, as the government has defined them, but not beyond, so that if anyone breaks the law, even on grounds of conscience, he must be punished. No doubt any government will make mistakes, and will regret decisions once taken. That is inevitable. But this middle policy will ensure that errors on one side will balance out errors on the other over the long run.

The first model, described in this way, has great plausibility, and most laymen and lawyers, I think, would respond to it warmly. The metaphor of balancing the public interest against personal claims is established in our political and judicial rhetoric, and this metaphor gives the model both familiarity and appeal. Nevertheless, the first model is a false one, certainly in the case of rights generally regarded as important, and the metaphor is the heart of its error.

The institution of rights against the government is not a gift of God, or an ancient ritual, or a national sport. It is a complex and troublesome practice that makes the government's job of securing the general benefit more difficult and more expensive, and it would be a frivolous and wrongful practice unless it served some point. Anyone who professes to take rights seriously, and who praises our government for respecting them, must have some sense of what that point is. He must accept, at the minimum, one or both of two important ideas. The first is the vague but powerful idea of human dignity. This idea, associated with Kant, but defended by philosophers of different schools, supposes that there are ways of treating a man that are inconsistent with recognizing him as a full member of the human community, and holds that such treatment is profoundly unjust. The second is the more familiar idea of political equality. This supposes that the weaker members of a political community are entitled to the same concern and respect of their government as the more powerful members have secured for themselves, so that if some men have freedom of decision, whatever the effect on the general good, then all men must have the same freedom. I do not want to defend or elaborate these ideas here, but only to insist that anyone who claims that citizens have rights must accept ideas very close to these.[1] It makes sense to say that a man has a fundamental right against the government, in the strong sense,

---

[1] He need not consider these ideas to be axiomatic. He may, that is, have reasons for insisting that dignity or equality are important values, and these reasons may be utilitarian. He may believe, for example, that the general good will be advanced, *in the long run,* only if we treat indignity or inequality as very great injustices, and never allow our *opinions* about the general good to justify them. I do not know of any good arguments for or against this sort of "institutional" utilitarianism, but it is consistent with my point, because it argues that we must treat violations of dignity and equality as special moral crimes, beyond the reach of ordinary utilitarian justification.

like free speech, if that right is necessary to protect his dignity, or his standing as equally entitled to concern and respect, or some other personal value of like consequence. It does not make sense otherwise.

So if rights make sense at all, then the invasion of a right must be a very serious matter. It means treating a man as less than a man, or as less worthy of concern than other men. The institution of rights rests on the conviction that this is a grave injustice, and that it is worth paying the incremental cost in social policy or efficiency that is necessary to prevent it. But then it must be wrong to say that inflating rights is as serious as invading them. If the government errs on the side of the individual, then it simply pays a little more in social efficiency than it has to pay; it pays a little more, that is, of the same coin that it has already decided must be spent. But if it errs against the individual, it inflicts an insult upon him that, on its own reckoning, it is worth a great deal of that coin to avoid.

So the first model is indefensible. It rests, in fact, on a mistake I discussed earlier; namely, the confusion of society's rights with the rights of members of society. "Balancing" is appropriate when the government must choose between competing claims of right; between the southerner's claim to freedom of association, for example, and the black man's claim to an equal education. Then the government can do nothing but estimate the merits of the competing claims, and act on its estimate. The first model assumes that the "right" of the majority is a competing right that must be balanced in this way; but that, as I argued before, is a confusion that threatens to destroy the concept of individual rights. It is worth noticing that the community rejects the first model in that area where the stakes for the individual are highest, the criminal process. We say that it is better that a great many guilty men go free than that one innocent man be punished, and that homily rests on the choice of the second model for government.

The second model treats abridging a right as much more serious than inflating one, and its recommendations follow from that judgment. It stipulates that once a right is recognized in clearcut cases, then the government should act to cut off that right only when some compelling reason is presented, some reason that is consistent with the suppositions on which the original right must be based. It cannot be an argument for curtailing a right, once granted, simply that society would pay a further price in extending it. There must be something special about that further cost, or there must be some other feature of the case, that makes it sensible to say that although great social cost is warranted to protect the original right, this particular cost is not necessary. Otherwise, the government's failure to extend the right will show that its recognition of the right in the original case is a sham, a promise that it intends to keep only until that becomes inconvenient.

How can we show that a particular cost is not worth paying without taking back the initial recognition of a right? I can think of only three sorts of grounds that can consistently be used to limit the definition of a particular right. First, the government might show that the values protected by the original right are not really at stake in the marginal case, or are at stake only in some attenuated form. Second, it might show that if the right is defined to include the marginal case, then some competing right, in the strong sense I described earlier, would be abridged. Third, it might show that if the right were so defined, then the cost to society would not be simply incremental but would be of a degree far beyond the cost paid to grant the original right, a degree great enough to justify whatever assault on dignity or equality might be involved.

It is fairly easy to apply these grounds to one problem the Supreme Court has recently faced, and must face soon again. The draft law provides an exemption for conscientious objectors, but this exemption, as interpreted by the draft boards, has been limited to those who object to *all* wars on *religious* grounds. If we suppose that the exemption is justified on the ground that an individual has a moral right not to kill in violation of his own principles, then the question is raised whether it is proper to exclude those whose morality is not based on religion, or whose morality is sufficiently complex to distinguish among wars. The Court has held that the draft boards are wrong to exclude the former, and it will soon be asked to decide whether it is wrong to exclude the latter as well.

None of the three grounds I listed can justify either of these exclusions. The invasion of personality in forcing men to kill when they believe killing immoral is just as great when these beliefs are based on secular grounds, or take account of the fact that wars differ in morally relevant ways, and there is no pertinent difference in competing rights or in national emergency. There are differences among the cases, of course, but they are insufficient to justify the distinction. A government that is secular on principal cannot prefer a religious to a nonreligious morality as such. There are utilitarian arguments in favor of limiting the exemption to religious or universal grounds—an exemption so limited may be less expensive to administer, and may allow easier discrimination between sincere and insincere applicants. But these utilitarian reasons are irrelevant, because they cannot count as grounds for limiting a right.

What about the anti-riot law as applied in the Chicago trial? Does that law represent an improper limitation of the right to free speech, supposedly protected by the First Amendment? If we were to apply the first model for government to this issue, the argument for the anti-riot law would look strong. But if we set aside talk of balancing as inappropriate, and turn to the proper grounds for limiting a right, then the argument becomes a great deal weaker. The original right of free speech must suppose that it is an assault on human personality to stop a man from expressing what he honestly believes, particularly on issues affecting how he is governed. Surely the assault is greater, and not less, when he is stopped from expressing those principles of political morality that he holds most passionately, in the face of what he takes to be outrageous violations of these principles. It may be said that the anti-riot law leaves him free to express these principles in a non-provocative way. But that misses the point of the connection between expression and dignity. A man cannot express himself freely when he cannot match his rhetoric to his outrage, or when he must trim his sails to protect values he counts as nothing next to those he is trying to vindicate. It is true that some political dissenters speak in ways that shock the majority, but it is arrogant for the majority to suppose that the orthodox methods of expression are the proper ways to speak, for this is a denial of equal concern and respect. If the point of the right is to protect the dignity of dissenters, then we must make judgments about appropriate speech with the personality of the dissenters in mind, not the personality of the "silent" majority for whom the anti-riot law is no restraint at all.

So the argument that the personal values protected by the original right are less at stake in this marginal case fails. We must consider whether competing rights, or some grave threat to society, nevertheless justify the anti-riot law. We can consider these two grounds together, because the only plausible competing rights are rights to be free from violence, and violence is the only plausible threat to society that the context provides.

I have no right to burn your house, or stone you or your car, or swing a bicycle chain against your skull, even if I find these natural means of expression. But the defendants in the Chicago trial were not accused of direct violence; the argument runs that the acts of speech they planned made it likely that others would do acts of violence, either in support of or out of hostility to what they said. Does this provide a justification?

The question would be different if we could say with any confidence how much and what sort of violence the anti-riot law might be expected to prevent. Will it save two lives a year, or two hundred, or two thousand? Two thousand dollars' worth of property, or two hundred thousand, or two million? No one can say, not simply because prediction is next to impossible, but because we have no firm understanding of the process whereby demonstration disintegrates into riot, and in particular of the part played by inflammatory speech, as distinct from poverty, police brutality, blood lust, and all the rest of human and economic failure. The government must try, of course, to reduce the violent waste of lives and property, but it must recognize that any attempt to locate and remove a cause of riot, short of a reorganization of society, must be an exercise in speculation, trial and error. It must make its decisions under conditions of high uncertainty, and the institution of rights, taken seriously, limits its freedom to experiment under such conditions.

It forces the government to bear in mind that preventing a man from speaking or demonstrating offers him a certain and profound insult, in return for a speculative benefit that may in any event be achieved in other if more expensive ways. When lawyers say that rights may be limited to protect other rights, or to prevent catastrophe, they have in mind cases in which cause and effect are relatively clear, like the familiar example of a man falsely crying "Fire" in a crowded theater. But the Chicago story shows how obscure the causal connections can become. Were the speeches of Hoffman or Rubin necessary conditions of the riot? Or had thousands of people come to Chicago for the purpose of rioting anyway, as the government also argues? Were they in any case sufficient conditions? Or could the police have contained the violence if they had not been so busy contributing to it, as the staff of the President's Commission on Violence said they were? These are not easy questions, but if rights mean anything, then the government cannot simply assume answers that justify its conduct. If a man has a right to speak, if the reasons that support that right extend to provocative political speech, and if the effects of such speech on violence are unclear, then the government is not entitled to make its first attack on that problem by denying that right. It may be that abridging the right to speak is the least expensive course, or the least damaging to police morale, or the most popular politically. But these are utilitarian arguments in favor of starting one place rather than another, and such arguments are ruled out by the concept of rights.

This point may be obscured by the popular belief that political activists look forward to violence and "ask for trouble" in what they say. They can hardly complain, in the general view, if they are taken to be the authors of the violence they expect, and treated accordingly. But this repeats the confusion I tried to explain earlier, between having a right and doing the right thing. The speaker's motives may be relevant in deciding whether he does the right thing in speaking passionately about issues that may inflame or enrage his audience. But if he has a right to speak, because the danger in allowing him to speak is speculative, his motives cannot count, as independent evidence, in the argument that justifies stopping him.

But what of the individual rights of those who will be destroyed by a riot, of the passerby who will be killed by a sniper's bullet, or the shopkeeper who will be ruined by looting? Putting the issue this way, in terms of competing rights, suggests a principle that would undercut the effect of uncertainty. Shall we say that some rights to protection are so important that the government is justified in doing all it can to maintain them? Shall we therefore say that the government may abridge the rights of others to act when their acts might simply increase the risk, by however slight or speculative a margin, that some person's rights to life or property will be violated?

Some such principle is relied on by those who oppose the Supreme Court's liberal rulings on police procedure. These rulings increase the chance that a guilty man will go free, and therefore marginally increase the risk that any particular member of the community will be murdered or raped or robbed. Some critics believe that the Court's decisions must therefore be wrong.

But no society that purports to recognize a variety of rights, on the ground that a man's dignity or equality may be invaded in a variety of ways, can accept such a principle. If forcing a man to testify against himself, or forbidding him to speak, does the damage that the rights against self-incrimination and the right of free speech assume, then it would be contemptuous for the state to tell a man that he must suffer this damage against the possibility that other men's risk of loss may be marginally reduced. If rights make sense, then the degrees of their importance cannot be so different that some count not at all when others are mentioned. Of course the government may discriminate and may stop a man from exercising his right to speak when there is a clear and substantial risk that his speech will do great damage to the person or property of others, and no other means of preventing this are at hand, as in the case of a man falsely shouting "Fire" in a theater. But we must reject the suggested principle that the government can ignore rights to speak when life and property are in question. So long as the impact of speech on these other rights remains speculative and marginal, it must look elsewhere for levers to pull.

IV

I said, at the beginning of this essay, that I wanted to show what a government must do that professes to recognize individual rights. It must dispense with the claim that citizens never have a right to break its law, and it must not define citizens' rights so that these are cut off for supposed reasons of the general good. The present government's policy toward civil disobedience, and its companion against vocal protest, its enforcement of the anti-riot law, may therefore be thought to count against its sincerity.

One might well ask, however, whether it is wise to take rights all that seriously after all. America's genius, at least in her own legend, lies in not taking any abstract doctrine to its logical extreme. It may be time to ignore abstractions, and concentrate instead on giving the majority of our citizens a new sense of their government's concern for their welfare, and of their title to rule.

That, in any event, is what the Vice-President seems to believe. In a policy statement on the issue of weirdoes and social misfits, he said that the liberals' concern for individual rights was a headwind blowing in the face of the ship of state. That is a poor metaphor, but the philosophical point it expresses is very well taken. He recognizes, as many liberals do not, that the majority cannot travel as fast or as far as it would like if it recognizes the rights of individuals to do what, in the majority's terms, is the wrong thing to do.

The Vice-President supposes that rights are divisive, and that national unity and a new respect for law may be developed by taking them more skeptically. But he is wrong. Our country will continue to be divided by its social and foreign policy, and if the economy grows weaker the divisions will become more bitter. If we want our laws and our legal institutions to provide the ground rules within which these issues will be contested, then these ground rules must not be the conqueror's law that the dominant class imposes on the weaker, as Marx supposed the law of a capitalist society must be. The bulk of the law—that part which defines and implements social, economic and foreign policy—cannot be neutral. It must state, in its greatest part, the majority's view of the common good. The institution of rights is therefore crucial, because it represents the majority's promise to the minorities that their dignity and equality will be respected. When the divisions among the groups are most violent, then this gesture, if law is to work, must be most sincere.

The institution requires an act of faith on the part of the minorities, because the scope of their rights will be controversial whenever they are important, and because the officers of the majority will act on their own notions of what these rights really are. Of course these officials will disagree with many of the claims that a minority makes. That makes it all the more important that they take their decisions gravely. They must show that they understand what rights are, and they must not cheat on the full implications of the doctrine. The government will not re-establish respect for law without giving the law some claim to respect. It cannot do that if it neglects the one feature that distinguishes law from ordered brutality, and makes that claim plausible. If the government does not take rights seriously, then it does not take law seriously either.

COMMENT
by Gidon Gottlieb

I

The most salient feature of recent forms of disobedience is the communal or group character of the phenomenon. This is the feature which requires emphasis most for an understanding of the rejection of law by important elements in our society.

Professor Ronald Dworkin continues, however, the analysis of this subject in the received tradition. He studies civil disobedience in the context of the relationship between the state and the individual. The individual's conscience is then characteristically pitted against the power of the state as when Socrates and Thoreau invoked their personal convictions in matters of great public moment. In the same spirit, Dworkin invokes the personal rights of individuals against their government and transposes some of our constitutional theories to the satisfying rhetoric of modern philosophical discourse. He would apparently side with Mr. Justice Black who rejects the "balancing" doctrine of the majority of the Supreme Court under which competing rights and values are weighed in a pragmatic fashion. He advocates instead "taking rights seriously"; that is, giving a preferred status to personal rights. He also argues for restraint in government prosecutions threatening to infringe upon them, for treading softly near the hallowed garden of these delicate rights. These are scarcely propositions with which I would quarrel. They are, however, somewhat remote from the causes, rhetoric, and justifications of contemporary practitioners of civil disobedience.

Much more than an individual moral problem, civil disobedience is now a societal and political phenomenon, an indicator of the disaffection of whole segments of our society, evidence of the rejection of the authority of the state. Dean Rostow is therefore quite right in perceiving the issue in terms of legitimacy, in terms of the acceptance of authority, in terms of what he calls a "society of consent." In such a society, "the powers of government are just . . . that is, they are legitimate, because authorized and renewed by procedures of voting all must respect." It is indeed the withdrawal of acceptance by powerful groups that now threatens faith in law (I prefer "acceptance" to the somewhat more mythical concept of "consent"). But on this point, a major source of confusion must be avoided: The withdrawal of acceptance of state authority is not tantamount to an assertion of the right to revolution. The withdrawal of acceptance may only be a strategic device for a restoration of legitimate rule by vigorous dissent, by protest, by resistance, or even by rebellion. It may, however, admittedly also pave the way for a complete take-over and transformation of state authority structures fully deserving the name of revolution. Not all group resistance is therefore revolutionary—quite the contrary. Some such resistance may be designed to realize the full promise of accepted constitutional texts and political pledges. All group resistance does, however, stimulate confrontation, social tensions, backlashes, and raises the threat of reaction and repression. Violent dissent, uprisings, and limited sporadic civil strife are evil genies that are hard to control once released from the body politic, but they should not be confused with the specter of revolution. Indeed, it is by no means clear that in an advanced society such as ours revolution is at all possible. What has been called the advent of the "technetronic age" could well render revolutions obsolete. Securing physical control of power centers such as communications facilities and transportation networks is a manageable task in many countries—as colonels thinking of military coups know well. But in our highly computerized society with its intricate technology and diffusion of power centers not much can be achieved by raw power alone—save, that is, the paralysis and the terrorization of the population. The dictates of long-term corporate planning, of capital management, of orderly administration, of demand control, and of technocratic manpower have been vividly and provocatively portrayed in Galbraith's *New Industrial State* and in Marcuse's *One-Dimensional Man*. While the delicate apparatus of modern power, communication and information systems is a helpless hostage to violent minorities, it remains nevertheless immune to control by revolutionary cliques of any kind. Unless, that is, the full weight of modern surveillance and repressive technologies is brought to bear by a ruthless bureaucratic and technological elite in a fully totalitarian regime along the lines of Orwell's *1984,* the feasibility of which we still mercifully have not discovered.

Having thus summarily disposed of the specter of revolution, I would like to return to the question of civil disobedience, or what should be more aptly called group disobedience or group resistance. The groups challenging the state's authority in our society are characterized by their ability to inflict severe civil disorder, to tear society apart, and to bring it to a near standstill. Black militants, student radicals, white supremacists, rebellious labor unions, militant police forces and national guardsmen, as well as other extremist groups, all have the power to bring the nation to the edge of civil strife if not beyond. None of them, either singly or in combination, could conceivably operate the vast and intricate administrative-technetronic machinery of the modern industrial state. Yet all of them have acquired in a sense a *"veto"* over the *status quo,* a power to bring business-as-usual to a stop, a power to make other groups painfully aware of a *status quo* they reject. This is a very real kind of power, for it does endow these groups with a measure of capability to gain their ends over the opposition of other centers of power—even, at times, over the opposition of a disorganized majority.

To put the matter differently, the business of the nation cannot be harmoniously conducted without a measure of consensus embracing these *"veto-communities."* This sets a serious limitation on the effectiveness of majority rule and one that should be borne carefully in mind by designers of a Southern Strategy or of any other strategy consciously intended to neglect a relevant community of the nation. It is a limitation bound to gain significance as administrations seek to legitimize policies in opinion polls that do not reflect the vehemence of veto-community attitudes. It is a limitation that new technology will make even more significant. The possible onset of direct, computerized television-audience-polling on national or local issues requires that such limitations on the workability of majority rule be restudied and that the pitfalls of government by referendum be kept clearly in mind.

It should be fairly plain that veto-communities cannot be effectively repressed by the state without a substantial transformation in our system of government. The first chilling symptoms of such modification are already manifest. Effective repression would require a measure of suspension of our cherished civil liberties, invasions of privacy with the help of electronic spying devices, police surveillance of dissenters, centralized and computerized data banks of information on every citizen, preventive detention of agitators, control of the media especially of television and its news coverage, the intimidation of universities, and financial pressures on educational and research foundations engaged in social and political concerns, as well as occasional bloodbaths to discourage public confrontations.

Effective repression, in other words, would take us down the road toward a dreaded fully administered bureaucratic-technological-authoritarian state in which not only probing investigations and unorthodox ideas but also deviant life-styles would be heavily penalized. The veto-communities of the nation wield power therefore not only over the *status quo* but also on the quality and character of our system of government. They have become in the process important instrumentalities for change, and not always for the good. Ironically, not even the reactionary veto-communities can protect the *status quo*. The very resort to violent clashes, to brutality, and to reprisals, to which some police and labor elements are increasingly prone, merely fans the fires of civil disorder and the anguish of the majority. They, no less than the advocates of change, thus pave the way either to social change or to repressive rule but in no case to the maintenance of the *status quo*.

Government dependent on a tacit concert of veto-communities is an ugly prospect for our political future. It suggests that our domestic order increasingly resembles the unquiet and threatening world of international relations. These semiautonomous communities—autonomous, that is, in a sociological and not in a legal sense—now reject majority rule in the country. Their expectations and demands are legitimated in their own groups' perceptions—not in community acceptance of their demands. They are prepared to hold the nation to ransom to achieve their objectives. Already, in the wake of the Newark riots in 1967, the mayor of that city sought to restore peace by obtaining the collaboration of his city's veto-communities: the white militants, the black militants and the police. With the spread of veto-communities on the national and local levels, realistic strategies taking this phenomenon into account must be designed for securing compliance with the law. Student disruptions on campuses have thus led some university administrators to adopt a delicate balance between policies of conciliation and of enforcement. University presidents, not unlike United Nations diplomats, are frequently divided between resort to "Chapter VI" procedures for peaceful settlement and "Chapter VII" procedures for enforcement actions. Indeed the similarities between key stages in the crisis at Columbia and, for example, the 1956 crisis in the Middle East are not fortuitous. In both places, accommodation and enforcement strategies were tried out and peace-keeping forces established. In both places the conflict involved large and powerful groups in the context in which they operated.

Spreading doubts about the feasibility of law enforcement against veto-communities are leading to second thoughts about coercive peace-enforcement strategies both domestically and internationally. Accommodation between hostile communities and the maintenance of some form of peaceful coexistence appear increasingly attractive as against the exorbitant societal and political costs of strict law enforcement.

II

The trouble with our legal order is that it is utterly unprepared to respond to the political and societal developments that have already taken place. Expectations about law and order, about the enforcement of laws, about punishment, about hierarchical authority structures, about the state as the alleged repository of a monopoly of power, about the expression of consent through elections, about the illegitimacy of resistance to validly elected authorities, about the shared values or "concordia" of society—all these expectations are being challenged. All require reassessment in light of group resistance. They must all be looked at again in light of the widening distribution of power between communities and groups within the state. For what has happened is not only the actual erosion of the state's monopoly of power but also the widespread realization that such loss of power has taken place. Nothing has done more than television to bring home the horrors and uselessness of violence and repression. From Khesan, to Chicago, to Kent, to Berkeley, and to Jackson, the failure of coercion was made apparent to millions of viewers. Unchecked riots were followed by unchecked illegal labor strikes. Sanitation men, transportation workers, policemen, teachers, firemen, and postal workers all joined the parade of lawbreakers. They were all put in that position by unenforceable legislation prohibiting strikes of public employees, which did not provide effective procedures to meet labor claims. The disappointment of expectations resulting from the failure to enforce the laws spread even more in the wake of the black riots in which the police stood by while businesses were looted and property was destroyed. The belief accordingly grew that the law did not matter as much as those who occupied the seat of power. It may have had something to do with the rise of confrontations aimed at the "power structure," with the pitting of power against power, of black power against white racism, and of student power against police power. Law and its enforcement became a paper tiger. Staggering crime statistics, corruption in the police and in local government, corporate frauds, the immunity of organized crime, the mounting evidence of lawlessness at all levels of society, massive drug addiction problems—all these merely compound the evident failure of coercive action rendered so obvious in confrontations with the veto-communities.

These phenomena can perhaps be given some degree of ordered expression on the more arid plane of analytic discourse. Governing elites, the legal profession, and the "man on the Queens subway" share a fairly uniform implicit theory of law. That theory of law received its classical exposition in the writings of John Austin in the nineteenth century. It was strongly anchored in a Hobbesian view, in a hierarchical conception of the state, is the relationship between a political sovereign and political subordinates, in a relationship of authority and obedience. The pyramidal concept of state power made it possible to ground the law in the capability to inflict sanctions. The close conceptual ties between law and sanctions is still the basis of the implicit theory of law of our society. For law without penalty, law without credible sanctions—international law, for example—is still taken lightly by a legal profession reluctant to revise inherited modes of thought and expectations.

The emergence in this century of new centers of power in a position to compete with the power of the state has radically altered the political realities in which the vertical, pyramidal, sanction-oriented concept of law originally evolved. But the stubborn refusal to alter conceptual expectations in the face of contrary social trends continues. It received perhaps its purest expression in Hans Kelsen's *Principles of International Law* in which he postulated a monopoly of coercive forces in a nonexistent world order in which international enforcement actions would sanction breaches of international law. Though the necessary connections between a legal system and its societal context are now gaining increasing recognition, legal theory is still largely dominated by the nation-state model allegedly endowed with a monopoly of coercive power. In international law studies, however, concern with legal arrangements in horizontal or non-hierarchical systems between fairly equal centers of power has led to the growth of new theories, but these studies have as yet scarcely penetrated the mainstream of juridical consciousness.

In speaking of the "death of law" we should make the identity of the patient no less clear than the fatal diagnosis itself. What is dying, I would submit, is a concept of law peculiar to a vanishing society, to a hierarchically organized society, relying upon the state's omnipotence against isolated, relatively helpless individuals. What is dying is a set of expectations accompanying the simple vision of law as superior power. What is dying is the pretense of enforcement in the face of an unbridgeable credibility gap. *What is also dying is the faith that democracy can rely on the consent of individuals alone, paying no heed to the acceptance of authority by distinct communities and by groups.*

Much of what is now perceived as the pathology of a decaying legal order may soon be perceived as the emergence of a new concept of law. This new concept would set realistic expectations for an increasingly egalitarian system of power relationships between semiautonomous communities and the state. Such a system may look to accommodation rather than to sanctions in group conflicts; it may look to a consensus about accepted principles and policies—accepted, that is, by all relevant communities including the veto-communities. It may look to mediation, collective bargaining, negotiations, and to new imaginative settlement procedures. An *acceptance-oriented concept of law* may gradually displace the now unworkable sanction-oriented model at least insofar as veto-communities are concerned. The traditional, hierarchical concept of law, freed of its burden of failure, may then operate more effectively in the sphere that is properly its own: where the society and the individual—not groups—are involved. Admittedly, the emergence of a new concept of law might raise formidable new problems on a practical as well as on an analytic plane. Yet the shape of the new concept is already discernible in horizontalist legal theories. The erosion of monolithic national authority structures, the proliferation of domestic power centers and of multinational corporations and agencies are all factors contributing to the cracking of outworn expectations.

Confusion about the nature of the legal order tragically obscures urgent new institutional arrangements. Peaceful settlement techniques in collective strife situations are now exposed to the hazards of local politics and prejudices. Conflict *control* mechanisms are almost nonexistent—use of the police and of the National Guard in civil disorders constitutes in itself a source of such disorders. The absence of peace-keeping—as distinct from law-enforcement instrumentalities for conflict control—has left the field open for the escalation of violence. The two functions of law enforcement and of peace-keeping cannot be performed by the same instrumentalities.

New legal arrangements are also needed where the poor, the blacks, and ethnic minorities are concerned. Effective grievance machinery for terminating the malignant neglect of millions of American poor has yet to be established. Legal doctrines recognizing the group consciousness and the *group rights* of American blacks are yet to be articulated. The development of "class actions" has not successfully met the acute needs for the juridical organization of students, the poor, slum dwellers, consumers, and other dissatisfied segments of the society. Indeed, problem clusters relating to veto-communities still go largely without legal recognition. The connections between racism, poverty, unemployment, urban decay, crime, and alienation still defy comprehensive *juridical* analysis. In vital respects, group rights lack effective legal vehicles for their defense. The law of unincorporated associations, labor law, certification and representation problems and class actions have all been resorted to in pressing for such rights. The law's coolness to group rights, its resistance to the growth of powerful organizations largely immune to state pressure, has been overcome in the past to permit the development of labor unions and of vast corporations and conglomerates. Churches, foundations and universities, together with business and labor, secured juridical forms for their activities. The question is whether the same will now be true for some of the veto-communities in our country.

III

No discussion of the "death of law" would be complete without reference to the black community. I would like to use this opportunity to raise some fresh concepts. Viewed from the blacks' perspective, the death of law is a misnomer. As far as they can see, it has never lived enough to die—it was stillborn. The promise of our most cherished legal and constitutional instruments was at no time fulfilled for the vast majority of black citizens. The apparatus of law appears to them as an oppressive enforcement system designed to protect neighboring white communities while abandoning black communities to their local violence and lawlessness. Remedial social, rent, rehabilitation, health, grant, and welfare legislation was in large measure defeated by profiteering bureaucracies and corrupt inspection and enforcement personnel. Despite the selfless devotion and courage of civil rights advocates, the attempt to bring the black population of the nation *as individuals* into the community of consent failed for the majority. The path outlined by the Fourteenth Amendment and followed with determination by the Warren Court was to provide an *individual* solution to black citizens as American citizens with their rights to the equal protection of the laws. The civil rights decisions and the attempted removal of racial barriers were among the noblest efforts in twentieth-century American history, but they still left the situation of the black community as a whole relatively intolerable. They certainly failed to bring black Americans into the community of consent from which they had been excluded when the Federation was established. Neither the black population nor the Indian nations were parties to the original social contract, and the attempt to recuperate them as individuals has failed for most of them. Militant elements in the black population—despite the rapid growth of a black middle class—have largely succeeded in establishing a veto-community which must now be brought into the social compact as one people.

The emancipation of the blacks as one people may demand that our legal structure grant recognition to the rights of "peoples" under our system of government. Claims about the cultural and linguistic rights of blacks are already advanced in the courts. Black power and Black Panther ideologies argue for collective black action and interests.

The concept of a distinct black people, all of whose members are American citizens, is one that could sadden some selfless enemies of racism—it is one nevertheless that would provide an emotional, conceptual, and juridical framework for approaching the problems of the black community as a whole without precluding the pursuit of individual solutions and of integration made possible by the Warren Court decisions. Community and racial relations might well be improved in the United States by the extension of juridical and institutional recognition to the separate rights and claims of the black, Indian, and Hispanic *peoples as such*. The unity of the nation and the equality of citizenship could be reinforced by an acceptance of the fact that this nation is made up of separate peoples, and that personal integration does not work for all. For many may indeed prefer to continue their association with the rest of the nation as a separate "people," endowed with group rights and duties of its own. *Nationality, citizenship, and peoplehood are not interchangeable concepts.*

As we near the bicentennial of the Declaration of Independence, fresh thought should be given to the fate of the black, Indian, and Hispanic peoples in this nation. The integration of immigrants into one nation, which characterized the first two centuries of independence, should now be followed by the acceptance of the black people, of the Indian people, and of the Hispanic people as equal partners in our national life. These peoples are now the suffering groups in this nation, every member of which is an equal citizen under the law but considers his group as a distinct people nevertheless. Where appropriate they should be entitled to reparations, restitution, to respect for their cultural rights, and to the development of institutions for the defense of their group rights. Such juridical developments would parallel the legal recognition of labor unions in the last century. But these legal changes would be meaningful only if accompanied by effective measures designed to meet the needs and to honor the rights of all our "national peoples." The alteration of expectations and the new machinery for social change that such juridical innovations may introduce could play a role in improving the fabric of our national life. Imaginative institutional and normative design on a large scale is now urgently required. Our law schools and universities should work on blueprints and models to house the fresh needs and expectations of the nation and to provide well-tooled machinery for conflict control and social change. Institutional and legal designing is now no less urgently needed than urban designing and housing for a rising population. It is needed if only to restore the reality of a society of consent, in which consent rests not merely on the participation of individuals and on procedures of voting but also on the acceptance of the authority of the state by all relevant communities.

IV

Finally, in considering the "death of the law," attention should be paid to the law killers, to the *legicides*. It can be fairly maintained that the entrenchment of dissatisfied veto-communities is not the only cause for the decline of the authority of the state and its legitimacy. Other factors directly attributable to the state itself do also come into play.

Claims for resistance to legitimate holders of authority have been founded on a number of alternative propositions. Significantly only a few express a demand for revolution or for a change in constitutional arrangements. Most of the claims are for a *jus resistendi* under a legitimate ruler. They complement the claims to revolution under a tyranny —that is, government without the consent of the governed—but must not otherwise be confused with revolutionary rhetoric. Claims to resist a legitimate ruler distinguish between his legitimacy as a ruler and the legitimacy of his policies and actions. For even the most legitimate ruler could conceivably commit acts abhorrent to the conscience of mankind or fail to perform the most necessary responsibilities of his office. Essentially, these claims fall under eight main headings:

1. On the right of the ruled to resist the ruler, if need be by means of violence, in case of any unlawful usurpation of power (under national law or international law) that is not met by effective checks from other branches of the government;

2. On the right of the ruled to resist the ruler when the laws of God or the dictates of morality so require;

3. On the right of the ruled to resist the ruler when fundamental human rights are not protected by the rule of law or when the basic needs of a community are callously neglected;

4. On the right of the ruled to resist the ruler when there is a general and drastic deterioration of legality or pervasive uncertainty about judicial neutrality and the legality of the ruler's own actions;

5. On the right of the ruled to resist the ruler in the absence of effective procedures for peaceful change or of an opportunity to participate in decisions substantially affecting his material interests;

6. On the right of the ruled to resist the ruler in the absence of a meaningful political choice between genuinely different policies;

7. On the right of the ruled to resist the ruler who breaks faith with the people by not honoring his pledges;

8. On the right of communities to resist the ruler and all other communities when their legitimate vital interests are threatened and when accommodation procedures have failed.

The legitimacy of these eight claims and the premises on which they rest need not detain us. What does matter is that they are widely entertained. A government that is indifferent to or careless of these claims cannot but weaken general respect for law and erode the foundations of its own legitimacy. When in addition that government fans the passions of the veto-communities and exacerbates the confrontation of groups, then the prospects for the free acceptance of government authority become dim indeed.

On these counts, the actions of our public officials could amount to culpable legicide. These bear detailing, for they illustrate the eight claims and provide a handy guidebook of grievances that frequently explode into civil disorders:

—the constitutionally unauthorized Presidential war in Indochina and the very questionable legality under international law of his prosecution of the war in these countries; the gross immorality and doubtful legality of the methods of warfare adopted against the enemy;

—the infidelity of the Administration to the spirit of the desegregation decisions in a wide range of administrative rulings, and failure to effectively protect the human rights of the black community;

—the brutal and murderous confrontations between police, guardsmen and students in the Chicago police riots, in the Berkeley riots, at Kent State, in Jackson and elsewhere, eroding student acceptance of the authority of the state;

—the exacerbation of group tensions by trials that are widely interpreted as political; that is, designed to repress and brand members of a group rather than to reform, deter, punish, and prevent crime. Such trials appear to run counter to the legitimate functions of nonpolitical criminal justice;

—the unchecked militancy of some brutal and lawless police elements against student protesters expressed also in anti-Panther violence, and failure to protect the human rights of youth communities with a deviant life-style;

—erosion of faith in the credibility and impartiality of the judiciary in the wake of ad hominem attacks on prominent judges, and the damaging controversies surrounding the nomination of Supreme Court Justices occurring shortly after the controversy about the performance of Judge Hoffman in the Chicago trial;

—erosion of the faith of the legal profession in the neutrality of a judicial philosophy in which competing societal values are admittedly balanced on an unprincipled basis by justices in our appellate courts, ultimately vindicating faith in power rather than faith in law;

—timid law enforcement against organized crime and corporate lawlessness, and corruption in police forces leading to the non-enforcement of much urban, housing, traffic, and pollution legislation;

—inefficiency in the capture and trial of criminals, coupled with costly and lengthy trial delays aggravated by a cruel and anachronistic prison system;

—Administration rhetoric enhancing expectations about law enforcement and the identification of law with order without sufficient emphasis on social justice, bringing the very concept of law into disrepute among large elements of the citizenry;

—malignant neglect of the needs of the blacks, slum dwellers, the old, the underfed, and the poor of the nation;

—neglect of the environment, toleration of industrial pollution practices, of land speculations and other commercial ventures destructive of the quality of life;

—the absence of a meaningful choice of policies between the major national political parties, and the manipulated selection of major national political candidates;

—unresponsive government bureaucracies neglectful of the vital interests of communities directly affected by their decisions in which such communities have little or no meaningful opportunity to participate;

—the initiation of repressive government policies in response to the violence, vituperation, and vandalism of extremist groups;

—neglect of the claims and needs of veto-communities in the belief that government need only rely on electoral majorities and on favorable opinion polls.

The seriousness and cumulative impact of all these charges of legicide that can be leveled against the Administration and other government and party officials account in good measure for the disrepair of our domestic legal order.

The eight claims to resist authority help us focus on some of the profound causes for the national malaise. Their utility in this regard may be of greater moment than their acceptability. At a time when authority structures of all sorts come tumbling down, particular heed should be paid to these claims. The advent of veto-communities and of a developing *jus resistendi* call for a reassessment of our expectations about legal ordering. They demand a new agenda for legal reform and for institutional design—a new agenda for legal theory and for the schools of the nation.

COMMENT

by Carl A. Auerbach

Professor Dworkin's attempt to solve our problem by explicating the ordinary language of "rights" is more confusing than helpful. In assuming an opposition between "personal rights" and society's welfare, Dworkin forgets or ignores what Dean Pound taught us many years ago. To judge between conflicting interests, Pound insisted, they must be placed "on the same level." [1] "Individual" interests should never be opposed to "social" interests. When the legal system recognizes certain individual rights, it does so because it has been decided that society as a whole will benefit by satisfying the individual claims in question; for example, when the legal system guarantees the individual freedom of speech, it advances society's interest in facilitating social, political, and cultural progress. This interest, it has been decided, is more important than society's interest in preserving existing institutions.

It is misleading, therefore, to speak, as Dworkin does, of the law's recognition of certain "personal rights" to do what is "wrong" from society's point of view. Moreover, the "government" does not "think" any way to behave is "wrong," except the ways of behavior prohibited by law.

[1] Roscoe Pound, "Survey of Social Interests," 57 Harv. L. Rev. 1, 2 (1943).

Dworkin poses and answers three questions, on which I shall comment briefly.

1. "If a man in fact has a personal right to do something, or to be free from some demand, and the government passes a law that wrongly invades that right, does he have a personal right to break that law?" Dworkin's answer to this question is incomprehensible. If by "personal right" he means an individual right guaranteed by the Constitution, then of course the answer to his question is yes. A law passed by the government invading this right is not only "wrong"; it is unconstitutional and will be declared so by the Supreme Court. When an individual "breaks" an invalid law, he does not commit an illegal act.

If by "personal right" Dworkin does not mean an individual right guaranteed by the Constitution, his question is meaningless. The government cannot "wrongly"—in any legal sense—invade a right not so guaranteed. If "personal right" means a "moral right," then Dworkin asks us to assume the law invading that right is morally wrong, and, as I pointed out in answer to Professor Wolff, Dworkin's question cannot be answered Yes or No in absolute terms.

It is muddling to say that a "personal right" is "a right to do something even when it is wrong to do it, and even though society in general would be worse off for having it done." As I pointed out, society recognizes no such personal right as a legal right. Nor does it recognize that an individual has a moral right to do something inimical to its welfare. This is not to deny that, under some circumstances, individuals who are impelled to such action by their moral convictions may be respected for it by some other individuals, even some who do not share these convictions. But then it is more understandable to pose the problem of individuals who violate the law because they feel morally obligated to do so, not because they have a moral right to do so. The notion of "moral right" in this context is mischievous. Who is the arbiter of such rights?

2. "If a man thinks he has such a personal right and that the government has wrongly invaded it, does he do the right thing to break the law?" This question is as confusingly put as the first one, for the reasons indicated above. Furthermore, it is not clear for what purpose Dworkin thinks it important to distinguish between the case of an individual who "in fact" has such a "personal right" and one who

merely "thinks he has." If "personal right" refers to a right which the individual thinks is guaranteed by the Constitution, then if he violates a law which invades that right in order to determine whether it is so guaranteed, he is not committing an act of civil disobedience even if the Supreme Court eventually decides that he does not in fact have that right.

If "personal right" does not refer to a legal right, society cannot acknowledge that the individual has done the "right thing" to break a law prohibiting the exercise of that nonlegal "right." Nor may prosecutorial discretion properly be used as a way for society to make such an acknowledgment. Its legal institutions have decided that the social interests promoted by the law are more important than the social interests sought to be promoted through recognition of the individual claim in question.

Whether other individuals may conclude that the individual has done the right thing to break the law depends, again, on the circumstances of the particular case.

3. "If an individual thinks he has such a right [to do something] and breaks the law on that ground, does the government," Dworkin asks, "do the right thing to punish him?"

No, of course, if the law is unconstitutional. Yes, if it is. Now, it is true that prosecutors have discretion whether to institute proceedings to punish violators and that they do not prosecute every violator who is apprehended. What influences their exercise of discretion is not always known, but their attitudes toward the policy reflected in the law and the circumstances of particular cases undoubtedly are important factors.

I agree with Dworkin that prosecutors should exercise this discretion, in doubtful cases, not to restrict but to enlarge the scope of the fundamental liberties guaranteed by the Constitution. I would urge the same consideration upon policemen who exercise discretion in making arrests; trial juries which exercise discretion in returning verdicts of guilty or not guilty; judges who exercise discretion in sentencing; and Chief Executives who exercise discretion in commuting sentences and pardoning criminals.

But Dworkin seeks to go further. He urges prosecutors to take the position that the government is not doing the "right thing" to prosecute an individual who violated the law if that individual believed "that he had a duty to act as he did" and "if that belief is sincere and plausible." This is a dangerous standard for the exercise of prosecutorial discretion because it would enhance the possibility of discrimination. All of us would think it wrong for a prosecutor to prosecute Professor Wolff's Stephen, whom he did not know, because he did not believe Stephen was sincere, but not some other young man of whom the prosecutor thought more highly because he was acquainted with his family.

Even more important, when the prosecutor decides to forgo prosecution, not because of the exigencies of a particular case but because of the attributes of whole classes of cases, he is usurping legislative authority. For example, prosecutors have not been delegated authority to withhold prosecution of all young men who refuse to submit to induction into the army because they think the American cause in Vietnam is wrong, while prosecuting young men who refuse to submit to induction because they are afraid of combat. Nor have prosecutors been delegated authority to withhold prosecution of all young men who refuse to submit to induction because the prosecutors believe that only volunteers should fight in Vietnam.

It still lies open to Congress—if it is persuaded by Dworkin—to extend the magnanimity it has shown conscientious objectors to all wars to those who would fight in some wars but are conscientiously opposed to the Vietnam war. It is also conceivable—though not very probable —that the Supreme Court may declare a refusal to fight in Vietnam because of such conscientious opposition to be a fundamental liberty guaranteed by the Constitution.[2] In either case, our problem would be resolved; refusal to fight in Vietnam would no longer be an act of civil disobedience.

[2] On March 8, 1971, the U. S. Supreme Court decided that neither the Constitution nor the Military Selective Service Act of 1967 requires exemption of individuals from military service because of their conscientious objections to participation in the Vietnam conflict which they regard as an "unjust war." The 1967 Act exempts those who oppose participating in all war and not those who object to participation in a particular war only, even if their objection is religious in character. Gillette v. U.S., 39 LW 4305.

CHAPTER 6

CIVIL DISOBEDIENCE

by Hannah Arendt

I

The Bar Association of the City of New York celebrated its centennial this year with a symposium on the rather dismal question "Is law dead?" The participants, divided into two panels, were asked by Eugene V. Rostow to prepare papers on "the citizen's moral relation to the law in a society of consent" and on "the capacity of American society to meet changing demands for social justice in peace, and through the processes of law and of democratic policymaking"—two topics that seemed to encourage a somewhat brighter outlook. The following remarks are in answer to the first question.

Asked to consider the citizen's *moral* relation to the law, one is inclined to think first of two men in prison—Socrates, in Athens, and Thoreau, in Concord, both of whom appear regularly in the literature on the subject. Many, indeed, share Senator Philip A. Hart's position: "Any tolerance that I might feel toward the disobeyer is dependent on his willingness to accept whatever punishment the law might impose" [1]—an argument whose plausibility gains in strength in a country where "an individual, through one of the most serious oddities of our law, is encouraged or in some sense

[1] In *To Establish Justice, to Insure Domestic Tranquility*, Final Report of the National Commission on the Causes and the Prevention of Violence, December 1969, p. 108. For the use of Socrates and Thoreau in these discussions, see also Eugene V. Rostow, "The Consent of the Governed," in *The Virginia Quarterly*, Autumn 1968.

compelled to establish a significant legal right through a personal act of civil disobedience." Yet all these models of civil disobedience may be seriously misleading when we try to come to terms with our present predicament, and not only because "the distinction between such acts"—in which an individual breaks the law in order to test its constitutionality or legitimacy—"and ordinary violations becomes much more fragile in a period of turmoil." [2]

As for Socrates, the argument in the *Crito* is less unequivocal than it is usually accepted as being. Socrates had never challenged the laws themselves—only this particular miscarriage of justice, which he spoke of as the "accident" ($\tau\acute{v}\chi\eta$) that had befallen him. His personal misfortune did not entitle him to "break his contracts and agreements" with the laws; his quarrel was not with the laws but with the judges. Moreover, as Socrates pointed out to Crito (who tried to persuade him to escape and go into exile), at the time of the trial the laws themselves had offered him this choice: "At that time you could have done with the state's consent what you are trying now to do without it. But then you gloried in being willing to die. You said that you preferred death to exile." We also know, from the *Apology,* that he had the option of desisting from his public examination of things, which doubtless spread uncertainty about established customs and beliefs, and that again he had preferred death, because "an unexamined life is not worth living." That is, Socrates would not have honored his own words if he had

---

[2] Edward H. Levi, "The Crisis in the Nature of Law," in *The Record* of the Association of the Bar of the City of New York, March 1970. Mr. Rostow, on the contrary, holds that "it is a common error to think of such breaches of the law as acts of disobedience to law" (*op. cit.*), and Wilson Carey McWilliams in one of the most interesting essays on the subject—"Civil Disobedience and Contemporary Constitutionalism," in *Comparative Politics,* Vol. I, 1969—seems to agree by implication. Stressing that the Court's "tasks depend, in part, on public action," he concludes: "The Court acts, in fact, to authorize disobedience to otherwise legitimate authority, and it depends on citizens who will take advantage of its authorization [p. 216]." I fail to see how this can remedy Mr. Levi's "oddity"; the lawbreaking citizen who wishes to persuade the courts to pass on the constitutionality of some statute must be willing to pay the price like any other lawbreaker for the act—either until the court has decided the case or if it should decide against him.

tried to escape; he would have undone all he had done during his trial—would have "confirmed the judges in their opinion, and made it seem that their verdict was a just one." He owed it *to himself* as well as to the citizens he had addressed to stay and die. "It is the payment of a debt of honor, the payment of a gentleman who has lost a wager and who pays because he cannot otherwise live with himself. There has indeed been a contract, and the notion of a contract pervades the latter half of the *Crito,* but . . . the contract which is binding is . . . *the commitment involved in the trial."* (My italics.)[3]

Thoreau's case, though much less dramatic (he spent one night in jail for refusing to pay his poll tax to a government that permitted slavery, but he let his aunt pay it for him the next morning), seems at first glance more pertinent to our current debates, for, in contradistinction to Socrates, he protested against the injustice of the laws themselves. The trouble with this example is that in "On the Duty of Civil Disobedience," the famous essay that grew out of the incident and made the term "civil disobedience" part of our political vocabulary, he argued his case not on the ground of a *citizen's* moral relation to the law but on the ground of individual conscience and conscience's moral obligation: "It is not a man's duty, as a matter of course, to devote himself to the eradication of any, even the most enormous, wrong; he may still properly have other concerns to engage him; but it is his duty, at least, to wash his hands of it, and, if he gives it no thought longer, not to give it practically his support." Thoreau did not pretend that a man's washing his hands of it would make the world better or that a man had any obligation to do so. He "came into this world, not chiefly to make this a good place to live in, but to live in it, be it good or bad." Indeed, this is how we all come into the world—lucky if the world and the part of it we arrive in is a good place to live in at the time of our arrival, or at least a place where the wrongs committed are not "of such a nature that it requires you to be the agent of injustice to another." For only if this is the case, "then, I say, break

---

[3] See N. A. Greenberg's excellent analysis, "Socrates' Choice in the *Crito,"* in *Harvard Studies in Classical Philology,* Vol. 70, No. 1, 1965. The *Crito* is properly understood only if read in conjunction with the *Apology.*

the law." And Thoreau was right: Individual conscience requires nothing more.[4]

Here, as elsewhere, conscience is unpolitical. It is not primarily interested in the world where the wrong is committed or in the consequences that the wrong will have for the future course of the world. It does not say, with Jefferson, "I tremble *for my country* when I reflect that God is just; that His justice cannot sleep forever," because it trembles for the individual self and its integrity.[5] It can therefore be much more radical and say, with Thoreau, "This people must cease to hold slaves, and to make war on Mexico, *though it cost them their existence as a people* (my italics)," whereas for Lincoln "the paramount object," even in the struggle for the emancipation of the slaves, remained, as he wrote in 1862, "to save the Union, and . . . not either to save or to destroy slavery." [6] This does not mean that Lincoln was unaware of "the monstrous injustice of slavery itself," as he had called it eight years earlier; it means that he was also aware of the distinction between his "official duty" and his "personal wish that all men everywhere could be free." [7] And this distinction, if one strips it of the always complex and equivocal historical circumstances, is ultimately the same as Machiavelli's when he said, "I love my native city more than my own soul." [8] The discrepancy between "official duty" and "personal wish" in Lincoln's case no more indicates a lack of moral commitment than the discrepancy between city and soul indicates that Machiavelli was an atheist and did not believe in eternal salvation and damnation.

This possible conflict between "the good man" and "the good citizen" (according to Aristotle, the good man could be a good citizen only in a good state), between the individual self, with or without belief in an afterlife, and the member of the community,

---

[4] All quotations are from Thoreau's "On the Duty of Civil Disobedience," 1849.

[5] *Notes on the State of Virginia,* 1781–85, Query XVIII.

[6] In his famous letter to Horace Greeley, quoted here from Hans Morgenthau, *The Dilemmas of Politics,* Chicago, 1958, p. 80.

[7] Quoted from Richard Hofstadter, *The American Political Tradition,* 1948, p. 110.

[8] Allan Gilbert, ed., *The Letters of Machiavelli,* 1961, Letter 225.

or, as we would say today, between morality and politics, is very old—older, even, than the word "conscience," which in its present connotation is of relatively recent origin. And almost equally old are the justifications for the position of either. Thoreau was consistent enough to recognize and admit that he was open to the charge of irresponsibility, the oldest charge against "the good man." He said explicitly that he was "not responsible for the successful working of the machinery of society," he was "not the son of the engineer." The adage *Fiat justitia et pereat mundus*—"Let justice be done even if the world perishes"—which is usually invoked rhetorically against the defenders of absolute justice, often for the purpose of excusing wrongs and crimes, neatly expresses the gist of the dilemma.

However, the reason that "at the level of individual morality, the problem of disobedience to the law is wholly intractable" [9] is of still a different order. The counsels of conscience are not only unpolitical; they are always expressed in purely subjective statements. When Socrates stated that "it is better to suffer wrong than to do wrong," he clearly meant that it was better *for him,* just as it was better for him "to be in disagreement with multitudes than, being one, to be in disagreement with [himself]." [10] What counts politically is that a wrong has been done; to the law it is irrelevant who is better off as a result—the doer or the sufferer. Our legal codes distinguish between crimes in which indictment is mandatory, because the community as a whole has been violated, and offenses in which only doers and sufferers are involved, who may or may not want to sue. In the case of the former, the states of mind of those involved are irrelevant, except insofar as intent is part of the overt act, or mitigating circumstances are taken into account; it makes no difference whether the one who suffered is willing to forgive or the one who did is entirely unlikely to do it again.

In the *Gorgias,* from which I just quoted, Socrates does not address the citizens, as he does in the *Apology* and, in support of the *Apology,* in the *Crito.* Here Plato lets Socrates speak as the philosopher who has discovered that men have intercourse not only with

9 *To Establish Justice, op. cit.* (note 1), p. 98.
10 *Gorgias,* 482, 489.

their fellow men but also with themselves, and that the latter form of intercourse—my being with and by myself—prescribes certain rules for the former. These are the rules of conscience, and they are—like those which Thoreau announced in his essay—entirely negative. They do not say what to do; they say what not to do. They do not spell out certain principles for taking action; they lay down the boundaries no act should transgress. They say: Don't do wrong, for then you will have to live together with a wrongdoer. Plato, in the later dialogues (the *Sophist* and the *Theaetetus*), elaborated on this Socratic intercourse of me with myself and defined thinking as the soundless dialogue between me and myself; existentially speaking, it requires that the partners be friends. The validity of the Socratic propositions depends upon the kind of man who utters them and the kind of man to whom they are addressed.[11] They are self-evident truths for man insofar as he is a thinking being; to those who don't think, who don't have intercourse with themselves, they are not self-evident, nor can they be proved. Those men—and they are the "multitudes"—can gain a proper interest in themselves only, according to Plato, by believing in a mythical hereafter with rewards and punishments.

Hence, the rules of conscience hinge on interest in the self. They say: Beware of doing something that you will not be able to live with. It is the same argument that led to "Camus's . . . stress on the necessity of resistance to injustice *for the resisting individual's own health and welfare.*" (My italics.)[12] The political and legal trouble with such justification is twofold. First, it cannot be generalized; in order to keep its validity, it must remain subjective. What I cannot live with may not bother another man's conscience. The result is that conscience will stand against conscience. "If the decision to break the law really turned on individual conscience, it is hard to see in law how Dr. King is better off than Governor Ross Barnett of Mississippi, who also believed deeply in his cause and

---

[11] This is made quite clear in the second book of the *Republic* where Socrates' own pupils "can plead the cause of injustice most eloquently and still not be convinced themselves," 357–367.

[12] Christian Bay, "Civil Disobedience," in the *International Encyclopedia of the Social Sciences,* 1968, Vol. II, p. 486.

was willing to go to jail." [13] The second, and perhaps even more serious, trouble is that conscience, if it is defined in secular terms, presupposes not only that man possesses the innate faculty of telling right from wrong but that man is interested in himself, for the obligation arises from this interest alone. And this kind of self-interest can hardly be taken for granted. Although we know that human beings are capable of thinking—of having intercourse with themselves—we do not know how many indulge in this rather profitless enterprise; all we can say is that the habit of thinking, of reflecting on what one is doing, is independent of the individual's social, educational, or intellectual standing. In this respect, as in so many others, "the good man" and "the good citizen" are by no means the same, and not only in the Aristotelian sense. Good men become manifest only in emergencies, when they suddenly appear, as if from nowhere, in all social strata. The good citizen, on the contrary, must be conspicuous; he can be studied, with the also not so very comforting result that he turns out to belong to a small minority—tends to be educated and a member of the upper social classes.[14]

This whole question of the political weight to be accorded moral decisions—decisions arrived at *in foro conscientiae*—has been greatly complicated by the originally religious and later secularized associations that the notion of conscience acquired under the influence of Christian philosophy. As we use the word today, in both moral and legal matters, conscience is supposed to be always present within us, as though it were identical with consciousness. (It is true that it took language a long time to distinguish between the two, and in some languages—French, for instance—the separation of conscience and consciousness has never taken place.) The voice of conscience was the voice of God, and announced the Divine Law, before it became the *lumen naturale* that informed men of a higher law. As the voice of God, it gave positive prescriptions whose validity rested on the command "Obey God rather than men"—a command that was objectively binding without any reference to human institutions and that could be turned, as in the Ref-

---

13 *To Establish Justice, op. cit.* (note 1), p. 99.
14 McWilliams, *op. cit.* (note 2), p. 223.

ormation, even against what was alleged to be the divinely inspired institution of the Church. To modern ears, this must sound like "self-certification," which "borders on blasphemy"—the presumptuous pretension that one knows the will of God and is sure of his eventual justification.[15] It did not sound that way to the believer in a creator God who has revealed Himself to the one creature He created in His own image. But the anarchic nature of divinely inspired consciences, so blatantly manifest in the beginnings of Christianity, cannot be denied. The law, therefore—rather late, and by no means in all countries—recognized religiously inspired conscientious objectors but recognized them only when they appealed to a Divine Law that was also claimed by a recognized religious group, which could not well be ignored by a Christian community. The present deep crisis in the churches and the increasing number of objectors who claim no relation to any religious institution, whether or not they claim divinely informed consciences, have thus created great difficulties.

However that may be, the conscience of the believer who listens to and obeys the voice of God or the commands of the *lumen naturale* is a far cry from the strictly secular conscience—this knowing, and speaking with, myself, which, in Ciceronian language, better than a thousand witnesses testifies to deeds that otherwise may remain unknown forever. It is this conscience that we find in such magnificence in *Richard III*. It does no more than "fill a man full of obstacles"; it is not always with him but awaits him when he is alone, and loses its hold when midnight is over and he has rejoined the company of his peers. Then only, when he is no longer by himself, will he say, "Conscience is but a word that cowards use,/ Devised at first to keep the strong in awe." The fear of being alone and having to face oneself can be a very effective dissuader from wrongdoing, but this fear, by its very nature, is unpersuasive of others. No doubt even this kind of conscientious objection can become politically significant when a number of consciences happen to coincide and the conscientious objectors decide to enter the mar-

---

[15] Thus Leslie Dunbar as quoted in "On Civil Disobedience in Recent American Democratic Thought," by Paul F. Power in *The American Political Science Review*, March 1970.

ketplace and make their voices heard in public. But then we are no longer dealing with individuals, or with a phenomenon whose criteria can be derived from Socrates or Thoreau. What had been decided *in foro conscientiae* has now become part of public opinion, and although this particular group of civil disobedients may still claim the initial validation—their consciences—they actually rely no longer on themselves alone. In the marketplace, the fate of conscience is not much different from the fate of the philosopher's truth: It becomes an opinion, indistinguishable from other opinions.

To sum up: We must distinguish between conscientious objectors and civil disobedients. The arguments raised in defense of individual conscience and the conditions prescribing the limitations on its rights—the "willingness to accept whatever punishment the law might impose"—are inadequate when applied to civil disobedience. Civil disobedients are in fact organized minorities, bound together by their decision to take a stand against an assumed majority.

II

Disobedience to the law, civil and criminal, has become a mass phenomenon in recent years, not only in America but in a great many other parts of the world. The defiance of established authority, religious and secular, social and political, as a worldwide phenomenon may well one day be accounted the outstanding event of the last decade. Indeed, "the laws seem to have lost their power." [16] Viewed from the outside and considered in historical perspective, no clearer writing on the wall—no more explicit sign of the inner instability and vulnerability of existing governments and legal systems—could be imagined. If history teaches anything about the causes of revolution—and history does not teach much but still teaches considerably more than social-science theories—it is that a disintegration of political systems precedes revolutions, that the telling symptom of disintegration is a progressive erosion of gov-

[16] McWilliams, *op. cit.* (note 2), p. 211.

ernmental authority, and that this erosion is caused by the government's inability to function properly, from which spring the citizens' doubts about its legitimacy. This is what the Marxists used to call a revolutionary situation—which, of course, more often than not does not develop into a revolution.

In our context, the grave threat to the judicial system of the United States is a case in point. To lament "the cancerous growth of disobediences" [17] does not make much sense unless one recognizes that for many years now the law-enforcement agencies have been unable to enforce the statutes against drug traffic, mugging, and burglary. Considering that the chances that criminal offenders in these categories will never be detected at all are better than 9 to 1, there is every reason to be surprised that such crime is not worse than it is. (According to the 1967 report of the President's Commission on Law Enforcement and Administration of Justice, "well over half of all crimes are never reported to the police," and "of those which are, fewer than one quarter are cleared by arrest. Nearly half of all arrests result in the dismissal of charges.")[18] It is as though we were engaged in a nationwide experiment to find out how many potential criminals—that is, people who are prevented from committing crimes only by the deterrent force of the law—actually exist in a given society. The results may not be encouraging to those who hold that all criminal impulses are aberrations; that is, are the impulses of mentally sick people acting under the compulsion of their illness. The simple and rather frightening truth is that under circumstances of legal and social permissiveness people will engage in the most outrageous criminal behavior who under normal circumstances perhaps dreamed of such crimes but never considered actually committing them.[19] In today's society, neither the po-

[17] *To Establish Justice, op. cit.* (note 1), p. 89.
[18] *Law and Order Reconsidered,* Report of the Task Force on Law and Law Enforcement to the National Commission on the Causes and Prevention of Violence, n.d., p. 266.
[19] Horrible examples of this truth were presented during the so-called Auschwitz trial in Germany whose proceedings are reported by Bernd Naumann, *Auschwitz,* New York, 1966. The defendants were "a mere handful of intolerable cases" selected from about 2,000 S.S. men posted at the camps between 1940 and 1945. All of them were charged with murder, the only offense which in 1963, when the trial began, was not covered by the statute

tential lawbreakers (that is, the nonprofessional and unorganized criminals) nor the law-abiding citizens need elaborate studies to tell them that criminal acts will probably—which is to say, predictably—have no legal consequences whatsoever. We have learned, to our sorrow, that organized crime is less to be feared than nonprofessional hoodlums—who profit from opportunity—and their entirely justified "lack of concern about being punished"; and this state of affairs is neither altered nor clarified by research into "the public's confidence in the American judicial process." [20] What we are up against is not the judicial process but the simple fact that criminal acts usually have no legal consequences whatsoever. What has broken down is not the legal system but its enforcement. On the other hand, one must ask what would happen if police power were restored to the reasonable point where from 60 to 70 percent of all criminal offenses were properly cleared by arrest and properly judged. Is there any doubt that it would mean the collapse of the already disastrously overburdened courts ("the proportion of cases which actually go to trial is tiny, representing less than one percent of all crimes committed"), and would have quite terrifying consequences for the just as badly overloaded prison system? What is so frightening in the present situation is not the failure of police power per se—and not even the constant increase of crime in the streets—but that to remedy this condition radically would spell dis-

---

of limitations. Auschwitz was the camp of systematic extermination, but the atrocities almost all the accused had committed had nothing to do with the order for the "final solution"; their crimes were punishable under Nazi law, and in rare cases the perpetrators were actually punished by the Nazi government. And these defendants had not been specially selected for duty at an extermination camp; they had come to Auschwitz for no other reason than that they were unfit for military service. Hardly any of them had a criminal record of any sort, and none of them a record of sadism and murder. Before they had come to Auschwitz and during the eighteen years they had lived in postwar Germany, they had been respectable and respected citizens, undistinguishable from their neighbors.

[20] The allusion is to the $1 million grant by the Ford Foundation "for studies of the public's confidence in the American judicial process" in contrast to the "survey of law-enforcement officials by Fred P. Graham of *The New York Times*" which without a research team came to the obvious conclusion "that the criminal's lack of concern about being punished is causing a major and immediate crisis." Tom Wicker, "Crime and the Courts," in *The New York Times,* April 7, 1970.

aster for these other, equally important branches of the judicial system.

The answer of the government to this, and to similarly obvious breakdowns of public services, has invariably been the creation of study commissions, whose fantastic proliferation in recent years has probably made the United States the most researched country on earth. No doubt the commissions, after spending much time and money in order to find out that "the poorer you are, the more likely you are to suffer from serious malnutrition" (a piece of wisdom that even made *The New York Times* "Quotation of the Day"),[21] often come up with reasonable recommendations. These, however, are seldom acted on but, rather, are subjected to a new panel of researchers. What all the commissions have in common is a desperate attempt to find out something about the "deeper causes" of whatever the problem happens to be—especially if it is the problem of violence—and since "deeper" causes are, by definition, concealed, the final result of such team research is all too often nothing but hypothesis and undemonstrated theory. The net effect is that not only has research become a substitute for action, but the "deeper causes"—with which it is hard to deal in any event, because they are too complex and often totally uncertain—are overgrowing the obvious ones, which are frequently so simple that no "serious" and "learned" person could be asked to give them any attention. To be sure, to find remedies for obvious shortcomings does not guarantee solution of the problem, but to neglect them means that the problem will not even be properly defined. (There is, for example, the well-known overresearched fact that children in slum schools do not learn. Among the more obvious causes is that many such children arrive in school without breakfast and are desperately hungry. There are a number of "deeper causes" for their failure to learn, and it is very uncertain that breakfast in school would help. What is not at all uncertain is that even a class of geniuses could not be taught if they happened to be hungry.) Research has become a technique of evasion, and this has surely not helped the reputation of science, which has been undermined in any event by other experiences.

[21] April 28, 1970.

Since disobedience and defiance of authority are such a general
mark of our time, it is tempting to view civil disobedience as a mere
special case. From the jurist's viewpoint, the law is violated by the
civil no less than the criminal disobedient, and it is understandable
that people, especially if they happen to be lawyers, should suspect
that civil disobedience, precisely because it is exerted in public, is
at the root of the criminal variety[22]—all evidence and arguments to
the contrary notwithstanding, for evidence "to demonstrate that
acts of civil disobedience . . . lead to . . . a propensity toward
crime" is not only "insufficient" but nonexistent.[23] Although it is
true that radical movements and, certainly, revolutions attract
criminal elements, it would be neither correct nor wise to equate
the two; criminals are as dangerous to political movements as they
are to society as a whole. If one wishes to establish a "causal" connection between the two, it is much more likely that it is the other
way around—that the impotence of institutional power has persuaded many otherwise complacent people of the legitimacy of civil
disobedience. (Nothing, indeed, is less likely than that the planned
expansion of the domestic intelligence apparatus to be directed at
the militants of the extreme left will do anything to bring down
crime in the streets, and it will, of course, not, as one official argued, according to *The New York Times,* "increase safeguards of
the civil liberties of individuals.")[24] Moreover, while civil disobedience may be considered an indication of a significant loss of the
law's authority (though it can hardly be seen as its cause), criminal
disobedience is nothing more than the inevitable consequence of a
disastrous erosion of police competence and power. Proposals for
probing the "criminal mind" either with Rorschach tests or by intelligence agents sound sinister, but they, too, belong among the
techniques of evasion. An incessant flow of sophisticated hypothe-
ses about the mind—this most elusive of man's properties—of the
criminal submerges the solid fact that no one is able to catch his
body, just as the hypothetical assumption of policemen's *"latent*

[22] Justice Charles E. Whittaker, like many others in the legal profession,
"attributes the crisis to ideas of civil disobedience." McWilliams, *op. cit.*
(note 2), p. 211.

[23] *To Establish Justice, op. cit.* (note 1), p. 109.

[24] *The New York Times,* April 12, 1970, p. 69.

negative attitudes" covers up their overt negative record in solving crimes.[25]

Civil disobedience arises when a significant number of citizens have become convinced either that the normal channels of change no longer function, and grievances will not be heard or acted upon —as in the case of the striking mailmen—or that, on the contrary, the government is about to change, and has embarked upon and persists in modes of action whose legality and constitutionality are open to grave doubt. Instances are numerous: six years of an undeclared war in Vietnam; the growing influence of secret agencies on public affairs; open or thinly veiled threats to liberties guaranteed under the First Amendment; attempts to deprive the Senate of its constitutional powers, followed by the President's invasion of Cambodia in open disregard of the Constitution, which explicitly requires congressional approval for the beginning of a war; not to mention the Vice-President's even more ominous reference to resisters and dissenters as " 'vultures' . . . and 'parasites' [whom] we can afford to separate . . . from our society with no more regret than we should feel over discarding rotten apples from a barrel"— a reference that challenges not only the laws of the United States but every legal order.[26] In other words, civil disobedience can be tuned to necessary and desirable change or to necessary and desirable preservation or restoration of the *status quo*—the preservation of rights guaranteed under the First Amendment, or the restoration of the proper balance of power in the government, which is jeopardized by the executive branch as well as by the enormous growth of Federal power at the expense of states' rights. In neither case can civil disobedience be equated with criminal disobedience.

There is all the difference in the world between the criminal's avoiding the public eye and the civil disobedient's taking the law into his own hands in open defiance. The former, even if he belongs to a criminal organization, acts for his own benefit alone; he refuses to be overpowered by the consent of all others and will yield only to the violence of the law-enforcement agencies. The civil disobedi-

---

[25] *Law and Order Reconsidered, op. cit.* (note 18), p. 291.

[26] *The New Yorker*'s excellent comment in The Talk of the Town is especially recommended. See f.i. February 28, 1970, and May 16, 1970.

ent, though he is usually dissenting from a majority, acts in the name and for the sake of a group; he defies the law and the established authorities on the ground of basic dissent, and not because he as an individual wishes to make an exception for himself and to get away with it. If the group he belongs to is significant in numbers and standing, one is tempted to classify him as a member of one of John C. Calhoun's "concurrent majorities"; that is, sections of the population that are unanimous in their dissent. The term, unfortunately, is tainted by proslavery and racist arguments, and in the *Disquisition on Government,* where it occurs, it covers only interests, not opinions and convictions, of minorities that feel threatened by "dominant majorities." The point, at any rate, is that we are dealing here with organized minorities that are too important not merely in numbers but in *quality of opinion* to be safely disregarded. For Calhoun was certainly right when he held that in questions of great national importance the "concurrence or acquiescence of the various portions of the community" are a prerequisite of constitutional government.[27] To think of disobedient minorities in terms of rebels and traitors is against the letter and spirit of a Constitution whose framers were especially sensitive to the dangers of unbridled majority rule. Of all the means that civil disobedients may use in the course of persuasion and of the dramatization of issues, the only one that can justify their being called rebels is the means of violence.

"Things of this world are in so constant a flux that nothing remains long in the same state." [28] If this sentence, written by Locke about three hundred years ago, were uttered today, it would sound like the understatement of the century. Still, it may remind us that change is not a modern phenomenon but is inherent in a world inhabited and established by human beings, who come into it, by birth, as strangers and newcomers (νέοι, "the new ones," as the

[27] *A Disquisition on Government* (1853), Poli Sci Classics, New York, 1947, p. 67. For a recent discussion of Calhoun's position, see George Kateb, "The Majority Principle: Calhoun and His Antecedents," in *Political Science Quarterly,* December 1969.

[28] Locke, *The Second Treatise of Government,* section 157.

Greeks used to call the young), and depart from it just when they have acquired the experience and familiarity that may in certain rare cases enable them to be "wise" in the ways of the world. "Wise men" have played various and sometimes significant roles in human affairs, but the point is that they have always been old men, about to disappear from the world. Their wisdom, acquired in the proximity of departure, cannot rule a world exposed to the constant onslaught of the inexperience and "foolishness" of newcomers, and it is likely that without this interrelated condition of natality and mortality, which guarantees change and makes the rule of wisdom impossible, the human race would have become extinct long ago out of unbearable boredom.

Change is constant, the velocity of change is not. It varies greatly from country to country, from century to century. Compared to the coming and going of the generations, the flux of the world's things occurs so slowly that the world can almost be called stable. Or so it was for thousands of years—including the early centuries of the modern age, when first the notion of change for change's sake, under the name of progress, made its appearance. Ours is perhaps the first century in which the speed of change in the things of the world has outstripped the change inherent in the human condition. (An alarming symptom of this turnabout is the steadily shrinking span of the generations. From the traditional standard of three or four generations to a century we have now come to a life expectancy per generation of four or five years.) But even under the extraordinary conditions of the twentieth century, which make Marx's admonition to change the world sound like an exhortation to carry coals to Newcastle, it can hardly be said that man's appetite for change has canceled his drive for stability. It is well known that the most radical revolutionary will become a conservative on the day after the revolution. Obviously, neither man's capacity for change nor his capacity for preservation is boundless, the former being limited by the extension of the past into the present—no man begins *ab ovo*—and the latter by the unpredictability of the future. Man's urge for change and his need for stability have always balanced and checked each other, and our current vocabulary, which distinguishes between two factions, the progressives and the con-

servatives, indicates a state of affairs in which this balance has been
thrown out of order.

No civilization—the man-made artifact to house successive generations—would ever have been possible without a framework of
stability, to provide the wherein for the flux of change. Foremost
among the stabilizing factors, more enduring than customs, manners, and traditions, are the legal systems that regulate our life in
the world and our daily affairs with each other. (This is the reason
it is inevitable that law in a time of rapid change will appear as "a
restraining force, thus a negative influence in a world which ad-
mires positive action.")[29] The variety of such systems is very great
both in time and in space, but they all have one thing in common—
the thing that justifies us in using the same word for phenomena as
different as the Roman *lx,* the Greek νόμος, the Hebrew *torah*—
and this is that they were designed to insure stability. (We are not
concerned here with the second universal characteristic of the law
—that it is not universally valid but is either territorially bound or,
as in the instance of Jewish law, ethnically restricted. Where both
characteristics, stability and limited validity, are absent—where the
so-called laws of history or nature, for instance, as they are interpreted by the head of state, maintain a "legality" that can change
from day to day and that claims validity for all mankind—we are
in fact confronted with lawlessness, though not with anarchy, since
order can be maintained by means of compulsive organization. The
net result, at any rate, is criminalization of the whole governmental
apparatus, as we know from totalitarian government.)

Because of the unprecedented rate of change in our time and
because of the challenge that change poses to the legal order—
from the side of the government, as we have seen, as well as from
the side of disobedient citizens—it is now widely held that changes
can be effected by law, as distinguished from the earlier notion that
"legal action [that is, Supreme Court decisions] can influence ways
of living."[30] Both opinions seem to me to be based on an error

---

[29] Levi, *op. cit.* (note 2).

[30] J. D. Hyman, "Segregation and the Fourteenth Amendment," in *Essays
in Constitutional Law,* ed. by Robert G. McCloskey, New York, 1957, p.
379.

about what the law can achieve and what it cannot. The law can indeed stabilize and legalize change once it has occurred, but the change itself is always the result of extralegal action. To be sure, the Constitution itself offers a quasi-legal way to challenge the law by breaking it, but, quite apart from the question of whether or not such breaches are acts of disobedience, the Supreme Court has the right to choose among the cases brought before it, and this choice is inevitably influenced by public opinion. The bill recently passed in Massachusetts to force a test of the legality of the Vietnam war is a case in point. Is it not obvious that this legal action—very significant indeed—is the result of the civil disobedience of draft resisters, and that its aim is to legalize servicemen's refusal of combat duty? The whole body of labor legislation—the right of collective bargaining, the right to organize and to strike—was preceded by decades of frequently very violent disobedience of what ultimately proved to be obsolete laws.

The history of the Fourteenth Amendment perhaps offers an especially instructive example of the relation between law and change. It was meant to translate into constitutional terms the change that had come about as the result of the Civil War. This change was not accepted by the southern states, with the result that the provisions for racial equality were not enforced for roughly a hundred years. An even more striking example of the inability of the law to enforce change is, of course, the Eighteenth Amendment, concerning Prohibition, which had to be repealed because it proved to be unenforceable. The Fourteenth Amendment, on the other hand, was finally enforced by the legal action of the Supreme Court, but although one may argue that it had always been "the plain responsibility of the Supreme Court to cope with state laws that deny racial equality," [31] the plain fact is that the Court chose to do so only when civil rights movements that, as far as southern laws were concerned, were clearly movements of civil disobedience had brought about a drastic change in the attitudes of both black and white citizens. Not the law but civil disobedience brought into the open "the American dilemma" and, perhaps for the first time, forced upon the nation the recognition of the enormity of the crime

[31] Robert G. McCloskey in *Essays in Constitutional Law, op. cit.,* p. 352.

not just of slavery but of chattel slavery—"unique among all such systems known to civilization" [32]—the responsibility for which the people have inherited, together with so many blessings, from their forefathers.

III

The perspective of very rapid change suggests that there is "every likelihood of a progressively expanding role for civil disobedience in . . . modern democracies." [33] And the central question here is not whether, and to what extent, civil disobedience can be justified by the First Amendment but, rather, with what concept of law it is compatible. I shall argue in what follows that although the phenomenon of civil disobedience is today a worldwide phenomenon, no other country, and no other language, has even a word for it, and that the American republic is the only government that has at least a chance to cope with it—not, perhaps, in accordance with the statutes but in accordance with the *spirit* of its laws. The United States owes its origin to the American Revolution, and this revolution carried within it a new, never fully articulated concept of law, which was the result of no theory but had been formed by the extraordinary experiences of the early colonists. It would be an event of great significance to find a legal niche for civil disobedience—of no less significance, perhaps, than the event of the founding of the *constitutio libertatis,* nearly two hundred years ago.

The citizen's moral obligation to obey the laws has traditionally been derived from the assumption that he either consented to them or actually was his own legislator; that under the rule of law men are not subject to an alien will but obey only themselves—with the result, of course, that every person is at the same time his own master and his own slave, and that what is seen as the original conflict between the citizen, concerned with the public good, and

---

[32] On this important point, which explains why the emancipation had such disastrous consequences in the United States, see the splendid study entitled *Slavery* by Stanley M. Elkins, New York, 1959.

[33] Christian Bay, *op. cit.* (note 12), p. 483.

the self, pursuing his private happiness, is internalized. This is in essence the Rousseauean-Kantian solution to the problem of obligation, and its defect, from my point of view, is that it turns again on conscience—on the relation between me and myself. (Another important defect has been pointed out by Hegel: "To be one's own master and servant seems to be better than to be somebody else's servant. However, the relation between freedom and nature, if . . . nature is being oppressed by one's own self, is much more artificial than the relation in natural law, according to which the domineering and commanding part is outside the living individual. In the latter case, the individual as a living entity retains its autonomous identity. . . . It is opposed by an alien power. . . . [Otherwise] its inner harmony is destroyed.")[34] From the point of view of modern political science, the trouble lies in the fictitious origin of consent—"Many . . . write as if there were a social contract or some similar basis for political obligation to obey the majority's will"—wherefore the argument usually preferred is: We in a democracy have to obey the law because we have the right to vote.[35] It is precisely these voting rights, universal suffrage in free elections, as a sufficient basis for a democracy and for the claim of public freedom, that have come under attack.

Still, the proposition set forth by Eugene Rostow that what needs to be considered is "the citizen's moral obligation to the law *in a society of consent*" seems to me crucial. If Montesquieu was right—and I believe he was—that there is such a thing as "the spirit of the laws," which varies from country to country and is different in the various forms of government, then we may say that consent, not in the very old sense of mere acquiescence, with its distinction between rule over willing subjects and rule over unwilling ones, but in the sense of active support and continuing participation in all matters of public interest, is the spirit of American law. Theoretically, this consent has been construed to be the result of a social contract, which in its more common form—the contract between a people and its government—is indeed easy to denounce

[34] *Differenz des Fichte'schen and Schelling'schen Systems der Philosophie,* 1801, Edition F. Meiner, p. 70.
[35] Bay, *op. cit.* (note 12), p. 483.

as mere fiction. However, the point is that it was no mere fiction in the American pre-Revolutionary experience, with its numerous covenants and agreements, from the Mayflower Compact to the establishment of the thirteen colonies as an entity. When Locke formulated his social-contract theory, which supposedly explained the aboriginal beginnings of civil society, he indicated in a side remark which model he actually had in mind: "In the beginning, all the world was America." [36]

In theory, the seventeenth century knew and combined under the name of social contract three altogether different kinds of such aboriginal agreements. There was, first, the example of the Biblical Covenant, which was concluded between a people as a whole and its God, and by virtue of which the people consented to obey whatever laws an all-powerful divinity might choose to reveal to it. Had this Puritan version of consent prevailed, it would, as John Cotton rightly remarked, have "set up Theocracy . . . as the best form of government." [37] There was, second, the Hobbesian variety, according to which every individual concludes an agreement with the strictly secular authorities to insure his safety, for the protection of which he relinquishes all rights and powers. I shall call this the vertical version of the social contract. It is, of course, inconsistent with the American understanding of government, because it claims for the government a monopoly of power for the benefit of all subjects, who themselves have neither rights nor powers as long as their physical safety is guaranteed; the American republic, in contrast, rests on the power of the people—the old Roman *potestas in populo*—and power granted to the authorities is delegated power, which can be revoked. There was, third, Locke's aboriginal social contract, which brought about not government but society—the word being understood in the sense of the Latin *societas,* an "alliance" between all individual members, who contract for their government after they have mutually bound themselves. I shall call this the horizontal version of the social contract. This contract limits the power of each individual member but leaves intact the power of

[36] Locke, *op. cit.* (note 28), section 157.
[37] See my discussion of Puritanism and its influence on the American Revolution in *On Revolution,* 1963, pp. 171 f.

society; society then establishes government "upon the plain ground of an original contract among independent individuals." [38]

All contracts, covenants, and agreements rest on mutuality, and the great advantage of the horizontal version of the social contract is that this mutuality binds each member to his fellow citizens. This is the only form of government in which people are bound together not through historical memories or ethnic homogeneity, as in the nation-state, and not through Hobbes's Leviathan, which "over-awes them all" and thus unites them, but through the strength of mutual promises. In Locke's view, this meant that society remains intact even if "the government is dissolved" or breaks its agreement with society, developing into a tyranny. Once established, society, as long as it exists at all, can never be thrown back into the lawless-ness and anarchy of the state of nature. In Locke's words, "the power that every individual gave the society, when he entered into it, can never revert to the individuals again, as long as the society lasts, but will always remain in the community." [39] This is indeed a new version of the old *potestas in populo,* for the consequence is that, in contrast to earlier theories of the right to resistance, whereby the people could act only "when their Chains are on," they now had the right, again in Locke's words, "to prevent" the chaining.[40] When the signers of the Declaration of Independence "mutually pledged" their lives, their fortunes, and their sacred honor, they were thinking in this vein of specifically American ex-periences as well as in terms of the generalization and conceptuali-zation of these experiences by Locke.

Consent—meaning that voluntary membership must be assumed for every citizen in the community—is obviously (except in the case of naturalization) at least as open to the reproach of being a fiction as the aboriginal contract. The argument is correct legally and theoretically but not existentially. Every man is born a member of a particular community and can survive only if he is welcomed and made at home within it. A kind of consent is implied in every newborn's factual situation; namely, a kind of conformity to the

[38] John Adams, *Novanglus. Works,* Vol. IV, p. 110.
[39] Locke, *op. cit.* (note 28), section 49.
[40] *Ibid.,* section 220.

rules under which the great game of the world is played in the
particular group to which he belongs by birth. We all live and survive by a kind of *tacit consent,* which, however, it would be difficult
to call voluntary. How can we will what is there anyhow? We
might call it voluntary, though, when the child happens to be born
into a community in which dissent is also a legal and *de facto* possibility once he has grown into a man. Dissent implies consent, and
is the hallmark of free government; one who knows that he may
dissent knows also that he somehow consents when he does not
dissent.

Consent as it is implied in the right to dissent—the spirit of
American law and the quintessence of American government—
spells out and articulates the tacit consent given in exchange for the
community's tacit welcome of new arrivals, of the inner immigra-
tion through which it constantly renews itself. Seen in this perspective, tacit consent is not a fiction; it is inherent in the human condition. This *consensus universalis* does not, however, cover consent
to specific laws or specific policies, even if they are the result of
majority decisions.[41] It is often argued that the consent to the Constitution, the *consensus universalis,* implies consent to statutory
laws as well, because in representative government the people have
helped to make them. This consent, I think, is indeed entirely fictitious; under the present circumstances, at any rate, it has lost all
plausibility. Representative government itself is in a crisis today,
partly because it has lost, in the course of time, all institutions that
permitted the citizens' actual participation, and partly because it is
now gravely affected by the disease from which the party system
suffers: bureaucratization and the two parties' tendency to represent nobody except the party machines.

At any rate, the current danger of rebellion in the United States
arises not from dissent and resistance to particular laws, and not

[41] I borrow the term from Tocqueville: "The republican government exists
in America, without contention or opposition, without proofs or arguments,
by a tacit agreement, a sort of *consensus universalis.*" *Democracy in
America,* Knopf edition, New York, 1945. Vol. I, p. 419.

For the important distinction between consent to particular politics and
the general *consensus,* see Hans J. Morgenthau, *Truth and Power,* 1970,
pp. 19 f., and *The New Republic,* Jan. 22, 1966, pp. 16–18.

even from denunciation of the "system" or the "Establishment," but from the challenge to the Constitution (partly from the side of the Administration) and the unwillingness of certain sections of the population to recognize the *consensus universalis*. Tocqueville predicted almost a hundred and fifty years ago that "the most formidable of all the ills that threaten the future of the Union arises" not from slavery, whose abolition he foresaw, but "from the presence of a black population upon its territory." [42] And the reason he could predict the future of Negroes and Indians for more than a century lies in the simple and frightening fact that these people had never been included in the original *consensus universalis* of the American republic. (It was the tragedy of the abolitionist movement that it could appeal only to conscience, and not to the law of the land. There was nothing in the Constitution or in the intent of the framers that could be so construed as to include the slave people in the original compact.[43] And the strong anti-institutional bias of the antislavery movement—its abstract morality, which condemned all institutions as evil because they tolerated the evil of slavery—certainly did not help in promoting those elementary measures of humane reform by which in all other countries the slaves were gradually emancipated into the free society.)[44] We know that this original crime could not be remedied by the Fourteenth and Fifteenth Amendments; on the contrary, the tacit exclusion from the tacit consensus was made more conspicuous by the inability or unwillingness of the Federal government to enforce its own laws, and as time went by and wave after wave of immigrants came to the country, it grew more poignant that blacks, now free,

[42] Tocqueville, *op. cit.* (note 41).

[43] From Jefferson to Lincoln, there is hardly an important statesman in American history who was not convinced that emancipation of the slaves meant segregation of the Negro people or, preferably, deportation. Jefferson: "Nothing is more certain written in the book of fate than that these people are to be free; nor is it less certain that the two races, equally free, cannot live in the same government." And Lincoln who, in agreement with the earlier abolitionist movement, had thought of Liberia as a proper place for colonizing the liberated slave population, tried even in 1862 "when a deputation of colored men came to see [him] . . . to persuade them to set up a colony in Central America." Hofstadter, *op. cit.* (note 7), p. 130.

[44] Elkins—*op. cit.* (note 32), Pt. IV—gives an excellent analysis of the sterility of the abolitionist movement.

and born and bred in the country, were the only ones for whom it was not true that, in Bancroft's words, "the welcome of the Commonwealth was as wide as sorrow." [45] We know the result, and we need not be surprised that the present belated attempts to welcome the Negro population explicitly into the otherwise tacit *consensus universalis* of the nation are not trusted. (An explicit constitutional amendment, addressed specifically to the Negro people of America, might have underlined the great change more dramatically for these people who had never been welcome, assuring them of its finality. Supreme Court decisions are constitutional interpretations, of which the Dred Scott decision is one.[46] The failure of Congress to propose such an amendment is striking in the light of the overwhelming vote for a constitutional amendment to cure the infinitely milder discriminatory practices against women.) At any rate, such attempts are met by rebuffs from black organizations, which care little about the rules of nonviolence for civil disobedience and, often, just as little about the issues at stake—the Vietnam war, specific defects in our institutions—because they are in open rebellion against all of them. And although they have been able to attract to their cause the extreme fringe of radical disobedience, which without them would probably have withered away long ago, their instinct tells them to disengage themselves even from these supporters, who, their rebellious spirit notwithstanding, were included in the original contract out of which rose the tacit *consensus universalis*.

Consent, in the American understanding of the term, relies on the horizontal version of the social contract, and not on majority decisions. (On the contrary, much of the thinking of the framers of the Constitution concerned safeguards for dissenting minorities.)

[45] George Bancroft, *The History of the United States,* abridged edition by Russel B. Nye, Chicago, 1966, p. 44.

[46] The case of Dred Scott vs. Sanford came before the Supreme Court in 1856. Scott, a slave from Missouri, had been taken by his owner to Illinois and other states where slavery was outlawed. Back in Missouri Scott sued his owner, "arguing that these journeys to free areas had made him a free man." The Court decided that Scott could "not bring suit in federal courts . . . because Negroes are not and cannot be citizens in the meaning of the federal Constitution." Robert McCloskey, *The American Supreme Court,* Chicago, 1966, pp. 93–95.

The moral content of this consent is like the moral content of all agreements and contracts; namely, the obligation to keep them. This obligation is inherent in all promises. Thoreau's often quoted statement "The only obligation which I have a right to assume is to do at any time what I think right" might well be varied to: The only obligation which I as a citizen have a right to assume is to make and to keep promises. Promises are the uniquely human way of ordering the future, making it predictable and reliable to the extent that this is humanly possible. And since the predictability of the future can never be absolute, promises are qualified by two tacit limitations. We are bound to keep our promises provided that no unexpected circumstances arise, and provided that the mutuality inherent in all promises is not broken. There exist a great number of circumstances that may cause a promise to be broken, the most important one in our context being the general circumstance of change. And violation of the inherent mutuality of promises can also be caused by many factors, the only relevant one in our context being the failure of the established authorities to keep to the original conditions. Examples of such failures have become only too numerous; there is the case of an "illegal and immoral war," the case of an increasingly impatient claim to power by the executive branch of government, and the case of violations (in the form of war-oriented or other government-directed research) of the specific trust of the universities which gave them protection against political interference and social pressure. As to the debates about the last, those who attack these misuses and those who defend them unfortunately incline to agree on the basically wrong premise that the universities are mere "mirrors for the larger society," an argument best answered by Edward H. Levi, the president of the University of Chicago: "It is sometimes said that society will achieve the kind of education it deserves. Heaven help us if this is so." [47]

"The spirit of the laws," as Montesquieu understood it, is the principle by which people living under a particular legal system act and are inspired to act. Consent, the spirit of American laws, is based on the notion of a mutually binding contract, which estab-

[47] Edward H. Levi, *Point of View: Talks on Education,* Chicago, 1969, pp. 139, 170.

lished first the individual colonies and then the Union. A contract presupposes a plurality of at least two, and every association established and acting according to the principle of consent, based on mutual promise, presupposes a plurality that does not dissolve but is shaped into the form of a union—*e pluribus unum*. If the individual members of the community thus formed should choose not to retain a restricted autonomy, if they should choose to disappear into complete unity, such as the *union sacrée* of the French nation, all talk about the citizen's *moral* relation to the law would be mere rhetoric.

Consent and the right to dissent became the inspiring and organizing principles of action that taught the inhabitants of this continent the "art of associating together," from which sprang those voluntary associations whose role Tocqueville was the first to notice, with amazement, admiration, and some misgiving; he thought them the peculiar strength of the American political system.[48] The few chapters he devoted to them are still by far the best in the not very large literature on the subject. The words with which he introduced it—"In no country in the world has the principle of association been more successfully used or applied to a greater multitude of objects than in America"—are no less true today than they were nearly a hundred and fifty years ago; and neither is the conclusion that "nothing . . . is more deserving of our attention than the moral and intellectual associations of America." Voluntary associations are not parties; they are *ad hoc* organizations that pursue short-term goals and disappear when the goal has been reached. Only in the case of their prolonged failure and of an aim of great importance may they "constitute, as it were, a separate nation in the midst of the nation, a government within the government." (This happened in 1861, about thirty years after Tocqueville wrote these words, and it could happen again; the challenge of the Massachusetts legislature to the foreign policy of the Administration is a clear warning.) Alas, it is no longer true that their spirit "pervades every act of social life," and while this may have resulted in a

[48] All the following citations of Tocqueville are from *op. cit.* (note 41), Vol. I, Ch. 12, and Vol. II, Bk. ii, Ch. 5.

certain decline in the huge number of joiners in the population—of Babbitts, who are the specifically American version of Philistines —the refusal to form associations "for the smallest undertakings" is paid for by an evident decline in the appetite for action. For Americans still regard association as "the only means they have for acting," and rightly so. In short, "as soon as several of the inhabitants of the United States have taken up an opinion or a feeling which they wish to promote in the world," or have found some fault they wish to correct, "they look out for mutual assistance, and as soon as they have found one another out, they combine. *From that moment, they are no longer isolated men but a power seen from afar,* whose actions serve for an example and whose language is listened to." (My italics.)

It is my contention that civil disobedients are nothing but the latest form of voluntary association, and that they are thus quite in tune with the oldest traditions of the country. What could better describe them than Tocqueville's words "The citizens who form the minority associate in order, first, to show their numerical strength and so to diminish the moral power of the majority"? To be sure, it has been a long time since "moral and intellectual associations" could be found among voluntary associations—which, on the contrary, seem to have been formed only for the protection of special interests, of pressure groups and the lobbyists who represented them in Washington. I do not doubt that the dubious reputation of the lobbyists is deserved, just as the dubious reputation of the politician in this country has frequently been amply deserved. However, the fact is that the pressure groups are also voluntary associations, and that they are recognized in Washington, where their influence is sufficiently great to be called an "assistant government";[49] indeed, the number of registered lobbyists exceeds by far the number of congressmen.[50] (This public recognition is no small matter, for, surprisingly, such "assistance," like the freedom of association in general, was in no way foreseen in the Constitution and

[49] Carl Joachim Friedrich, *Constitutional Government and Democracy,* 1950, p. 464.
[50] Max Lerner, *America as a Civilization,* New York, 1957, p. 399.

its First Amendment, which protects no more than a kind of negative right—"peaceably to assemble and to petition the Government
for a redress of grievances.")

The dangers inherent in civil disobedience are no greater than
the dangers inherent in the right to free association, and of these
Tocqueville, his admiration notwithstanding, was not unaware.
(John Stuart Mill, in his review of the first volume of *Democracy in
America,* interpreted them: "The capacity of coöperation for a
common purpose, heretofore a monopolized instrument of power
in the hands of the higher classes, is now a most formidable one in
those of the lowest.") [51] Tocqueville knew that "the tyrannical control that these societies exercise is often far more insupportable
than the authority possessed over society by the government which
they attack." But he knew also that "the liberty of association has
become a necessary guarantee against the tyranny of the majority,"
that "a dangerous expedient is used to obviate a still more formidable danger," and, finally, that "it is by the enjoyment of dangerous freedom that the Americans learn the art of rendering the dangers of freedom less formidable." In any event, "if men are to
remain civilized or to become so, the art of associating together
must grow and improve *in the same ratio in which the equality of
conditions is increased."* (My italics.)

We need not go into the old debates about the glories and the
dangers of equality, the good and the evil of democracy, to understand that all evil demons could be let loose if the original contractual model of the associations—mutual promises with the moral
imperative *pacta sunt servanda*—should be lost. Under today's circumstances, this could happen if these groups, like their counterparts in other countries, were to substitute ideological commitments, political or other, for actual goals. When an association is
no longer capable or willing to unite "into one channel the efforts
of *divergent* minds" (Tocqueville), it has lost its gift for action.
What threatens the student movement, the chief civil-disobedience
group of the moment, is not just vandalism, violence, bad temper,
and worse manners but the growing infection of the movement with

[51] Reprinted as Introduction to the Schocken Paperback edition of
Tocqueville, 1961.

ideologies (Maoism, Castroism, Stalinism, Marxism-Leninism, and the like), which in fact split and dissolve the association.

Civil disobedience and voluntary association are phenomena practically unknown anywhere else. (The political terminology that surrounds them yields only with great difficulty to translation.) It has often been said that the genius of the English people is to muddle through and that the genius of the American people is to disregard theoretical considerations in favor of pragmatic experience and practical action. However that may be, the fact is that the phenomenon of voluntary association has been neglected and that the notion of civil disobedience has only recently received the attention it deserves. In contrast to the conscientious objector, the civil disobedient is a member of a group, and this group, whether we like it or not, is formed in accordance with the same spirit that has informed voluntary associations. The greatest fallacy in the present debate seems to me that assumption that we are dealing with individuals, who pit themselves subjectively and conscientiously against the laws and customs of the community—an assumption that is shared by the defenders and the detractors of civil disobedience. The fact is that we are dealing with organized minorities, who stand against assumed and nonvocal, though hardly "silent," majorities, and I think it is undeniable that these majorities have changed in mood and opinion to an astounding degree under the pressure of the minorities. It has been the misfortune of recent debates that they have been dominated largely by jurists—lawyers, judges, and other men of law—for they must find it difficult to recognize the civil disobedient as a member of a group rather than to see him as an individual lawbreaker, and hence a potential defendant in court. It is, indeed, the grandeur of court procedure that it is concerned with meting out justice to an individual, and remains unconcerned with everything else—with the *Zeitgeist* or with opinions that the defendant may share with others and try to present in court. The only non-criminal lawbreaker the court recognizes is the conscientious objector, and the only group adherence it is aware of is called conspiracy—an utterly misleading charge in such cases, since conspiracy requires not only "breathing together" but secrecy, and civil disobedience occurs in public.

As I noted earlier, civil disobedience, though it is compatible with the spirit of American laws, has not yet found a niche in the American legal system. The first step would be to obtain the same recognition for the civil-disobedient minorities that is accorded the numerous special interests (minority interests, by definition) in the country, and to deal with civil-disobedient groups in the same way as with pressure groups, which, through their representatives—that is, registered lobbyists—are permitted to influence and "assist" Congress by means of persuasion, qualified opinion, and the numbers of their constituents. These minorities of opinion would thus be able to establish themselves as a power that not only is "seen from afar" during demonstrations and other dramatizations of their viewpoint but is always present and to be reckoned with. The next step would be to admit publicly that the First Amendment covers neither in language nor in spirit the right of association as it is actually practiced in this country—this precious privilege whose exercise has in fact been (as Tocqueville noted) "incorporated with the manners and customs of the people" for centuries. If there is anything that urgently requires a new constitutional amendment and is worth all the trouble that goes with it, it is certainly this.

Perhaps an emergency was needed before we could find a home for civil disobedience not only in our political language but in our legal system as well. An emergency is certainly at hand when the established institutions of a country fail to function properly and its authority loses its power, and it is such an emergency in the United States today that has changed voluntary association into civil disobedience and transformed dissent into resistance. It is common knowledge that this condition prevails at present—and, indeed, has prevailed for some time—in large parts of the world; what is new is that this country is no longer an exception. Whether our form of government will survive this century is uncertain, but it is also uncertain that it will not. Wilson Carey McWilliams has wisely said, "When institutions fail, political society depends on men, and men are feeble reeds, prone to acquiesce in—if not to commit—iniquity." [52] Ever since the Mayflower Compact was drafted and signed under a different kind of emergency, voluntary associations

[52] McWilliams, *op. cit.* (note 2), p. 226.

have been the specifically American remedy for the failure of institutions, the unreliability of men, and the uncertain nature of the future. As distinguished from other countries, this republic, despite the great turmoil of change and of failure through which it is going at present, may still be in possession of its traditional instruments for facing the future with some measure of confidence.

COMMENT

by Edgar S. Cahn

If I understand what Dr. Arendt has said, she has politely indicted the entire legal system and legal profession. Let me be a little more explicit as to why I believe that is what she has done.

As a profession committed to the rule of law, we have no forum, no means to accommodate, to cope with, the realities to which she has addressed herself. And they are indeed the most pressing realities that pose any kind of menace to the rule of law in this society.

To be more specific, current discussions about the limits of civil disobedience characteristically suffer from two major defects:

1. They speak in terms of individual disobedience: the right of an individual in the Thoreau tradition to violate the social compact and ask whether a price—and what price—should be exacted for such an act.

2. Discussions of civil disobedience treat the social compact itself as a static order to which the individual as an individual should be viewed as giving implied or actual consent.

The realities with which we deal are at odds with both premises.

It is not individuals but entire groups which are dissenting. To speak of individual disobedience, or individual guilt and liability, would generally be understood to be of little analytical use in, for instance, the context of international war or civil war. There it would be understood that the problem was not one primarily of individual guilt—but rather of negotiation of the terms of an equitable truce between two nations or two segments of a nation. The question would then not be one of "disobedience" or violation of an international social compact by individuals. The issue would be redefined—as it was by President Wilson—in terms of devising an honorable peace and a way in which nations could live together with each other in the future—not how they could engage in a constant process of affixing blame for the past.

In fact, this is what we deal with today—not individual disobedience, but secession or, more accurately, expulsion of major groups of disenfranchised citizens from society, who in turn are viewed as engaged in individual isolated acts of civil disobedience.

As a result, we talk nonfunctionally in terms of what rules to apply in judging individual guilt—rules designed *not* for a forum of negotiation, like peace talks or truce negotiations or union negotiations, but rules of fault and liability designed for application in one and only one forum, the courts.

And this is fundamentally the wrong forum and the wrong set of rules with which to deal with major and sustained outbreaks of protest or dissent where large segments of the population are demanding a fundamental restructuring of the ground rules which have disenfranchised or oppressed them.

This raises the second issue: that of a static social compact. One may haggle about whether the black or the Indian ever can be said to have consented to accept the social compact voluntarily. With college students, the case is obviously stronger, since they have been nurtured by and have partaken of the blessings of this society. What one must challenge is the notion of a static social compact—for we have never had that, despite the formal appearance of one in the Constitution and laws of the land. Our social compact as a nation is always being renegotiated on a grand scale. When attempts were made rigidly to interpose a static format on that process, violence erupted. The Dred Scott Decision illustrates what can happen when attempts are made to impose the logic of a static social compact on a changing order.

Since our nation's origin, that social compact has always been renegotiated—first in seemingly grand terms, with westward expansion and the admission of new states. But now the renegotiation taking place is just as massive, just as cosmic, even though it is not accorded formal recognition. That renegotiation is the renegotiation taking place as a result of Federally subsidized flight to the suburbs, now given constitutional status in the reapportionment cases. That dynamic social compact is being altered by the civil rights revolution and student revolutions on campus. These, too, are renegotiations of a social compact which has never been static and which we cannot assume should be viewed as static. That renegotiation is taking place in every city and county in this country, through the Model Cities Act, the poverty program, the welfare program, and so on—all of which fundamentally redefine the relationship of the individual to the state and the states' relation to the national government.

As a profession we have spent little time and intellect in concerning ourselves with the constitutional challenge of the dimensions that Dr. Arendt has thrown down.

I do not speak about this from an abstract sense, because I am afraid that I do not deal day to day with abstractions.

I deal with realities, since I come from the banks of the Columbia where the State of Washington denies to Indians the exercising of their treaty rights and the privilege of fishing for sustenance, while the very same State of Washington will spend up to $2,000 *per salmon* on the upper reaches of the Columbia to save them for sportsmen fishers and commercial fishermen.

I speak as the attorney who represented ten counties in Alabama, where our contention was that the government refused to declare them emergency counties for purposes of getting emergency food and commodities in those counties. We claimed it was an emergency because it was the worst winter since 1887, because of the failure of the cotton crop and because of an influenza epidemic, and were told that this was no emergency; that, in the words of the United States attorney, "death was a chronic condition." Only later did we find out those very same counties had been declared emergency counties in order to give emergency loans to plantation owners because it was the worst cotton crop since 1887, because it was the worst winter since 1887, and also because the peanut crop had failed.

I am talking about situations like that in Dayton, Ohio, where my wife and I spent six weeks this past winter under twenty-four-hour armed guard that I assure you was not provided by the police, where the school board had unilaterally repudiated a renegotiated social compact with the black community for the purpose of improving the quality of education. That compact had been incorporated in the Model Cities plan and approved by the Federal government. The school board and the community were, by agreement, to be the joint beneficiaries of some $70,000 in programs until the school board decided it could be the sole beneficiary. I am talking about a government which is lawless, a government which violates its own compacts.

I speak, for instance, about the relocation programs, and I can cite to you relocation requirement after relocation requirement, enacted by the Congress, which the executive branch knowingly refuses to enforce.

I speak of highways built with Department of Transportation money, dozens of which are planned to go through areas being built up by the Department of Housing and Urban Development with urban renewal and model cities.

This is a lawless society, and it is the executive branch that is acting lawlessly. When we speak about groups and social compacts, we have no forums to deal with these grievances, whether they are the *de minimis* grievances of rotten heads of lettuce in supermarkets or taxicabs that will not pick up black passengers, or the kind of grievance that is so woven into the fabric of community perceptions that to wrest it from that fabric and put it in an adversary context is to do violence not only to the reality of that grievance but also to the entire community's perception of that grievance.

As a profession we have in effect neglected our responsibilities in the use of intellect. I favor the use of intellect and craftsmanship. But any profession that is devoted and dedicated to law ought to spend time thinking through where *these* issues are to be heard, and lawful resolutions evolved.

Moreover we cannot talk about renegotiation of the social compact purely on a nationwide basis. That is too general and undifferentiating.

We ought to recognize by now that the school system and hospital system, the zoning boards and welfare departments, are as much a part of the legislative and judicial process as the formal political and legal system which we study in the law schools. In our obsession with law, as we know it, we have lost sight of the true institutional dimensions of lawlessness.

Having spent as much time as I have on Indian reservations, I am reminded of an event that occurred last Law Day in the State of Washington, where a member of the Tulalip tribe rose and said:

"You have a very complicated legal system. It is not that way with my people. I have always thought that you had so many laws because you were a lawless people, why else would you need so many laws?

"After all, Europe opened up its prisons and penitentiaries and sent their criminals to this country. Perhaps that is why you need so many laws. I hope we never have to reach such an advanced state of civilization."

We have failed to think in terms of effective intragroup sanctions, or to learn from a culture within our midst that uses group sanctions, such as community ostracism and disapproval. These were the alternatives.

Thomas Jefferson noted, "Imperfect as this system of coercion may seem, crimes are very rare among them," speaking of the Indians of Virginia.

Then Jefferson went on to observe, "It will be said that great societies cannot exist without government, the savages therefore break them into small ones."

I wonder who are the savages.

I think of the instance that the explorer in the Arctic, Peter Freuchen, records when he was sharing food with an Eskimo hunter. He was reproved for thanking him for the food: "You must not thank me for your meat; it is your right to get it; in this country nobody wishes to be dependent on others. With gifts you make slaves just as with whips you make dogs."

I am talking about a culture and society which evolved other kinds of tribunals and began to build ways in which community grievances could be heard, and new sanctions levied.

I am talking about the evolution of institutions such as neighborhood courts, and the use of boards of inquiry such as were used in connection with *Hunger USA*.

Recently a People's Forum was established in Memphis, where black members of the city council requested hearings on police brutality and prominent jurists and lawyers came in to hear them.

It is perhaps symptomatic that the first and only jurist who was prepared to come down was the only Indian who is a judge outside the tribal court system in the United States.

We must consider how to create forums where entire groups can be incorporated into the social structure, where one can begin, in effect, to renegotiate the social compact.

Must we abandon the notion of community, or is democracy, as Tocqueville observed, just a way in which men live alone? Is it true, as one Indian told me, that "Law among you is the way in which strangers live with one another"?

Have we lost the entire capacity to create any kind of community that can live with itself?

When one thinks of the communications media and particularly the effect that television has had, we have in certain respects become a national community. And yet we have no way in which this community, this great nation of ours, and groups in it, can begin to speak to each other. We limit ourselves to fights about renewal of TV licenses.

But we fail to explore, as a legal instrumentality, the use of the media whereby groups can begin to levy sanctions on themselves and one another, talk to each other and form consensus.

The legal profession in the past has made its greatest contributions, not by creating a dependency upon itself, but rather by creating institutions and constitutions and corporate charters where people could function without lawyers to create, to fulfill their own desires, to realize their own potentials. What we need to do as a profession is to create institutions, forums, and ways for people to air their grievances and construct systems in which welfare workers and school officials can be held accountable.

The alternative is to increase dependency on ourselves and on others. That approach is epitomized by our treatment of the Indian, which offers a kind of microcosm of our society as a whole. On one reservation in South Dakota, one of the largest in this country, we have finally reached the ratio of one helping official to every single Indian family. Total expenditures on that reservation averaged a little over $8,000 per Indian family, but the median income of an Indian family of five on that reservation was less than $1,900. One might say there is some slippage. If that is the way we will renegotiate the social compact, then the greatest growth industry we have is that charged with the care and tending of the poor. It is a profitable industry for the caretakers. One cartoonist depicted it in the form of an Indian behind barbed wire saying to a black man, "Let me tell you, brother, there is no neglect like benign neglect."

The challenge we face today, and that Dr. Arendt has correctly diagnosed, is one of group dissent from the social compact of the past. We cannot cope with this challenge simply by viewing it as a matter of rules to be tried in only one forum, the courts. That forum primarily looks at the past. But the question we must face is how we live with each other in the future. It is not appropriate to talk purely about individual liability, individual guilt and responsibility. The real questions are: How can groups of communities, the conquered and the conquerors, live together in terms of a just peace? How can one renegotiate today's terms in a way that makes sense and will make it possible for the bitterness of the past to be mitigated to the greatest extent possible?

The legal profession itself has abdicated responsibility by concern with rules, by faultfinding, by notions of a social compact artificially restricted to a very limited notion of the political process and the legal process as we know it.

It is perhaps the words of the poet, the artist, as expressed by Kahlil Gibran, in *The Prophet,* that are sounder as points of departure for legal analysis: "The righteous is not innocent of the deeds of the wicked. You cannot separate the just from the unjust, and the good from the wicked, for they stand together before the face of the sun, even as the black thread and the white thread are woven together, and if the black thread breaks, the weaver shall look to the whole cloth and he shall examine the loom also."

That is, I believe, a challenge that Dr. Arendt has put to the legal profession and those who are truly dedicated to the rule of law.

PART II

The Capacity of the American
Social Order to Meet
the Changing Demands
for Social Justice
Through the Methods of Law

INTRODUCTION

by Eugene V. Rostow

We have contemplated the fate of Socrates. Even if we all agreed with the interpretation of the *Crito* which I put forward, and pledged ourselves to abide by it as the first law of social life, our vows would not of themselves advance the cause of social peace very far. The obligation to law would not survive if the social order crumbled all around us. No society can expect the loyalty of obedience to law if it fails consistently to meet the challenge of changing ideals of social justice. And the pressure for change has never been more insistent within the American community.

The question to be examined in Part II therefore is whether the society, the economy, and the legal and political system we have inherited can be adapted to these pressures wisely and justly, in time, and in peace.

The answer to these questions is far from self-evident. Our loose and flexible social and political order is dominated by the principle of divided power as a bulwark against tyranny. As Justice Brandeis once remarked, an efficient government is not the primary goal of the Constitution. Its purpose, rather, is to maintain a state of tension within society, through the inevitable friction of its various parts, as the safest and most favorable setting for personal freedom. In that perspective, the Constitution has been an immense success. We have friction galore—between cities and states, between states and the nation, among the three branches of government at every level. No single center of power can possibly seize command. But no political machinery requires more of its votaries, or can be paralyzed more easily by determined and well-placed opposition.

This strong, slow, resilient, and deeply rooted political order, spun out of an eighteenth-century parchment by practical men in the heat of a thousand crises, now faces a difficult agenda of social action—equality for blacks, rational government for our swollen cities, rethinking and renewed agreement on foreign policy, educational reform, address to the disaffection of some young people.

Hard as these problems of tangible policy are—and they are very difficult indeed—they impose less stress on those who must decide than the changes which are taking place in the climate of opinion. I find it hard to think of a period in our history when the prevailing outlook changed so quickly. Was the gap between 1850 and 1870, or between 1910 and 1920, as wide as the gap between President Eisenhower and President Nixon? I wonder.

Whether the pace of change in ideas is unusually rapid at this stage, it is surely rapid. Consider just one factor in the process, as an example. The experience of war has always been a prodigious catalyst of social change, and America has been at war, almost without relief, for thirty years. It is not surprising that ideas and taboos about dress, sex, language, and many other familiar habits have been transformed. The code of social justice has not been exempted from the storm. The notion of a minimal income as a legal right, for example, would have seemed a fantasy from the realm of science fiction to President Hoover, and even to his successor.

Nonetheless, during the last forty years we have lived through an immense and an immensely rapid change in the prevailing American code of social justice. A review of that experience is indispensable, I think, in considering the question before us today: Does our social order have the capacity to meet and master the new tides of change which are pressing in upon us now, in their appointed turn?

If the social revolutions of the last forty years are viewed in perspective, they appear as among the greatest historic achievements of our political system. The bitter years of depression and war, and the political leadership of President Roosevelt, galvanized the progressive impulses of American life into a moral and political force that transformed the nation. Later Presidents of both parties accepted the basic rightness of what had been accomplished, and built on it.

What have we done?

First of all, I should say, we have developed and accepted a theory and practice in economic planning which should guarantee society against great depressions, and hopefully against great inflations as well, even under the pressure of war. These methods are not much more than a quarter-century old. They are still crude and imperfect. They do not solve all economic and social problems, nor do they guarantee capitalist societies prosperity, growth, and stable prices without thought and effort. But they indubitably work. At a minimum, they have eliminated the specter of a Great Depression, like that of the thirties, from the expectations of man. And they have been supplemented by measures against fraud in finance, by special policies with regard to transportation, agriculture, power, and the provision of credit, which have helped (and sometimes hindered) the responsiveness of the economy to the stimuli of fiscal and monetary controls.

Secondly, we have undertaken other experiments in planning— not the detailed, overall fixing of employment and production quotas, but experiments in regional and urban planning, where again, through trial and error, we have confirmed the promise of such methods in enabling us to solve the problems generated by the prodigious movements of people which have so altered the life of the nation. Perhaps in this area we should state our hopes more modestly. The social costs of the free movement of our people— from rural areas to cities, from South to North, from East to West —are so enormous, and the human dislocations so deep, that perhaps we should be content not to "solve" these problems, or to "master" them, but simply to cope with them.

Third, in this generation the national government has assumed primary responsibility in education, in the provision of medical care, and in social welfare. These titanic steps are remaking the social order, and the universe of men's minds.

Fourth, in the area of law itself, the Supreme Court has led a far-reaching movement for law reform which has involved Congress, the bar associations, the state legislatures, and the political process as well. That movement has steadily gained in momentum, despite the opposition it has provoked. It has accomplished much, although, naturally, even more remains to be done. Our concepts of individual liberty have been broadened. Criminal law administration has been improved, and the use of the third degree reduced as a method of law enforcement. The guarantees of the Bill of Rights have never been more intensively enforced. Stirred by the Supreme Court, and those who brought cases before it, the nation was aroused at long last to insist on the enforcement of the Fourteenth and Fifteenth Amendments in behalf of the Negro.

Responding to the stresses of its experience with depression and war, the nation deeply altered its conception of social justice, through programs carried out by judicial and parliamentary means and conceived in terms which confirmed and fulfilled its own aspirations. Violence played a minimal part in these events, and often a negative one. The most open act of political coercion of the entire period was President Roosevelt's court-packing plan. It failed. The Supreme Court emerged from that trial, as it has emerged from all its historic trials, stronger than ever as the guarantor of the Constitution. The great social legislation of the last forty years, from AAA, SEC, and social security to poverty, housing, and education, was not easily achieved, and it was often resisted. Its enactment, however, was the achievement of virile democratic politics, not the threats of armed mobs, or the equivalent. The agony of prolonged depression stirred the country not to massacre, or to suicidal violence, but to effective and constructive political action.

In the field of Negro rights, the civil rights movement brought about a profound and continuing process of change in custom and in outlook not, in the main, by using tactics of civil disobedience, but by a full use of lawful methods of peaceful assembly and of protest, and above all by calling on the courts and the nation to enforce the Constitution against the civil disobedience of those who had resisted the law for a century. The nation responded positively to court decisions, and to peaceful and legal demonstrations against unconstitutional laws or practices. It was aroused to righteousness by the spectacle of men of law in the South, who had sworn to uphold the Constitution, using force to resist its command, and the orders of United States courts.

But the response of the nation to the more recent riots and disorders in the ghettos of our cities has been troubled, and, on the whole, negative. Congressional appropriations for poverty and urban programs have been adversely affected by outbreaks of violence. People and business enterprise move away from the areas of violence, making the disease worse. Small tactical improvements may occur here and there, stirred by the threat of violence or disruption. But the strategic lesson, I believe, is clear. The social progress of the nation during the last forty years has been the achievement primarily of democratic law and politics, not of revolutionary methods. In the course of that titanic social effort, the violent and revolutionary resistance of a minority to the valid command of the nation was overcome, not by force, or by force alone, but by the repeated assertion of the nation's political will. Over and over again, the nation showed its distaste for tactics of violence and coercion, and its capacity to be stirred by the active but peaceful methods of its own politics.

It is often claimed, as a justification for violence as a political method, that in the struggle for labor's rights, illegal and sometimes violent tactics were justified in the end by their success in raising the status and rewards of labor, and bringing labor relations within the reach of law.

The transformation of labor law in the century before 1935, and the changed public attitude toward trade unions, was a process which surely included recourse to violence, illegal coercion, and other forms of illegality both by labor and by employers. A limited right to strike was recognized in some states toward the middle of the nineteenth century. And doubt was cast on yellow-dog contracts in the same period, or somewhat later. But the legal rights of labor were cloudy and uncertain. Judicial opinions were not followed up by statutory codes. Practice often failed to recognize even rights about which the courts were clear. And modern statutes did not begin to take shape much before the Clayton Act in 1914.

Under these circumstances, the struggle for labor's rights took place in large part without real guidance from the positive law.

The more violent episodes in labor history—going well beyond what custom regarded as reasonable—were almost invariably counter-productive in immediate effect. Progress occurred when labor respected boundaries public opinion could accept. Often, labor made progress when it was the clear victim of violence or unfairness on the part of employers. And it lost ground when it resorted to tactics the public regarded as wrong.

The moral of labor history, I believe, is not that violence and disobedience to law on the part of labor were justified by the passage of the Wagner Act and the recognition of labor's rights, but that those goals were achieved in the main by political means, after violence and counterviolence had produced nothing but bitter exhaustion. In labor, as in civil rights, those who relied primarily on force and coercion lost in the end—the southern segregationists in the field of civil rights, and the anti-union employers in the field of labor.

This is not to suggest that all is well with our society, and that the social tensions we feel all about us are an illusion. Not at all. As in every other period of rapid progress in history, hope based on the experience of progress has generated a deep and urgent restlessness—a desire to press forward more rapidly still, for more progress. Explosive and even revolutionary impatience in societies, as many students of the phenomenon of revolution have remarked, usually develops not in situations of hopelessness, of poverty, and of hunger, but at times when social conditions are improving.

The agenda for social action in the United States is formidable. The process of change has generated its own momentum. Many institutions and arrangements have been left behind by the uneven pace of change in different sectors of society.

But nothing in our experience should lead us to suppose that the agenda is beyond the capacity of our social order. It surely is less formidable than the perspectives which faced us in 1930.

It is bracing to recall 1930. We were in the midst of a depression, which most of us regarded as a phenomenon of nature, beyond the reach of impious man. Economic orthodoxy—and even most economic heterodoxy—did not offer politicians the intellectual tools with which they could hope to devise a policy to end the Depression. And we lived in a constitutional universe which would have denied the government power to carry out a full employment policy, even if at that point we could have devised one.

We are surely in trouble again—but not nearly so badly off as we were in 1930.

CHAPTER 7

CHANGING PATTERNS OF SOCIAL COHESION AND THE CRISIS OF LAW UNDER A SYSTEM OF GOVERNMENT BY CONSENT

by David M. Potter

When we attempt to appraise the place which law occupies in any given society, it is a good point of departure, I believe, to start by recognizing that the law is a uniform system of social control for the entire population living within a given jurisdiction. Its rules apply to everyone within the area of this jurisdiction. Other institutions may have rules which apply to parts of the population—churches, for instance, may do so, or labor unions—and they may impose penalties for violation of their rules. But these institutions do not apply uniformly to everyone, while, on the contrary, the law does. Since the law is uniform, it will, of course, operate most effectively when the population to which it applies is also uniform, or, as we might say, homogeneous. Or conversely, it may operate least effectively where the population is heterogeneous. In treating the relationship of law to society, legal thinkers commonly assume that the population, or society, to which the law applies *is* homogeneous —is a holistic community. One finds this assumption, for instance, in the criterion that obscenity can be defined by "prevailing community standards." This is well and good if there is one community which coincides with the jurisdiction. But suppose there is no community; or suppose there are two or more separate and somewhat antagonistic communities, all within the same jurisdiction. Then there can be no holistic "prevailing community standards," and therefore no criterion for the law—perhaps no social "legitimacy" for it.

This is a point to which I must return later, but first I should observe that this problem does not arise in all systems of government. Historically, even the potentiality of such a dilemma could scarcely have arisen more than two hundred years ago, for up to that time legitimacy was regarded as residing in a single ruler rather than in a multiplicity of people—in a unitary authority rather than in a pluralistic one. Of course, as we all know, this theory had been modified in various ways, by making the ruler an institution ("the crown") rather than a man ("the king"), and by avoiding the enactment of laws that would arouse popular hostility. But still, authority, and also legitimacy, were believed to come from above, and so long as this was true, the question of what happened to the legitimacy of law when it was vested in a society which might be deeply divided—that question did not arise. The kind of sanctions that would justify an authority as universal as that of the law seemed to be of so transcendent a nature that men tended to attribute a supernatural quality to them—the law was from the king and the king was from God. Such authority could hardly present problems of heterogeneity.

But the Americans of the late eighteenth century broke new ground by everlastingly rejecting the idea of authority from above, and by repudiating the notions of rank which had buttressed such authority. America, they decided, was to be a society of men equal in formal rank. Without rank, there could be no hierarchical class of "natural" rulers, and government was specifically declared to derive its sanction ("its just powers") from the "consent of the governed."

Among the innumerable writers who have celebrated the advent two centuries ago, of the principle of government by the consent of the governed, it is remarkable how few have ever recognized that this principle contained a built-in dilemma, and one which might have been seriously regarded as an insoluble dilemma: When the governed include the entire body of citizens (and even noncitizens), it is inevitable that they will disagree on many matters and that policies which win the consent of some will never gain the consent of others—perhaps of very numerous others. Therefore, at an operative level, government by the consent of the governed really means government according to the wishes of some of the governed and contrary to the wishes of some others of the governed. The phrase "consent of the governed," under the cover of a false assumption that the governed will always and inevitably be an integral body, concealed the imminent hazard that government by citizens might simply mean government by any combination of citizens strong enough to overpower any other combination or combinations of citizens. In this sense, the principle of "consent" might become an ironic fiction to cover the process by which a more powerful component in society would trample upon the deepest convictions of a less powerful component.

There was nothing inherent in the doctrine of consent itself—nothing in the logic of the idea—which would have prevented such a travesty. In terms of theory, one might say that the United States became exposed almost two centuries ago to the potentiality that conflicting popular factions might destroy the society by dividing it into irreconcilable opposing groups, for there was no authority higher than the people's own consent to restrain them. Once, of course, at the time of the Civil War, this potential hazard became a terrible reality. But it was only once, and otherwise, for two centuries, the hazard remained potential only. Thus, by now, when divisiveness endangers our public policy as never before, we are so accustomed to the routines of government by consent and so in the habit of assuming that consent can always be attained at some kind of price that we have ceased to realize that our mechanism provides no recourse for society in situations where consent is really withheld. This lack of recourse constitutes a vulnerability in our system —an acute, distinctive, but largely unrecognized vulnerability— which renders the society almost helpless in the face of divisions which cannot be reconciled. This vulnerability is peculiar to the system of government by consent and is basic to the present crisis of law in a divided society.

Historically, the system of government by consent succeeded so well that we are now most inclined to take it for granted, at a time when we can least afford to take it for granted. At the beginning of the American experiment, there were men who felt acutely apprehensive about the cohesiveness of a system which gave a broad franchise to dissent and which sanctioned organized opposition to the policies of the government. Most of the founders were decidedly uneasy about the danger of political parties, because they felt that the creation of parties would deepen divisions in the society and would perpetuate strife. Strife was generally regarded as likely to tear the social fabric, and traditional governments had customarily sought to suppress it. Now the United States was about to incorporate political strife as a regular part of the system. Not unnaturally, some political sages viewed such a step with deep misgivings. Further, it was generally recognized that by sanctioning a high degree of freedom for individual citizens, the founders were releasing a force which might weaken the claims of the community as a whole—as an organism—vis-à-vis the claims of the unrestrained individual.

Thus, men recognized that democracy was a peculiarly fragile system, especially dependent upon the responsibility and self-restraint with which citizens exercised their freedom. Long after the Revolution, pundits continued to repeat these warnings and the public continued to nod approval of the repetitions. But the fact is that after a time, while still affirming these propositions ritualistically, we ceased to believe them. One may say that the system worked so well that it inspired faith in democracy, or one may say that America got along so well under the system (which is by no means the same thing), that people ceased to worry about it. Certainly the United States, under the Constitution of 1787, did grow with incredible rapidity in area and in population. It experienced a total economic transformation from a land of small farmers, producing food for their own use, to what some social analysts call a post-industrial society, with the immensely complex and interdependent economy which we have today. Democracy survived this transformation. It survived the transition from a horse-and-buggy technology based on the muscle of men and animals, the power of wind in a sail, and water in a waterwheel, and heat from fossilized plants, to a technology which could put men on the moon and—what was even more remarkable—could bring them back. Naturally, we began to think that if democracy can flourish under such varied conditions, and can contribute in a significant way to such remarkable achievements, it must be tough, adaptable, and resilient —not brittle or fragile after all.

Our confidence in the indestructibility of the democratic system was strengthened when we saw it survive crises which other, seemingly "stronger" systems might not have survived. To begin with, in the Civil War, more than a century ago, the nation faced a test of whether a democratic government can be, at the same time, strong enough to defeat its embattled adversaries and weak enough (or limited enough) to insure that freedoms would not be sacrificed by the very severity of the measures required to protect them. Abraham Lincoln was deeply concerned with this problem, and he spoke very feelingly of "the necessity that is upon us of proving that popular government is not an absurdity." Before he was assassinated, he knew that the government of the Union—a democratic government—had vindicated itself, and that Old World critics could never again speak with their former confidence when they said that a republic might be all right in times of tranquility but that it would fall apart at the first real test of strength.

Eight decades after the Civil War, the "inefficient" and hopelessly civilianized American democracy administered total defeat to the most "efficient" and powerful military machine that the world had ever seen up to that time. Meanwhile, on many fronts— industrial, and technological, and scientific—the country had passed from triumph to triumph in a way which further assured Americans of the invulnerability of their system.

Yet, all the while, we had been operating on a principle of government by consent, of which it might plausibly be said that the reason we trusted it so completely was that we had never taken the trouble to understand it. When we thought about it at all, it was usually in the simplistic terms of "majority rule." The consent of the governed, operationally, we thought was the will of the majority, and even while upholding individual rights and freedoms, we have been chronically oblivious to the contradiction between the principle of majority rule and the principle of individual rights, just as we have been uncritically susceptible to such unsophisticated corollaries of the majoritarian fallacy as the "one man, one vote" slogan. But as almost everyone would recognize, if he would only stop to reflect, the process of government in the United States has never been one of an omnipotent majority imposing its will upon a defenseless and unresisting minority. Rather, the process has been one by which the majority and the minority arrived at an understanding—not necessarily an amicable one, and indeed usually an arrangement by which the majority settled for less than it wanted to attain and the minority yielded more than it wanted to concede. Both accepted terms with which they were not entirely satisfied. While actual coercion was avoided, heavy pressure was frequently used, but even when pressure was heaviest a kind of understanding was involved, and this was what was meant by government by consent.

I doubt whether history or political science has ever done full justice to the subtlety and also to the pervasiveness of the arrangements by which the principle of consent—seldom totally voluntary, seldom entirely coercive—was woven into the fabric of our institutions. Politically, consent did not mean what we now sometimes mean when we speak of "consensus," and if my interpretation here should be damned as "consensus history," at least it is not consensus history of the orthodox kind. Consent did not mean either bland agreement on all questions, or a decision to confine public dispute to nonessential or trivial questions. It did not mean that there would be no conflict. On the contrary, many contests have been waged with heat and acrimony over issues that were felt to be fearfully urgent. For instance, in the struggles between Thomas Jefferson and Alexander Hamilton, Jefferson felt that he was saving the country, as he expressed it, from "monarchism and militarism." After Andrew Jackson's conflicts with the Bank of the United States and with the South Carolina nullificationists, Jackson is said to have expressed regret, when he left the White House, for two pieces of unfinished business—he had neither shot Henry Clay nor hanged John C. Calhoun. In 1884, when Grover Cleveland was being nominated for the Presidency, one of his nominators declaimed, "We love him for the enemies he has made." So, we must certainly recognize, many of the contests were real, and many of the rivalries were intense. Also, as Richard Hofstadter asserted, many of the issues—the American Revolution, the Civil War, and many ethnic and immigrant divisions—represented conflict of the most genuine kind.

But if the principle of consent did not mean the elimination of conflict, what it did mean was that conflict should be limited. Adversaries might pit all their strength against one another, but they would not engage in remorseless attempts to destroy one another. There are many ways in which we have shown our purpose to avoid struggles leading to political extermination. The provisions in the Constitution against ex post facto laws and bills of attainder are pertinent examples. But far more telling, perhaps, is the habitual pattern of our political contests—notably our Presidential elections. During these quadrennial episodes, the element of conflict has customarily been highly conspicuous. Almost every election was hotly contested, and if there were no important issues involved, the heat of the contest might be even more intense. Rhetoric, customarily, became very highly charged. Both parties talked big and denounced each other most abusively, and it was not unusual for one party to claim that if the rival party were elected it would be the end of republican government in the United States. Men made frenzied efforts to gain electoral victory, as if the future of mankind were at stake.

But after the election was over, what happened? We all know the scenario. The loser could send his congratulations to the winner; the newspapers which had supported the loser would begin to publish more flattering pictures of the winner than they had published during the campaign. One or two members of the losing party, after what we may call a decent interval, might agree to take positions in the new Administration. When the Congress met, the majority party would assign a certain number of places on each committee to be filled by the minority party. They would do this as a matter of course, without even discussing whether to do so. Pretty soon they would be busily working out legislative compromises in the cloakroom while hurling rhetorical thunderbolts at one another on the floor.

In fact, the very structure of the parties themselves reflected this pattern of limited conflict, for the traditional two parties of American history—Federalists versus Jeffersonians, or Whigs versus Democrats, or Republicans versus Democrats—have been very unlike the ideologically "pure" splinter parties which have arisen so often in central and western Europe. The ideological parties have consisted of adherents from only one segment of the political spectrum, united in support of one particular doctrine, rather like small religious sects in this country. But the American political parties have been coalitions of conservative southern Democrats and reformist northern Democrats, or in the first half of the present century, of stand-pat Republicans from the East and progressive Republicans from the West, working together more or less reluctantly and with more or less internal friction.

Since both parties represented a coalition of men of diverse views, it followed that neither party was ideologically very different from its rival. Both tended to take what are called "moderate" positions and to avoid going very far to the Right or very far to the Left. This made it easier for them to reach accommodations with one another. So long as this relationship prevailed, it was always possible to evoke a spirit of unity between the parties as well as to rouse angry strife between them. In fact, this dualism became, as I have suggested, almost a ritual in which the parties were expected to assail each other vigorously in election campaigns, but never so vigorously that they could not be reminded, after the election was over, that what they shared as Americans far outweighed what they disagreed about as party members, and that the President, once elected, ceased to be merely a partisan leader and became President of all the people.

Thomas Jefferson was the first President to articulate this view of our political system, and no President has ever stated it better. At his first inaugural in 1801, Jefferson, addressing himself to both his supporters and his recent adversaries, stated a profound truth—a truth that was valid on several levels—when he declared, "Every difference of opinion is not a difference of principle. We have called by different names brethren of the same principle. We are all Republicans; we are all Federalists." At the lowest level this meant that each party constituted a kind of brokerage house, and that the brokerage houses can, as the phrase goes, "do business" with one another—a little opportunism along with the principle. At a higher level, it meant that once the contest was over, both parties would abide by the results of the contest, and the country would be spared the disruptive consequences of an endless feud. As Jefferson himself expressed it, since the "contest of opinion" had been "now decided by the voice of the nation . . . all will, of course, arrange themselves under the will of the law and unite in common efforts for the common good. All, too, will bear in mind this sacred principle, that, though the will of the majority is in all cases to prevail, that will, to be rightful must be reasonable; that the minority possess their equal rights, which equal law must protect, and to violate would be oppression." At the highest level of all, the principle of consent was based not only on a contract, but upon the recognition of a reality. The reality was that areas of agreement were always present among the American people—that these areas were more important than the areas of disagreement, which were also always present, and that therefore the factors of union and cohesion must take a priority over the factors of dissension and disruption. This preponderance of factors shared in common was what made it possible for Americans to maintain a system of consent, even though limited conflicts over specific issues were always being waged.

It had been a quarter of a century earlier that Jefferson had coined his immortal phrase about governments deriving their just powers from the consent of the governed. I would suggest that in the passages I have just quoted he was at last defining what "consent of the governed" really meant. It meant, above all, that conflicting parties would constantly remember that they could be adversaries without being enemies, would observe the distinction between differences of opinion and differences of principle, and would work out more or less voluntary solutions to their differences of opinion, recognizing the obligation of the majority to respect the rights of the minority and the obligation of the minority to respect the popular mandate held up by the majority.

Such, as it appears to me, was government by consent—a system which prevailed in the United States for well over a century, and which is not yet terminated, though it is, I believe, badly impaired.

As we look back at it, we are apt to romanticize it, and indeed, I may have idealized it somewhat in my description here. Therefore, I must point out, for the sake of verisimilitude, as Mark Twain used to say, that the system had some rather unlovely features. Sometimes, in the quest for accommodation, it reduced principles to such a negligible point that parties indulged in shameless bargaining, and thought more about how to win elections than about what to do with the elections they had won. "What are we here for," asked a delegate to the Republican convention of 1868, "except the offices?" Further, to mention a more serious flaw, the principle of consent exaggerated one of its own chief virtues into a vice. The virtue was the principle of compromise. The willingness to compromise was what enabled adversaries to get along with one another even when they disagreed. Compromise of all kinds—between large states and small states, between slavery and antislavery, between mercantile interests and planter interests, between advocates and opponents of national power—was what made "a more perfect union" possible in 1787. Great compromises again—in 1820, in 1832–33, in 1850, and finally at the expense of the blacks, in 1877—had either avoided or liquidated major crises in the republic. Partly because of this experience, compromise was almost sanctified, and men who rejected compromise were often written off as "fanatics" or "zealots" who refused the "tolerance" and the "give-and-take" of the American way. At times, it seemed that there was no principle which could not be compromised if the parties to the transaction were sufficiently "reasonable."

The greatest flaw of all in the system of consent was one that was perhaps least recognized. The system had a fatal tendency to bring in those who could be conveniently included, but if there were groups whose voices would not harmonize, it practiced the brutally simple expedient of denying them a voice altogether. These excluded groups were just not regarded as, in the terminology of the sociologist, "significant others." Thus, the American Indians were denied a voice. Negroes, both slave and free, were denied a voice. Also, occasional strong efforts were made to deny immigrants a voice. The denial of a voice to immigrants never succeeded in a formal sense, but, realistically, many immigrants were made to understand that they were on probation, and that if they behaved themselves, their children might be admitted to full membership in American society. Strange as it may now seem, for many of them, this was enough, and they gave patient support to a system in which they occupied a very marginal position.

These major faults in the system of consent cannot and should not be extenuated, and indeed they were so serious that they might be regarded, in the eyes of some critics, as completely vitiating the entire structure. I certainly do not want to idealize it. I would not conceal the fact that compromise was often given a priority over principle, harmony over morality, and agreement over clarity of decision. I would not gloss over the fact that shameless bargaining and relentless arm-twisting were frequently employed to secure agreements in situations where direct coercion was taboo. But with all its faults, the system allowed for a measure of internal criticism and dissent such as few societies have known, and it reduced the factor of direct physical coercion to about as low a point as is possible in a complex and highly structured society. In fact this avoidance of coercion was the chief glory of the system, and the devices for obtaining consent were important primarily because they made the avoidance of coercion possible. To an astonishing degree in America, public affairs have been conducted on a basis that nothing could be done until it had been put into a form such that the opposition could be induced to agree to it. The use of the filibuster in the Senate, the copious devices for obstruction in both houses of Congress, the bicameral system itself, the arrangements for checks and balances, have all contributed to make it virtually impossible to enact a Federal law if an opposition group of appreciable size is irreconcilably determined to prevent it.

But this emphasis upon more or less voluntary consent is by no means confined to the political sphere. Throughout the society, we regard the use of force in almost any situation as a confession of moral failure, whether it involves the use of a birch rod in the school, or of militia in the streets. We even construct our buildings in a way which suggests our faith that people will accept the prevailing practices of the society without any duress to compel them to do so. In the past, tellers in banks sat guarded in little metal cages, but we have taken them out of these barricades and placed them behind low counters in rooms designed to look as little like a countinghouse as possible. In the past, honest burghers built their houses with heavy, solid shutters at the windows to repel marauders, but today we have turned to building and living in glass houses whose walls can be shattered with a small stone. Where loans were once granted only in return for formidable mortgages, we now flood the mails with unsolicited cards extending credit with a bounty so overflowing that it sometimes extends beyond adults to infants, deceased persons, and domestic animals. In place of compulsion we substitute agreement, but this substitution makes the necessity for agreement truly vital, so that when an important issue is in dispute, we are obsessively concerned that the negotiations that may lead to agreement shall never stop. The cessation of talk means crisis, and negotiations must go on, day and night. In a government by consent, the default of consent is the paralysis of authority.

Such was the system of government by the consent of the governed that prevailed in the United States for about two centuries. It never meant consent in the simple sense of spontaneous agreement by everyone. Sometimes the minority blackmailed the majority and sometimes the majority put intolerable pressure upon the minority. Always, certain disadvantaged groups were disregarded and left out. But withal, the fact remained that the majority refrained from pushing the minority to the point of actual resistance and the minority recognized an obligation, at a certain point, to abide by the terms of a settlement which they did not like—not an obligation to approve of it or even to agree to it, but at least to acquiesce in it, or as we say, "to go along" with it. Within this framework, men enjoyed remarkable opportunities to oppose the existing authority and to dissent from prevailing opinion. This system could operate without producing crises of social disorder because it was understood by all parties concerned that after the dissent had been heard and the issues had been canvassed, an arrangement would be worked out which the majority could accept as good enough and which the minority could tolerate as not utterly bad.

When the matter is viewed in this way, one might suppose the principle of consent succeeded simply because of the rationality or the tolerance of the American people—because men were logical enough to appreciate the philosophical elegance of this beautifully balanced political device, and tolerant enough to cherish the mutual concessions by which the invocation of *force majeure* was avoided. But in fact, human behavior is seldom this reasonable, and the ways and means by which society induces its members to do what is expected of them are never this voluntary. Government by consent may have succeeded partly because men recognized that submission to the majority is the price of democracy, and that compliance with society's basic creed is the price of freedom within the context of that creed. But it succeeded less for these reasons than for two others: First, the American people were remarkably homogeneous, and were well aware that the values which they shared were far more important to them than the values on which they disagreed; second, government by consent did not abolish the principle of authority—instead it substituted the equalitarian authority of the community as a whole for the hierarchical authority of a designated ruling class. It accomplished this transition by making conformity rather than obedience the device by which authority was enforced.

Social critics from Tocqueville to the present have, of course, given a great deal of attention to conformity in American life. They have pointed out how strong, and sometimes relentless, the pressure toward conformity has been. They have deplored its effects in stunting the growth of individualism and creativity, and even in making a travesty of freedom. Many of these criticisms are quite justified, and I would not gainsay them. But they have already been stated over and over again with skillful insight and with strong emphasis. At the same time, certain other aspects of social conformity have been relatively neglected, except by some sociologists. To begin with, it has been poorly understood that conformity has an important constructive function, especially in a society which avoids the use of physical force or coercion. Every society has to have ways of coordinating the activities of its members, and this means that it has to have ways of inducing individuals to behave in ways in which they may not wish to behave and to do things which they would prefer not to do. This is almost what we mean when we speak of civilization. Some of the modes of inducing such behavior are quite formalized, and we have the law, the courts, the police, and the prisons. But on the whole, American society has relied less on formal authoritarian devices than almost any important society in history, and the force of law, for instance, has derived more from its claim to embody society's concept of justice than from its threat of penalties. In this situation of minimal direct coercive control, conformity has imposed the coordinating arrangements in American society which authority has imposed in other societies. Our society demands "cooperation" with the community rather than "obedience" to the rulers, but both "socialize" the individual to behave as his society expects him to behave. Erich Fromm has expressed the essence of socialization in an elegant and subtle formulation: "In order that any society may function well, its members must acquire the kind of character which makes them *want* to act in the way they *have* to act. . . . They have to *desire* what objectively is *necessary* for them to do. *Outer force* is to be replaced by *inner compulsion*. . . ."

This is, I think, a perfect statement of what conformity is all about. But men in Jacksonian America anticipated Fromm by a century with a less learned but no less perceptive formulation. With a kind of subtle crudity, they asserted that "this is a free country, and every man does as he pleases, and if he don't, we make him do so." This too was conformity, and, as I have suggested, I feel that scholars have not given enough attention to the social function of conformity in an anti-authoritarian society.

But if they have neglected the function of conformity, they have neglected even more the means by which conformity was enforced. It is, I believe, partly because we have never adequately recognized what these means were that we fail to understand, today, why values which, as recently as a decade ago, appeared to rest upon granite foundations have suddenly proved vulnerable to basic attack.

In brief, I would argue, conformity, and also the whole system of government by consent and law by consent, were based upon the sanction of community sentiment. But this statement can have no meaning until the term "community" has meaning, and the term "community" [1] is one of the most loosely used words in the language. If the etymology is to count for anything, a community ought to mean an aggregate of people, living in propinquity, who share the same basic values, attitudes, and outlook upon their social and physical environment. In brief, we might say that they share a common culture. But we all, apparently, have a tendency to believe that any aggregate of people living in propinquity *ought to* have these shared qualities, or we wish that they did, and therefore we have gotten into the habit of speaking of any localized aggregate as a community, whether this aggregate has any shared values and attitudes or not. Thus we beg the question of whether it is a community, and we sometimes try to make it a community by pretending that it is one. I recently heard a university administrator, in the midst of a campus crisis, state, "This disruption will end when the community decides that it must end, and no sooner." Of course, a public leader must assume the existence of a community, for, without one, there is nothing for him to lead. Also, sometimes, by a moving appeal, it is possible to invoke a spirit of community. But in realistic terms, the question was not whether the community would decide; it was the question whether a community existed to decide—whether the aggregate of people in the situation was enough of a corporate group to be able to reach a collective decision.

Because of this practice of confusing actual community with mere physical propinquity or formal membership in a particular institution, it may be worth pausing to ask how the demographic, economic, and social circumstances of an earlier America contributed to the process of community formation. Briefly, let us consider the situation a century ago. At that time 34,427,000 Americans lived in rural areas, or in cities or towns of less than 100,000 population. Another 4,128,000 lived in cities of between 100,000 and 1,000,000. There were no cities of more than 1,000,000. This is to

[1] A community is usually more or less coterminous with a society, but the two may be theoretically distinguished on the ground that a society is an aggregate of people who are interdependent in their activities, without any necessary compatibility of ideas, while a community implies shared beliefs and values as well as activities.

say that demographically about 88 percent of the population was distributed in a great multiplicity of small clusters of people. There were, in fact, 611 towns with between 2,500 and 25,000 population. There were only 14 cities of over 100,000 and only two over 500,000. These clusters of population were economically tied together by a network of railroads, rivers and canals and they were politically unified by national political parties, a strong but much limited national government, and a strong spirit of American nationalism. National church organizations and publishing houses, with a small but nationally distributed market, gave a limited degree of centralization to religious and cultural life—or at least the more elite and self-conscious aspects of cultural life. But, by modern standards, America's towns and villages were remarkably isolated from one another. America's system of roads and automobiles was still more than half a century in the future, and the only practicable way to make any journey of more than 100 miles was to go by rail. Electronic communication was even more than half a century away, and the chief medium of public communication was the local newspaper. Even the smaller towns had their own dailies or weeklies, with no national columnists, no syndicated news, and a remarkable degree of self-sufficiency. The local editor, the local clergyman, the local political leader, were not overshadowed by the quick accessibility and the technological dominance of the cities.

Population clusters of this kind tended to form strong cohesive communities. Their spatial isolation defined them as units. Their small size was conducive to a high degree of personal acquaintance and frequent contact among the people. The limitations of their technology intensified their cohesiveness, for the orbit of social interaction was effectively circumscribed by a circle whose radius was the distance that a person could conveniently walk (or, if a farmer, drive his wagon) to the corner grocery, to the neighborhood school—which really was a neighborhood school—or to the druggist a few blocks away. Their orientation to the physical environment gave them a good bit in common, for in a society which still relied primarily upon agriculture and did much of its work outdoors, they shared a common concern with the weather and a common adjustment to nature—to the phases of the moon, the rhythm of the seasons, the fatefulness of drought and flood and untimely freezes. The social institutions which flourished within a population cluster of this kind also greatly reinforced the cohesiveness of the cluster itself, for they were what the sociologists call primary institutions—family, church congregation, neighborhood—which emphasize the personal bond of relationship among their members and the loyalties of one for all and all for one.

The strength and cohesiveness of the communities of this world we have lost are so well recognized that there is no need for me to dwell upon them. In fact they may have been too much sentimentalized and exaggerated. But there is a further point, quite crucial to the concept of consent, which I believe has not been sufficiently recognized. This is the fact that the traditional community was a preclusive community. As I have observed, it certainly did not lovingly embrace everyone, and draw together all the human beings within its orbit. It restricted active participation to the "significant others" and it openly excluded Negroes, slighted immigrants, and made life difficult for any square pegs which did not fit into the round holes with which the society was equipped. But even for those who were excluded, the community exercised such a strong gravitational force that though they had been rejected, they usually displayed compulsive impulses to qualify as insiders by adopting the values and the behavior of the insiders. For instance, the few Negroes who had attained middle-class status rejected Negro mores and zealously imitated the follies as well as the values of white middle-class life. The outsiders were culturally assimilated though not structurally assimilated: They tried to be like insiders though not accepted as insiders. To state this another way, they gave their allegiance to the *dominant* community and this meant that there could be no competing community.

Of course there have always been dissenters—men who did not want to pay the price of community membership. It is possible to identify a few of these in almost any community, and American history is rich in its record of dissent. But in the traditional community which I have been trying to sketch out, the outlook for a consistent dissenter was bleak. The community frowned upon his deviance and it had a whole arsenal of social weapons, ranging from social snubs to outright ostracism, with which to whip him into line. It could easily isolate him, and make him feel his isolation, because the population of the community was small and did not provide enough dissenters to form a socially self-sufficient group (or rival community) of their own. As for other dissenters in other communities, the dissenter might get some meager psychological support from reading what they had to say (Elbert Hubbard, H. L. Mencken, Brann the Iconoclast, Bob Ingersoll), but they were too remote to protect him from the dreadful anxieties of the socially isolated. He could not join them in the togetherness of sit-ins, be-ins, or marches on Washington. His lot was a lonely one, and indeed the brooding spirit of loneliness which pervades nineteenth-century American literature may be a reflex of this loneliness of the dissenter.

Thus, the community was not only holistic in the positive sense of being strong, cohesive, and integrated, but it was monolithic in the negative sense of inhibiting the development of social units which might deviate from the patterns of the dominant community. The basic American social structure until nearly the middle of the present century was a world of tight and tiny local communities, heavily insulated against external influences, but strikingly resembling and strongly reinforcing one another because of their generally homogeneous character. Such communities exercised a monolithic cultural control over all who lived within their orbits. Men who marched to the beat of a different drummer paid a high price for their singularity and were therefore few.

It was the fundamental structuring of American society into such communities that formed the functional basis for an informal system of conformity. And it was the prevalence of the system of conformity that made possible the formal system of consent as the basis for government and law. It is true, no doubt, that political philosophy encouraged both the forbearance of majorities and the acquiescence of minorities, both of which are essential to a consensual system. But the very notion of majorities and minorities is meaningless without the concept of a whole—a community—of which majority and minority are both parts. What, after all, is a

majority? It is a number greater than half, just as a minority is a
number less than half. But this must mean more than or less than
half of a whole. If a large number tries to control a smaller number,
and they are not parts of a whole but are separate peoples, we
regard the control as tyranny. If they are parts of a whole, and the
whole is a community, then, under the doctrine of majority rule
and consent of the governed, the control, if it does not violate basic
individual rights, is legitimate. It is hard to say precisely why the
fact of community makes such a vital difference, but it must be
partly because of a recognition that the community is more or less
homogeneous. Perhaps it is only a restatement of this same point in
a more specific way to say that there is a recognition that the values
on which the members of the community agree are more important
to them than the matters on which they disagree, and therefore that
the matters of disagreement must be subordinated to the matters of
agreement, which means that conflict over the matters of disagreement must be limited.

Fundamentally, there are two ways of looking at the system of
control by communities, whose outlines I have tried to sketch.
From an adverse point of view, it can be regarded as a system of
majoritarian control by a dominating group which demanded blind
conformity and used the informal penalties of social disapproval
and isolation to exercise a coercion just as forcible as the authoritarian control of an earlier time, which had used flogging, ear-
cropping, and imprisonment to exercise a more naked coercion.
This is a view with which all the most vociferous critics of conformity and the Establishment would agree. On the other hand, it
can be regarded as a system which encouraged men to comply with
accepted standards of decent behavior, to recognize the importance
of the values they shared, to settle their disagreements with a minimum of strife, and to operate their society with a minimum use of
force. It also encouraged them to base the legitimacy of law upon
public consent. No matter which of these views one adopts, it is
clear that the power of community sentiment was crucial, and that
such sentiment was not generated by just any kind of community.
It was generated by somewhat isolated and autonomous communities which were more or less homogeneous to begin with, and in

which particular factors of size, technology, primary institutions, and general orientation strengthened the cohesive effect.

To say this is to say that if this particular kind of community disappeared, the means by which the consent or conformity of the reluctant was procured might disappear also, and with it the sanction for the kind of government and the kind of law which a system of consent makes possible. It is to say further that the unique vulnerability of a consent society, of which I spoke earlier, would be exposed, and that many of the institutions of the society would be revealed to have no defenses. They would be exposed to assault—both verbal and physical assault, since this country has largely renounced the kind of coercive legal controls with which most countries still defend their institutions. Being based upon the assumption that any opposition from within will always be limited opposition, and that any internal issues are always negotiable, the system of consent provides no mechanism for the contingency of unlimited opposition and nonnegotiable issues.

What I am contending here is that the system of consent succeeded historically because the American people lived in population aggregates of a certain kind. These aggregates formed communities which were homogeneous with one another, strongly cohesive, and equipped with the means of inducing virtually everyone in the aggregate to accede to the decisions of the dominant elements —decisions which were in turn modulated by the right of those who were acceding to demand certain concessions. Most of all, communities of this kind were able to monopolize the field of social organization in such a way that no effective communities incompatible with the standard type of community could be created. The consent that followed was not really the consent of millions of individual persons; it was the consent of many hundreds of individual communities. But what I would contend further is that the traditional kind of community has deteriorated or even disappeared. As it has done so, it has left the field open for the emergence of a variety of different kinds of communities—each with something of the strength, cohesiveness, and self-sufficiency which result from personal association and shared values. But these new-style communities, far from being traditional or standard or homogeneous with one another, frequently hold values in conflict with one another's—even values antithetical to one another's. In a social structure of conflicting communities, there is no longer a sanction for consent, and the whole system of law and government based upon consent faces a supreme crisis.

It is almost too well known for me to go into any detail about what happened to the nineteenth-century constellation of more or less autonomous, small communities. The automobile multiplied manyfold the radius of men's mobility. This fact itself destroyed countless cherished community institutions. It also greatly increased the distance between men's work and their homes, and thus began to shatter the integration of both their personalities and their lives. Technological changes reared secondary environments—the office, the university, the ghetto—which stood between man and the primary environment. These secondary environments diminished the shared experience which exposure to the primary environment had offered. They also made possible the concentration of large populations in cities. By 1968, 63 percent of the population of the country lived in places of more than 250,000 population. The impersonality of city life, in turn, gave men an anonymity which was sometimes welcome, sometimes unwelcome, but, in either case, which relieved them of the personal impact of social pressures and social expectations. At the same time, city life was more secular than the church-oriented life of the rural community, and this secularism encouraged a skepticism in the higher learning—a skepticism that began to strip away the mystique with which a religious society will always sanctify its civil institutions: the Constitution, the flag, the majesty of the law, the mandate of the people.

By the 1950's the solidarity of communities was fractured, their cohesion was diluted, and their power over individuals was but a shadow of what it had been. As patterns became diffused, the processes of socialization for children became blurred. Boys who had identified fairly readily with fathers who plowed a furrow on the farm could not take their cues so readily from fathers who were away most of the time, engaged in incomprehensible work at places which one had never seen. Boys and girls whose sex roles were no longer codified all too frequently wound up feeling uncertain about their identities. Communities were divided in voice, bewildered by the rapidity of social change, bullied by "experts" who told them what to believe, and silenced by the voices of the electronic media, which came from the metropolis and to which they could not talk back. As instruments of social control, communities became faint shadows of what they once had been. They could no longer speak to the dissenters in tones of authority, nor could they monitor the behavior of deviant individuals.

But these changes are well known, and what I would like to focus upon is a less recognized and perhaps more important aspect of this revolution in the patterns of social relatedness. This is a change in the scale of society, which has destroyed the power of traditional communities to control dissenters by isolating or ostracizing them, and has now given to those who reject or are rejected by the community a power to form communities of their own. This change is vital, because when the traditional community loses its power to deny the blessings of social relatedness to those who reject it, the principle of social control by communities is left with no effective means of enforcement.

The readiness with which alienated or nonconformist groups can now form communities of their own is cogently suggested by a comment of Daniel Bell's in the Spring 1970 issue of *The Public Interest*. Bell asks how many constitute the "mass" of the radicals, and he cites *Fortune* surveys which indicate that as many as 30 percent "in the elite schools" may be significantly radical. But then he adds: "A more important consideration, however, and a crucial one for all our problems is less the percentage than the change of scale. In an arena of ten thousand students, five percent comes to 500, and these can form a powerful striking force."

No doubt this is true, but the power of the striking force which they can form is perhaps less important than the strength of the community that they can form. A community of 500 is large enough to give the person who joins it a sense of belonging, large enough to protect him against the snubs and slights and disapproval of the larger society, large enough to isolate him from outgroups, as all communities do with their members. Five hundred strongly cohesive people can devise standards of dress, speech, and belief for their own group, and impose these as rigidly as if they were the most orthodox of conformists. David Riesman has touched this point rather effectively in his observation that "The Bohemians and the rebels are not usually autonomous; on the contrary, they are zealously tuned in to the signals of a defiant group that finds the meaning of life in a compulsive non-conformity to the majority group."

We still speak of the Bohemians and the rebels as dissenters, which means that we are still held in the grip of the illusion that there is one "community" which includes everyone except those who opt out and float about as displaced persons on the margins of society. But the fact that large numbers of people, living in propinquity, on campuses, in communes, in Bohemias, or whatever, may share common values and even impose standards of conformity upon their members means that these people are not dissenters at all. Rather, they are conforming members of new kinds of communities. Not only new kinds of communities, but communities which are committed to a cultural separation from communities of the standard kind. To embark on an extended scrutiny of these new social organisms is beyond the scope of this paper, for all that we are immediately concerned with here is the impact of these changes upon a system of law based upon consent and uniformity. But the fact that they are communities, and communities of a special kind, is beginning to be recognized. J. Milton Yinger has already written about what he calls a "contra-culture," and Theodore Roszak about a "counter-culture." The "spirit of Woodstock" is a manifestation of an urge toward community in these new groups. This spirit in some ways is very different from the spirit of traditional communities. For instance, the traditional community was highly structured by a network of explicit commitments and loyalties binding individuals to one another in an intricate cohesive pattern. The spirit of the commune is much more an unstructured diffuse sense of "love" toward everyone in general and no one in particular. But in many respects, we have new communities whose relation to the traditional community is as negative as their culture is negative toward the traditional culture, and if we are to speak of contra-cultures or counter-cultures, we might as well also speak of contra-communities and counter-communities. It is such social entities as these which now withhold the consent which has been vital to our non-coercive society and which thus present a challenge to the legitimacy of law such as this basic institution has never before faced in America.

In sum, we have lived for some two centuries in a society which has minimized the use of physical compulsion at all levels and has used less compulsion than almost any society in history. Socially we have abandoned chastisement for children, both at home and in school. We have abolished, in law and almost in practice, the domination of husbands over wives. We have operated with a Congress in which it has remained almost impossible to enact a law to which a handful of senators are deeply and irrevocably opposed. We have operated with a court system in which there is no good way to induce the accused to let his trial proceed if he is not willing to let it proceed. The unanimity with which, in the past, accused persons accepted this system was so total that we were not even aware of the naked vulnerability of the courts until the Chicago Seven disclosed it to us.

Having rejected compulsion as a means of social control, except in the cases of punishment of palpable felons whose offenses were condemned by almost everyone, we became desperately dependent upon "agreement"—perhaps under pressure, perhaps reluctant, perhaps secured by bullying or bartering or bribery, but still with some measure of voluntarism or at least acquiescence in the result. Since agreement was the alternative to deadlock and paralysis, we became compulsively addicted to negotiation. I suppose that most legislation is negotiated before it is enacted, and that more legal disputes are negotiated than are ever brought to trial. In important disputes in the area of labor relations, we insist, above all, that the parties must never stop talking; and if the matter is urgent, they must negotiate around the clock. Since our only truly instrumental device for resolving disputes is by talk, the prospect that the contestants might actually quit talking is too awful to contemplate. Agreement or what passes for agreement *must* be reached, because if agreement fails, our system offers no recourse.

For two centuries, this system of government by consent operated, sometimes creaking loudly, sometimes brought to a dead halt, sometimes imposing injustice and hardship upon groups who were forced to the mockery of pretending to accept by agreement what they were compelled to accept by irresistible pressure. But on the whole, the system worked reasonably well, not because it was intrinsically workable, but because the dominant communities wanted it to work. People truly regarded the points on which they agreed as more important than the points on which they disagreed. When they did disagree, it was as adversaries, and not as enemies. We were "all Republicans and all Federalists," and for all its imperfections, the operation of the system might well have gratified Thomas Jefferson.

But today, we face confrontations with men who believe in revolution—believe in it, in a good many cases, with genuine conviction. They do not want to reach agreement. Their demands are, by stipulation, nonnegotiable. Their adversary may give in, but they will not let him agree. Often their terms are stated in a way carefully designed to make agreement impossible.

Thus we approach the answer to a question which most people never recognized as a question and to which those who did recognize it hoped never to have to learn the answer. What happens to law based upon the norms of the community if there is no prevailing community but only a multiplicity of conflicting communities? What happens to the principle of consent if the social structure has no center which can even speak the voice of consent?

The answers are far from clear. But perhaps it is important to remember that while consent requires what Richard Hofstadter has called an attitude of comity on the part of conflicting parties, and while even minimum comity seems unattainable in many confrontations today, still the principle of consent was never predicated upon the idea of bland agreement and readiness to avoid issues for the sake of superficial harmony. It was predicated upon the idea that adverse parties can limit their conflict, and can recognize the values they share, even while contesting the points on which they disagree. Whether the communities and counter-communities of America in the 1970's may be able to hold such a balanced view in the heat of the antagonisms and extremisms that now prevail is questionable indeed. But if it is possible to contest social issues without destroying essential institutions, it will have to be done by the difficult feat of combining tolerance with idealism. The more we fall to lumping men and women into opposing categories, the more we need to look at people as individuals and not as types. To whatever extent attitudes of hostility threaten to destroy the shared features which cause society to hang together, to that same extent it will be pertinent to remember with Thomas Jefferson that "every difference of opinion is not a difference of principle," that every political issue does not involve a moral absolute, and that men may be adversaries in sturdy conflict without being mortal enemies, rending the fabric of society in a struggle fueled by intolerance and hate.

COMMENT

by C. Vann Woodward

Driving through New Haven to catch the train to New York, where I was to comment on David Potter's paper, I thought of how accurately his reflections applied to the scene that spread before me. The city, where I make my home, and where Potter until a few years ago made his home, was a strange sight in the morning rush hour. The streets were largely empty, the big windows of the stores were covered with plywood, and though it was a Friday morning, most of the shops were closed for business.[1] Nearly everything movable had been carted away. Even the lids of the manholes in the streets had been welded closed to protect the city's vital communication system. Virtually the only

[1] Reference is to the demonstration on May 1, 1970, in support of the Black Panthers on trial for murder in New Haven.

thing open in the city was the university that lies at its heart. Its wide-openness and patent vulnerability was its only hope of immunity. Diagonally across the Green from where the mass demonstrations would take place is located another vulnerable institution, the Superior Court of the State of Connecticut.

It is about what was happening there, and what might happen in that building, that all the turmoil in my city and the crisis that had befallen it was concerned. This was a crisis of law, the validity and sanction of law, and it arose out of just those areas of deterioration that David Potter unerringly identified—where consensus becomes impossible when membership is not shared. Without community, as he said, there can be no membership. Without membership, no relatedness of the members. Without relatedness, no consensus, no democratic process; in fact, no democracy.

New Haven is in many ways an illustration of the social picture that Mr. Potter painted. Its openness, its vulnerability, its form of government by consent rather than coercion, combine with the illusory assumption of an overriding consensus of community. Now it suddenly found itself the center of a nationwide conversion of the forces of counter-community with which a heroic local resurgence of community and consensus were attempting an uneasy alliance in the name of justice.

Ironically, the word *community* is heard most often these days from the black people. In a little over two decades the proportion of black people in New Haven has increased about tenfold, from about 3 percent to more than 30 percent. Nine out of ten of them are relative newcomers, mainly from the South. Whatever community they shared in their native region they have had little success in reconstructing in their new surroundings. Their white hosts were ill-prepared for their coming, lacking in understanding of them, and no more hospitable toward them than those of other northern cities. They constituted a potential counter-community from the start. Negroes generally constitute an exception—the large exception of which Mr. Potter is thoroughly aware—to his important generalizations about consensus, about coercion, about negotiation and compromise and agreement, and about consent of the governed.

Historically, and of course not only in remote historical terms, Negroes were never included in the great American consensus. They did not even figure as a consentual minority whose opinions the majorities traditionally respected, for they were never really members of the community. Whatever reluctance white Americans have traditionally shown in resort to compulsion and force as a means of social control, and whatever their compulsive preference for consensus and agreement as a means of social control, they have not felt bound by the tradition in their dealings with black Americans. With Negroes it has been a long history of coercion and force. For the greater part of their history in the new world, it was force in its most naked and brutal form, the form of slavery.

Afterwards, the law nominally came to apply equally to black and white. But actually it was applied, as we know, quite unequally. It still is.

That is what the crisis in New Haven was about. It was a crisis of confidence in the rule of law. Should this failure of confidence come to pervade black America, it would unite a counter-community, by far the greatest counter-community of all, with numerous tiny counter-communities, or counter-cultures, of alienated white youth in an ominous and dangerous alliance.

It would be a great mistake, I believe, to think, as many now do, of blacks and of youth in stereotypes of conformity. It is a terrible mistake to think of either group as a block of united alienation, however loud the alienated and often revolutionary minorities of both groups may now seem.

In particular, one should give heed to what Kingman Brewster has described as the relatively sound student majority. They also suffer more now than in the recent past from disenchantment, deteriorating morale, and from malaise of several kinds. A great struggle now rages for their allegiance. They are asking many questions. They are even questioning the validity of law itself. The outcome of the struggle for their allegiance will, I think, determine in large measure the future of community, of consensus, and of the democratic process and probably of democracy itself.

CHAPTER 8

THE ROOTS OF SOCIAL NEGLECT IN THE UNITED STATES

by Robert L. Heilbroner[1]

I wish to pose a question that is at once central and critical, and yet singularly elusive and perplexing. It is the question of why the United States, which is by all conventional measures the wealthiest nation in the world, is not at the same time the most socially advanced. To put the question differently, I wish to ask why a nation that could, more easily than any other, afford to remove social and economic inequities has been among the more laggard in doing so.

Note that my question hinges on the *comparative* performance of the United States. I am not concerned with measuring the absolute level of neglect in America, or in assessing the trend of that neglect, or in trying to estimate by how much it could or should be reduced in the future.[2] My problem is broader and more far-reaching, and perhaps correspondingly more difficult. It is why social neglect in the United States is greater than in other nations with similar institutions, such as Norway, Sweden, Denmark, Switzerland, New Zealand, England, or Canada. In the end, of course, the matter that concerns us is the alleviation of neglect in this country—a matter to which I shall turn at the end of this essay—but the primary focus of my inquiry lies in the roots of the problem rather than in the specifics of its remedy.

[1] I am indebted to many helpful suggestion from Daniel Bell, Victor Fuchs, Adolph Lowe, and David Schwartzman, as well as to statistical assistance from Peter Anthony. Of course none is responsible for any conclusions in the paper.

[2] For estimates along this line see *Annual Report of the Council of Economic Advisers*, January 1969, pp. 158 ff.

Let me begin by documenting briefly the premise from which I start. I shall do so in broad brushstrokes, partly because the statistical information is lacking to make finer comparisons, and partly because I do not think the basic evidence is apt to be called into question.

I start with habitat itself. It is not a simple matter to make precise comparisons of social neglect with regard to housing and living environment among nations, because accepted standards differ from one country to the next: Swedish housing projects, for example, have fewer rooms per family and less room space per person than similar projects in the United States, while in Japan only 13 percent of all urban and less than 2 percent of all rural dwellings have flush toilets, a condition that in the United States is virtually prima facie evidence of extreme social disrepair.[3] Thus the unwary statistical comparison shopper could easily come to the conclusion that American housing projects are better than Swedish, or that the vast bulk of Japanese live in conditions similar to those of the worst of our slums.

Such considerations make it exceedingly difficult, or even impossible, to arrive at a simple ranking of living habitats that will disclose where the United States belongs on an international spectrum of neglect. Hence I shall content myself with two generalizations based on personal observations at home and abroad. First, I believe that in no large city in the United States do we find a concern for the living habitat comparable to that commonly found in the cities of such nations as the Netherlands, Switzerland, or the countries of Scandinavia; and second, I maintain that to match the squalor of the worst of the American habitat, one must descend to the middle range of the underdeveloped lands. These are, I repeat, "impressionistic" statements, for which quantitative documentation is lacking, but I do not think they will be challenged on that account.

Let me now turn to another and somewhat more objective indi-

[3] *World Health Statistics*, World Health Organization, Geneva, 1968.

cator of the comparative performance of the United States with
regard to social well-being—the neglect of poverty. Here again, a
degree of statistical prudence is necessary. The income of a family
of four at the "official" threshold of poverty in the United States is
roughly $3,500. This is an income approximately equivalent to
that of a family in the middle brackets in Norway. Poverty is therefore a matter of relative affluence quite as much as absolute income. On the other hand, just as the definition of poverty reflects
the differing levels of productivity of different countries, so the neglect of poverty also mirrors the differing capabilities of nations to
create a surplus that can be transferred to those in need. Thus, a
rich nation may define its level of need higher than its poor neighbor, but it should also be in a better position to devote more of its
income to the remedy of that need.

Unfortunately, we do not have detailed statistics that allow us to
match the specific anti-poverty efforts of different nations, as
percentages of their national incomes. But as a very rough indicator of the allocation of resources for this purpose we can turn to the
percentage of gross national product used for income transfers of
all kinds. In the 1960's, for the nations of the European community the average ratio of social security expenditure to GNP was
approximately 14 percent; for the Scandinavian trio it was around
12 to 13 percent; for Canada 9.9 percent. In the United States the
ratio was 6.5 percent, barely above the level for Portugal.[4]

Furthermore, to this general indicator of comparative performance we can add a second consideration. The existential quality of
poverty is profoundly affected by the surrounding conditions in
which it is experienced. The difference between "genteel" and "de-
grading" poverty is not alone one of private income but of public
environment. Thus a factor worsening the relative neglect of poverty in the United States is that it is here concentrated in the
noisome slums of our cities or rural backwaters, rather than being
alleviated, as in the Scandinavian or more enlightened European
nations, by clean cities, attractive public parks, and a high general
level of basic life-support.

[4] *Basic Statistics of the Community,* Statistical Office of the European
Community, 1967, p. 132.

I move on to another related, and yet distinct, area of social neglect—public health. Here we possess the most detailed statistics of international performance, but once again the results are not comforting for the United States.

At first blush, one would expect to find the United States as a world leader in the field of health. No nation devotes as large a fraction of its gross output—some 6.5 percent—to health services. None has produced more important advances in drugs or medical techniques or spent more on basic research. Yet the comparative showing of the United States can only be described as disastrous. In 1950 the United States ranked fifth safest in the world in risk of infant mortality. This less-than-best rating could perhaps be explained by the generally admitted inferior health services provided to the Negro population, much of which still lived in rural areas in the South. Since then, however, the Negro has moved northward and to the cities, but despite (or because of?) this migration, our infant mortality rate has steadily worsened. By 1955 we had fallen to eighth place; by 1960 to twelfth. Today it is estimated that we rank eighteenth, just above Hong Kong.[5]

It is not only in infant mortality where comparative neglect in matters of health is visible in the United States. Despite our overall expenditure on health services, we ranked only twenty-second in male life expectancy in 1965 (down from thirteenth in 1959); tenth in female life expectancy (down from seventh in 1959).[6] Our death rates from pneumonia and TB are far from the best. Diseases of malnutrition, including kwashiorkor—long considered a disease specific to underdeveloped areas—have been discovered in the United States.

The causes for this deplorable showing are complex, and involve many cultural attributes of Americans, who overeat and oversmoke, as well as reflecting the effects of sheer neglect. But the steady deterioration of our *comparative* showing does not result from an absolute impairment of American health (with minor exceptions),

[5] *Toward a Social Report,* Department of Health, Education and Welfare, 1969, p. 7. Most recent estimate from *American Journal of Obstetrics and Gynecology,* November 1, 1969, p. 653.

[6] *American Journal of Obstetrics and Gynecology, ibid.*

as much as from the spectacular successes of other nations in applying social effort to the improvement of their national health.[7]
Judged against this steady comparative decline, the finding of extreme social neglect in the area of health seems inescapable.

Last, let me direct attention to a somewhat unrelated but surely
no less important area of social concern. This is the manner in
which we and other advanced nations treat that aberrant fraction
of the population that is apprehended for criminality. I put the
matter this way since it is well known that the infringement of laws
is much more widespread than the prosecution of illegality. Estimates of crimes committed, but unreported, range from twice the
number of recorded instances of criminality to much larger than
that. Indeed, a recently reported survey of 1,700 adults without
criminal records brought out that 99 percent of them had committed offenses for which they could have ended in prison.[8] Furthermore it is clear that among those who do commit crimes, it is
the economically and socially least privileged that bear by far the
heaviest incidence of prosecution and punishment. In 1967 the
President's Crime Commission reported that 90 percent of American youth had done something for which they could have been
committed by a juvenile court.[9] Yet only 5 percent of the children
in institutions for juvenile delinquency came from families in
"comfortable circumstances." [10]

I have no evidence to indicate that this differential apportion-
ment of punishment is more pronounced in this nation than in
others. But I have some distressing statistics with regard to the
measures taken by our nation in its treatment of the "criminal"
stratum compared with the measures taken by other nations. The
total population of Sweden, for example, is roughly 40 percent of
that of California. Yet its prison population is 20 percent of that of

[7] "The average Swedish worker who pays $3 a week for complete medical
care for himself and his family is likely to live eight years longer than his
American counterpart who pays perhaps five times as much." *The New
York Times*, March 29, 1970.

[8] *New Republic*, November 1, 1969, p. 16. See also the famous study by
E. H. Sutherland, *White Collar Crime*, 1949.

[9] "Juvenile Profile," *Task Force Report: Corrections*, U.S. President's
Commission, Washington, D. C., 1967.

[10] *New Republic*, op. cit. (note 8), p. 17.

California, and one third of that prison population is in small light-security camps enjoying "open" conditions. In the United States, such work-release camps are available in only four states.[11] The case loads of prison psychologists in Denmark average 20 to 30 per doctor;[12] in the United States the average ratio of psychiatrists or trained therapists per inmate is 1 to 179, and this ratio is for our Federal penal institutions which are far superior to our state institutions. In no Scandinavian (or European) country have prison camps or institutions been reported that can match for brutality the conditions recently discovered at the Arkansas State Farm. All this must have some bearing on the fact that recidivism in Scandinavia runs from 20 to 40 percent, compared with an average of 73 percent in the United States.[13]

It would not be difficult to add further evidence of neglect in other areas of American social life. One thinks, for example, of the niggardliness of American social security payments as a percentage of pre-retirement earnings compared with those of Sweden, or of the greater American than European indifference with regard to the protection of the consumer in many areas.[14] But I think the basic premise does not require further detailed argument. Instead, let us now turn to the central and critical question with which we began. How can we account for the anomaly that the United States, which among all nations can most easily afford to remedy social neglect, has been so lax in doing so?

II

We move now from the reasonably solid ground of evidence to the quicksands of explanation. Any effort to unravel the problem of American relative social backwardness must be suppositious and conjectural. Perhaps its main purpose is to make us thoughtful

[11] *Prison Journal,* Spring 1964.

[12] John P. Conrad, *Crime and Its Correction,* Berkeley, 1965.

[13] Conrad, *ibid.*

[14] *Sweden's Social Security System* by Carl G. Uhr, H. E. W. Research Report No. 14, 1966, and *Economic and Business Bulletin,* Temple University, Winter 1970, p. 38.

rather than to bring in a clear-cut verdict. But let us defer that
question until we have had a chance to see what the quest for explanation can unearth.

Let me begin by stressing an essential aspect of our inquiry. It is
that the terms of the problem, as we have posed it, make it impossible simply to declare that the social neglect all too visible in
America is nothing but the "natural" result of the class stratifica-
tion, the hegemony of property interests, or the blind play of
market forces characteristic of capitalism. Speaking of the failure
of American society to provide low-cost housing, two radical critics
have declared. "Such planning and such action [that is, the provision of low-rent housing] will never be undertaken by a government run by and for the rich, as every capitalist government is
and must be." [15] The trouble with such an explanation is that it
overlooks the fact that there is no significant difference in income
distribution, concentration of private or corporate wealth, or play
of market forces among the various countries that we have used to
establish the laggard social record of the United States.[16] It may
very well be that the institutions and ideologies of capitalism place
fundamental inhibitions on the reach of social amelioration in all
capitalist nations, but the problem remains as to why the United
States has not reached the limits of improvement that have been
attained by other nations in which the same basic inhibitions exist.

This initial orientation to our inquiry suggests that the reasons
must be sought in the most treacherous of all quicksand regions—
those that account for the subtle differences in basic institutions,
attitudes, or responses that we call "national character." Evidently

[15] Baran and Sweezy, *Monopoly Capital,* New York, 1966, p. 300.
[16] Kuznets, *Modern Economic Growth,* pp. 168–169; 208–211. The top
5 percent of income receivers in Denmark received 17.5 percent of national
income in 1955; 19 percent in (urban) Norway in 1948; 24 percent in Sweden in 1945; 20 percent in the United States in 1955–59 (before tax). See
also closeness of Gini indices of inequality as between United States and
Scandinavian nations: Russet, *World Handbook of Political and Social Indi-
cators,* 1964, p. 247. Concentration of corporate assets and sales among all
capitalist nations is also roughly similar. See Schonfield, *Modern Capitalism,* p. 241 n., and M. M. Postan, *An Economic History of Western Europe,*
p. 196. Nor does the degree of intervention into the market seem inordinately different as between, say, Switzerland on the one hand and the United
States on the other.

factors and forces in the American past made American capitalism less attentive, or less responsive, to large areas of social neglect than was the case with its sister societies abroad. Can we venture to guess what these elements may have been?

We might start by considering what is perhaps the most obvious differentiating factor between the United States and the European nations—the matter of size. One hypothesis would then be that the higher level of American neglect could be ascribed to social changes induced by the larger scale of our continent, with its obvious spatial obstacles in the way of creating a tight-knit society with a strongly felt sense of communal responsibility and concern.

The hypothesis is a tempting one, and perhaps contains a modicum of explanatory power. Sheer distance undoubtedly works against the growth of community spirit. But the effects of scale cannot possibly bear the whole burden of the problem. Canada, with a better record of legislative social concern than we, has an even larger territory. More to the point, the density of population per square mile, which is perhaps the most important way in which scale becomes translated into human experience, is not markedly different in the United States from that of many smaller nations. The United States averages 55 persons per square mile; Sweden averages 44; Norway 31; New Zealand 26; Canada 5.[17] Thus the effects of scale in separating man from man, and presumably thereby reducing the level of shared concerns and mutual responsibilities, should operate in the opposite direction, toward a higher level of concern in the United States than in any of the above countries.

A second intuitive possibility seems more convincing. If size does not provide a convincing answer to the problem of why America lacks a relatively high-ranking program of social repair, the striking diversity of the American scene may serve as a better reason. In the heterogeneity of the American population there would seem to be a prima facie cause for its lack of community feeling.

As with the matter of size, it may be that heterogeneity has its role to play, but—with one special exception to which I will shortly turn—I do not believe it can be made a central causative factor.

[17] *Statistical Abstract,* 1969, p. 828.

There is, to begin with, the awkward fact that the most heterogeneous of all European nations—Switzerland with its three language groups—is certainly one with a high level of public amenities. Canada is another example of a culturally diverse nation, in which political frictions have not stood in the way of the development of an advanced welfare system. Perhaps even more telling, we cannot easily establish within the United States any strong association between homogeneity of culture and community concern. The high level of social neglect among the white population of the southern states, and the inattention paid to the decline of Appalachia by its white kinsmen in more affluent areas of the affected region, are cases in point.

However, if homogeneity, in itself, seems an uncertain source of social concern, there is no doubt that the special case of *racial* heterogeneity is an all too certain cause of social neglect. The problem of racial animosity is by no means confined to this country and, wherever it appears, greatly intensifies the problem of neglect; witness the Maoris in New Zealand and the Ainu in Japan. But there is no parallel to the corrosive and pervasive role played by race in the problem of social neglect in the United States. It is the obvious fact that the persons who suffer most from the kinds of neglect we have mentioned—residents of the slums, recipients of welfare payments, the medically deprived, and the inmates of prisons—are disproportionately Negro. This merging of the racial issue with that of neglect serves as a rationalization for the policies of inaction that have characterized so much of the American response to need. Programs to improve slums are seen by many as programs to "subsidize" Negroes; proposals to improve the conditions of prisons are seen as measures to coddle black criminals; and so on. In such cases, the fear and resentment of the Negro takes precedence over the social problem itself. The result, unfortunately, is that the entire society suffers from the results of a failure to correct social evils whose ill effects refuse to obey the rules of segregation.

III

If the subject of race is discouraging, at least it gives us a clue as to where to search for the causes of the comparative social neglect in the United States. For the important role played by race in the etiology of the problem gives us one clear-cut reason why the institutions of capitalism in America have failed to develop in the same way as in other nations. Moreover, the importance of this special factor in our past suggests that other distinctively "American" facets of our history should also be examined to see if they too bear on the problem.

Whoever searches for such distinctive shaping forces of our past quickly fastens on two: the unique role of democracy and the extraordinary success of the economic system in shaping the American heritage. But if democracy and economic success are familiar touchstones in our history, they are surely disconcerting candidates for the role of social retardants. We are accustomed to pointing to our strong egalitarian sentiments and to the exuberant pace of economic progress when asked why we did so much "better" than Europe in the nineteenth century, not why we are doing so much "worse" in the twentieth century. To consider the possibility that these very elements of our past success may now act as social retardants would seem to require us to reverse the verdict of considered historical judgment.

That is not, however, what I intend. My thought, rather, is to suggest that the traits and institutions that admirably served the needs of one period may not be equally well suited to those of another. Consider, to begin with, the much admired democratic cast of American political thought. This is usually extolled for the impetus it gave to self-government, the limits it established against tendencies to tyranny, and so on. That judgment remains valid. But the democratic bias of American thought can also be seen in another light, when we consider it as a background factor that has conditioned our attitude to social need. The idea of the self-government of equals, as has often been remarked, has brought with it a deep suspicion of government for any purposes other than to facilitate the intercourse of the (presumably) successful majority. And beyond that, it has meant as well a denigration of an important aspect of the more ancient conception of a government of unequals; namely, that one of the justifications of government was the dispensation of charity and social justice to the neediest by those entrusted with the power of the state.

I have no wish to romanticize this elitist ideal of government. Indeed, it is probable that the homely realities of American democratic social justice were preferable by far to those of the "benevolence" of the rulers of nineteenth-century Europe. Nonetheless there remained within the older "feudal" conception of government a latent legitimization of authority that, once given the changed mandates of the twentieth century, provided the basis for a much stronger and more penetrative attack on social neglect than did the much more restricted democratic concept. In a word, the elitist tradition was ultimately more compatible with the exercise of a compassionate and magnanimous policy than was the democratic.

As always, Tocqueville sensed the difference. "The bonds of human affection," he wrote, "with regard to the democratic state, are wider but more relaxed" than those of the aristocratic:

> Aristocracy links everybody, from peasant to king, in one long chain. Democracy breaks the chain and frees each link. As social equality spreads there are more and more people who, though neither rich nor powerful enough to have much hold over others, have gained or kept enough wealth and enough understanding to look after their own needs. Such folk owe no man anything and hardly expect anything from anybody. They form the habit of thinking of themselves in isolation and imagine that their whole destiny is in their own hands. Thus, not only does democracy make men forget their ancestors, it also clouds their view of their descendants, and isolates them from their contemporaries. Each man is forever thrown back on himself alone, and there is danger that he may be shut up in the solitude of his own heart.[18]

What Tocqueville alerts us to is a restriction of the reach of concern in democratic societies—a tendency to cultivate a general solicitude for those who remain within a few standard deviations

18 *Democracy in America,* Mayer and Lerner, eds., 1966, p. 478.

from the norm of success, but that ignores those who drop beyond the norm into the limbo of failure.

In its general antipathy for government policies that transgressed these narrow boundaries of social concern, the "anti-welfare" animus of American democracy was further abetted by two other attributes of our experience. One of these was the frontier spirit with its encouragement of extreme individualism and self-reliance. The other was the enormous influence of economic growth. What E. H. Kirkland has called "that great human referendum on human conditions, the number of immigrants," [19] provided striking confirmation throughout the late nineteenth and early twentieth centuries of the relative superiority of life chances in America to those elsewhere, including the Scandinavian countries that now appear as paragons of capitalism. This vast encouragement in the field of economic life powerfully reinforced the prevailing political belief that those who failed to reach the general level of average well-being had no one to blame but themselves. Not only among the upper classes, but in the middle and working classes as well, the conviction was gained that social failure was more a matter for scolding than for indignation. Thus the rampage of social Darwinism in late nineteenth-century America, with its long-abiding legacy of anti-welfare attitudes in the twentieth, cannot be divorced from the myth (or the reality) of the frontier or the facts of economic life itself.

The result was a peculiarly American anesthetizing of the public's social conscience which, coupled with its profound suspicions of government "from above," led toward a mixed indifference and impotence with regard to social neglect. This is not to say that American culture produced a people that was less sensitive to suffering than other peoples—on the contrary, Americans have shown their quick human sympathies more readily than many other nationalities, especially for victims of misfortune in *other* parts of the world. It is rather that the ingredients of the American experience made Americans loath to acknowledge the *social* causes of neglect and reluctant to use public authority to attend to them.

It is informative in this regard to reflect on how much of the

[19] *Industry Comes of Age,* p. 6.

social legislation in America has come about as the result of determined work by the "aristocrats" of the system, against the opposition of the middle classes. Today as well, proposals for the elimination of social grievances receive much more support from the elites
of national government than from the county administrators, state
legislators, or small-town congressmen who continue to express the
traditional philosophy of the American past.[20] When it comes to the
alleviation of the specific forms of neglect we have discussed in this
essay, it is not a pinch on the profits of the great corporation, but a
pinch on the principles of middle-class Americans that often stands
in the way. As Adam Walinsky has aptly observed, "The middle
class knows that the economists are right when they say that poverty could be eliminated if we only will it; they simply do not will
it." [21]

To this enthronement of middle-class attitudes must be added
one last and exceedingly important supplement. This is the combined efficacy of the American democratic ethos and the American
economic *élan* in preventing the socialist movement from gaining a
foothold in the United States. On the one hand, as Leon Samson
has pointed out, the political ideology of America, with its stress on
equality, came very close to that of socialism, to the detriment of
the special appeal of the latter in less democratic milieux.[22] On the
other hand, the sheer economic advance of the United States
greatly lessened the traditional appeal of socialism in terms of its
promised economic benefits. As Werner Sombart remarked crudely
but tellingly, "On the reefs of roast beef and apple pie, socialist
Utopias of all sorts are sent to their doom." [23]

The absence of a socialist movement in turn exerted two effects.
On the one hand it removed from American political life the abrasive friends of a class-oriented politics that proved the undoing of
parliamentary government in many nations of Europe. That was
sheer gain. On the other hand, it also removed the combination of

[20] Robert Sherrill, "Why Can't We Just Give Them Food?" in *The New
York Times Magazine,* March 22, 1970, esp. pp. 93 ff.

[21] *New Republic,* July 4, 1965, p. 15.

[22] S. M. Lipset, *The First New Nation,* 1963, p. 178.

[23] Quoted in Daniel Bell, *Marxian Socialism in the United States,* p. 4.

working-class political power and intellectual concern for social reform that provided the moving force behind much of the reform legislation that eventually emerged in the rest of the Western world. If there seems to be one common denominator within the variety of capitalist governments that have developed a high level of response to social neglect, it is the presence within all of them of powerful social democratic parties combining trade-union strength and moderate socialist ideology. Per contra, one cause for the relative neglect of social ills in this country seems to be the failure of a comparable alliance to emerge in America.

In focusing attention on the roles played by the democratic and economic elements of American history in giving rise to its present condition of relative social backwardness, I do not wish to overlook consideration of numerous other factors that we have not considered, primary among them the peculiarly tangled and ineffective structure of American political power. The impotence of city government, the rivalry of the streets, the power of sabotage inherent in the seniority system in Congress—all these and still other factors surely deserve their places in an examination of the roots of social neglect. Nevertheless, with all the risks inherent in an effort to simplify a multi-causal phenomenon, I believe that we can offer a reasonably cogent answer to the question with which we began: Why has American capitalism lagged bethind other capitalist nations in the repair of its social defects?

The reasons, as I see them, are threefold. First, the remedy of neglect has been stymied because of the identification of need with race, and the unwillingness to take measures of which a principal effect would have to be a marked improvement in the condition of the Negro. Second, social reform has been retarded due to the lingering heritage of the democratic conception of limited government and to its lack of the ideal of social magnanimity. Finally, social neglect has persisted because the American credo and the American experience have inhibited the formation of a social-democratic, working-class party dedicated to the improvement of the lower classes.

IV

Is it possible to go beyond diagnosis to prognosis? Can an examination of the roots of American inertia give us some clues to chances for remedying the neglect from which the country suffers? From the material we have covered I shall venture a few comments which may be somewhat surprising, for in an age of general pessimism they carry a message of qualified optimism. By this I mean that new social forces capable of bringing about a substantial betterment of the prevailing level of social neglect seem to me to be at hand, but that we cannot yet say whether the potential for change inherent in these forces will be allowed to exert its influence.

Few would deny the presence of the first force. It is the belated arrival on the American scene of significant improvement in the relative economic well-being of the Negro community. Median incomes of black families, which averaged 55 percent of white incomes at the beginning of the decade, moved up to 63 percent at the end. Moreover, the preconditions for further increases are present in the existence of legislative measures that, however inadequately, bring some power of remedy against the remaining barriers of discrimination. I do not wish in any way either to exaggerate the progress of the average black family, which is still much too little, or to brush aside as inconsequential the obstacles to social equality that remain, which are immense; but only to state as an indisputable fact that a beginning has been made, and that it seems unlikely that it will come to a halt.

My second cause for qualified optimism is the tardy arrival of another necessary force for the repair of social neglect in America. This is the basis for a possible new New Deal—that is, for a second great massing of public energies for the improvement of social conditions in the United States. Here, the stimulus is provided by the challenge of the ecological crisis which, in the short run, threatens the comfort, decency, and convenience of life in America, and in the long run imperils its very continuance. There is no doubt that the reckless abuse of the environment must come to an end and that the present mindless extraction of raw materials and heedless disposal of wastes must give way to an orderly administration of the entire economic process from start to finish. In this imperious requirement, imposed on us not by a division within society but by a potentially fatal imbalance between the system as a whole and its adjustment to nature, there lies an issue that may be sufficiently impelling—and yet also homely and personal enough—to bring about the needed public acquiescence in the bold use of government authority for social ends. What the ecological crisis offers, in other words, is the basis for a new reform movement in America whose potential for improving our habitat, health, and general well-being could be very great.

My third cause for qualified optimism lies in the presence of still a last necessary ingredient for social change. This is the discovery in our midst of a social force that may provide a substitute for the social-democratic political conscience which has been missing from the American experience. That substitute is the party of the young.

I am aware that the young are not currently in full favor with Americans of our generation, and I shall have something to say about their shortcomings. But at this juncture, while we are looking for possible counterforces against the traditional American inertia in the face of social neglect, surely we must count the energy and idealism of the youth movement as one of these. Whatever their faults, the vanguard of angry young people has succeeded, where all else has failed, in causing Americans to re-examine the condition of their own house. Do not forget that the movement for civil rights was begun by the young; that the opposition to the war has been led by it; that the "discovery" of the ecological crisis was and is their special concern. It would be foolish to glorify everything that the youth movement has produced in America, but it would be wrong to deny the role that the young have played as the enforcement agents for the nation's conscience.

The presence within contemporary America of the first real signs of racial improvement, of the basis for a new New Deal, and of a corps of idealistic and determined youth, constitute new and promising possibilities for the repair of social neglect. Yet I would be

remiss in my role as social critic if I did not make clear the basis
for the qualifications that I must also place against these optimistic
possibilities.

Let me begin with the risks that must be faced in the rise of
black well-being. They derive from the fact that we cannot expect a
continued improvement in the social neglect suffered by blacks to
follow "automatically" from the workings of a growing economy,
or even from a rise in the average income of blacks. On the contrary, the past decade of "average" improvement tells us that the
deprivations of black ghetto life, the prison brutalities suffered by
blacks, the terrible differentials in conditions of health, or the persistent poverty of the black fatherless slum family, will not melt
away quickly even under the warming sun of a general rise in relative Negro incomes. To repair these resistant areas of social failure
will require continued agitation on the part of the black community
to bring its neglect incessantly and insistently before the attention
of the white community. The prerequisite for improvement, in a
word, is a continuation of black militancy; that is, demonstrations,
confrontations, and so on.

The dangers here are twofold. On the one hand, the prospect of
a decade or more of continual turmoil and pressure from the black
minority hardly promises a peaceful or easy political atmosphere
for the nation as a whole. More ominous, there is the risk that
black militancy, if pushed beyond the never clearly demarcated line
of social tolerance, may result in white counter-militancy, with the
possibility of an annulment of black gains, or even of a retrograde
movement. If the rise of black power thus opens the way to a long
overdue repair of the single greatest source of social neglect in
America, it also holds the worrisome prospect of a polarization of
race relations that could result in a major social catastrophe, for
whites as well as blacks.

Second, the possible basis for a new New Deal—the need to
work toward an intelligent management of our economy—also
brings with it considerable price. For the achievement of an ecological balance in America will not be won by the imposition of a few
anti-pollution measures. In the long run it will require an unremitting vigilance over and a penetrative regulation of large areas of

both production and consumption.[24] In a word, the functional requirements of a new New Deal must include a far-reaching system of national planning.

Is it possible that such a profound change in the structure of the American economy will be easy to achieve? The experience of the first New Deal is hardly reassuring in this regard. Yet the problem this time may not lie at first with the recalcitrance of business management; it is significant that two major corporate leaders, Robert W. Sarnoff of RCA and Thomas J. Watson, Jr., of IBM, have already called for national planning as the necessary first step if we are to exert effective control over the future.[25] The difficulties may lie, instead, with the unwillingness of the great mass of average Americans to give up the easy freedom of an unrestrained economic carnival for the much more self-denying life-style necessary for a truly balanced economic equilibrium. And beyond that lies the still more difficult problem of reorienting our whole economic system away from its accustomed goals of growth to new goals of a cautiously watched relationship with nature itself. In the end, the demands placed on the adaptive powers of the system by the requirements of ecology may constitute the life-or-death test of capitalism itself.

Finally, there are the qualifications with regard to the young. These are of two kinds. The first I need not dwell upon. It is the risk that the energies and idealism of the young will focus on petty issues rather than central ones, will be directed to rhetoric rather than remedies, or will culminate in a senseless fury that will only bring upon itself the repressive countermeasures of their elders. The second danger is perhaps even greater, although it is one to which we usually pay less attention. It is simply that the party of the young will vitiate its strength in internecine quarrels, as have so many parties of reform, or will become a party of the few rather than one of the many. The danger, in a word, is that the present energy and idealism of the young will peter out into exhaustion and futility. There are those in our generation, I know, who would wel-

[24] See R. Heilbroner, *Between Capitalism and Socialism,* 1970, ch. 16.
[25] Sarnoff at the 1969 annual meeting of the National Industrial Conference Board; Watson in January 1970 before the New York Bond Club.

come such a disappearance of youthful activism. But where, we must ask ourselves, would we then find an equally effective force of conscience in America?

All these qualifications come as chastening offsets to the optimism offered by the advent of new forces for social change. The threat of the difficult adjustments, clashes, and crises that seem certain to arise from the need for continued black militancy and for expanded government planning, and from the uncertain temper, appeal, or staying power of youth, make it impossible to look forward to a smooth transition from a relatively neglectful America to a relatively concerned one. Indeed, it is entirely possible that the decade ahead will not be one of improvement at all, but only one of growing tensions between the forces for change and those of indifference or inertia, and that the indices of social neglect will show little or no gain. In a word, America ten or twenty years hence may be as ugly, slum-ridden, unconcerned with poverty, unhealthy, negligent in its treatment of criminals—in short, as laggard with regard to its social problems—as it is today.

Before this indeterminate outlook, predictions can only be fatuous. More important, they are beside the point. For what our diagnosis has brought to the fore is a recognition that social neglect in America is but the tip of an iceberg of attitudes and institutions that deter our society, not alone in dealing generously with respect to its least fortunate members, but in dealing effectively with respect to the most pressing issues—racial, ecological, ideological— of our times. In this sense, the remedy of neglect in America comes as a challenge much larger than the immediate problems to which it addresses itself. What is at stake is not only whether the richest nation in the world will finally become the most decent; but whether a nation whose very greatness is now in jeopardy can recognize—and thus perhaps begin to remedy—the degree to which its present failures are rooted in its past success.

COMMENT

by Carl A. Auerbach

I question the significance of some of the basic evidence Professor Heilbroner relies upon to support his premise that "social neglect" in the United States is greater than in other western, democratic countries.

1. The *percentage* of gross national product used for *income transfers* of all kinds should not be the exclusive basis upon which to compare the anti-poverty efforts of different nations.

In the first place, it fails to take account of the greater prevalence in the United States than in other western, democratic countries of *private* social insurance systems. This may explain, in part, why social security legislation is less developed, and why social security payments as a percentage of pre-retirement earnings is less, in the United States than in other countries.

American trade unions, for example, have used collective bargaining to gain supplementary retirement pensions, sickness benefits and comprehensive medical and dental treatment, supplementary unemployment insurance and compensation for redundancy. They have not had the incentive or the strength to press for legislation to provide the population at large with the benefits they hope to secure for their members through collective bargaining. By contrast, the scope of collective bargaining is confined to more traditional areas in Great Britain. But British social security legislation is much more pervasive. Yet this very fact may serve to confine the scope of collective bargaining in Britain and to deprive the union member there of certain benefits his American brother enjoys.

There is a dilemma here. All-inclusive social security legislation tends to pull standards to minimum-subsistence levels. Gaps in such legislation tend to encourage the strong to fend for themselves and leave the weak without even minimum protection. Hopefully, the current drive of the American labor movement for national health insurance may signify a renewed effort on its part to close the gaps in social security for all our citizens.

Part of the differences in the percentages of GNP used for income transfers upon which Heilbroner relies is due to the differences in the public-private mix in the provision of health care. Yet Heilbroner points out that no nation devotes as large a fraction of its gross output—some 6.5 percent—to health services. This fact, together with the other facts he adduces as to the state of our public health, leads me to think that the situation does not support his "finding of extreme social neglect in the area of health," but rather a finding that we do not seem to know how to buy and deliver the health care we should have for the money we are spending.

It may be interesting in this connection to note that the British National Health Service is not solely an anti-poverty measure. The middle classes in Britain benefit greatly from the improved medical care made possible by the Health Service. The middle classes in the United States would also benefit greatly from a national health insurance program that would finance an efficiently organized health care delivery system.

Relative expenditures on public education (including manpower training) are not included in Heilbroner's comparisons. Yet such expenditures cannot be ignored in any study of comparative social welfare. I think it is safe to say that a comparison of public spending on education would favor the United States. For example, by 1968 there were 434,000 Negro college students in the United States out of a total Negro population of about 22,000,000. Out of a total population of 55,000,000 in Great Britain, there were 200,000 university students.

Heilbroner is comparing the United States as a whole with other European countries, ignoring the fact that we are a federal union. Yet this fact is responsible, to a signficant degree, for the comparatively poor showing—in Heilbroner's terms—reflected by figures for the country as a whole. Social security standards vary appreciably from state to state; the President's proposed welfare program is designed to build a minimum national floor which does not now exist.

Yet I daresay it would be possible to select particular combinations of states with populations as great as the European countries taken for comparison by Heilbroner and show that the ratio of their social security expenditures to their total income compares favorably with the ratios in these countries.

My principal objection is to Heilbroner's implicit assumption that the same or a higher percentage of a compassionate society's GNP must be spent on social welfare as the GNP grows larger. I would argue that this need not be so.

First, it is clear that one of the consequences of economic growth has been to lessen poverty. The incidence of poverty fell from 22 percent to 17 percent from 1959 to 1966 and has undoubtedly fallen still further since 1966. To the extent that poverty lessens with increases of GNP, the same percentage of a larger GNP devoted to social security can produce greater ameliorative effects. And of course the United States GNP is many times greater than the GNP's of the other countries taken by Heilbroner for purposes of comparison.

The point I am trying to make can be illustrated in a striking manner. If the ratio of social security expenditure to GNP in the United States rose from 6.5 percent to 8.5 percent, it would still compare unfavorably, percentagewise, with Canada's 9.9 percent, Scandinavia's 12 to 13 percent, and the European community's 14 percent. Yet it is estimated that such an increase of expenditure would eliminate poverty in the United States, in the sense that every family could be assured an income above the current poverty line.

Heilbroner acknowledges that the "income of a family of four at the 'official' threshold of poverty in the United States [roughly $3,500] . . . is an income approximately equivalent to that of a family in the middle brackets in Norway." I might add that Negroes in the United States have a per capita income about equal to that of a British subject and in 1969 spent more than $35 billion on goods and services, an amount only slightly less than that spent by the total population of Canada, which is about 1,000,000 less than the Negro population of the United States.

For these reasons, Heilbroner defines "poverty" as "a matter of relative affluence quite as much as absolute income." But if this concept of relative affluence means that the requirements of a minimum decent life in America will constantly increase in public estimation—a conclusion I am quite prepared to accept—I wonder how much is to be gained by clinging to the notion of "poverty" to describe the ensuing problem which, by definition, will be with us forever. Measures to assure a richer content to a minimum decent life in the United States and to reduce inequalities in income and wealth may take forms other than social security expenditures—such as further spread of unionization, higher minimum wages, wage-price-profit ("incomes") policy, more progressive taxation, particularly on inheritance and free university education.

It should be mentioned here, as Heilbroner points out, that income is distributed about as equally in the United States as in the countries he has taken for comparison. In this respect, too, we have made great progress, even though a more affluent society might be expected to be less concerned with economic inequality. From 1929 to 1963, the percentage of households earning incomes of less than $4,000 a year (in constant 1963 dollars) declined from 68 to 29. The percentage earning incomes in excess of $4,000 but less than $10,000 increased from 26 to 50. The percentage earning $10,000 and more went up from 6 to 21.

I should emphasize that I am questioning only Heilbroner's comparisons. I do not deny that we can and should do much better than we are doing to assure a minimum decent life for everyone, particularly decent housing, adequate medical care, and the necessary public amenities and services which will benefit all our people and not only the poor. Nor do I deny the fact of mistreatment of the Negro American, whose situation so terribly mars the record of American social performance.

Undoubtedly, there are elements of truth in the reasons Heilbroner advances to explain why we have not done better. But many factors also militate against total acceptance of his explanations. I am skeptical of any explanation put in terms of "national character." The "national character" is as much the product of circumstances as it is a molder of circumstances. It is not to be taken as given but as changing. Professor C. Vann Woodward has written that over the centuries American character has been described as "puritanic and hedonistic, idealistic and materialistic, peaceful and warlike, isolationist and interventionist, conformist and individualistic, consensus-minded and conflict-prone." Whatever our national character has been, it is obvious from our history that it has tolerated great, and even revolutionary, changes in our institutions and public policy.

I do not accept Heilbroner's contention that the elitist tradition is ultimately more compatible than the democratic with the adoption by government of a compassionate and magnanimous policy. Nor do I think that the quotation from Tocqueville—stressing alienation as a feature of life in a democracy—gives a fair picture of that writer's whole thought. Tocqueville's writings, as Raymond Aron has reminded us, are "full of rhetorical antitheses." Tocqueville thought that the great growth of voluntary associations—so characteristic of American democracy and so favored by the American legal system—would help to overcome the tendency toward alienation of the individual. Tocqueville also wrote:

> . . . if you hold it expedient to divert the moral and intellectual activity of man to the production of comfort and the promotion of well-being; . . . if, instead of living in the midst of a brilliant society, you are contented to have prosperity around you; if, in short, you are of the opinion that the principal object of a government is not to confer the greatest possible power and glory upon the body of the nation, but to ensure the greatest enjoyment and to avoid the most misery to each of the individuals who compose it—if such be your desire, then equalize the conditions of men and establish democratic institutions.

I do not agree with Heilbroner that "the frontier spirit with its encouragement of extreme individualism and self-reliance" abetted the " 'anti-welfare' animus" of American democracy. The frontier spirit, let us not forget, was also one of cooperation without which our country could never have been settled. Our people have never hesitated to use government and law to further their ends—and not only, as Heilbroner argues, "to facilitate the intercourse of the (presumably) successful majority." The social legislation of the nineteenth century and early twentieth century acknowledged the social causes of neglect and demonstrated concern for the less fortunate in our society. Certainly, since the New Deal period, our society has undertaken increasing responsibility to assure a minimum decent standard of life for everyone. In a recent case, the Supreme Court has assumed that the discharge of this responsibility is an accepted feature of public policy.

I would maintain that this extension of the horizons of human sympathy, not an anti-welfare animus, has been characteristic of American democracy. It has certainly manifested itself, as Heilbroner agrees, in the vast sums which Americans have given to aid foreign peoples. It has also manifested itself at home. Even if we accept Heilbroner's comparative evaluation, the relative deficiencies in the American system of social welfare are not so great as to warrant attributing them to an anti-welfare animus in the American national character. Nor do I agree that "social legislation in America has come about as the result of determined work by the 'aristocrats' of the system." This sweeping statement ignores the whole history of social struggle in the United States. Furthermore, I do not see what warrant Heilbroner has for saying that "the combination of working-class political power and intellectual concern for social reform" was any less a moving force behind reform legislation in the United States than in the rest of the Western world.

I grant that the American ideal of equality has often come into conflict with the high value Americans—not only middle-class Americans—put on achievement. To this day, for example, reputable scholars debate the question whether a guaranteed income in an amount Heilbroner would think adequate will so reduce the incentive to achievement as not only to be socially undesirable but also to be destructive of the status and self-respect of employable individuals receiving such an income. While I would discount this fear, I would not attribute it to an anti-welfare animus on the part of those whose views are influenced by it.

Furthermore, I would contend that the welfare state came into its own in the countries of western Europe with which Heilbroner compares the United States only when socialist ideology was declining in these countries. The absence of socialist ideology, therefore, is not a plausible cause of the supposed relative neglect of social ills in this country. Nor do I know of a social-democratic, working-class party in the rest of the Western world that has been more effective in improving the lot of the lower classes than the lower-class-based Democratic party of the United States which, Martin Lipset has demonstrated, has represented an alliance of urban workers, minority ethnic groups, and middle-class intellectuals.

Why, then, have we not done better in ameliorating the lot of the less fortunate in our society? I do not think the answer lies entirely in the tension that exists between the values of equality and achievement. Ignorance is a factor; it is a constant surprise to me, for example, how many people in the United States do not know what life is like in an urban or rural slum. Inertia is always a factor. So is the recalcitrance of the human material which we always encounter in trying to effect social change.

Lastly, our law-making institutions are problem-oriented. We seem able to concentrate only upon a small number of problems at a time. And wars and race aside, it would be difficult to say that we have not shown a proper sense of priority in the problems we have chosen to tackle. To try to deal with everything at the same time may threaten national sanity. The problem of race has been dominant since the end of World War II, and is still urgent, yet a Presidential adviser thinks it has been "up" for long enough; it is now time benignly to neglect it. Now it seems environmental problems are "up." One of the principal functions the legal system can perform is to assure a conscious and rational choice of priorities.

But I do not think it will facilitate the changes necessary to remedy the social neglect of which Heilbroner rightly complains if the progress made to date is disparaged or if the causes of neglect are attributed to factors inherent in our culture. No one should withhold the truth just because it may be discouraging and dispiriting. But there is no point in deprecating the country's achievements when the truth does not justify it.

I am happy, therefore, that Heilbroner concludes by expressing "qualified optimism" about the country's future, though it should not be surprising that I do not accept some of his reasons for optimism, and that the qualifications on my optimism are different from his. For example, I do not see the requirements of ecology as constituting a particular test of our kind of society. The Soviet Union—despite its comprehensive national planning—has despoiled the environment to no lesser extent than any capitalist country. Nor do I think Heilbroner's "party of the young" is a substitute for the "social-democratic political conscience." That conscience exists as a matter of political fact, and, in time, I hope it will be shared by many of the young who now fail to understand it. I do not accept Heilbroner's estimate of the accomplishments of the "youth movement." I am astounded, for example, by his statement that "the movement for civil rights was begun by the young." And I shiver a little when he speaks of the "role that the young have played as the enforcement agents for the nation's conscience." It is chimerical to envisage the "youth movement" as an independent political force, let alone a unified force for progressive social change. Obviously there are differences of opinion and political divisions among the young as among their elders. For example, the polls indicate that the college-educated young voted for President Nixon, and still support him. Polls in some states also show that opposition to the war in Vietnam increases with age.

I wish that Heilbroner's hopes for the presently young materialize, and that the country experiences as much social progress in the next forty years as it has experienced in the last forty years.

CHAPTER 9

THE HISTORICAL ROOTS OF AMERICAN SOCIAL CHANGE AND SOCIAL THEORY

---

by Harold Cruse

I

Alexis de Tocqueville, writing about America of the 1830's, made the following observation:

> If ever America undergoes great revolutions, they will be brought about by the presence of the black race on the soil of the United States; that is to say, they will owe their origin, not to the equality, but to the inequality of condition.[1]

He added:

> I do not assert that democratic nations are secure from revolutions; I merely say that the state of society in those nations does not lead to revolutions, but rather wards them off. A democratic people left to itself will not easily embark in great hazards; it is only led to revolutions unawares; it may sometimes undergo them, but it does not make them: and I will add that when such a people has been allowed to acquire sufficient knowledge and experience, it will not allow them to be made.[2]

Tocqueville made these observations about America during the years 1831–1835, or some fifteen to seventeen years before Marx and Engels produced their famous document on revolution—the *Communist Manifesto*.

During this period, Americans experienced the great nullification

[1] *Democracy in America,* Vintage Book Edition, Vol. II, p. 270.
[2] *Ibid.,* p. 271.

controversy—the states' rights crusade of the slave states against the Federal power. There were also the slave uprisings, capped by the Nat Turner revolt in 1831. New Indian policies were promulgated by Congress in 1834, setting up special Indian territories as another phase in the process of the extermination and pacification of the Indians. At the same time there was a marked increase in the number of black Africans entering the United States by way of the slave trade. This stepped-up influx of black slaves occurred despite the fact that the trade had been rendered illegal by the Congressional Act of March 2, 1807, prohibiting the slave trade.

In 1830 the total population of the United States was estimated at 12,866,020 (17,069,453 by 1840). Despite the Act of 1807 prohibiting the slave trade, the slave population increased from 893,602 in 1800 to 2,000,000 plus in 1830, and was steadily rising when Alexis de Tocqueville arrived in 1831 to study the American penal system and make his observations on democracy in America.

Writing in 1896, W. E. B. Du Bois said of slavery:

> The history of slavery and the slave trade after 1820 must be read in the light of the industrial revolution through which the civilized world passed in the first half of the 19th century.[3]

In other words, powerful economic forces intervened during the early years of the nineteenth-century evolution of the American nation and proceeded to impose on this nation the kind of racial ingredient, the kind of racial juxtaposition of cultural group encounter, not at all in keeping with the social philosophy motivating the original Anglo-American founders of the American nation. Which is to say that the human commonwealth envisaged by the original English settlers of the American colonies was not deputed in their minds as a society that would include African blacks and Indian reds on a democratic par with white people.

Thus, when one talks about the viability of the idea of "revolution" in contemporary American society, one cannot avoid casting a critical view backward into the very crucial forging of racial ele-

---

[3] *The Suppression of the Slave Trade in the United States,* Shocken, 1969, p. 151.

ments that characterized the formation of this American nation. This was why Tocqueville was so much intrigued with the future destinies of the white, black, and red races in America when he was here in the early 1830's. He pointed out that slavery could not survive.[4] He added:

> The destiny of the Negroes is in some measure interwoven with that of the Europeans. These two races are fastened to each other without intermingling; and they are alike unable to separate entirely or to combine.[5]

In contemplating the probable future of the American union of states in the 1830's, Tocqueville was led to observe this:

> The most formidable of all ills that threaten the future of the union arises from the presence of a black population upon its territory.[6]

This was a fact, yet traditional American history written by Americans obscures this fact. In their attempts to explain the causes of the Civil War, American historians conjure up every possible reason other than black slavery. They also seek out every secondary threat to the stability of the early American unity except the presence of blacks—the primary threat. The historiography of the Civil War—the ultimate rupture of America's unity—is a massive compendium of all kinds of "causes" ranging from "clashing economic systems" to "conflicts between cultures" to antagonisms stemming from "divergent political theories and moral codes." All of these opinions depart from the clear vision of Tocqueville in the 1830's who called the presence of blacks, as a threat to American unity, "a primary fact." The American historian Lee Bemson, writing in 1961, remarks:

> The number of studies touching on the causes of the American Civil War has already reached awesome proportions. The number of different explanations advanced is not as large but is almost as awesome.[7]

[4] *Democracy in America, op. cit.* (note 1), Vol. I, p. 397.
[5] *Ibid.*, p. 370.
[6] *Ibid.*
[7] A. S. Eisenstaat, ed., *Causation and the Civil War: The Craft of American History,* Vol. 1, p. 43.

The story of white people in America during the nineteenth century is a story of a people whose imaginations were haunted by the terrible fear of an impending conflict between black and white. In the North Tocqueville observed that whites made it a common topic of conversation, but this fact does not often come through in the history books. Consider the powerful impact Frederick Jackson Turner's "frontier hypothesis" had on the thinking of American scholars at the turn of this century. Turner stated that the differences between European and American civilization were based, in part, on the influence of the frontier in shaping American character. Ray Allen Billington, although alleging that Turner oversimplified the early American migratory patterns of life, insisted that "the anti-intellectualism and materialism which are national traits can . . . be traced to the frontier experience." [8]

I consider it possible to say that the presence of black people in America influenced the American character just as much as the frontier. Consider, in fact, how the reality of slavery dictated political and economic decisions relating to the western expansion. The burning question was always: shall the West be slave or free? Shall the West be for white men, red men, or black men? (Never for the equal occupation and use of all three.) Western expansion was always pursued in the interests of white people. However, the evolving "national character" of these American whites was strongly influenced by the presence of the red man and the black man, but these two non-European people did not influence the white man in the same way. Tocqueville wrote:

> The Negro, who earnestly desires to mingle his race with that of the European, cannot do so. While the Indian, who might succeed to a certain extent, disdains to make the attempt. The servility of one dooms him to slavery, the pride of the other to death.[9]

Note that Tocqueville equated an alleged desire on the part of blacks to amalgamate or assimilate with black "servility." He makes little or no mention of the slave revolts—for example, the Nat Turner uprising of 1831—or the general slave unrest which

---

[8] *Ibid.*, p. 144.
[9] *Democracy in America, op. cit.* (note 1), Vol. I, p. 347.

was on the increase at that time. Nevertheless, Tocqueville's views tell us much more about the basic ingredients that went into the formation of the American nation than many writers who followed.

I think that Tocqueville affords us more historical guidelines to understanding America than any other writer. Phillips Bradley, the editor of the Vintage Edition, was right when he said in 1945:

> (Tocqueville's) *Democracy in America* speaks to our condition, while we are in the midst of war and even now searching for stable foundations for our own future and the world's, as freshly as when it was written just over a century ago. The present is not an inopportune time to bring *Democracy in America* again into circulation—as a guide and inspiration for the task ahead.[10]

In the decade of the 1960's just recently passed into history, we have seen how apt were the prophecies of Tocqueville regarding the roots of revolution for America as existing in the presence of a considerable black population. The 1960's were the decade of the incipient "black revolution." I say "incipient" because it was not really a "revolution" in the strict classical or societal sense of the term. It was a rebellion.

Back in 1963 I wrote a series of articles for the *Liberator* magazine in New York, titled "Rebellion or Revolution?" in which I posed the question: "Would the 1960's black movement just then getting into high gear—would that movement lead to a 'revolution' or was it a rebellion only?"

I was then absorbed in the writings of Albert Camus who, in dealing with such concepts as "rebellion" and "revolution," wrote:

> Rebellion is, by nature, limited in scope. It is no more than an incoherent pronouncement. Revolution, on the contrary, originates in the realm of ideas. Specifically, it is the injection of ideas into historical experience, while rebellion is only the movement that leads from individual experience into the realm of ideas.

On this specific point I am in full agreement with Camus. In the 1960's, I did not believe that the black rebellion was a revolution, merely a threat thereof, but a threat that struck deep into the recesses of fear, chagrin, and guilt in America. The very idea of a

[10] *Ibid.,* p. 3.

revolution, especially a revolutionary thrust from the blacks, out-
raged most Americans. To many the very thought of revolution
was sacrilegious and an insult to the hallowed traditions of American democratic ideals. One hundred and ninety years after the
American Revolution, with its resort to arms, its force and violence, and its noble aims, the American people find the black revolution an outrageous possibility.

But the attitude of whites toward the black revolution is not
based on any such thing as an assessment of American history.
However, the attitude of whites is an outgrowth of American racial
history. The Americans today are acting out their historic role
against the idea of revolution precisely the way Tocqueville proph-
esied they would in the 1830's when he wrote that "A democratic
people left to itself will not easily embark in great hazards; it is
only led to revolutions unawares," and moreover "will not allow
them to be made," if they can be avoided.

The question today is: Can the American people avoid the black
revolution? Certainly the great majority do not want a revolution.
But another way of asking the same question is: Can the American
people avoid "social change"? The great majority of American
people (silent or otherwise) do not really want social change, but
they cannot avoid it. Which is to say that the majority of Americans cannot avoid the inner social thrust for the *basic aims* of the
black rebellion. Which is to say the American people must accede
to these basic aims—that is, must incorporate them in their society
or see their society rent into a state of chaos, wholesale repression,
sectional division, race war, and social retrogression. It will be out
of such a state of irresponsible social breakdown that a genuine
revolution will emerge. This is the generically true nature of American society.

We reach certain conclusions from this: Ever since the disappearance of the American frontier—that is, the era of nineteenth-
century expansionist violence that characterized American growth
—this nation has had two options in the province of progressive
social change—slow social reformist methods, and social change
spurred by violent protest and coercion. We still have these options
today with regard to the aims of the black rebellion. The nation *has*

the capacity and the material resources and the organizational capacity to meet the demands of the black rebellion. What the nation
lacks is the will, the vision, and the complete understanding of the
real nature of these demands.

The term "revolution" conjures up visions of blacks running
amok in the streets of the big cities, threatening law and order, and
other social horrors. These visions do have the prophecy of possible truths to come. However, what Americans do not compre-
hend is that the general demands of the black rebellion are projec-
tions of what paths of social change the American nation must
tread if the nation is ever to realize its full social potential as a
nation. The fact that the Founding Fathers who guided the establishment of the American nation looked upon blacks and Indians
as second- and third-class humans outside the purview of the new
Anglo-American commonwealth of the eighteenth and early nineteenth centuries only meant that the Founding Fathers (such as
Thomas Jefferson) were unable to grasp the full historical implications of what they had initiated. They had the illusion that they
could build a nation for whites only. This was the historical misconception in which most white Americans have since indulged.
But the prime imperatives behind the conception of an all-white
nation in the eighteenth and nineteenth centuries ceased to be the
prime imperatives after the Civil War. Before the Civil War, the
whites failed to stop the slave trade; they failed to abolish slavery
by constructive social and political action. And, as a result, they
invited military violence, coercion, and destruction. But once the
Civil War was over and the Thirteenth, Fourteenth, and Fifteenth
Amendments were added to the Constitution, nation-building on
the American continent took on social dimensions not dreamed of
by the Founding Fathers. Other social, racial, cultural, economic,
and political imperatives became the order of the day. Thus, that
new post-Civil War era placed nation-building on another historical level. Problems were posed for the American people which have
not yet been solved, the basic problem being: How do we incorporate the black population into the social structure of the nation?
Many whites and many blacks have always assumed that incorpo-
ration meant assimilation or amalgamation. But this is not neces-

sarily so. Blacks can be incorporated into the national polity on a multi-group, multi-cultural basis. But that is another question for other experts.

Another level of social engineering is demanded that is not beyond the capacities of Americans at all. More to the point, it is certainly not beyond the capacities of the oncoming young leadership that is protesting legally and also illegally in the streets.

But back to American history. I would like to discuss the thoughts of a prominent black American of the nineteenth century on the future of the race problem in American. He was the eminent Reverend Alexander Crummell, a full-blooded black man, born in New York in 1819. He was a product of the Free African School located in New York City at that time. He became one of the two most highly educated black men of his time, receiving his higher education in Quaker religious schools of the North and Queens College of Cambridge in England, receiving his Cambridge degree in 1853. It was said of him that "he brought a scholar's temper, a knowledge of history, and a familiarity with the sciences, languages, and literature to the writing of essays and articles on a remarkable range of Negro themes." His work directed sober thought to the controversy over the Negro's physical and moral equality with the rest of the human race.

Crummell's views on race relations in America were extraordinary, considering the bitter racial temper of his time. In a speech to his congregation in Buffalo, New York, in 1888, he said:

> The residence of various races of men in the same national community is a fact which has occurred in every period of time and in every quarter of the globe.

He went on to describe such racially mixed civilizations that developed in Egypt, on the shores of the Mediterranean, in ancient Rome, and elsewhere. Then he said:

> It might be supposed that an historical fact so large and multiform would furnish a solution of the great race problem which now invites attention in American society.

However:

There is no fixed law of history by which to determine the probabilities of the race problem in the United States.

Alexander Crummell, like Tocqueville, was originally perceptive enough to see that multiracial America was a uniquely new social phenomenon on the stage of history. Hence he said:

> Nevertheless we are not entirely at sea with regard to this problem. There are certain tendencies, seen for over 200 years in our population, which indicate settled, determinate proclivities, and which show, if I mistake not, the destiny of races. What, then, are the probabilities of the future?

He went on to discuss the imperatives of race differences, problems of amalgamation, the nature of the Anglo-Saxon race in America, the Celts, the French, the Puritan tradition in New England, the German influx, pointing out that "the Negro contingent was one of the earliest contributions to the American population." He asked the question:

> Has a new race, the product of our diverse elements, sprung up here in America? Or, is there any such a probability for the future?

He pointed out that all over the civilized world was revealed the strong tendency toward race cohesion, but at the same time the process of unification of races. "Indeed, on all sides, in Europe, we see the consolidation of states, and at the same time the integration of races."

Alexander Crummell was not a believer in race mixing or assimilation, but concluded:

> When a race once seats itself permanently in a land it is almost as impossible to get rid of it as it is to extirpate a plant that is indigenous to its soil.

Hence, the black race and the white are in America to stay, and there was and is nothing anyone can do about it but live with it. Crummell believed that history, more precisely the intimate history of the three races in America, ordained that "the probabilities tend toward the complete and entire civil and political equality of all the people of this land."

Being a minister, he called it "God's hand in history" (which reminds us of how Marx accused Hegel of leaving the door open to naming God Almighty as the generator of the dialectical flow of history). However, Alexander Crummell was very worldly in his social and historical judgments. He concluded that American democracy must solve the race problem because it is historically necessary. He said:

> It is not the case of the Negro in this land. It is the nation which is on trial. The Negro is only the touchstone. By this black man, she [the nation] stands or falls. . . . If this nation is not truly democratic, then she must die.[11]

Aside from everything else we know that has gone into the broad contours of American history, it is fatal to forget the underlying dynamics of race conflict as a social determinant. The black presence is a factor that can no longer be seen as a something "outside the pale" or as a ploy for the maintenance of liberal guilt or paternalistic guidance. Black people are an integral determining factor in the future destiny of this nation, which must stand or fall on the question of group democracy. There is no other way; there is no escaping this historical judgment.

Yet the black group's leadership never really rose to the occasion of exercising the group's potential until the 1960's. This upsurge could not have failed to impart a traumatic shock reaction across the nation. The nation had to be shocked into the realization that it was living in the midst of an unsolved problem handed down from the national past—from the nineteenth century when Alexander Crummell tendered his judgment on the future of race relations. Riot and violence were unavoidable when seen in context, past and present. The black rebellion said: "Take measures to solve this problem in this century—the twentieth—or America will not be preserved for the twenty-first century in its present state of national unification."

For black people it is the 1970's, the 1980's, the 1990's, or it is never. The same can be said for the entire nation.

[11] All quotes from Alexander Crummell's address "The Race Problem in America" in *Africa and America: Addresses and Discourses*, 1891, pp. 39–57.

This need not be taken as the fatefully frightening kind of ultimatum it seems to be. I am of the belief that the coming phase in race relations will be like a crucible out of which will emerge a new kind of social engineering. This nation has too much talent for it to be otherwise. I believe it will represent this country's coming of age in the very age in which its raw and crude capabilities have been called upon to give world leadership.

The black rebellion has forced this extrovert nation for the first time to take a painful look into itself. It does not always like the truth of what it sees as it is forced into these trying moods of historical introspection. But if the nation and its chosen policy makers are forced to look deeply enough, they will begin to see that the social ingredients and the institutional and organizational means for reorganizing and revamping our social system are, in fact, built into the system itself. This most highly developed nation in the world possesses every latitude and option permitting a reordering of its priorities. Being, historically, a nation of practical people, it is a nation which needs a new social theory predicated on its living actualities. America is a multi-group, a culturally pluralistic society, a multiracial nation. It must restructure its institutions to accommodate that reality.

II

I would now like to deal briefly with one specific example of the need for a reorienting of institutions. I would like to speak to the capacity of the American social order to meet the changing demands for social justice through the methods of law. This presents two problems, it seems to me—one in the character of the American development, the other in the nature of the evolution of American law. These two questions are intertwined in a very peculiar way, it turns out, particularly due to the fact that the nation was born out of the crucible of a revolution, which, in addition to establishing a new nation, also founded a new kind of legal code—in other words, a new basis of law.

We are now asking if the American social system, as it has

evolved, can accommodate peaceful social change to the methods of the same law. This posits a contradictory proposition for many reasons, because this nation has not developed societally in accordance with the original constitutional concept of the nation, and the legal philosophy permeating the spirit of the Constitution is inadequate in that it does not reflect the true nature of the kind of society that has evolved in the late nineteenth and the twentieth centuries. Yet there does exist, it seems, something of a legal basis through which social change can be accommodated, whether it is peaceful or violent.

Now, the elements, or the ingredients of social change, are built both legally and racially into the American system. The elements have been molded by the singular American historical development, and have a direct relationship to the problem of social change, it seems to me. America can change in a peaceful, legal fashion, or the adjustment can be in response to a violent coercion instituted rapidly. Dean Rostow has pointed this out in his references to the New Deal type of social change. This is instructive, but I think for other reasons than Dean Rostow has meant, because labor was never, or hardly ever, a revolutionary trend in this society. Therefore, as a result of the activities of labor in the thirties, it was possible for the New Deal to bring about social reform in a gradual manner. For this reason, I don't see any correlation here between the changes wrought because of labor action and the changes that have to be wrought in this society as a result of current black action, or future black action. Labor was never revolutionary despite what the Marxists have long maintained, but it does have missionary overtones. This historical fact says in effect that whatever radical or revolutionary philosophy one adheres to, one should not overlook the fact that there are imbedded in our historical antecedents revolutionary ingredients which are native to our traditions.

Tocqueville pointed out in the last century that the black presence has been revolutionary, because the blacks were left out of the democratic equation in the evolution of this nation. Hence, from the very outset, the law was always dead or ineffective for blacks. For blacks, the democratic rule of the majority meant a white majority, a negation of democracy for the blacks. In very real terms the law to black people means the police, jail, prejudiced judges, racist sheriffs, and not legal theory—and this despite the achievements of the NAACP in its pursuit of legal redress. Speaking of the rule of the majority means speaking to the fact that the entire history of black people in America is one of being tyrannized by the will of the majority, without consent or assent.

To discuss social change within this view of the legal order becomes rather ridiculous. The black rebellion today is a manifest protest, violent or peaceful, against the will, the historical will, of this majority.

Constitutional law, it seems to me, can legitimize protest, but it cannot legitimize revolution or radical social change. It cannot legitimize the kind of social change that the black rebellion is demanding and will demand more of in the future, because historically the black population—and, as a result, the black movement today—is beyond constitutional purview; ultimately it must alter and revamp this Constitution if it is ever to achieve its aims in the context of this American nation.

The problem here, and this is implicit, is that the Constitution defends individual rights, especially those of the group blessed with social power bestowed upon it by history. The Constitution does not safeguard, and never has safeguarded, the rights of outgroups, the blacks or the Indians. Only when constitutional law is expanded to prevent a majority social group from oppressing a minority group without its consent can we talk seriously of the sanctity of constitutional safeguards with respect to the black condition in this country. From a legal point of view, then, part of the revolution to come must be a radical development of the actual present philosophy contained in constitutional law.

The conclusion I draw from the symposium is that the legal profession, as it now stands, is not intellectually oriented, is not equipped theoretically, to deal with social change, even the peaceful social change so fervently espoused by Dean Rostow and others. It is incorrect to approach the black revolt in terms of the old libertarian legality, vouchsafed for those individuals, black or white, who conform. Blacks today are not conformists. At least

black militants are not conforming. To explain all of this, it is unnecessary to say that the black rebellion has profound historical
roots. We are now in a transitional phase. The black rebellion that
started in the sixties and continues in the seventies results from the
lack of liberty the blacks have suffered. The legal profession, then,
in order to cope with this contingency in our society, must remake
itself in the history of this movement. Its members are called upon
to become the founding fathers of a revamped and altered Constitution, to make it conform to group equality, as Professor Gottlieb
has suggested. The legal profession cannot aid social change in this
country through the individualistically oriented philosophy now expressed in the Constitution.

We recognize the need for social change. The political fashion
seems not to be aware of the fact that the black movement will
eventually make more advanced demands on American society. At
this moment, believe it or not, the demands of the black movement
are limited to generalities—equality, for example, but you must
prepare for the time when its tactics are going to change and become geared to revolutionary change, because the movement has
not yet taken up advanced questions involving power and other
problems that are inherent in the movement. It is one thing for the
legal profession at this stage to concern itself with the limited goals
of the black movement in its deliberations, its search for liberation,
freedom, and equality. It is quite another, and more taxing, requirement to ask the legal profession to look down the road into
the future, and to understand that this movement is going to develop and put forth more advanced demands, demands relating to
the actualities of group power; that is, political power in the cities,
where blacks will become the vast and overwhelming majority.
And even the problem of land power is going to come up, and the
problem of institutional power, and that of the distribution of
power. Problems peculiar to this society and its structure will soon
begin to be taken up by the more advanced young generation of
black leadership.

The legal profession must be able to see these problems. And so
must black leadership. But the ultimate problem at this stage is

lack of comprehension, total comprehension, on the part of each group, as to what the basic necessities are for dealing with the structural realities of each side. This problem, then, is an intellectual one, a theoretical one, a legal problem, an organizational problem; it is a problem which demands profound study.

The legal profession has its work cut out.

I say it must remake itself, and not keep thinking within the framework of old constitutional guarantees concerning individual liberties and rights. We are dealing with a group problem here, and the imperative of the black situation is the demand that the solutions be predicated upon group survival, the survival of the black group as a group, not the survival of a group of disparate individuals, but a group with a growing sense of community, a group which sees its community as one that is being prevented from achieving the kind of critical, cultural, economic autonomy that is necessary in order for it to achieve its ultimate goal of freedom, equality, liberation.

III

The prospects, then, are not easy, but neither are the goals impossible. The solution demands the harnessing of native talent, black and white, existing and emerging in the social sciences, and giving them the option of establishing a new set of norms for a new set of priorities in economics, politics, culture, the arts, sociology, social psychology, the techniques of mass communications, the ecological sciences.

Along this path lie the possibilities that progressive social change can be pursued minimally free from the coercive drive of violence. But the pursuit of reforms must be resolute and determined because anything less constitutes the main cause of violence and disorder.

It is my contention that there is an implied social theory for democratic social change inherently built into the material, ideological, and legal scheme of American society. I believe that it is objectively possible to effect social change through the processes of law and of democratic policy making. What blocks the path is the subjective factors motivating the present brand of policy-making decisions on all levels—political, economic, institutional, legislative, judicial, and executive. These subjective motivations behind traditional American policy making are governed by an institutionalized set of social values of ancient vintage, hallowed into myths and reactionary biases. There is the myth of American "free enterprise," the myth of individualism unlimited, unfettered states' rights, the myth of the separation of Federal power from laissez-faire economic life, and so on. Subjective factors in policy making serve to prevent the necessary reordering of social, economic, and political priorities that would implement the progressive policies of law and real democratic policy making. Is the space race a priority established by real democratic policy making? Is it not true that the priorities given to conducting the Vietnam war are the result of subjective factors in policy making that fear the consequences of peace more than they actually fear black urban uprisings and crime and violence in the streets? What are those of us who favor social change through the processes of law and of democratic policy making to do about stopping this war through "legal" channels? I, for one, do not see how I can morally condemn anti-war violence in the streets of New York and Chicago and Washington, D.C., when there is no "legal" path open to those who would demand from our policy makers a reordering of priorities. And unless there is a fundamental reordering of national priorities, there will be no access to "changing demands for social justice in peace"; there will be available no remedies for crime and violence in the streets; nor will there be any major shift to the very radical kinds of change in policy making necessary to meet the demands of the black rebellion.

A report from the National Commission on the Causes and Prevention of Violence states the following:

> The response of the nation to the more recent riots and disorders in the ghettos of our cities has been troubled, and on the whole, negative. Congressional appropriations for poverty and for urban programs have been adversely affected by outbreaks of urban violence.

The answer to this is that the nation does not understand what must be done to eradicate the causes of riots and disorders—any more than the nation understands how and why it must stop the Vietnam war and the violence this war wreaks on Vietnam. Connecting the Vietnam war with urban uprisings is not being done here for purely propaganda motives. It is a question of the relationship of peace and new priorities. We know that the Vietnam war is a race war, but that is not the point being stressed here, although the young black militants duly emphasize this fact in their assessment of American racism at home and abroad.

The United States is grossly misapplying its world-leadership role, which role it cannot avoid, by setting a poor example in the handling of its domestic problems. America will begin to play its genuinely progressive world-leadership role only when it begins to solve its internal race problem. This is what the world is looking at when it contemplates the role of the United States in world affairs. This is what the young black militants think when they connect the policies of the United States in the Vietnam war with the policies toward the black ghettoes. This is what the Spanish scholar Enrique Tierno Galván meant when he spoke on America at Princeton University in December 1968:

> In the near future, the United States of America may offer to the world two different models—outlooks—of life:
> One, by solving the internal problems now dogging the American people. Considering the vital importance of the essential problems challenging the structure, and even the existence, of the American people, their solution will provide the world with a feasible model (positive or negative) for the Western world. These problems are, to my way of thinking, the following:
> A. the intellectual rebellion;
> B. the racial disorders;
> C. the latent problem of generalized class struggle;
> D. the problem of harmonizing United States foreign policy with the internal moral crisis.
> How will the American people solve these outstanding problems? This is the question that the old European nations are asking themselves. Perhaps the future role of the United States

of America will consist—from the standpoint of people—in the providing of new answers and cultural challenges that are the common heritage of the old European nations.[12]

The situation is one of historical development. But the ingredients of social change, whether violent or gradual, are contained in the intimate history of the black and white encounter.

I take this to mean that insofar as the black influence on the society is concerned, neither black nor white nor any other race should go, but all must come to some kind of rapprochement or our society will perish.

COMMENT

by *Charles L. Black, Jr.*

I believe Professor Cruse has implied something to the effect that his posture has become less favorable toward revolution as he has grown older.

I am older than he is, and I have even less of the potential revolutionary in me. I find that prospect hard to evaluate, accordingly, but I think that the word "revolution" (as is implicit in Professor Cruse's paper) is really an ambiguous word.

What he would look for, and what I think the rest of us must be looking for, *is* a revolution—not in terms of the overthrow of a government and the attempted substitution of another government for that one, in power and legitimacy, but in terms of a total overhaul of all our attitudes and actions on racial questions.

It is interesting to note how the question whether "law is dead" so easily becomes the question whether law has enough life in it to do justice to black people. I thoroughly agree with Professor Cruse, and I think we all ought to take this message to the laity, that the question of justice to black people has been and is by a long lead the major

[12] Enrique Tierno Galván, "The United States and the Future Atlantic Model," a paper delivered at Princeton University, December 4, 1968.

question about the United States and about our significance in history. Our survival as a nation with any morality or any dignity, anything but a shell held together by a Cromwellian sort of army, hangs altogether on the capacity of our legal institutions to meet this challenge.

We cannot walk away from it. We are, as Tocqueville saw, bound to it; we whites and blacks are bound to each other, and we will either solve this problem or, in some manner, in some sense of the word, simply die, with our law as well as with everything else.

I strongly agree that American history needs to be totally rewritten, and re-evaluated in the light of this thought.

I think of such things as that we celebrate with dinners the birthday of Andrew Jackson. Well, now, that is something that really ought to be thought about. One should look into it freshly, into the actions and expressions of Andrew Jackson on the subject of race, on the subject of the American Indian, and on the subject of slavery.

Then we should ask ourselves freshly: Can we put ourselves forward as objects of trust, as people to be trusted, if we are getting together annually and making a hero out of a man with this kind of record?

But of course, though the rewriting needs to be done, the need is much more fundamental and basic than that. The mere statement of agreement is not enough. I would say that the beginning of our legal institutions and our constitutional system toward meeting the challenge which history has placed before us inescapably, has to start— the danger, of course, is that it will end, but it has to start—with great ideas; and the first function, I think, that the legal profession in this field has to take on itself, as lawyers have so often done, is the job of communicating some great ideas, in an intelligible form, to the laity, because I think the laity has more difficulty than we have in understanding.

I just want to say briefly what I think should be the great strategic ideas dominating our legal system in the immediate and indeed in the long future.

First of all—and this is trite, but I think when you turn to the laity they don't fully understand it—there is such a thing as *distributive* justice.

That concept, which is rather in mothballs in our society, should be refurbished and restudied, and it should be made plain that injustice may quite as well consist in an inadequate distribution of the goods of life as in definite and episodic invasions of a man's personality and individuality.

When you run that concept through the racial question, and through the poverty question, the demands of justice become more intelligible, only as a beginning, of course, but as a necessary beginning.

Secondly, the law can contribute out of its own body the idea of *restitution,* which is a lawyers' idea.

Many of us tend to feel that when we bring blacks up to a position of sheer formal equality, we have done enough. The simplest notions of restitution begin to suggest the contrary: that there is an obligation that can be given structure, which goes a whole lot further than that.

I think, thirdly, that we should accept and develop throughout the fabric of law the great idea which is latent and sleeping in the Slaughterhouse Cases decision of 1873—the idea, namely, that our Constitution does contain material which justifies us in treating racism as a *special* subject, that what we do about racism substantively, evidentially and remedially does not have to respond to analogical questioning from other fields, any more than the law of land finance need be brought into exact analogy with the law of marriage contracts. It is the race problem that is the special problem in the United States, and our dealings with it should be devoted uniquely to it. Here again I think the laity does not understand.

But getting past this sort of thing I think we have to take up as lawyers Mr. Cahn's notion, expressed in this symposium, that we have the specific job of building *structures* to contain and channel the necessary distributive and restitutive processes—structures for the administration of those things to which we ought to be led by reflection on distributive justice, on the concept of restitution, and on the uniqueness of the race problem. Those structures call for creative thinking.

I should think that the bar associations—this great one, for example—should be thinking very actively along these lines, perhaps as to something within themselves, or perhaps as to a joint committee of Congress on the conduct of the war against racism and against the clearly associated evil of poverty.

We have to retool ourselves along these lines. I don't know that I disagree with Professor Cruse, but I do disagree with what I have taken to be his implication, that our Constitution is not adequate to this task.

Our Constitution, in my view, is entirely adequate to it. The question is whether our will is up to it.

The Constitution is, in a way, an empty vessel into which we can pour what we are willing to pour.

CHAPTER 10

REVOLUTION

by Michael Harrington

Legalize a revolution?

The answer to this question, both the Left and Right would say at first glance, is that it is preposterous even to ask it. For Karl Marx and his followers, it would seem, law is simply an instrument of class justice, a juridical façade for an unjust system, the target, not the means, of revolution. And Edmund Burke and his descendants would warn that any conscious and abrupt attempt to alter social relationships which have developed organically will inevitably lead to disaster.

It is now necessary to amend the conventional wisdom of this united front of the revolutionaries and conservatives. It is, to be sure, quite possible that the upheavals of these times will overwhelm American society and that there will be no democratic transition to a new order. But *if* the future is to be created humanely, a revolution must be legalized. It is, in short, necessary to define a kind of political process which is not dreamed of in the traditional philosophy of either the Left or the Right.

But the work of definition is made all the more difficult by a certain debasement of language in the United States. In this somewhat frenzied, and electronic age, the word "revolution" has been used to describe everything from the modest progress of Negroes in the sixties to a Dodge automobile. The editors of *Fortune* magazine once even borrowed a phrase from Leon Trotsky, "the permanent revolution," in order to describe, of all things, the happy prodigies of which capitalism is capable. So the first task is to impart some precision to the meaning of "revolution."

In doing this, I will carry on something of a dialogue with the shades of Karl Marx and Friedrich Engels.[1] One reason for doing so is obvious: Marxism is the most profound and influential theory of revolution in modern times, and the term can hardly be defined without reference to it. But another reason is not so apparent. It is that there is a tendency within the Marxian tradition which is actually congenial to the notion of legalizing a revolution.

So the second section of this essay will propose a Marxist analysis of why the Marxist scenario has to be somewhat rewritten. It will suggest that the evolution of the modern economy has made revolution as Marx usually—but not always—imagined it impossible. Yet the necessity for basic structural change which he defined, arising out of the contradiction between a revolutionary technology and a conservative social system, becomes more urgent every day. And that is why a legal revolution is the only way out of our plight.

The final portion of my discussion will try to give some specific, and American, content to the idea of legalizing a revolution. Space will not, of course, permit a comprehensive statement of a program, for that requires a book-length treatment, at least. So I have concentrated on two limited, related aspects of my theme: the way in which basic transformations in the very structure of inequality in this society are imperative; and, in broad outline, the role of the legal system in this process.

I

First of all one must do away with the simplification that a revolution is necessarily violent.

Marx and Engels distinguished between a political revolution, in which one faction within a system displaced another, and a social

---

[1] If I may quote from my *The Accidental Century:* "The Karl Marx to whom I refer here . . . is not the mythic figure to whom the Russians assign the honor, and the Americans the shame, of being the father of totalitarianism. He is the revolutionary and democratic humanist who reveals himself in his own writings, those books which most people with opinions about him have never read."

revolution, which alters the very forms of property and power. But even though the transition from capitalism to socialism which they envisioned involved epochal changes in the basic institutions of society, they did not think that violence was necessarily essential to it. In 1847, when he was particularly optimistic about the potential of democracy,[2] Engels wrote the *Grundsatzen des Kommunismus,* which turned out to be a kind of first draft of the *Communist Manifesto.* "Which path of development," he asked, "will the socialist revolution take? It will above all establish a *democratic constitution* and thereby establish the political rule of the proletariat either directly or indirectly."[3] In an article written in the same period he was even more precise about his hopes, arguing that "in all civilized lands, democracy has the rule of the proletariat as its natural consequence."[4]

But a comment by Marx in 1852 is even more interesting than these references by Engels. For it dates from the period of Marx's anger with the bourgeois democrats and is all the more compelling for that reason. "Universal suffrage," he wrote, "is equivalent to political power for the English working class; for there the proletar-

[2] Despite the effort of some of the keepers of the true faith to picture Marx and Engels as oracles who were born with their wisdom completely intact, or at least defined it *in toto* by 1845, they were human beings who changed their minds regularly and responded to events. This is particularly true of their attitude toward democracy, and it is important to outline their evolution in this area so that their remarks can be understood in the context of their own history. In the period before 1848 they were in favor of a united front with the bourgeois democrats, and they therefore stressed the value of democracy; after the defeats of 1848 and 1849 they were bitter about their former allies and made an uneasy alliance with their conspiratorial Blanquists; in the 1860's, the period of the First International, they were in coalition with non-socialist trade unionists and emphasized the worth of reforms like the Ten Hours Law; after the Paris Commune, their defense of that upheaval revived some of their earlier, insurrectionary attitudes; and Engels, as will be seen, read enormous and positive significance into the electoral victories of the German Social Democrats in the eighties and nineties. The texts which I will focus upon in my analysis come, of course, from those periods in which they were most impressed by the value of democracy, and I therefore feel impelled to warn the reader that somewhat contrary precedents exist in their work.

[3] *Marx-Engels Werke,* Berlin, 1953–1963 (cited here as *MEW*), Vol. IV, pp. 372–3.

[4] *Ibid.,* p. 317.

iat composes the great majority of the population and, through a long, hidden civil war has struggled to a clear consciousness of its class position. . . . The establishment of universal suffrage would in England have a much greater socialist content than any similar measure on the continent." [5]

Twenty years later Marx gave a speech in Holland after the Hague Congress of the International Working Men's Association. He spoke on the socialist revolution and said, "We do not believe that the way to achieve this goal is everywhere the same. We know that one must take account of the institutions, the mores and the traditions of different countries. We do not deny that there are nations like England and America—and if I knew your institutions better, I might add Holland—where the workers can achieve their goals by peaceful means." And finally, Engels, in a famous and controversial document written near the end of his life, was even more explicit on the value of elections and democratic institutions (it will be discussed in some detail in Section II).

This brief recapitulation is, of course, sketchy and incomplete. And it certainly should be noted that Lenin interpreted these remarks in a way diametrically opposed to the reading made here; that is, he held that history had made them obsolete, not more relevant.[6] That is a matter which can be settled only by reference to the actual course of events, not by the citations of texts. But however one concludes on that issue, it is clear that both Marx and Engels conceived of the *possibility* of a nonviolent and democratic revolution. Whether the revolution can be legalized, they said, can be determined only by a careful, empirical examination of a specific country at a given point in historical time.

But then I do not quote Marx and Engels on this question because their opinions are of historical interest or represent some kind of argument from revolutionary authority. I also think, and hope to show, that they were right in saying that a legal revolution

[5] *MEW,* Vol. VIII, p. 344.

[6] In his polemic "The Proletarian Revolution and the Renegade Kautsky," Lenin held that Marx and Engels had made England and America exceptional cases because they lacked militarism and a bureaucracy. And he added, "They do exist in Britain and America *now.*" Cf. *Lenin on the United States,* International Publishers, New York, 1970, p. 365.

is possible. And that judgment requires me to confront America as it is today rather than as it was in the days of Marx. How, someone might plausibly ask, can you persuade us that America under Richard Nixon is in the throes of a revolution?

If you look for barricades and masses in the streets, you will not find them. But if, understanding along with Marx and Engels that a revolution does not have to be as obvious as that, more subtle data are examined, one must conclude that this country is in the midst of profound transformations. Consider, for instance, the enormous distance we have traveled in the few years since the consensus theory of American history and society dominated the country's thinking.

In the 1950's a number of very influential analyses of the nation's past and present pictured America as relatively free of serious conflict. David Riesman described how the other-directed conformity of the lonely crowd had become our most characteristic trait; Daniel Bell proclaimed as end of ideology and the irrelevance of the traditional polarities of Left and Right; and Louis Hartz reread the American past and found there a record of cooperation and harmony. By the mid-sixties, Lyndon Johnson had turned these theories into a political program which called for "reasoning together" as the way to solve problems. In the 1964 campaign, Barry Goldwater's candidacy allowed Mr. Johnson to build the broadest middle of the road in modern times, stretching from Henry Ford to Walter Reuther and from Governor Connolly to Martin Luther King, Jr.

In an article in *Fortune* in 1966 Max Ways generalized these themes into an apotheosis of "creative federalism." Ways wrote that "United States history is making a major turn from the politics of issues to the politics of problems, from an emphasis on need to an emphasis on opportunity, from struggle over the redistribution of what we have to the less crude and more intricate decision about what we have become." The old politics of the thirties, he said, were based on "taking from group A to give to group B"; but now, in the Johnson programs, "every group is . . . believed capable of advancing under its own steam" and Medicare, aid to education, anti-pollution, and all the rest of the measures are "not ideological *issues*. They are efforts to deal with *problems*." [7]

Yet American society has not exactly developed according to these consensus scenarios. In a remarkable reversal of historic precedent, a mass movement effectively forced an incumbent President to resign from politics in 1968. In a decade of unrivaled prosperity there were tremendous eruptions of black violence in cities like New York, Detroit, Chicago, and Newark, and nationalist and separatist tendencies emerged among Negroes, Mexican Americans, Puerto Ricans, and American Indians. Instead of an end to ideology some of the brightest students at elite colleges and universities became more ideological, and the revival of Leftist thought— or at least of Leftist emotions—was greater than at any time since the thirties.

There were even tragically misguided youths who turned to terrorism. As one of them told William Worthy, ". . . this is a technological society which is extremely vulnerable because the people who are attacking it from within are not foreigners—not anarchist terrorists in the classic sense—they are the children of this society who had their eyes opened to the nature of this society and they refuse to be part of it." [8]

Perhaps one might dismiss that young man's Dostoevskian politics as telling more about his psychology than about the society. But the National Commission on the Causes and Prevention of Violence can hardly be discounted on grounds of ultra-radicalism. It was appointed by Lyndon B. Johnson, chaired by Dr. Milton Eisenhower, and it was composed of the usual stratum of sober leaders ranging from the moderate Right to the moderate Left. And it said that "in a few more years, lacking effective public action," the central cities would be deserted at night, the high-rise apartment buildings of the affluent would be "fortified cells," the slums would be places of terror. Private automobiles, taxis, and commer-

[7] Max Ways, " 'Creative Federalism' and the Great Society," *Fortune*, January 1966.

[8] William Worthy, "A Real Bomber's Chilling Reasons," *Life*, March 27, 1970.

cial vehicles, the Commission predicted, would be "routinely equipped with unbreakable glass, light armor and other security features," and armed guards would "ride shotgun" on all public transportation and patrol all public facilities.

And the Commission commented: "Individually and to a considerable extent unintentionally, we are closing ourselves into fortresses when collectively we should be building the great, open, humane city-societies of which we are capable." [9]

But how did America change its image of itself in the matter of a few years from one of consensus and cooperation to this anti-Utopia of the Violence Commission? Part of the answer is to be found in the combination of technological revolution and the relatively conservative politics which have been the rule during the past decade. This, I would suggest, is the basic, objective contradiction in the society, and although it takes place in a setting of capitalist affluence which Marx never anticipated, it has an extraordinary similarity to the problem which he identified more than a century ago.

Since the end of World War II, that large-scale production which is crucial to the American economy has been producing more and more social costs. Either the market system did not work at all, as in the case of those corporations which administer prices, or else it misallocated resources by making some of the most important social goods—like air and water—"free" and therefore encouraged their reckless, antisocial use.[10] Carl Keysen made a brilliant summary of one aspect of this trend:

> The interrelated set of questions involving urban renewal, urban planning and transportation planning raises questions that go right to the heart of the usual value assumptions of the economist. The whole field is dominated by the existence of externalities, i.e., it is clear that there is no simple meaningful sense in which the range of decisions can be left to market forces. It is further clear that our

[9] *To Establish Justice, to Insure Domestic Tranquility,* Final Report of the National Commission on the Causes and the Prevention of Violence, GPO, Washington, 1969, pp. 44–45.

[10] This discussion of technology and the welfare state will be relatively brief. For an extended analysis and documentation the reader is referred to my "Why America Needs Socialism" in *Dissent,* May–June 1970.

past methods for dealing with the major externalities are increasingly inadequate. Zoning by a fragmented set of competing jurisdictions, highway planning uncoordinated with land-use planning or without comprehensive transportation planning simply fail to meet the issues. What alternate decision mechanisms are available?

The natural bias of economists is toward believing that consumers "ought" to get what they want in some ethical sense of the word. Economists accordingly tend to resist, as a matter of fundamental principle, changes in decision-making processes that substitute planners' choices for consumers' choices. Yet in the face of what consumers' choices are leading to, some such substitution appears inevitable. At the very least, planners will determine, much more narrowly than present processes do, the range of alternatives from which consumers may choose. The key question becomes, "By what political mechanism are planners' choices to be reviewed and controlled." [11]

So there is a systematic tendency in the American economy to create congestion, suburban sprawl, pollution, and the like. And it is this objective trend which, in part, gives rise to all those discontents which contradict the consensus scenarios (the question of motivation will be considered in some detail shortly). But, as I showed in *Toward a Democratic Left,* government policies encourage and subsidize the very crises which the government deplores. In the area of housing, for instance, Washington helped finance the middle-class desertion of the city through tax policy (the write-off for interest payments on the mortgage; the exclusion of the rental value of a privately owned house from the owner's income), below-market rates of interest and multi-billion-dollar highway programs.

In other words, the political system has not checked the destructive tendencies of corporate allocation but actually encouraged them. It does so, not because Washington has been peopled by individuals with an antisocial bias—during this period most of the officials had liberal values—but because the welfare state used the same commercial priorities as the private sector. Low-cost housing

[1] Carl Keysen, "Model Makers and Decision Makers," in *Economic Means and Social Ends,* Robert Heilbroner, ed., Prentice-Hall, Englewood, N.J., 1969, p. 149.

simply does not pay enough in conventional terms to motivate either builders or Federal administrators to build very much of it. That is why the Kerner Commission reported that the United States helped in the construction of more than 10,000,000 new homes— that is, dwellings for the white middle and upper classes, over about a thirty-year period—and financed only 650,000 units of low-cost housing in roughly the same period.

So America is undergoing a technological revolution with enor-mously high social costs; there must be structural changes moving from consumers' choices to planners' choices; and the political in-stitutions have yet to demonstrate that they are capable of making this transition. If violent change, as I will show, cannot deal with this situation, only profound nonviolent change can. In the sophis-ticated, but unromantic, meaning of the word *revolution,* the histor-ical period requires one.

But secondly, these crises of the times express themselves in people's minds and actions. And here the peculiarity of the mo-ment is best seen in terms of relative deprivation. For that is a major source of rebellion under conditions of affluence.

The term "relative deprivation" is a sociological cliché. And yet the consensus theorists did not give it a proper place in their projec-tions, for almost all of them assumed that, as the conditions of life got objectively better, people would become more content and less prone to conflict. In point of fact, it is precisely in a period of prosperity, when expectations are so encouraged that they some-times outstrip performance, that groups become most demanding. As far back as 1906, when Werner Sombart developed his famous thesis that socialism was not developing in America because the standard of living was so high, he overlooked the fact that he was writing in a period of extremely violent class struggle and the rapid growth of the Debsian Socialist party.[12]

This process of good times radicalizing people has been known for a long time. As far back as 1849, Marx wrote that under pros-

12 Werner Sombart, *Warum gibt es in den Vereinigten Staaten keinem Sozialismus,* Mohr, Tubingen, 1906. For the extraordinary intensity of class conflict in the period see Philip Taft and Philip Ross, "American Labor Violence: Its Causes, Character and Outcome" in *Violence in America,* Graham and Gurr, eds., Vol. I, GPO, Washington, 1969.

perity "although the enjoyments of the worker have risen, the social satisfactions which they give him fall in comparison with the increased enjoyments of the capitalists. . . . Our desires and pleasures spring from society; we measure them, therefore, by society." [13] But commonplace as the proposition is, it was effectively ignored by the consensus theorists of the fifties. But now there is another danger: that the idea of relative deprivation will be used to underestimate our present crisis by saying that it is *only* psychological. This is the tactic of Professor Edward C. Banfield of Harvard in *The Un-Heavenly City.*

Banfield writes that "To a large extent . . . our urban problems are like the mechanical rabbit at the race track, which is set to keep just ahead of the dogs no matter how fast they run. Our performance is better and better, but because we set our standards and expectations to keep ahead of performance, the problems are never any nearer to solution. . . . After all, an 'urban crisis' that results largely from rising standards and expectation is not the sort of crisis that, unless something drastic is done, is bound to lead to a disaster." [14]

That is a dangerous simplification—and in Banfield's case, a rationale for telling policy makers that they don't have to be overly disturbed about our crises (that, I suspect, is the kind of scholarship which President Nixon appreciates). All of those externalities of pollution, congestion, overcrowding, slum deterioration, and fear of crime are not psychic inventions but objective facts. Moreover, Professor Banfield ignores the fact that *needs* become greater as society becomes more sophisticated. He cites the enormous number of high school graduates in 1970 as compared to 1900 but forgets to add that, in order to maintain a relative position within the class structure, that additional education has become a necessity, not a case of extravagant expectation.

So in emphasizing relative deprivation as a discontent typical to affluence, I am not suggesting that our problems are simply a result of our standards. There is quite real deprivation as well as a height-

[13] *MEW, op. cit.* (note 3), Vol. VI, p. 412.
[14] Edward C. Banfield, *The Un-Heavenly City.* Little, Brown, Boston, 1970, p. 21.

ened awareness of it.[15] And used in this way, I think that the term can be quite helpful to an understanding of what one might call the "cultural revolution" of our times: the way in which some of the most basic institutions for evoking loyalty and enforcing discipline in society are breaking down. I refer to the labor market, the family, and the church.

Up until quite recently, the overwhelming majority of the population were subjected to that most basic of disciplines immortalized in the cruel motto: "He who does not work shall not eat." But in the upper and lower reaches of the class system and particularly among the young this imperative is now weakening. As a result this society does not simply need planned social investments but a new system of motivation as well.

In the middle and upper classes, parents fervently believe that education is the key to future status and income for their children. As a result, there has been a vast increase in spending on higher education. For some time now, as Christopher Jencks and David Riesman point out in their brilliant study, *The Academic Revolution,* these outlays have been increasing faster than the gross national product. Since they are, to a considerable measure, subsidized with tax funds, this is one more way in which the government funds the crises it decries: the largest amounts are spent at elite schools, particularly elite public universities, where white children from culturally advantaged homes have an unbeatable edge in a "democratic" competition. So these programs tend to institutionalize, or even worsen, the class divisions of the society at public expense.

One result of this emergence of a knowledge economy is a new social-biological stage of life. Kenneth Keniston calls it "youth." [16]

[15] I have given particular attention to Professor Banfield's book because I believe it represents a major intellectual trend of playing down the gravity of our situation. Other important works in this mood are *The Myths and Reality of Our Urban Problems* by Raymond Vernon (Harvard University Press, 1966) and *The Metropolitan Enigma: Inquiries into the Nature and Dimension of America's "Urban Crisis,"* ed. by James Q. Wilson (U.S. Chamber of Commerce, 1967). I discussed these earlier optimistic statements in Chapter II of *Toward a Democratic Left* (Macmillan, 1968).

[16] Kenneth Keniston, *Young Radicals: Notes on Contemporary Youth.* Harcourt, Brace & World, New York, 1967.

Adolescence was an innovation of capitalist society. Prior to capitalism, children entered the working world (or, for royalty, the political world) as soon as they were physically able. But in the nineteenth century society grew wealthy enough to establish a "moratorium" between childhood and adulthood for the children of the privileged (the term is Erik Erikson's). So "teen age," as a social phenomenon, is of rather recent date and located primarily in the middle and upper strata of the class structure. Now, however, this moratorium is being extended as more and more of the advantaged young prolong their education, formally or informally, into their twenties. And it is within this new age grouping of the young—post-adolescent but not yet taking adult responsibilities— that some of the most tumultuous protests of recent years have taken place.

In part, this discontent arises out of a dissatisfaction with the college student's place in the society. For, to a considerable extent, his degrees are not meant to represent scholarly achievement so much as to function as credentials which certify a young person as having the proper qualifications for a good job. Consequently there is a sharp contrast between the quality education which the student receives, particularly in the humanities and social sciences, and the kind of work he is expected to perform after graduation. That is one of the reasons why so many of the talented young are turning their backs on business and volunteering in community action projects; it is also a cause of hippie disaffiliation from the entire society. Their intellectual abilities and training are excessive in terms of the roles offered them, so it is precisely their advantages which make them feel deprived. That paradox is, I suspect, difficult for their parents to understand; but it is real.

The relative deprivation of the activist young also has a component which is quite idealistic, and not so much concerned with their own future. These students have the time (which is to say, the money) to examine the society and to measure it against their values. And part of their anger has come from the perception of the systematic inequities of the American class structure. They experience a sort of vicarious relative deprivation by identifying with the poor, the blacks, the minorities, and, intellectually at least, examining the allocation of roles and power in the society from their point of view.

In both its aspects, the self-interested and the idealistic, I believe that the activism of the educated young is going to continue and even increase. It is not a fad, as was swallowing goldfish in the thirties; it expresses important reactions to the evolution of our class structure. Ironically, American society is paying millions for the privilege of creating its most bitter critics.

At the other end of the class structure, among the poor, a parallel phenomenon occurs. A good many of minority youth are neither educated nor motivated to participate in the increasingly sophisticated labor market. They qualify for unemployment or for dead-end jobs. In past periods they would have competed for the latter if only to avoid starvation. But now in the most conscientious states, Aid for Dependent Children becomes competitive with the worst jobs, and a good many poor women see no point in working hard with no prospect of improving their lot.[17] Others, who don't qualify for welfare (that is, able-bodied men, for—contrary to popular myths about people loafing on relief payments—only a negligible percentage of this category receives any assistance), turn to "hustling," and to crime.

One possible consequence of this development was recently suggested by Robert Heilbroner: that overt coercion will replace the indirect discipline which the labor market used to enforce. This is certainly an aspect of the compulsory work requirement in President Nixon's welfare reform proposal. Another, infinitely more humane, way of dealing with the question would be to design interesting and creative jobs which would utilize the wasted talents of the poor. In 1966, the Automation Commission identified some 5,300,000 jobs in public service which could provide an opportunity to engage in this kind of innovation and to improve the quality of life of the entire society.[18]

But I do not raise this last point here for extended discussion.

[17] Cf. Nathan Glazer, "Beyond Income Maintenance" in The Public Interest, Summer 1969.

[18] Technology and the American Economy: Report of the National Commission on Technology, Automation and Economic Progress. GPO, Washington, 1966, Vol. I, p. 36.

Rather I cite the dispossessed poor in this context as another case of relative deprivation. For there is no question that their anger at their plight is intensified by the fact that it takes place in the richest society in human history. And their refusal to take menial jobs represents, in part at least, a heightened sense of expectation and self-esteem which has been encouraged by the ubiquitous education system run by the advertising industry.

At the same time that the traditional discipline of the labor market falters, so does that of both the family and the church. In the case of the family, the event is clearly related to the economic change that has just been analyzed. At the upper end of the class structure, affluence has created leisure for the young; at the lower end, more idleness. In each case, as Richard Lowenthal has pointed out,[19] there is a growing population which does not take part in the production process. "What appears today as a widespread rebellion of youth versus authority is, I suspect, largely born of frustration caused by the absence of authority. . . ."[20]

If this is indeed the cause—and I think it quite possible that it is—then conservative proposals to bring these young people back to the old ways by being tough with them are doomed to failure. *For society does not, and cannot, provide roles for them under present conditions which elicit voluntary loyalty and self-discipline, and external pressure will only serve to further embitter them.* It is necessary, in short, to define new kinds of work, new kinds of roles, if the social contract is to be restored—and that means moving toward a new kind of society.

So in this first attempt to give some contemporary meaning to the word *revolution,* it is clear one does not exist in America in the popular, and less profound, definition of the term. But there are technological transformations which are radically reshaping the very character of the society and they cannot be contained within our current political-economic structure. And there is a kind of cultural revolution taking place among the young in which the three most formidable sources of authority in the bad old days—

[19] Richard Lowenthal, "Unreason and Revolution" in *Encounter,* November 1969.
[20] *Ibid.,* p. 20.

the labor market, the church and the family—have all been called into question. In the sense of those very profound social happenings, we are living through a new kind of revolution.

II

But does this then mean, as some of the enthusiastic young radicals conclude, that these various tumults will goad America to a revolution in which violence will solve our contradictions? I think not. For the daring proposition about our present plight is that it has not, and *cannot,* generate a revolution on the nineteenth-century model. A counterrevolution, yes; but not a revolution. And secondly, even if a brutal upheaval were to take place, it could not solve any of the nation's basic problems.

Or, to put my analysis in another context, I am challenging Mr. Justice Douglas's dictum (while obviously agreeing with most of the other ideas in his book) that "We must realize that today's Establishment is the new George III. Whether it will continue to adhere to his tactics, we do not know. If it does, the redress, honored in tradition, is also revolution." [21] That tradition, I am saying, is obsolete. If the Establishment (and I do not like the imprecision of the term, but let that pass) continues in its present way, it will move to the Right, perhaps to the far Right. And if the crisis is to be resolved progressively, it will be because a new kind of revolution—nonviolent and democratic, legal—will take place, unlike anything the Founding Fathers or Marx and Engels ever dreamed.

Once again, my method will be to compare classic revolutionary texts to our very unclassic reality, first as regards the possibility of violent change, and then in terms of its potential for solving our woes.

To begin with, one must understand that Karl Marx changed his mind about revolution but died before he could work out the full implications of his mature view.[22] In the projections of the *Commu-*

William O. Douglas, *Points of Rebellion.* Vintage Books, 1970, p. 95.
[22] My reading and thinking on this issue were very much stimulated by "Proletariat and Middle Class in Marx: Hegelian Choreography and the

nist Manifesto, the "distinctive feature" of the modern epoch was that "it has simplified class contradictions. The entire society more and more divides itself into two great, hostile camps, into two classes directly counterposed to one another: the bourgeoisie and the proletariat." [23] In this view, the petty bourgeoisie and even the solid middle class would be proletarianized, and the suffering and misery of their condition would drive them, and the workers, to overthrow the established order.

But in later years, Marx recognized that the basic economic and sociological calculations on which his revolutionary politics rested had to be modified. As capitalism developed, he said, it economized on labor through investment in machines. As a result, it had the resources to spend on "non-productive" consumption and the motive to provide for it; that is, a desire to see to it that all the wealth of society was consumed. In the heroic days of the struggle against feudalism, the bourgeois was frugal, thrifty, even ascetic; but after the conquest of power, he grew to appreciate the enjoyment, and the economic function, of luxuries and took a much more tolerant view of those people who consumed his products but did not produce any surplus value themselves. "What a fine arrangement," Marx wrote, "that permits a factory girl to sweat for twelve hours so that the employer can use a portion of her unpaid labor to hire her sister as a maid, her brother as a groom and her cousin as a soldier or a policeman." [24]

And, in a much more fundamental intimation of the same trend, Marx argued that the evolution of capitalist society results "in the constant increase of a middle class standing between the workers on the one side and the capitalists and landlords on the other, which is, for the most part, fed directly by income ["income," in Marx's terminology, is money which does not come from producing surplus value in capitalist production, but from providing serv-

---

Capitalist Dialectic," by Martin Nicolaus in *For a New America* (James Weinstein and David W. Eakins, eds., Vintage Books, New York, 1970). However, Nicolaus and I draw quite different political conclusions from a similar historical interpretation of Marx's development.

[23] *MEW, op. cit.* (note 3), Vol. IV, p. 463.

[24] *Theorien über den Mehrwert,* the posthumously published "Fourth Volume" of *Das Kapital: MEW, op. cit.* (note 3), Vol. XXVI, Pt. I, p. 171.

ices—like law] and which is a burden on the working people but increases the social security and power of the upper ten thousand." [25] And this insight is repeated, but its implications are not explored, in the third volume of *Das Kapital* itself.[26]

It was precisely this trend which was the subject of the great debate over revisionism in the German social democracy at the turn of the century. Eduard Bernstein noted that the polarization of society predicted in the *Manifesto* was not taking place, and it was on that basis that he argued for a moderate, evolutionary tactic.[27] Karl Kautsky, who had edited the posthumous volume of Marx's *Theories of Surplus Value,* where some of the most striking anticipations of the growth of the middle class are to be found, replied that there was no question that the intermediate strata were increasing. But ultimately, Kautsky said, economic crisis would proletarianize that middle class, "at which moment they will discover their proletarian heart." [28]

The proletarianization of the middle class did take place in Germany in the late twenties and early thirties when there were so many lawyers without clients and doctors without patients. But they turned not to the Left but toward Adolf Hitler.

I review this history because I think it points to why our current crises have not, and cannot, give rise to a revolution. For the evolution of the class structure of advanced capitalist society is even less like the model in the *Communist Manifesto* today than it was in the era of classic Marxism before World War I. The blue-collar workers have become a declining percentage of the labor force (though they are still increasing in absolute numbers), and the category of "professional, technical and kindred workers" is making the most dramatic gains.

Under these circumstances, the decisive condition for revolution in Lenin's analysis of the subject—a revolutionary class strong enough to break a government which can no longer rule in the old

[25] *MEW,* Vol. XXVI, Pt. 2, p. 576.

[26] *Ibid.,* Vol. XXV, p. 310.

[27] *Die Voraussetzungen des Sozialismus,* Dietz Verlag, Berlin, 1923.

[28] Quoted by Peter Gay, *The Dilemma of Democratic Socialism.* Columbia University Press, New York, 1952, p. 204.

way—is absent.[29] Moreover, every indication of economic and class trends shows that this possibility will become even more remote in the future. It is on these grounds that I would argue that the revolution hypothesized by Justice Douglas—and planned by a tiny minority of the most imaginative and tragically misdirected young of the New Left—cannot possibly take place.

Indeed I would give my analysis its most paradoxical form by arguing that Willy Brandt and Harold Wilson have proved themselves more genuinely in the Marxist tradition than almost all of the fervid quoters of Marx to be found on the Left. For they have actually responded politically to profound changes in historic circumstance. If I am critical of some of their revisions, I cannot help being impressed by the fact that they are the true radicals, the ones with the greatest irreverence toward received authority.[30]

But if a revolution on the early Marxian model of the *Manifesto* has been ruled out by the facts of historical development, a counterrevolution has not. And here we encounter one of the most disturbing aspects of the present situation. The various discontents and insurgencies do not lead to the creation of a revolutionary class or mass; they are too disparate, too heterogeneous, for that. But they do raise questions about, and threaten, some of the most basic assumptions of the society. To put the situation in Lenin's terms, the old order cannot rule in the old way—but there is no revolutionary alternative to it, at least in the violent, insurrectionary sense of the word. Under those circumstances, the old order might be persuaded to rule in a new way. That is to say that America will move further and further to the Right—and even to the ultra Right. This danger, I believe, becomes particularly acute if, in the absence of any real possibility for an abrupt revolutionary change, militants from among the middle- and upper-class young and from the minorities act as if the scenario of the *Communist Manifesto* were still in force. By doing so they could have a very real, but unintended, impact upon the United States: driving it to the Right.

[29] V. I. Lenin, *Collected Works*. International Publishers, New York, 1930, Vol. XIII, pp. 281–82.
[30] See my "Whatever Happened to Socialism?" in *Harper's*, February 1970.

But secondly, even if the old-style revolution were possible, it could not solve our problems.

In *The New Industrial State,* John Kenneth Galbraith raised the crucial problem:

> When the case of democratic socialism began to emerge in the clos-
> ing decades of the last century, the capitalist entrepreneur was
> still in authority. The firm was small enough and the state of
> technology simple enough so that he could wield substantial power
> of decision. The belief that his power could be exercised instead by
> a parliament or by a directly responsible agency was not an idle
> dream. Certainly a public body could supersede his power to set
> prices and wages and therewith his power to exploit the consumer
> and the wage-earner.
>
> The misfortune of democratic socialism has been the misfor-
> tune of the capitalist. When the latter could no longer control,
> democratic socialism was no longer an alternative. The technical
> complexity and planning and associated scale of operations, that
> took power from the capitalist entrepreneur and lodged it with the
> technostructure, removed it also from the reach of social con-
> trol.[31]

I disagree with part of this analysis, yet the aspect of it which is relevant here is quite persuasive. Just as the evolution of the class structure of modern capitalism has subverted the preconditions for a revolutionary rising, so the evolution of its technology has rendered obsolete the concept of "seizing" power. For, as Galbraith rightly notes, economic power is no longer a factory which can be taken over by a detachment of armed men and administered by a revolutionary council. It is also a vast structure of highly skilled individuals who must give their assent if the system is to work at all.

But finally, I fear that the analysis of this section might lead to complacency. The conservative could say to himself that, for all the Marxist historiography, I have simply demonstrated that the United States is revolution-proof, that there will be no insurrection, and that it couldn't run the economy if it did take place. And so I

[31] John Kenneth Galbraith, *The New Industrial State.* Houghton Mifflin, Boston, 1967, pp. 103–104.

must once again stress the conclusions of Section I: There are profound crises which, if the term is carefully defined, might even be said to be revolutionary in nature, and they require changes in some of the most basic institutions of the society.

Under those circumstances, to conclude that revolution on the old style has been rendered obsolete is not necessarily a happy discovery. For if a new way to make fundamental transformations is not found, that means that the society may become the armed, paranoid camp described by the Violence Commission, conducive to a sort of Hobbesian war of each against all in which life will become nasty, brutish, and long. Or, to take up the possibility I just referred to, the government could institutionalize repression in some new version of American Rightism.

The alternative to violent revolution in the United States is not business-as-usual, or even moderate reform. It is nonviolent, legal revolution.

III

It is, then, both possible and urgently desirable to legalize a revolution. In this concluding section there is hardly space for even a sketchy outline of what this would mean in the United States.[32] But I can treat three important aspects of the transformation which I advocate: one of its basic themes, that of equality; some of its relationships to the legal profession itself; and how these measures, and the others which are necessary, must be thought of, not as discrete and separate reforms, but as components of an effort to change the basic institutional structure of the nation.

First of all, my analysis indicates that the issue of equality must once again be placed on the American agenda.

Relative deprivation is, as I indicated before, the source of much of the militancy and insurgency in American society. People have become radical, or at least profoundly discontented, in a period of prosperity. Their basic demand has not been the relatively simple

[32] For that I would again refer the reader to my "Why America Needs Socialism" in *Dissent,* May–June 1970.

one of "more," a proposal which can be dealt with by a shrewd conservative. There has been, rather, an insistence upon speeding up the process of social justice so that the deprived get a larger proportion of the increment in national wealth and much greater participation in political power. A positive response to such a movement requires that society redistribute its shares of both.

In the first section of this essay, I described this relative deprivation in terms of two of its most dramatic components, the affluent radicals and the slum dropouts. But, it is important to emphasize, this concept applies to the *majority* of the American society. In the official definitions of the Bureau of Labor Statistics, a "moderate" standard of living for an urban family of four cost over $9,000 a year in 1967—and, when adjusted for the rapid price inflation since then, more than $11,000 a year in 1970.[33] But only a minority of the American people have such an income. Not only the poor, but the near poor, most of the organized workers, and a goodly section of the lower middle class do not have that kind of money.

In a period of relative prosperity, rising expectations and then price inflation, the deprivations of this majority can become explosive precisely because its members measure their plight against the obvious and stupendous wealth of the society as a whole. Thus it was an explicit resentment against the fact that profits had risen much faster than wages during the first part of the sixties boom, and that inflation then eroded wage gains when they finally became possible, which was at the bottom of the labor militancy of 1969 and 1970.[34] The American workers, who, in the complacent myth, are supposed to be happy and integrated into the affluent society, became so restless that they regularly rejected even the contracts which their own leadership had negotiated for them.

Now, these working-class demands may not at first seem as radical as those of the slum and suburban Leftists. But in fact they raise the same basic issue: how to reallocate the shares of the various groups in the society so as to better the relative position of

[33] Rudolph Oswald, "The City Worker's Budget" in *The Federationist,* February 1969.

[34] "Corporate Profits and the Wage Gap" in *The Federationist,* July 1968.

labor.[35] And that means that the issue of equality, paradoxically, becomes more acute in good times than in bad. Therefore dealing with this question is one of the basic components of legalizing a revolution.

There has been no change in the basic position of social classes in this country since World War II.[36] Even more to the point, there have been no political movements raising the issue *as such*. It was, as I have indicated, an element in the resentment of many groups, but the idea of redistribution was absent from the formal programs. Even the civil rights movement was ambiguous on the issue. For a good many black activists and their white co-workers, the goal was to secure the right of minorities to *compete* on equal footing with whites; that is, to rise up within the existing class system as individuals rather than changing its structure for different groups. Others proposed a racial redistribution of income to compensate for past wrongs, or to get a fair share for the Negro, but even these propositions did not confront the class and power relations of the entire society.

What I propose here is not that the fortunes of the rich be expropriated but primarily that government policy—law—adopt the conscious goal of distributing much greater proportions of the *increment* in national wealth to the bottom 60 percent of the society. This can be done in a number of ways: first, by having a serious tax reform which would repeal the special protections given to high-income people, for example, capital gains privileges. For openers in such a project one might legislate that, for the purpose of income tax, income actually equals income. Secondly, the effective rate of

[35] In his *Theories of Surplus Value,* Marx made an early, and quite shrewd, statement of this process. "The position of classes in relation to one another," he wrote, "is more determined through proportional wages than through the absolute amount of wages." (*MEW,* Vol. XXVI, Pt. 2, pp. 420–421.) There is a fascinating discussion of how good times turn people to the Left under capitalism in *Labouring Men: Studies in the History of Labour,* by E. J. Hobsbawm (Basic Books, New York, 1964, pp. 128 ff). And some of the recent research is summarized in Vols. I and II of *Violence in America,* the staff reports of the Violence Commission ed. by Hugh Davis Graham and Ted Robert Gurr (GPO, Washington, D. C., 1969).

[36] Joseph Pechman, "The Rich, the Poor and the Taxes They Pay" in *Public Interest,* Fall 1969.

inheritance taxes on the very rich should be sharply increased. Here one might well consider the proposal made this year by Jean-Jacques Servan-Schreiber in his new role as leader of the French Radical party which would establish special—ultimately confiscatory—duties on the transfer of corporate ownership at the time of death.

But then tax measures are only the most obvious instruments of redistribution and primarily concern personal consumption income. But there are enormous deficits in social consumption for the poor, the near poor, many of the organized workers, the minorities, and the other militant or insurgent groups. The United States has betrayed all of its promises to low-income families with regard to housing ever since the 1949 Housing Act and it is doing so in spectacular fashion under Nixon in 1970. If the proposals for building ten new cities of 1,000,000 people each, and ten new towns of 100,000 each are to be acted upon, that will require a qualitative increase in the amount of planned social spending. In his introduction to the Urban Growth Policy report which suggested those targets, Vice-President Agnew was quite enthusiastic, and President Nixon, in his Population Message, even suggested that such goals were inadequate.[37] But if these ringing affirmations are to become reality, they require a major shift of resources from the private to the public sector.

Tax and housing policy are only two cases in point, but I think they make my attitude clear enough. Both of them would aim at beginning to restructure the society, to redistribute wealth. Both of them would be primarily directed not so much to the confiscation of existing riches as to having government direct more of the increments in GNP to those in greatest need of both private and social consumption—instead of doing the exact opposite, as now is the case.

Now, such a program requires legal innovation in the broadest sense of the term: by a new political majority winning the Presidency and control of the Congress, and enacting such measures

[37] Vice-President Agnew's statement is to be found in *The New City: Report of the National Committee on Urban Growth Policy,* published for Urban America by Frederick A. Praeger, New York, 1969.

into law. But law, in the narrower sense of the courts and the bar, has an important role to play. And here again the emphasis must be on equality: *genuine* equality before the law.

American justice is vitiated, and sometimes completely subverted, by the injustices of the social and economic system. That famous dictum of Anatole France—that the law in its impartial majesty forbids rich men and poor men alike from sleeping under bridges—still applies. In some instances this discrimination is formal and acknowledged: The wealthy can buy their way out of jail by paying fines or posting bonds; the poor cannot. But even more important than these manifest inequities—and much more difficult to change—is the institutional bias of the system based on social class and increasing in intensity when one reaches the world of poverty.

A rich, well-dressed citizen who speaks educated English is less likely to be arrested for any offense than a poor, cheaply dressed "equal" with the speech patterns of a functional illiterate. In jail and in the process of arraignment, the same advantage is afforded to those who are, or even seem, middle- or upper-class. If I may offer personal testimony, on one occasion, when I was arrested in New York in the course of a civil rights demonstration, I had a vivid experience of this bias. Waiting in the "tank" in the morning before facing the judge, I was treated with a modicum of courtesy by the guards (they called me "Mister" and did not curse). I, after all, was white, and even if I looked disheveled from a night in the cell, I spoke like someone who might know an influential politician. But the others in the group, mainly Negroes and Puerto Ricans charged with drunk and disorderly conduct or gambling, were the object of constant, and I suspect ingrained and unconscious, verbal abuse.

In the trial process itself similar factors work against the impoverished, or, for that matter, against the worker who can't afford a good lawyer. The help supplied by the court often comes from terribly overburdened advocates who have a relationship which they must maintain with the judges. As is well known, this can lead in some instances to a kind of collusive bargaining over sentences, more often than not carried out in good faith. In short, the social class and racial composition of the prison population is only partly explained by the tendencies to violence and crime associated with impoverishment and deprivation. It is also a consequence of the (usually unwitting, sincere) class character of American justice.

There have obviously been important gains in the struggle to correct this intolerable situation; and they are, just as obviously, still inadequate.

In a series of historic decisions, the Supreme Court has spoken out in defense of the rights of defendants to be represented by competent counsel. In a number of projects funded by the Office of Economic Opportunity, law offices have been set up to provide services for the poor and the minorities. In other cases, private foundations and individuals have established public interest firms, and universities have organized a number of centers which collect and publish material dealing with all the ramifications of poverty and civil rights law.

But even these commendable efforts are only the beginning of a beginning. There are two reasons why I make this pessimistic statement: One of them has to do with a fundamental limit contained within the present American system and it cannot be transcended under any circumstances; the other has to do with an insufficient willingness in the society to confront a correctable evil.

Strangely, let me begin my plea for a more profound reform of the system of justice with a frank statement of what cannot be accomplished, short of a fundamental structural change in the society. The reason I do this is that I do not want lawyers (or educators, or doctors) to promise too much to themselves or to the poor, for that is the way to disillusionment and bitterness on both sides. I would take as my text an extremely brilliant analysis of American higher education by Christopher Jencks and David Riesman. In the course of their analysis they take up the charge that IQ tests, because of their middle-class bias, are unfair to the poverty-stricken.

It is not the tests, Jencks and Riesman argue, which are unfair to the poor: "Life is unfair to the poor. Tests are merely the results. Urban middle class life in general and professional work in particular seem to nourish potential academic skills and interests in parents, while lower class life does the opposite." [38] Substitute law for education and the thesis applies. For, if I may lapse again into Marxian language because it is quite apt, even the most ranging changes in the superstructure of society—that is, in the administration of laws—are not going to get at the injustices inherent in the base. Increase the safeguards for the defendants, subsidize legal services for the poor at two, three, or four times the present rate—and, I suspect, a corporation executive will still be able to purchase higher-quality justice for himself.

Jencks and Riesman's conclusion also applies to the courts as well as to the schools: "So long as American life is premised on dramatic inequalities of wealth and power, *no* system for allocating social roles will be very satisfactory." [39] And that means that the most profound commitment of the lawyer to genuine equality before the law is social and political and must express itself outside the judicial system. If he is serious about changing the inequities of the present system, then he must also be committed to the political struggle to change those "dramatic inequalities of wealth and power."

This hardly means that I counterpose this involvement to the second aspect of the issue, the pursuit of reforms within the present, and inevitably unjust, system. For one thing, if the Nixon Administration persists to 1976, as it obviously intends to do, I do not anticipate too much (progressive) structural change in America. And impoverished defendants who are now languishing in jail, or soon will be, can hardly be told just to wait for the legalized revolution. So I believe that the legal profession must redouble the efforts that have already been made.

Here I have no suggestions as to detail. My expertise, such as it is, has to do with the criticism of the society, not with its administration. But with the start that has now been made by the Supreme Court, in the Office of Economic Opportunity, and with the private and foundation efforts, I would propose that the profession adopt

[38] Christopher Jencks and David Riesman, *The Academic Revolution.* Doubleday Anchor edition, New York, 1969, p. 125.
[39] *Ibid.,* p. 150.

an impossible goal—genuine equality before the law in a social and economic system of great inequality—and then try to test that limit, to approximate as much of that goal as is possible. And this will mean committing resources and energy to a major project.

Finally, a brief comment on the third aspect of legalizing a revolution in America: the necessity for structural change.

The classic Marxians before World War I thought that the new society would come in a sudden, gigantic leap.[40] For that reason some of the most sectarian among them tended to oppose many immediate reforms until the day after the revolution, for they would only prolong the wretched life of the old order. That perspective, as I have tried to demonstrate in this essay, is now irrelevant, for the historical evolution of advanced society has passed it by (if it ever had a chance). But it is wrong then to conclude that, properly chastened, the advocates of social change must now content themselves with an infinite series of finite reforms.

For the problem is, as Jencks and Riesman so well put it, that the systematic inequities of the society put sharp limits on the efficacy of reforms. If one posits a racially homogeneous, overcrowded slum, no matter how much sincerity and money the society invests in it, its schools and its system of justice are going to be less than satisfactory. That is why at every point in my analysis I have put the emphasis on reforms which are indeed limited, yet are designed to begin to get to the fundamental structural inequities. That is why, with all my qualifications and historical amendments, I believe that we must indeed talk about legalizing a *revolution*, a change in the distribution of both wealth and political power.

This will be done legally—nonviolently, through democratic process—or it will not be done at all. But to say that is not to invite people to continue with business-as-usual, for that will lead to an anti-Utopia like that of the Violence Commission, every bit as radical as any dream of mine, but in a wrong, frightful way. It is to say that we must find a way for law to do what it never has done before: help alter, rather than express, the determinants of power. And that will not take place in a courtroom, important as are the reforms of the judicial system itself.

[40] See my "Whatever Happened to Socialism?" in *Harper's*, February 1970.

It will take place only if there is a political movement which speaks to these various discontents, these relative deprivations, and offers them a way, not simply to fight for that simple demand of "more," but actually to win more justice.

COMMENT
by Daniel Bell

Mr. Harrington is a member of a secular church, and he spends considerable part of his paper wrestling with canonical texts to prove that Marx would have approved his idea of a peaceful revolution. No doubt he is right. But that subject is largely of interest to the sectarian faithful and not to me. The important question is to understand what is going on in the United States today.

Any meaningful discussion of a society has to try to identify the persisting elements which are the shaping forces of the society. These are in three realms: of culture, values, and social structure. The culture, that of the expressive and symbolic realm, is the effort of persons to find meaning in their experiences and to present them in some coherent, esthetic form. The values are the legitimating elements in the society; they state what is right and wrong, and provide the justifications for action. The social structure is the workaday world of social arrangements: the occupational positions, the mobilization of resources, their allocation through the market or by political decision, the constraints regarding their use. The analysis of change in any society has to deal with these three realms, of culture, values, and social structure. In these brief comments, I will restrict myself, necessarily, to social structure.

Mr. Harrington's central argument is that there is a "lag" between technology and the society. He feels that many of our problems are due to the concentrations of corporate power and the manipulation of the market by such corporations. I find such a view overly simple. Nor do I want to argue on the terms he has set, for that narrows the problem. What I would like to do is to set forth, necessarily schematically, an alternative scheme to identify the relevant structural changes which have shaped the social problems of the day.

1. *The Demographic Transformation*

Since the end of World War II—in a quarter of a century—90,000,-000 children were born in the society; subtracting for deaths, the net increase in population was from 140,000,000 to 200,000,000. The character of that change—the bulge in births—was to create a giant wave of young people which burst on the society in the 1960's. From 1950 to 1960, the number of young persons between the ages of fourteen and twenty-four remained almost constant (from 26,600,000 to 27,100,000). From 1960 to 1969, the number of young persons increased suddenly 44 percent (from 27,100,000 to 39,000,000). It is this sudden change—increasing the competition for place, forcing rapid expansion of schools—which has created a sense of disorientation, often a feeling of depersonalization, a new consciousness of generation. It is this change of scale which frames our youth problem.

The second major demographic change has been the changeover to an urban society. Since 1940, more than 25,000,000 persons have left the farms. About 70 percent of the population now live in urban areas.

The third major change was the transformation of the central cities. From 1960 to 1966, for the first time in American history, there was an absolute decline in the white population of the central cities (.3 percent) while in the same period the black population increased by 24 percent. If the present movements persist, ten major cities in the United States may be more than 50 percent Negro. Washington, D.C., passed that mark a decade ago and is today 66 percent black. Newark, which in the 1960 census was 34.4 percent Negro, is now more than 50 percent black. In New Orleans, Memphis, and Atlanta, blacks make up 40 percent of the population. In Detroit, Baltimore, Cleveland, and St. Louis, they compose more than a third.

2. *The National Society*

The United States has always been a nation, but only in the last quarter of a century has it become a national society—because of the revolution in communications and transportation—so that changes taking place in one part of the society have an immediate repercussion in every other.

Just as the New Deal in the 1930's had to grapple with the problem of a national economy—and create institutions for the regulation and management of the economy—so the Great Society has had to deal—in questions such as urban renewal, housing, health, welfare education, and environment—with a national society. And we are only now beginning to create the national mechanisms to deal with these problems.

If one grapples with the problems of national society, one can raise some questions about the adequacy of our administrative structure. What is the rationale for fifty states almost all based on some archaic, patchwork pattern? What is the rationale for such small entities as Rhode Island, Delaware, New Jersey, and Maryland? What is the rationale for the crazy-quilt pattern of townships, municipalities, cities, counties, and the multiplication of independent water districts, sewer districts, health districts, park districts, school districts, and the like? We do not have decentralization, but disarray. With a modern economy and technology we have an antiquated Tudor polity. One of the major problems in the next decades will be to redefine the administrative structure of the country: to specify the scope of the appropriate social unit to deal with the magnitudes of the relevant problems; what should be handled on a neighborhood and community basis, what on a city basis, what on a state, a regional, and a Federal level.

3. *The Communal Society*

In the last decade, we have seen the emergence of a communal society. This has two dimensions:

a) The rise of non-market, public decision making. A clumsy phrase, but the only one that fits. By non-market public decision making, I mean, simply, the emergence of problems which have to be decided by public authorities, rather than through the market. The laying out of roads, the creation of jetports, the planning of cities, the organization of health care, the payment for education, the cleaning up of the environment—all these problems, while performed often by private enterprise, are of public concern, become the subject of public debate, and often have to be settled by public decision.

This arises for two reasons: No one can buy his share of clear air or clean water in the marketplace; one has to use communal mechanisms to deal with pollution. The second is the rise of *externalities,* the social costs which are borne by the public or other individuals as a result of costs generated by firms, and even municipalities. The regulation of externalities—the decision who is to bear the costs and how —is a political matter.

The rise of non-market public decision making necessarily sharpens community conflicts. The virtue of the market is that it disperses responsibility. Where a decision is made by the multiple choice of thousands of consumers, acting individually in a marketplace, and if a product does not sell, or there is a shift of taste, or firms fail because they have failed to anticipate market changes or are crowded out by new products, no single group can be saddled with the responsibility, other than the managers of a firm itself. But in politicalized decision making—to locate a housing project, or a jetport, or the path of a highway—the decision points are visible, and everyone knows whose ox is being gored. One knows whom to fight. One—everybody —goes to fight City Hall.

These community conflicts, in the 1970's, will multiply. And without some organized bargaining and a schedule of trade-offs we are likely to see heightened tensions between different groups in the communities of this country.

b) The second dimension of the communal society is the emergence of "group rights." Increasingly, claims on the community are made on the basis of membership in a group, rather than as an individual. We see this, of course, in the case of the blacks. The demand for preferential hiring, special quotas, compensatory education, is made as a group demand. What this leads to, sometimes, as in the case of the New York City schools, where blacks have demanded the naming of black principals to schools with high concentrations of black students, is a conflict of rights: the principle of selection on the basis of achievement, as determined by test, and a principle of reducing cultural disadvantage by special exemptions. The world would be a much simpler place if conflicts of value were simply between good and bad, right and wrong. The nature of tragedy, and the definition of tragic politics, is that conflicts are between two rights; and there is no unambiguous ground of adjudication.

4. The Post-Industrial Society

The post-industrial society has a double aspect. There is, first, the fact that we have shifted from being a goods-producing to a service society. Today almost 66 percent of the labor force is in services. By 1980 almost seven out of ten will be in the service category.

More importantly, the nature of the post-industrial society is such that there is a change in the character of knowledge. Increasingly innovation takes place through the codification of theoretical knowledge. This is pre-eminently the case now in the changed relation of science to invention; it is demonstrable in the management of the economy through the application of theoretical principles to policy.

The nature of the post-industrial society is that the chief requirement, of course, is education and skill, and for that reason the university has become the gatekeeper to place and privilege in the society. This is one of the reasons why there is increased hostility by students to the power of the university, for when any institution assumes a quasi-monopoly position over the lives of individuals, it will be challenged. The attack on grades, on requirements, on tracks, is part of this attack. In the last two decades, too, the university has assumed some of the major burdens of research in the society, often at the expense of teaching; and this, too, has come under attack. In one sense, the present student agitations, one might say, are the beginning class struggles of the post-industrial society. Long after the Vietnam war is past, the problem of the structure of the university will remain problematic in the society, and working out new purposes and structures will be one of the chief problems in the decade ahead.

Let me summarize two of the central arguments that are being made here. First, there has been a major shift in the *arena* of decision making. The emergence of a national society has meant that a whole host of problems—health, education, welfare, urban renewal—which previously had been handled at the state and local level had now become matters of Federal concern. Just as in the 1930's the New Deal had to manage with the problems of a national economy, so, too, the New Frontier and the Great Society have had to deal with the problems of a national society. Over thirty years we have worked out the mechanisms for the regulation of the economy—in the fields of finance and securities, in labor relations, in fiscal and monetary policy. We are still trying to fashion, albeit inadequately, the institutions to deal with a national society.

One of the things we have learned is that there has been a failure of social science knowledge. The problem is not just money, real as it is. But we find, to our dismay, that we do not know how to organize an effective health care service, or whether education or housing has a greater social multiplier effect, or how to plan for cities. Even if we were to reorder the national priorities that Mr. Harrington wants, we would still face large problems in fashioning an adequate program—administratively and in social science knowledge—to achieve the objectives.

The second major argument is that we have seen, in crucial areas, a shift from market to political decision making. And for this reason, there has been a rise in community conflicts. Paradoxically, it has increased a sense of helplessness that individuals feel about the political system for a very quixotic reason. Today, I would argue that *more* people are aware of politics; *more* people, in the large urban centers, participate in organizations than ever before. But each acts as a veto group, checkmating the other. Fifty years ago, in a city like New York, one went to a political boss and made a deal for what one wanted. Today that system is gone. In its place we have a multiplicity of organizations each seeking to impose its single view on the polity. And with a consequent sense of helplessness.

But the most difficult dimension of this new rise of politicalized decision making is the emergence of the claim for *group* rights. The nature of tragedy, as Hegel said long ago, was not the problem of right and wrong, but right versus right. The claim for group rights necessarily invokes conflict in which there is no easy moral answer. Take the case of the New York City school situation. Fifty to sixty years ago, the system was riddled by favoritism and patronage. In order to assure equality of opportunity, reform groups fought for a merit system in which place in the schools was given on the basis of achievement. Now we face the demand that positions in schools, especially positions as principals, be given on the basis of cultural identity, so that a predominantly black school would be run by a black principal, and such allocation would cancel out the system of merit and achievement. It may be that we should modify a merit system and place black principals in black schools—so that the man who stands at the top of the list because of achievement has to step aside. But let us not be unaware of the relative injustice in either choice.

In a fundamental sense, there is an "overload" on a political system which has not been equipped to handle this kind of communal issues. In principle there is a solution. In the 1930's, the labor issue was as fractious and divisive—in the seizure of property, in the heated, violent conflicts—as many of the social ruptures today. Yet a solution was found through bargaining. Certainly it is easier to do collective economic bargaining because there is a single locus for decision—in the factory and the enterprise. Yet, particularly on the local level, one can envisage a greater degree of self-organization on the part of groups and a bargaining which would lead to a trade-off between groups as to what they want.

On a national level we do need a comprehensive social policy with a greater awareness of desirable priorities and some institutional mechanisms, such as a Council of Social Advisers, or an enlarged Council of Economic and Social Advisers, to measure our performance and to assess our shortcomings.

PUBLIC SAFETY AS A PUBLIC GOOD

by William H. Riker

On the one-hundredth anniversary of an organization devoted to the peaceful settlement of disputes, we are engaged in an urgent discussion of the nature of public peace. This ironic fact testifies both to the fragility of peace itself and, even more, to the paucity of our comprehension of it. Not only have we apparently lost public order; but, furthermore, we do not know how to get it back, partly because we are not even clear about what we have lost. We have, therefore, not only a practical crisis in public peace, but also an even deeper theoretical crisis in jurisprudence.

If we are to work our way out of this crisis by any means other than pure luck, we need a new jurisprudence, which is, I suppose, what this conference is all about. I do not know whether we have much chance to get what we need. Indeed, I am inclined to be pessimistic, given the ideological approach implicit in most of the companion papers of this conference. But I am certain that, given the failure of the old jurisprudence, we will not get much forwarder by recycling it. What we need, I think, are some new notions, new analogies, and new facts. My intention in this paper is to contribute at least one new notion, the concept of public goods. My strategy is, first, to transplant it from political economy into jurisprudence and then to draw a few inferences. Hopefully these will be useful in helping us to understand the nature of public peace a little better.

To begin with, I distinguish between, on the one hand, public goods, of which the primary and compelling example is an orderly nonviolent society, and, on the other hand, private goods, like apples or shirts or attorney's advice. Things in both categories are goods in the sense that a seller sells them and a buyer buys them. The seller of apples is the orchard operator; the seller of shirts is the haberdasher; the seller of legal services is the attorney; and the seller of public peace is the government at all levels. All of these sellers provide goods or services of high or low quality as the case may be; but regardless of quality, they are still things that are provided and sold. And they are bought: The hungry man buys apples; the chilly man buys shirts; the contentious man buys legal advice; and the frightened man buys peace. In every case these goods or services satisfy a human need and are therefore sought for and purchased.

To some it may seem absurd to reduce to a mere commodity so grand a thing as public order. Peace and public safety, it may be said, are inherent in the nature of the community. They occur because it exists. To speak, therefore, of buying them is to speak as if one can buy the community, a turn of speech that appears to be lèse majesté. I recognize, of course, that the community is not for sale, and I have no wish to offend the sensibilities of those who think the community itself is almost sacred. And yet there are very real senses in which one can say that public safety has a cost and a price. With one policeman, we may not have peace; with a hundred, we may. What makes the difference? Clearly, ninety-nine policemen or some indispensable part of them, whose cost is therefore a kind of marginal price of public safety. Or again: With income distributed in such a way that half of the society feels cheated, public safety may not exist even for the satisfied half. Yet with the proportion of dissatisfied reduced to, say, one percent, life may be safe for everyone. What makes the difference is the redistribution. From the point of view of the originally satisfied, what they lose in the redistribution may be interpreted also as the marginal price of public safety.

Even with these examples, some may yet think it is improper to speak of order as a commodity. To those I can simply ask that they suspend judgment until they hear the whole analysis. If the whole analysis leads to greater understanding, perhaps they can tolerate then the possible crudity of the premises. If, on the other hand, the analysis does not lead anywhere, the whole approach can be thrown out.

Although, as I therefore insist, public and private goods and services are all commodities that are bought and sold, the economic similarity ends there. And we here are much more concerned with the differences between them than we are with the similarities. The most obvious difference—the fundamental difference from which all other differences follow—is that the supply of public goods is quite unlike the supply of private ones. For a private good, the seller furnishes a unit of the good to a buyer who is distinguished by the fact that he pays for exactly that unit. Short of madness, the seller does not give a unit to anyone other than a buyer in the sense just defined as one who has contracted and paid for the good. In particular, when the orchardist sells a bushel of apples to one hungry man, he does not in celebration of the sale give away bushels of apples to all the onlookers who may themselves be hungry and therefore potential buyers. For a public good, however, the seller does almost that. He offers the good to a class of buyers that is defined in part by the good itself. And, if the good is produced and sold, every member of the class of purchasers receives it whether or not he is in fact a buyer or indeed whether or not he needs or wants the good. Consider, for contrast, an attorney who has several clients. For one he writes a will, for another he searches a title, for another he negotiates a settlement, and so on. His total production is the sum of the work done for each of his clients. Consider, on the other hand, a policeman on a beat. He produces peace, and his total production is used up on the first resident of the block. If there are additional residents, they get this same amount of peace and there is no increment in the amount of peace produced. Furthermore, the additional residents cannot be kept from enjoying the peace produced for the first.

So we say of a public good, to distinguish it from a private one, that it has jointness of supply; that is, once furnished to one member of a class of recipients, it is furnished without increase in production or cost to all other members of the class. Indeed, it cannot be withheld from them. It is, we say, supplied simultaneously and jointly.

Typically also, there is a kind of jointness of demand for at least those goods, like public peace, that are actually produced by public bodies. When a contentious man wants a lawyer, he hires one; when a hungry man wants an apple, he buys one—in both instances without consulting anyone else. For such private goods, every man makes his own budget. A man's house is his castle and he is lord of his pocketbook. Not so with "government issue." No matter how much a frightened man wants peace, he cannot buy it alone. Indeed, though he be willing to pay all he has, there is no place he can buy safety unless nearly everybody else wants to buy it too. For goods produced by governments, a man's personal budget is nevertheless beyond his personal control. The decision to buy or not to buy is made by governments, which are, for every single person in democracies, someone else. It is true that in democracies especially we try to involve citizens in making public budgetary decisions, but it remains the case that, for most citizens most of the time, involvement is a farce. Practically, the decisions are made in bodies and by processes that almost all the citizen buyers do not understand.

To summarize the definition of a public good, it is distinguished from an ordinary market good by

(1) jointness of supply, which means that everybody in the relevant public gets the public good, whether they want it or not; and, for a publicly produced good,

(2) jointness of demand, which means that nearly everyone must concur to buy it.

Now that I have defined a public good, let us look at the way reasonable people go about buying and selling this restricted commodity. By reasonable people, I mean of course people who are trying to get the most for their money—or, to use the jargon of social scientists—who are trying to maximize expected utility. I fully realize that not everybody is reasonable in this sense; nevertheless, it is the well-recognized experience of the world that a sufficient proportion of people behave this way to determine the way the world is. So it is their motives we will study.

The first question to ask about a public good in this setting is:

How does it ever come to be produced in the first place? Even if a vast majority want it, each single person in that majority can reason thus: "If the good is produced, I will get it even if I don't pay for it. Since others want it, they can be relied upon to pay for it. I need not do so." If everyone reasons this way, then the good is not produced. So in a society composed entirely of reasonable people, there are no public goods supplied, which is, of course, a social disaster. We have thus an instance of the well-known prisoners' dilemma, although here those impaled on the dilemma are those who want, but cannot get, a public good.[1] In a very simple way, the situation can be visualized thus: Suppose there is a society of two people, for each of whom the benefit from a public good is one unit of money, while the cost of production is one and one-half units. Each of the two persons has two possible courses of action, (a) to produce or (b) not to produce, and the total situation can be summarized thus:

	PERSON 2'S OUTCOMES Given Action a_1 or Action a_2	
	(*Produce*)	(*Not Produce*)
PERSON 1'S Action a_1 OUTCOMES (*Produce*) Given:	Persons 1 | 2 1/4 | 1/4	Persons 1 | 2 -1/2 | 1
Action a_2 (*Not Produce*)	Persons 1 | 2 1 | -1/2	Persons 1 | 2 0 | 0

In each cell of the foregoing table, I have filled in the net benefit to each person of the joint actions. In the upper left-hand corner, where they join to produce (call it cooperative production), the benefit for each is one unit. One-half the cost is three-fourths unit, leaving one-fourth unit positive benefit for each. In the upper right-hand corner, where 1 produces and 2 does not (call it noncooperative production), 1 gets a negative benefit of one-half unit which is the net benefit to him of one unit less the cost of one and one-half

[1] James M. Buchanan, "Cooperation and Conflict in Public Goods Interaction" in *Western Economic Review*, Vol. 1, December 1966, pp. 109–121.

units. In that cell, however, 2 gets the full unit of benefit with no cost. The situation is simply reversed in the lower left-hand cell. Finally, in the lower right cell, where neither produces (call it non-cooperative non-production), here is neither cost nor benefit for either one, so I have recorded zeros.

The remarkable feature about this table is that neither 1 nor 2 has a private incentive to produce, even though, if they do jointly produce, they both gain. Let person 1 compare his alternatives, a_1 and a_2, under two assumptions: that person 2 performs a_1 or a_2.

If person 2 performs a_1, then for person 1, a_2 is better than a_1, i.e., $1 > \frac{1}{4}$.

If person 2 performs a_2, then for person 1, a_2 is better than a_1, i.e., $0 > -\frac{1}{2}$.

So under either of the possible circumstances, it is better for person 1 to choose a_2, or not to produce. Since this situation is completely symmetric, the same holds true for person 2. Hence, if they look just to their own interests, no one has an incentive to produce a public good, which in this case I have supposed to be a public benefit. What happens in this simple case of a society of two persons happens equally in massive societies of many persons. So our question recurs: How do public goods ever come to be produced in the first place?

In the easiest case, there is no dilemma. Reverting to the two-person example just elaborated, suppose that person 2 actually receives a private benefit of five units from the public good. Then it pays him to produce it regardless of whether or not person 1 joins in. Of course, 2 would like it better if he could cozen 1 into sharing the cost or even bearing the cost entirely. But rather than permit the good to be unsupplied, person 2 is willing to supply it himself, even knowing that he cannot keep person 1 from getting it free. In this case there is no dilemma, and one can expect the public good to be produced. Surprisingly, as Mancur Olson has shown, there are many similar instances, especially when the public is quite small.[2] Suppose there is an industry with one dominant firm and

[2] Mancur Olson, Jr., *The Logic of Collective Action*. Cambridge, Harvard University Press, 1965.

many small ones and that all firms think it worthwhile to lobby for a tariff, which, with respect to these firms, is a public good, even though it may be a public evil for the society at large. If the expected effect of the tariff on the profits of the dominant firm is greater than the cost of the lobbying, then it pays this firm to produce the public good (that is, the lobbying), even if the smaller firms contribute nothing and gain a lot.[3] No dilemma exists.

Let us revert, however, to the harder case, where truly there is a dilemma. Whence comes the production of a public good then? The answer is: out of some combination of cooperation and force. Cooperation is possible because, as shown in our two-person example, everybody gets more out of cooperative production (the upper left cell) than out of noncooperative non-production (the lower right cell). Insofar as cooperation can be induced, therefore, production of the public good is mutually beneficial, and reasonable people can be expected to undertake it. On the other hand, each person in the two-person example gets more out of noncooperative production by the other person (the lower left and upper right cells) than he does out of cooperative production. Each has, therefore, a powerful incentive to defect from the agreement to cooperate. Insofar, however, as defection can be prevented by force or by a mutual recognition of the long-run advantages of cooperation, cooperative production can be maintained.

Cooperation begins when a political entrepreneur undertakes to produce it. In our two-person example, there is a net benefit of one-half unit to society from cooperative production over nonproduction, and each person gains one-fourth unit. A third person, a political entrepreneur or politician (as we usually call him), observes that potential benefit and notes that he might be paid some amount, say one-sixth unit, for bringing about cooperation. Many persons have believed that political leadership is unproductive; but as this example readily indicates, leaders who bring about that coopera-

---

[3] For all the customers of these firms, it may be a public good to lobby against the tariff. But with respect to this second and larger public, the dilemma applies with full force—which explains why we often have more lobbies for than against tariffs.

tion needed to produce beneficial public goods actually perform and are paid for a highly productive role.

Nevertheless, no matter how firm the agreement devised by politicians, there is a temptation to defect so long as the dilemma exists. What keeps the agreement in the face of such temptation? The answer is some combination of force and custom. This temptation is commonly called the free-rider problem in the field of labor organization where it is especially visible. I shall discuss it first in that simple form as a prelude to analyzing it in relation to the public peace. The public good that unions are here assumed to produce is negotiation with an employer for a whole class of workers. If the union succeeds, its benefits go to every worker in the class, whether or not any particular one is a union member. In such case, the worker has no motive to stay in the union, since he benefits even if he does not pay part of the cost. What do unions do to meet this problem? For one thing, they use force. They often threaten nonmembers with physical violence unless they join the union, and sometimes they carry out the threats. They write contracts with employers that provide for union shops or closed shops or merely checkoffs—so that in any of these cases the whole force of the judicial and police system is placed at the call of the union leadership to force workers to maintain membership. Force is expensive, however, not only to apply in the first place but also because of the animosity it arouses. So as an alternative to force, union leaders use persuasion. They create and propagate an ethic in which working-class solidarity and union membership are highly virtuous. And many workers, who of course themselves recognize the free-rider problem, are often eager to adopt the ethic. They know it makes cooperation easier.

So far I have described some of the problems of the production of public goods that arise out of the jointness of supply. Now I want to mention briefly some of the problems that arise out of the jointness of demand. These not only loom large in themselves but also tend to exacerbate problems arising on the supply side.

Parelling the free-rider problem is what can be called the unwilling-buyer problem, which comes about thus: When the producer of a given good is government (or at least endowed with force), it is possible to spread the cost by adding to the relevant public. The more persons taxed, the less each has to pay. Such addition creates no problem and indeed is welcomed by all, if the added public gets as much benefit from the good as did the original public. The new are at least as willing to buy as the old. But suppose the added public discerns no benefit to itself from the good in question. (For example, consider a union which expands its bargaining unit to include office workers, who, typically, believe they can do better for themselves in individual, as against group, negotiation. For the added workers, the union is at best of zero benefit.) Then the old public has simply created unwilling buyers. The obvious question then is: How does the existence of unwilling buyers affect the production of the public good?

For one thing, the presence of unwilling buyers surely pushes the costs up. In sharp contrast to the production of private goods, where all buyers are eager to buy, unwilling buyers must be manipulated. Whether they are forced by police action—as, for example, when losers in a bargaining unit election are forced to accept the union of the winners—or are forced by bribery—as when negotiations of the expanded unit are conducted in such a way as to contribute more than the new public might otherwise expect—no matter how the unwilling buyers are manipulated, the manipulation is itself a cost in addition to the other costs of production.

To revert to the example of the dilemma, suppose a third person is added to the public who personally gets zero benefits from the production of the good. Since he is part of the relevant public, he can be forced by the majority to bear part of the cost. And the old public of two has a strong motive to force him to share if they believe that they can thereby lower their individual costs from one-fourth unit to, say, one-sixth. We assume, however, that the third person's rancor occasions enforcement problems and raises costs to three units. Sharing these again equally means that even for the original public, benefits are no more than costs. Hence it is, by reason of the introduction of the third member, no longer feasible to produce the good. This is a typical consequence of unwilling buyers: They raise the price of a good so much that it is no longer feasible to produce it.

So far I have pointed out some of the special features of public goods generally as distinct from private goods. Now I want to show that these features particularly characterize the market for that most fundamental of all public goods, the maintenance of public peace. In this market, the dilemma of public goods is more intense than for any other public good known to me. This intensity arises, I believe, from the fact that the relevant public, for both the use of public safety and the production of public safety, is everybody.

That everybody is involved in producing public peace is easily recognized when one recalls the violence that even the least noticed member of society can let loose on the world if he chooses to do so. The boy in the ghetto who, though tempted, refrains from throwing a brick at a cop is just as vital to public order as the rich old tycoon whose taxes pay for a hundred policemen. Indeed, since anyone can break the peace, everyone is involved in keeping it. Similarly, that everybody is involved in consuming peace is recognized when one recalls that even the most disaffected benefit from some social stabilities. Revolutionaries, who are professional promoters of disorder, nevertheless rely on the existence of public order for raising children. In the United States revolutionaries even rely on the stability and order of the society they are seeking to disrupt for their civil rights—and typically they are actually accorded them. It is perhaps a little harder to recognize our essential equality as consumers of peace than to recognize our equality as producers. Riots are recent and vivid reminders of the potential destructiveness which everyone can restrain. But since the clever and diligent benefit far more from peace than do the stupid and lazy, we sometimes forget that everyone consumes peace. But everyone does. Even alms come easier when there is public order.

The inclusion of everybody in the class of producers is a way of saying that peace depends on more than policemen. It is certainly true that one of the reasons people obey laws and thus avoid violence is force. Force is involved in the physical restraint of those who are engaged in violence, and, even more widely, force is involved in arousing a fear of reprisal in those who are tempted to violence. But mere police action in itself is not sufficient to preclude violence.

Not to have unlawful violence means that everybody is restrained in some way. Suppose, for an imaginary extreme, that the only restraint is force and that everybody (including police) wished for some violence. In such circumstance, restraint would be possible only if police and law enforcement generally amounted to some very large proportion of society; say, 10 or 20 percent. This is, of course, a case of unwilling buyers. In effect the police must coerce everybody else into paying for them. And the cost of such an enormous police would be astronomical—all borne by unwilling buyers. Even in nondemocratic systems, this is a situation not likely to be endured for long. Noting the problem of unwilling buyers and the cost increases they engender, it is clear that unlawful violence cannot be restrained entirely by the counterforce of police. There must be some more powerful restraint than mere police, judges, and jails.

The only way that the cost of public peace can be kept within reasonable bounds is for each of the recipients—who are of course also producers—to bear the cost of production himself. And of course the way the citizen-producer-buyer does that is to refrain from violence, not out of fear of police, but out of internalized conviction that violence is undesirable. Much has been written about where such a conviction comes from: Some say it is Christian love. Others say it is a Kantian imperative to act as you would have others act. Many contemporary writers, without making a judgment on the source, speak of this internalized distaste for violence as socialization or education into the acceptance of society. In the political economy of obedience that I have developed here, internalized restraint is simply the recognition that a joint acceptance of restraint—a kind of unspoken coalition—is the only way to come out ahead, given the dilemma of public goods. But wherever the general citizen conviction that violence is undesirable comes from, it is necessarily the only feasible means to maintain an orderly and peaceful society.

The fact that everybody is both a producer and a consumer of public order implies much more, however, than merely the insufficiency of police. It implies also that the dilemma of public goods is invariably present.

As I indicated previously, there are many public goods around which no dilemma occurs simply because some one consumer makes enough from the use of the good to justify producing it himself. This cannot be true of a good like public safety, however, simply because everyone is both a producer and a consumer. Even though some consumers are richer than others and have more to lose in robberies and riots, still the personal safety of his body means about as much to any one man as to another—and in that sense the values of public order are about the same for everyone. Thus it is that our equality of dependence forces us into the dilemma.

Furthermore, since everyone is also a producer and hence bears some of the costs, the dilemma is always certain to exist for each citizen. Suppose some people could insist on the production of public order without bearing any of the costs. Then, referring to our earlier example, person 1 could get the same return in the upper left and lower left cells and would therefore be indifferent between them. This in turn would tend to make him indifferent between the non-production and production of the good, which would severely weaken or even wash out the dilemma. But, as I have already shown, the nature of public order is that everyone is involved in producing it. Hence everyone bears some of its costs. And so everyone also faces the dilemma of public goods.

Finally, with peace more than most public goods, the individual producer-consumer tends to be acutely conscious of the dilemma simply because all the values in the cells (that is, both the costs and benefits of peace) are wholly subjective. For public goods in which production and consumption are separated into mostly different persons (for example, education), there is for the consumer an objective cost. (In the example of education, this cost is teachers' salaries, school buildings, janitors, books, principals, and so on.) And with objective costs the values in the cells do not so easily fluctuate. With peace, however, the values are subject to sudden,

intense fluctuations: with fluctuations of anger and love, content-
ment and aggravation.

To summarize this portion of my argument, I observe that public
peace is a public good for which the dilemma of public goods is
always present in every citizen.

I turn now to some concluding remarks on how this dilemma is
resolved, which amounts to examining how the effect of the free-
rider problem is minimized.

The essence of the free-rider problem is that, while everybody
prospers when the whole society cooperates, it is nevertheless possible for each individual to prosper more when he refuses to cooperate. Referring back to our two-person example, let us expand it
by interpreting person 2 as a conglomerate of all the other persons
in a large society. Suppose, then, that person 1 can safely assume
that the whole society will adopt the cooperative strategy; namely,
to produce the public good. Then person 1 has simply to compare
the outcomes for himself in column one, where noncooperative behavior—that is, the lower left-hand cell—is clearly more advantageous. And where there exist opportunities for profit by behaving
uncooperatively, it seems to be regrettably true that there are some
people who are ready and willing to refuse to cooperate. That
crime and violence occur indicates that the perpetrators have, in
practical ways, studied the dilemma and found the uncooperative
strategy is advantageous for them. That crime and violence are increasing in our society simply indicates that more and more people
find noncooperation more and more advantageous.

The practical problem of this society and the subject of this conference is how to reconstruct the social situation so that fewer and
fewer people wish to adopt the noncooperative strategy. As is immediately apparent from the two-person example, there are two
main ways in which society as a whole can manipulate the dilemma
as it appears to individual people.

For one thing, society can attach a cost to noncooperation by
punishing people who fail to produce public order. This is, of
course, what we do when we add to the police, train them in riot

control, equip them with cattle prods, and so on. These actions have the effect of decreasing the value of noncooperation. To be effective they need not reduce the value of noncooperation to zero or a negative amount. They need merely to make violence less attractive than peace.

The other way to manipulate the dilemma as it appears for individuals is to increase the value of cooperation. That is, society increases the payoff to person 1 in the upper left cell. Naturally, with limited means, society cannot reward everyone this way. If, however, there are some people especially prone to violence because they have no stake in the system, then society can increase the gains through cooperation for that select class. This is what we do when we try to find jobs for unemployed young men who we suspect may be potential rioters.

The first method of manipulating the dilemma we can call reprisal; the second method, redistribution. The great question to be asked about these is whether or not one is more appropriate than the other. I cannot answer this question here, but I shall try to make a few remarks about factors I think are involved in the answer.

If the number of persons tempted by noncooperative behavior is relatively small—if, that is, the level of nonviolence is fairly high because most people appreciate the benefit of cooperation—then reprisal is doubtless a sufficient method. In such situations, violent crime is committed mostly by people who are either too sick or too stupid or too shortsighted to recognize the benefits of cooperation anyway. Physical restraint and reprisal are therefore about the only devices that can be expected to work with them.

If, on the other hand, the persons tempted to violence represent a large class of relatively normal people, then it is probably impossible to use only the method of reprisal. Large-scale reprisal on a scale sufficiently repressive to prevent violence in this case amounts to a police state or even a civil war. Both of these are inordinately costly, and furthermore they involve a society in the problem of unwilling buyers. Given a large enough number of such buyers, society may ultimately come to prefer the violence that is being put down to the violence involved in putting it down. So, if one cannot use reprisal exclusively, one must use redistribution, at least in part.

Redistribution is of course expensive also, especially when, in an effort to resolve the dilemma for one set of people, a new dilemma is revealed for another. This is what has happened in many cities with school desegregation, which is originally undertaken to offer greater benefits from the system to blacks in the hope of forestalling violence. But when these benefits are given, the delicate balance of cooperation is upset for those whites especially affected by the desegregation, and they in turn become violent. Typically, redistribution is possible, however, simply because society is constantly creating new values in much the same way it creates new capital. And new values can be distributed in ways other than the old ones in order to resolve the dilemma.

Quite a bit of laboratory research has been done on this dilemma, which is known in the scholarship of game theory as the prisoners' dilemma. While most of the inferences from laboratory experiments are irrelevant because the structures of the experiments are quite unlike the appearances of the dilemma in the natural world, still a few of the laboratory observations are relevant here.[4] In the laboratory at least, the amount of cooperation increases significantly as the difference between the payoff in the upper left and lower left cells decreases. That is to say that even if one does not resolve the dilemma but merely makes it less intense, people tend to increase cooperation. And this suggests that if there is any cohesion in society at all, people would rather cooperate than not—other things being approximately equal. I infer that even modest steps in redistribution can have significant effects on the reduction of violence.

I conclude with one final comment on methods of manipulating the dilemma. For reprisal, the crucial figures are the policeman and the soldier, all kinds of riot police, and the personnel of the judicial and penal systems; or, in short, police, lawyers, judges, and turnkeys. For redistribution, on the other hand, the crucial figures are

---

[4] Anatol Rapaport and Albert Chammah, *Prisoners' Dilemma*. Ann Arbor, University of Michigan Press, 1967.

politicians, for they are the ones who persuade people to cooperate and they are the ones who propose ways of dividing up new values. To a very considerable degree, therefore, the people who actually do one kind of manipulation to minimize violence are totally separate from the people who do the other kind. As a consequence the society is much confused by the cacophony of conflicting advice for more reprisal and more redistribution from the two classes of manipulators—both of whom, I regret to say, are professionally trained to be somewhat strident. My suggestion is that the general citizenry ought to recognize the partiality of each kind of advice and seek instead to create its own harmony of the two methods.

COMMENT

by Jean Camper Cahn

According to Professor Riker, one characteristic of a public good is that once it has been produced, it cannot be denied to anyone.

He offered as a prime example public peace—which, he asserted, was a public good in the sense that no private individual could purchase it alone, and that once it was produced, all could partake. Unfortunately that does not correspond with my experience with such public goods as law and order. They appear to be for the private consumption of a few only.

I remember the riots, too. We have had much mention of the riots here, but I am not certain any of the speakers was really there.

Edgar[1] and I were there, and we spent our time in the precinct station during the riot trying to keep people from being killed. It is difficult, using Professor Riker's terms, to determine who was producing the public good—the police restoring order, or the rioters redistributing wealth and engaging in instant urban renewal. Take, for example, one of the most common grievances in Washington, D.C., at the time of the riots: a grievance that people had previously tried to take care of

[1] Mrs. Cahn is the wife of Edgar S. Cahn.—Ed.

by seeking legal redress; namely, inferior quality and higher prices of merchandise in Safeway supermarkets located in black neighborhoods. For over a year, women had been going down to the Federal Trade Commission, to the City Council; they had asked for hearings in Congress; they had done everything to attempt to see if they couldn't get the Safeway to provide better service in the ghetto.

The Safeways in the ghetto had worse food at higher prices; the food that they discarded in the section of the city I lived in, they put in the ghetto.

Well, nobody did anything in response to petition after petition, and hearing after hearing. They took care of that during the riots. They burned all but two of the Safeways by the end of the riots. Within another week those two went also. Who are we to say produced a public good?

Now, another thing that I remember about the riots was the functioning of the legal system. Supposedly, we as lawyers are producers of the public good.

Well, all the lawyers—or rather those who were out, at least— were down at the courthouse. They were in the courthouse busy posturing, attempting to catch the glare of publicity, and working very hard for people to see them.

Strangely enough, in the precincts where people were being beaten —where people had ruptured appendixes—where they put nineteen in a cell that was meant for two, we found no lawyers. We found only fifty-six law students who were drafted into going down. They didn't want to go down but they were drafted into going down. The legal profession stayed far away from the precinct stations, which were, in fact, the actual tribunals of the law.

After you look at that and you think about public peace, if a riot is something that disrupts public peace, what were the police doing about taking care of public peace or public safety?

One of the strange things I realized about the third night of the riots was that nobody really gave a darn about what happened to people.

The police, the National Guard, the troops, and the tanks had been deployed in such a way as to protect private property.

I sometimes wonder what would have happened if things had been a little different and if rioters had peeped over into those diplomatic sections where embassies are located. There was no one there to protect the lives of the people at the embassies. There were no police up in the area where I live.

When I would go home at six o'clock in the morning, I would see paratroopers standing two to a door of every commercial establishment, but not one of them was where our houses were. That is a peculiarly selective definition of a "public good"—a selectiveness which draws into question the validity of the concept as a realistic analytic tool.

By June, the public definition of order as a public good became even more blatantly discriminatory. By the time June came, no one made any pretense anymore of attempting to get only those people who were rioting. The police simply took fourteen square blocks and tear-gassed them. Anybody who was in those fourteen square blocks, whether he was two years old or ninety years old, was tear-gassed.

What does all this have to do with what Professor Riker said?

He said when one produces a public good or public peace, it cannot be denied to anyone.

Presumably the police were producing public peace, or taking care of public safety.

But clearly there is a group that was involved in that situation which was being denied a public good.

It made no difference whether you were a person who was rioting. The only criterion for being in jail during the riot was to be black and out on the street.

The only criterion for the use of tear gas in June was to be black and living within a certain geographical section of the city.

In terms of other things which Professor Riker said, I think there is a basic misconception as to who causes the problems in terms of public peace.

I think that very, very often we forget that the problem is caused by the lawlessness of our institutions.

There is no attempt—or, more precisely, there is very little attempt —on the part of the legal profession to make the institutions that serve the great majority of our people into law-abiding institutions. When the police tear-gas a fourteen-block area, everybody overlooks the lawlessness of such indiscriminate use of legalized force and simply expresses relief that at least we didn't have any violence this time. I can assure you that those living in that area felt violence had been perpetrated on them. And when the Department of Health, Education and Welfare fails to find out how its money is being spent—in particular the funds under Title I of the Elementary and Secondary Education Act, which is failing to achieve the purposes for which it was authorized and appropriated—we turn our backs on that official lawlessness.

It doesn't occur to us that perhaps there is something unlawful in spending public money without accounting for its uses.

There are all kinds of things being produced by public institutions, but I don't see them as necessarily being a public good.

It seems to me that we give rise to the very wave of violence we have all agreed is threatening our society by the failure to police our institutions adequately, whether it is the police or the Federal government or the educators or the local officials who really do not intend to be bound by whatever the populace who elected some congressmen or senators wanted. And here I must add a footnote and say the fascinating thing about the bureaucracy in Washington is that it often makes no difference whom you elected to Congress, because once you have elected him and he has passed the laws, the bureaucracy will administer them in exactly the way they intended to administer them all along. Thus, your congressmen may decide you are going to get x amount of money for a particular good, a public good, but the Bureau of the Budget may decide that it will not allocate funds for those purposes.

One of the most recent instances of that was the failure to allocate money for a crash nationwide hunger survey that Congress told the executive branch it wanted conducted immediately. Funds were authorized, appropriated, and earmarked by Congress. A deadline of June 1968 was set for the initial report. A year was to be taken for the study. However, not until April of 1968, two months before the study was to have been completed, did the Bureau of the Budget release the money so that the study could actually take place. And Congress alone would have been powerless to break loose that money without the pressure that had been stimulated by the publishing of a report called *Hunger USA* and the work of six doctors who went to Mississippi and Alabama.

It seems to me that the real danger to our legal system comes from the producers of such defective public goods as public safety.

It seems to me it comes also from a kind of insulation of the profession.

It bothers me greatly—and that is a very mild word, *bothers,* because sometimes it becomes a matter of excruciating pain—that I belong to a profession that is 98.5 percent white.

There are moments when I realize we are not even talking the same language, because there is no basis to communicate certain kinds of experience. If I can't communicate my experiences to other members of my profession, then I wonder what the gap must be when white members of the profession talk to blacks who do not share the common language provided by the law.

This goes on day after day.

I see it most clearly in the performance of purely technical, professional tasks—the drawing up of a lawsuit, for instance.

When I say to a lawyer who has just graduated from law school that this plaintiff has a cause of action because his right to be black has been violated, I am told that he shouldn't have certain ethnic characteristics. The young lawyer's first response to me is that he can't find that in a casebook.

He doesn't understand the kind of thinking that went into making the case of Brown versus the Board of Education and all the other civil rights cases that came through—the formulation of new rights by the acknowledgment and legitimatizing of new portions of reality and new classes of grievances.

If the profession can't communicate with the disadvantaged of this society, it seems to me that we may well have answered the question that was the subject of this entire conference, and perhaps law can't answer the problems of change in the social order.

So in the end I find myself driven back to the basic—and, it seems to me, the fundamental—problem. The people who administer the system of justice, the people who administer our laws and who make up our institutions—who are they? What do they really know about what is going on in this country? Are they as far removed from reality as actually the prisoners' game that we had played here—the prisoners' dilemma?

Do they understand at all the reality of who makes criminals, and what happens?

Two years ago, officials said that there was no widespread hunger and malnutrition in this country. That is really surprising. Only a year ago our government had to face up to the fact that we had 10,000,000 people, and now they say it is more like 20,000,000 people, suffering from severe and chronic hunger and malnutrition. The officials charged with responsibility for food programs and for public health knew nothing about the conditions under which 20,000,000 Americans lived.

I submit that they still know nothing, and it is this insensitivity and indifference that in the end will threaten the legal order and any attempt at lawful change in the social order.

I would like to leave with you just one final thought.

Our legal system can either adapt by developing radically new and increased mechanisms of response to the demands for social justice— or it can perish either by fire or by ice.

Everybody is used to thinking of its perishing dramatically by fire. But I think increasingly that it may perish by ice, the ice of indifference.

Robert Frost said:

> Some say the world will end in fire,
> Some say in ice.
> From what I've tasted of desire
> I hold with those who favor fire.
> But if it had to perish twice,
> I think I know enough of hate
> To say that for destruction ice
> Is also great and would suffice.

That is the challenge to the social order.

NOTES ON CONTRIBUTORS

HANNAH ARENDT, the political scientist and social philosopher, received her academic training in Germany. Since 1940, when she came to the United States, she has served on several American faculties, being professor at the University of Chicago, 1963–67, and since 1967 at the New School for Social Research. Among her books are *The Human Condition* (1958), *On Revolution* (1963), and *The Origins of Totalitarianism* (1951). She has received many awards, notably that of the National Institute of Arts and Letters in 1954 and the Emerson-Thoreau Medal of the American Academy of Arts and Sciences in 1969.

CARL A. AUERBACH, Professor of Law at the University of Minnesota, graduated from the Harvard Law School, and served the government for nine years both in the military service and as a lawyer for several government agencies, being the general counsel of OPA in 1946–47, before joining the academic branch of the profession, first at Wisconsin and then at his present post. Professor Auerbach has been visiting scholar at the London School of Economics (1953–54), and at the Center for Advanced Study in the Behavioral Sciences at Stanford (1958–59), and visiting professor at Columbia (1965). He has written widely in his fields of specialization, and in journals of opinion.

DANIEL BELL is Professor of Sociology at Harvard University and co-editor of *The Public Interest*. He is the author of, among other works, *The End of Ideology*, and editor of *Towards the Year 2000*.

CHARLES L. BLACK, JR., Henry R. Luce Professor of Jurisprudence at Yale since 1956, is a poet and a classical scholar as well as a lawyer, and a crusader in behalf of blacks and Indians as well as the author of *The People and the Court* (1960), *The Occasions of Justice* (1963), *Structure and Relationship in Constitutional Law* (1969), and other books and articles. A graduate of the Yale Law School, he joined the

Columbia faculty in 1947. As consultant to the NAACP Legal Defense Fund, Mr. Black has contributed to the resolution of many of the most important constitutional controversies of the time.

DR. EDGAR S. CAHN earned a Ph.D. in English from Yale in 1960, and an LL.B. from the same university in 1963. As executive director of the Citizens Advocate Center in Washington, he is a leader in the theory and practice of law for the poor and the disadvantaged. He has served as consultant to foundations and government agencies concerned with the field, after three years of service (1963–66) on these problems in the Department of Justice, OEO, and AID. He has found time to write and edit a number of books and articles, several with his wife Jean Camper Cahn. His most recent book is *Our Brother's Keeper: The Indian in White America* (1969).

JEAN CAMPER CAHN, a graduate of Swarthmore and of the Yale Law School, is director of the Urban Law Institute of the George Washington University School of Law, and co-author, with her husband, Dr. Edgar S. Cahn, of a number of pioneering articles on the law of poverty. She helped found the OEO National Legal Services Program, and has been a catalytic force in the development of other programs addressed to urban reform and improvement in the lives of the poor. She also served for a time in the office of the legal adviser of the Department of State.

HAROLD CRUSE was born in Petersburg, Virginia. He is the author of *The Crises of the Negro Intellectual* and *Rebellion or Revolution,* plus many articles and reviews on Black American social and cultural affairs. Mr. Cruse is a Visiting Professor at the University of Michigan at Ann Arbor.

RONALD DWORKIN, Professor of Jurisprudence at the University of Oxford, and Lecturer in Law at the Yale Law School, had his undergraduate training at Harvard and Oxford, and received his law degree from the Harvard Law School. After four years of New York practice with Sullivan and Cromwell, he joined the Yale law faculty, where he was Wesley Newcomb Hohfeld Professor of Jurisprudence before going to Oxford in 1969. He has written widely in legal and philosophical journals, as well as in journals of opinion.

CHARLES DYKE received a Bachelor of Arts degree from Brandeis University in 1961, and a Ph.D. from Brown University in 1966. He has been teaching at Temple University since 1965.

PETER GAY, Professor of Comparative European Intellectual History at Yale, and formerly William R. Shepherd Professor of History at Columbia, has received the National Book Award and other prizes for several of his books, notably *The Enlightenment* (1966 and 1967), *A Loss of Mastery* (1964), and *The Rise of Modern Paganism* (1966).

GIDON GOTTLIEB, Associate Professor of Law at the New York University School of Law, and Barrister at Law of Lincoln's Inn, was trained at the London School of Economics, at Trinity College, Cambridge, and at the Harvard Law School, where he received the J.S.D. He is the author of *The Logic of Choice* (1967) and of professional articles, and has been a consultant to the United Nations.

MICHAEL HARRINGTON, the writer, received his academic training at Holy Cross, Yale, and the University of Chicago, and was associate editor for a time of *The Catholic Worker*. He has published *The Other America* (1963), *The Accidental Century* (1965), and *Towards a Democratic Left* (1968). Mr. Harrington is associated with the League for Industrial Democracy and is a leader of the American socialist movement and party.

HON. PATRICIA ROBERTS HARRIS, a Washington lawyer, was a member of the Howard University law faculty between 1961 and 1969, serving as dean at the end of that period, and, on leave, as United States Ambassador to Luxembourg between 1965 and 1967. Mrs. Harris has been, and is, a member of many important public bodies, among others, the NAACP Legal Defense Fund, the Advisory Committee on the Reform of the Federal Penal Code, and the National Commission on the Causes and Prevention of Violence.

ROBERT L. HEILBRONER, of the New School for Social Research in New York, is the author of *The Future as History* (1960), *The Worldly Philosophers* (1962), *The Limits of American Capitalism* (1966), and other works on economics and social affairs. He has also lectured at many institutions.

DAVID M. POTTER, who died in the winter of 1971, served at the University of Mississippi, Rice, and Yale before becoming the Coe Professor of American History at Stanford in 1961. Author of *People of Plenty* (1954), *The South and the Sectional Conflict* (1968), and other books and articles, Mr. Potter was Harmsworth Professor of American History at Oxford, 1947–48, and editor of the *Yale Review,* 1949–51.

WILLIAM H. RIKER, Wilson Professor of Political Science at the University of Rochester, is the author of *The Theory of Political Coalitions,* an application of game theory to politics; *Federalism,* a comparative study of federal governments; *Democracy in the United States,* an interpretation of American government; and papers in social science, philosophical, and historical journals.

EUGENE V. ROSTOW, Sterling Professor of Law and Public Affairs at Yale University, was dean of its Law School between 1955 and 1965; Pitt Professor of American History and Institutions, Cambridge University, 1959–60; Undersecretary of State for Political Affairs, 1966–69; and Eastman Professor at Oxford University, 1970–71. He is the author of *Planning for Freedom* (1959), *The Sovereign Prerogative* (1962), and *Law, Power and the Pursuit of Peace* (1968).

WHITNEY NORTH SEYMOUR has been president of the Association of the Bar of the City of New York (1950–52), president of the American Bar Association (1960–61), president of the American College of Trial Lawyers (1963–64), president of the American Bar Foundation (1960–64), president of The Legal Aid Society (1945–50), chairman of the International Legal Center, and Assistant Solicitor General of the United States (1931–33). He is a partner in the firm of Simpson, Thacher & Bartlett, New York.

CHRISTOPHER D. STONE, Associate Professor of Law at the University of Southern California, took his law degree at Yale in 1962, did a year's graduate work at Chicago in law and economics, and joined the U.S.C. faculty after two years' experience with the Cravath firm in New York. He has already developed new and imaginative courses at the law school, contributed to the law reviews, and served as consultant to a number of public bodies, including the President's Task Force on Communications Policy (1968), the National Institute of Mental Health (Hallucinogenic Drugs), and the Legal Educational Opportunities Program.

HARRIS WOFFORD, JR., President of Bryn Mawr College, was the first president of the College of Old Westbury of the University of the State of New York, 1966–1970. Before that, he practiced law with Covington and Burling in Washington; taught at the Notre Dame Law School; worked for the Civil Rights Commission (1958–59); was President Kennedy's Special Assistant for Civil Rights (1961–62); head of the Peace Corps program in Africa (1962–64) and Associate Director of the Peace Corps (1964–66). Mr. Wofford received his LL.B. both from the Howard University Law School and from Yale, and has published *India Afire*, written with his wife Clare (1951); *Embers of the World*, conversations with Scott Buchanan (1970); and a number of essays and speeches on education and other problems of public policy.

ROBERT PAUL WOLFF is Professor of Philosophy at the University of Massachusetts at Amherst. He studied at Harvard, and has taught at Harvard, the University of Chicago, and Columbia. Among his recent books are *The Poverty of Liberalism, The Ideal of the University,* and *In Defense of Anarchism.* Professor Wolff has also edited a recent collection of essays on the subject of law and society, entitled *The Rule of Law.*

C. VANN WOODWARD, Professor of History at Yale, and President (1969) of the American Historical Association, has published *The Origins of the New South, 1877–1913* (1952, awarded the Bancroft Prize in 1952); *Reunion and Reaction* (1951); *The Burden of South-*

ern History (1960); and other books and articles. Mr. Woodward served as Harmsworth Professor at Oxford in 1954–55, and received the Literary Award of the National Institute of Arts and Letters in 1954.

INDEX

AAA (Agricultural Adjustment Administration), 256
Abolitionist movement, 235
Academy, 33
Acceptance-oriented concept of law, 201
Actions as opposed to attitudes, 83–84
Administration, orderly, 196
Adolescence
as new phenomenon, 347
Africa, 145
Aggregative adequacy, 142–44, 147–48, 158
Aggressive war, 80
Agnew, Spiro, 33–35, 193, 225, 358
Agreements, establishment of, 139
Agriculture, 175–76
Aid for Dependent Children, 348
Ainu, 296
Alabama, 245
Alcatraz, 109
Ali, Muhammad, 173
Alternatives, voting and specification of, 148–49
American revolution, 230, 266
Anarchism, 78, 90, 105, 148
equalitarian, 92
natural, 56
neo-anarchism, 154
philosophical, 121, 128–33
Anarchy, two faces of, 33
Anti-authoritarian society, 273

Anti-intellectualism, 318
Anti-riot law, 184–85, 189–91, 193
Aquinas, Saint Thomas, 30, 35
Arendt, Hannah, 212–43, 391
Aristophanes, 78
Aristotle, 215
Arkansas State Farm, 293
Aron, Raymond, 311
Asia, 145
Atlanta, 364
Attitudes as opposed to actions, 83–84
Auerbach, Carl A., 130–33, 208–211, 307–14, 391
Austin, John, 200
Authority
from above, 261
by consent, 261
decentralization of, 58
definition of, 122
equalitarian, 272
hierarchical, 272
replaces power, 22
of state
rejection, 195–96, 205–8, 220–21, 224
Wolff on, 121–28
unitary, 261
Automation Commission, 348
Automobile, 280
Autonomy
definition of, 122
functional, 152–54